DATE DUE

FEB 0 7 2008		
OCT 1 6 2008		

COMPUTER NETWORKING
AND NETWORKS

COMPUTER NETWORKING
AND NETWORKS

SUSAN SHANNON
EDITOR

Nova Science Publishers, Inc.
New York

NOTICE TO THE READER

The Publisher has taken reasonable care in the preparation of this book, but makes no expressed or implied warranty of any kind and assumes no responsibility for any errors or omissions. No liability is assumed for incidental or consequential damages in connection with or arising out of information contained in this book. The Publisher shall not be liable for any special, consequential, or exemplary damages resulting, in whole or in part, from the readers' use of, or reliance upon, this material.

This publication is designed to provide accurate and authoritative information with regard to the subject matter covered herein. It is sold with the clear understanding that the Publisher is not engaged in rendering legal or any other professional services. If legal or any other expert assistance is required, the services of a competent person should be sought. FROM A DECLARATION OF PARTICIPANTS JOINTLY ADOPTED BY A COMMITTEE OF THE AMERICAN BAR ASSOCIATION AND A COMMITTEE OF PUBLISHERS.

LIBRARY OF CONGRESS CATALOGING-IN-PUBLICATION DATA
Computer networking and networks / Susan Shannon (editor).
    p. cm.
Includes index.
ISBN 1-59454-830-7
1. Computer networks. I. Shannon, Susan.
TK5105.5.C6424   2006
004.6--dc22   2005034395

Published by Nova Science Publishers, Inc. ✢ *New York*

CONTENTS

Preface   vii

Chapter 1   Early Detection and Prevention of Denial-of-Service   **1**
Attacks within the Routing Infrastructure
John Haggerty

Chapter 2   Automatic Creation of Agreements in a   **41**
Service-Oriented Scenario
Pablo Fernandez, Manuel Resinas and Rafael Corchuelo

Chapter 3   Broadband Residential Multiservices Access   **63**
S.W. Song and W. B. Gardner

Chapter 4   Flow-based Analysis of Internet Traffic   **99**
Andrei Sukhov, Warren Daly,
Fedor Afanasiev and Anton Petrov

Chapter 5   Dynamic Maintenance of a Given Proxy Cache Hit Ratio by   **115**
Leveraging the Relative Data Object Popularity Profile
Allan K.Y. Wong, Richard S. L. Wu and Tharam S. Dillon

Chapter 6   Vertical Handoff Schemes for Interworking of 3G Cellular   **141**
Networks and Wireless LAN
Maode Ma

Chapter 7   Innovative Network Emulations Using the NCTUns Tool   **157**
Shie-Yuan Wang and Kuo-Chiang Liao

Chapter 8   Quality of Service Provision in High-Speed Packet Switches   **189**
Qiang Duan

Index   **239**

PREFACE

Computer networks remain one of the central aspects of the computer world. This new book examines crucial issues and research under the following rubrics: Communication Network Architectures; Communication Network Protocols; 3. Network Services and Applications; 4. Network Security and Privacy; 5. Network Operation and Management; 6. Discrete Algorithms and Discrete Modeling Algorithmic and discrete aspects in the context of computer networking as well as mobile and wireless computing and communications.

As explained in Chapter 1, the flow of data is a primary concern for home and business users alike, facilitated by the growth of network and information technologies. Organisations today face a dichotomy. On the one hand, they must open their systems to make use of this information flow for competitive advantage; on the other, they must secure their systems in the face of threats and vulnerabilities that this technology harbours. A major threat is that of denial-of-service attacks. These attacks threaten the very heart of the information economy: connectivity and availability. Denial-of-service attacks pose a significant threat as they are easy for a malicious user to launch and difficult to defend against. Current countermeasures to these attacks rely on the perimeter model; a boundary is established and security devices are placed to protect the integrity of that boundary. However, this model has severe limitations in the face of denial-of-service attacks in that the attack has succeeded at the point of detection. Therefore, a new approach is required, one that provides early detection of denial of service prior to the attack reaching its intended victim. The DiDDeM system is located at key network infrastructure devices, such as routers, with dedicated server support to ensure the early detection and response required by network users. This system fulfils the requirements of early detection such as scalability, utilisation of both stateful and stateless signatures, cooperative working, and provision of early detection in a high-speed, high-volume environment.

New trends in Network Computing, such as SOA (Service Oriented Architecture), allow an easy integration of heterogeneous systems. Among other benefits, these advances make it possible to outsource several parts of the business process as services. Moreover, as a next step in that direction, we foresee an automatic outsourcing that allows the customer to choose at run-time the best provider according to its business rules. However, a significant gap still has to be solved: there is a need of an automated handling of the agreement process. Although several specifications and architectures have been proposed, no one covers, as far as we know, the agreement creation process completely because they focus on a one-to-one scenario and do not tackle the problem of searching and choosing the provider that better fits customer's needs and vice versa. In Chapter 2 we make an introduction to the state of the art in the automatic creation of agreements in a service-oriented scenario. In addition, we present a novel standards-based proposal that solves the above mentioned problems with a many-to-many architecture. It deals with the whole process of creating agreements automatically taking three major concerns into account: non-functional requirements, dynamic business policies and automated negotiation.

Chapter 3 presents a thorough discussion of broadband residential multiservices, also known as integrated access networks. Section X.1 provides an overview of broadband residential multiservices. Network architectures based on different network protocols, including the B-ISDN (Broadband Integrated Services Digital Network), the Ethernet, the SONET/SDH (Synchronous Optical Network/Digital Hierarchy), and the IP (Internet Protocol), are all introduced in Section X.1. In the following sections, X.2 to X.5, we discuss each of these network models in turn. Finally, a summary of these possible broadband residential access networks is presented in Section X.6.

We propose the use of flow-based analysis to estimate the quality of an Internet connection. Using results from queueing theory we compare two expressions for backbone traffic that have different applications. We will demonstrate in Chapter 4, a curve that shows the dependence of link utilization and the number of active flows in it, to describe different states of the network. We propose a methodology for plotting such a curve using data received from a Cisco router from the NetFlow protocol, and use this curve to show the working area and the overload point of the given network. Our test demonstrates an easy way to identify when a backbone upgrade is required.

Without caching support the Internet can easily become terribly congested, slow and lose its appeal. The danger of congestion is aggravated by the fact that the WWW (*World Wide Web*) volume of pages has a monthly growth rate of around 15% but the Internet backbone capacity increases only by 60% yearly. The massive amount of information needed to be transferred across the network in browsing and information retrieval can quickly deplete the amount of sharable bandwidth. This situation worsens if retransmissions are involved as a means to recover the information lost owing to different kinds of network faults, which are inevitable due to the sheer size and heterogeneous nature of the Internet. Caching alleviates network congestion and speeds up WWW information retrieval by providing two advantages. The explicit advantage is the shortening of the service roundtrip time (*RTT*) for WWW information retrieval. The service *RTT* is the time interval between sending a request by the client and getting the corresponding result from the server correctly. The service RTT in this client/server relationship conceptually consists of two legs. The first leg is for the roundtrip between the client and the proxy server, and the second leg is between the proxy server and the remote data source or web server. If the proxy server finds the data object in its cache, then the second leg is automatically obviated. The hit ratio is the probability of finding the required data locally in the proxy's cache. It fluctuates with the clients' shift of preference for certain data items. For a set of data objects this shift changes the relative popularity profile. If ψ is the cache hit ratio, and RTT_{leg1} and RTT_{leg2} as the average roundtrip times respectively for the first and second legs, then the retrieval speedup is

$$S_{cache} = \left(RTT_{leg1} + RTT_{leg2}\right) \Big/ \left(RTT_{leg1} + [1-\psi]*RTT_{leg2}\right),$$ where $[1-\psi]$ is the miss ratio of the

proxy cache. With hit ratio $\psi = 0.5$, $RTT_{leg1} = 10$ and $RTT_{leg2} = 40$ the speedup is

$S_{cache} = \dfrac{(10+40)}{(10+0.5*40)} = \dfrac{50}{30}$ or 1.67. It is advantageous to have a high proxy cache hit ratio because RTT_{leg2}, which involves the Domain Name Server (DNS), is usually very much longer than RTT_{leg1}. The DNS helps the proxy locate the required data objects in the right remote data source. The implicit advantage from S_{cache} is less data needed to be transferred across the network. This means more backbone bandwidth available for sharing and a reduction in the chance of network congestion. The explicit and implicit advantages from caching motivate different areas of relevant research. The most popular topic is how to design replacement strategies to effectively keep as many hot data objects in the cache as possible. Almost all the known replacement strategies work with a static cache size. They aim at yielding a high cache hit ratio but not necessarily maintaining it. For this reason the cache hit ratio fluctuates with respect to the system dynamics and the current data object popularity profile. Maintaining a given cache hit ratio needs dynamic cache size tuning. In Chapter 5, the novel MACSC (*Model for Adaptive Cache Size Control*) framework, which leverages the relative data object popularity profile as the sole parameter for this purpose, is proposed. It represents an important departure from previous work which always postulated static cache size. This new approach leads to significant improvements in cache hit ratios or allows one to maintain a prescribed hit ratio. It computes the tuning solution in a short time to avoid possible deleterious effects by the tuning process. Three different versions of the framework, namely, MACSC(PE), MACSC(M^3RT), and MACSC(F-PE) are presented.

The combination of cellular wireless technology and wireless LAN technology offers great possibility of achieving anywhere, anytime Internet access. Wireless LAN technology can provide high bandwidth data transmission within a small coverage while cellular wireless network including 3G cellular wireless networks can serve relative low bandwidth data transmission in a wider area. The integration of these two wireless technologies will enhance the Internet access ability of mobile users to achieve "Always Best Connected". Loosely coupled architecture seems to be prospective to implement. One of the important issues in loosely coupled approach is the handoff between wireless LAN and 3G cellular networks. Chapter 6 presents an overall view on various techniques to perform the vertical handoff. We describe several state-of-the-art schemes to implement the vertical handoff and seamless connection processes in quite detail. The objective of this review is to present a general picture on the topic and the relevant techniques for further research.

Network emulation is an important research approach. It allows real-world traffic to interact with simulated traffic and experience various user-specified packet delaying, dropping, reordering, and duplication treatments. With emulation, one can test the function and performance of a real-world network device under various simulated network conditions without the need to get, know, or modify its internal protocol stack. Due to these capabilities, emulation is widely used to test network protocols and network devices. In Chapter 7, we introduce NCTUns, an innovative network simulator and emulator. We explain the novel simulation methodology used by it, present its design and implementation, and show its emulation capabilities and performance. Several examples are presented to illustrate its uses in wired and wireless network emulations.

The wide range of emerging networking applications demand much stricter requirements on the quality of service (QoS) provided by computer networks. Packet switches play one of the most crucial roles in network QoS provision. Although the research community has achieved considerable results on both packet switch design and QoS support, these two aspects have not yet been neatly integrated together. Most research results for QoS provision assume a switch architecture with only output queueing, which is not practical for high-speed switches. Current research on switch design either mainly focuses on throughput and average performance that are not sufficient for QoS guarantee, or requires very complex control to support QoS that is not feasible in high-speed switches. Therefore, how to control traffic in high-speed packet switches to achieve QoS guarantees is an important issue; and this is the topic that we will discuss in Chapter 8.

First, we introduce a variety of typical switching fabric structures and queueing schemes, and discuss their influences on switch performance. We specifically describe the recently developed buffered crossbar architecture, which employs virtual output queueing scheme and a crossbar switching fabric with internal buffers. This switch architecture is expected to be widely applied in computer networks. Then we give a brief review about current research on high-speed switch design and network QoS provision, which shows that current available results are not sufficient in providing QoS in buffered crossbar switches. To tackle this problem, we develop a network calculus-based model and a set of analysis and design techniques for the traffic control system in buffered crossbar switches. Based on the model and techniques, we can evaluate the minimum bandwidth and maximum packet delay performance guaranteed by buffered crossbar switches, and can determine the amount of resources--service capacity and buffer space--that must be allocated in the switch for achieving given performance objectives. By applying this model, we show that buffered crossbar switches can provide very close bandwidth and delay guarantees to what can be achieved by the output-queueing switch. The developed model and techniques are also extended to study QoS provision in multistage buffered crossbar switches, which are constructed by interconnecting a set of single-stage switches. Traffic aggregation is typically employed in high-speed packet switches to simplify traffic control. We apply the network calculus-based model to examine the influence of traffic aggregation on resource utilization for QoS provision in buffered crossbar switches. Finally we investigate statistical QoS provision in buffered crossbar switches.

In: Computer Networking and Networks
Editor: Susan Shannon, pp. 1-39

ISBN: 1-59454-830-7
© 2006 Nova Science Publishers, Inc.

Chapter 1

EARLY DETECTION AND PREVENTION OF DENIAL-OF-SERVICE ATTACKS WITHIN THE ROUTING INFRASTRUCTURE

John Haggerty

Network Security Group, Liverpool John Moores
University, Liverpool UK

Abstract

The flow of data is a primary concern for home and business users alike, facilitated by the growth of network and information technologies. Organisations today face a dichotomy. On the one hand, they must open their systems to make use of this information flow for competitive advantage; on the other, they must secure their systems in the face of threats and vulnerabilities that this technology harbours. A major threat is that of denial-of-service attacks. These attacks threaten the very heart of the information economy: connectivity and availability. Denial-of-service attacks pose a significant threat as they are easy for a malicious user to launch and difficult to defend against. Current countermeasures to these attacks rely on the perimeter model; a boundary is established and security devices are placed to protect the integrity of that boundary. However, this model has severe limitations in the face of denial-of-service attacks in that the attack has succeeded at the point of detection. Therefore, a new approach is required, one that provides early detection of denial of service prior to the attack reaching its intended victim. The DiDDeM system is located at key network infrastructure devices, such as routers, with dedicated server support to ensure the early detection and response required by network users. This system fulfils the requirements of early detection such as scalability, utilisation of both stateful and stateless signatures, co-operative working, and provision of early detection in a high-speed, high-volume environment.

1 Introduction

The flow of information is the most valuable commodity for organisations and users alike. Financially unquantifiable assets, such as people, reputation, and business relations, have become of the utmost importance to businesses. This flow of information is facilitated by network technologies, and our reliance on these technologies is set to grow. Both fixed and wireless networks rely on the transmission control protocol/internet protocol (TCP/IP) model which underpins data transmission and reception. However, this model has a major flaw in its inherent lack of security, which can be exploited by malicious users of those networks. Organisations realise that they are facing a dichotomy. On the one hand, they must be interconnected to take advantage of information flow; on the other, they must secure their systems in the face of the number of threats and problems that networking harbours.

Computer security is emerging as the primary issue that organisations face today and attempts to redress this issue of secure interoperability within multi-user (insecure) environments. Computer security has the following three goals: confidentiality, integrity, and availability. Confidentiality requires that assets of a computer system are accessible by only those authorised to access them. Integrity is concerned with ensuring that the assets of a system can only be modified by authorised parties and only in prescribed ways. Availability refers to ensuring that system services and data are accessible to authorised users when needed. The information economy requires all three if it is to grow and increase consumer confidence in it.

Availability attacks, or *denial of service*, are a significant problem, e.g. forty-two per cent of US businesses in a recent survey indicated that they had suffered an attack of this type [66]. Denial of service attacks the core of the information economy paradigm: connectivity. These attacks halt or denigrate network connections. As will be demonstrated later in this chapter, such attacks can be launched in a number of ways, from malicious use of common applications such as e-mail, to subverting Internet protocols. Denial-of-service attacks may also be a side-effect of other types of attack, such as Internet worms. Irrespective of the *modus operandi*, denial-of-service attacks are prevalent as the tools required are freely available on the Internet, simple to launch, effective, and difficult to prevent. Thus, large numbers of attacks are continuously being launched [52].

Despite the prevalence of denial-of-service attacks, a cost-effective and efficient countermeasure has yet to be proposed. Current countermeasures rely on the perimeter model of network security, where a boundary is established around the nodes under protection. Through the deployment of firewalls and intrusion detection systems (IDS), inside the perimeter remains trusted, whilst outside is viewed as untrustworthy. Yet, in spite of the widespread deployment of these perimeter model countermeasures, denial-of-service attacks remain a significant problem.

Therefore, a number of alternative approaches to the denial-of-service problem have been posited. Proposed approaches fall into two categories, *application-based* approaches and *protocol-based* approaches. Application-based approaches focus on protecting applications, such as operating systems, e-mail, or routers, from both being the victim of, or the attacker in, denial of service. Protocol-based approaches are more diverse and attempt to enhance or protect existing protocols from attack. These approaches focus on longer-term issues of the inherent lack of security in the TCP/IP architecture, and often on how to prevent protocols from being subverted in the first place or used in an attack.

As will be demonstrated later in this chapter, these approaches to denial-of-service attacks have several weaknesses. Hence, there is a requirement for an alternative, yet complementary, approach to the denial-of-service problem. To meet this challenge, we have proposed a system for early defence against denial of service. At the heart of this system is a novel Distributed Denial of Service Detection Mechanism (DiDDeM) providing the means by which denial-of-service attacks are detected early, beyond the perimeter of the network under attack, so as to enable an early propagated response to block the attack through network routers, particularly those close to the attack sources. This chapter presents the way in which the DiDDeM achieves early detection through its novel design and use of stateful and stateless signatures. Results from a prototype implementation presented in this chapter demonstrate the applicability of this approach.

2   Denial-of-Service Attacks

Denial-of-service attacks can occur at different levels of network with varying intensity of effect. This effect has different degrees of cost impact to the organisation. For example, an attack on a single host, such as a home user, may prevent a transaction from taking place. At the LAN level, an organisation may be prevented from conducting its business due to key elements of the LAN infrastructure being affected by an attack. Irrespective of the level or size of network affected by an attack, the situation is unacceptable if information flow is considered more critical to business than any other factor [64].

It has been argued that denial-of-service attacks do little harm but waste people's time, bandwidth and occasionally crash a system [56]. However, they remain a sizeable problem and the ramifications of an attack severe. In February 2000, a number of ambassadors of the information economy paradigm, such as Yahoo and Amazon, suffered denial-of-service attacks. The cost to Yahoo alone was estimated at $500,000 or more in lost advertising and commerce revenue [54]. The success of these and other attacks has led to denial of service emerging as a tool for blackmail, whereby companies relying on their internet connections to conduct business have their Web presence threatened.

Whilst there are a number of options open to a malicious person wishing to cause denial of service, there are two principal classifications of attack; *resource starvation* and *bandwidth consumption*.

- *Resource starvation:* these attacks attempt to consume all resources on their target so that they are unable to process any new requests for legitimate users [52]. For example, TCP SYN flooding uses up all their victim's resources with half-open requests for connection [38, 46]. E-mail subscription attacks, where a user is signed up to receive a large amount of junk mail, uses up the e-mail resources of the victim [5, 31].
- *Bandwidth consumption:* these attacks occur when an attacker sends more data to the victim than they are able to deal with, filling all communications channels with traffic. For example, ICMP flooding and UDP flooding utilise connectionless protocols to consume bandwidth [22, 39, 50].

2.1   Resource Starvation

Resource starvation attacks prevent availability by consuming services or processing power of the victim that are required by legitimate users. To achieve the attack objective, an application is used to either replicate information on the victim host, to divert information away from the legitimate destination, to receive large amounts of information, or to tie-up resources with bogus connections. This can be achieved by either sending large data files, or by sending smaller amounts of data many times to achieve the volume required to affect the victim's resources [13].

Most organisations today use e-mail for the rapid dissemination of information and is a primary activity of those on-line. It is therefore a popular means of denial-of-service attack. One of the most simple e-mail attacks is to subscribe a victim's e-mail address to a large number of mailing lists or newsgroups to increase the amount of e-mail traffic to that address [5]. This type of attack can be conducted against a single person or against a server. Even if a large number of messages can be handled by the victim's mail server, the victim's desktop e-mail client will continue to fill with unwanted messages, consuming network and computer resources. Worse still, the sheer volume of traffic may crash their computer.

The very robustness of the e-mail infrastructure ensures that denial-of-service attacks succeed [5]. This infrastructure is illustrated in figure 1. A message sender forwards a message to the first Message Transfer Agent (MTA) via Simple Mail Transfer Protocol (SMTP). MTAs pass the message to the next mail router, until the messages reaches its destination. The message recipient is then able to retrieve the message from his/her local MTA via Post Office Protocol (POP). There are a number of attack scenarios that exploit e-mail message passing mechanisms. For example, "chain bombs" exploit the message handling process [5]. A large number of e-mails are directed at MTA_1, which attempts to deal with the messages that it has received. It passes as many messages as it is able to handle into its outbound queue for MTA_2 before it crashes owing to the large amount of data transfer. MTA_2 receives the traffic from MTA_1 and attempts to deal with the messages until it too crashes owing to the large amount of traffic. This process continues for all MTAs.

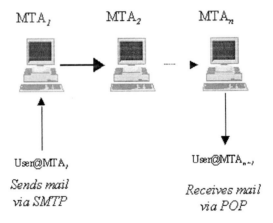

Figure 1. An e-mail traversing the Internet.

Another e-mail based denial-of-service method is message amplification [31]. This is especially pertinent to a large organisation with many users such as an academic institution or global business. In a case study described in [31], an attacker was able to circumvent mechanisms that blocked users from being able to send an e-mail to all users of a university mail system to cause major disruptions.

For example, as illustrated in figure 2, Alice, a user of the university e-mail system, decides to send an e-mail to all of the university system users, of which there are 20,000. Instead of selecting all users individually, Alice circumvents the mechanisms to prevent this by selecting all groups publicly available. This ensures that the majority of system users will be selected as it is assumed that they will be in one group or another. Alice then sends the message to the mail server. The mail server receives *message 1* and deciphers the individual mailboxes from the group address blocks. It then delivers the message to each of the recipients. Thus, *message 1* is duplicated 20,000 times and held on the server until the destination accounts are accessed. Bob, another user of the university e-mail system, reads *message 1* and decides to reply to it. Instead of replying to the individual that sent the message, Alice, he replies to all that received the message. By replying to all groups, like Alice, Bob is able to circumvent the mechanisms aimed at preventing this type of attack. *Message 2*, the reply, is sent to the server and the server dutifully delivers *message 2* to all 20,000 recipients. As we can see, 40,000 messages are created out of just two messages. As accounts are accessed, the server attempts to deliver *message 1* and *message 2* to recipients' desktops. Therefore, not only are server resources needlessly wasted with just two messages, but the network also has to deal with 40,000 messages, potentially bringing network resources to a standstill.

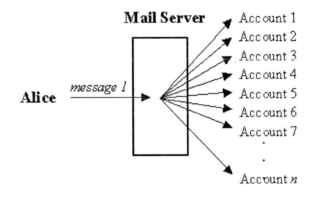

Figure 2. An amplification attack. One e-mail message is 'amplified' by a mail server.

Routing-based attacks target the network infrastructure. A router is a critical element of a network's infrastructure in that it passes packets to their destination. As such, it is an attractive target for an attacker as misrouting packets will ensure that packets will not reach their destination, causing denial of service [8]. This is achieved by compromising the router to ensure that packets are redirected or misrouted. If enough packets are redirected, the volume of traffic may cause additional denial of service at the address that the packets are redirected to, as illustrated in figure 3. Routers *A, B,* and *C* direct traffic to misconfigured router *D*. This traffic is intended for *V2*, but does not reach its destination, represented by the dashed line. Instead, traffic is sent to *V1*. The combined traffic eventually causes *V1* to crash. For example, on 20 January 2001, a number of routers redirected traffic intended for high volume sites such as Yahoo and Microsoft to a Bermuda-based Web hosting and domain registration firm. An estimated 100,000 users attempting to access various Web sites were redirected to the site in Bermuda, eventually causing this Web site to crash [73].

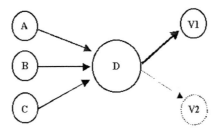

Figure 3. Router-based denial-of-service attack.

Bishop *et al* posit another router-based attack, again based on changing routing tables [7]. To reconfigure a network dynamically, routers periodically update each other's routing tables. If a router were configured to falsely announce that it was the closest router to a destination, all other routers would send their packets to that router to pass on to the destination. This misconfigured router would then attempt to pass on those incoming packets, but all paths would lead back to itself. The packets would not be able to reach their destination, and would cause denial of service in the victim router [7]. This attack is illustrated in figure 4. *Router 1* sends a packet to a misconfigured router. This attempts to pass the packet to its destination via *router 2*. *Router 2* sees in its tables that the misconfigured router is closest and passes the packet back to the misconfigured router.

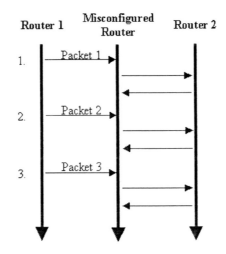

Figure 4. Misconfigured router denial of service.

Another example of resource starvation is that of malicious mobile code. These attacks centre around Java, the most widely used programming code by internet programmers. Java has been widely accepted due to its mobility, where a program can in principle be loaded and executed locally by any user on his or her machine [23]. Java-based attacks are mostly launched by applets executing on a user's system, so they can misbehave in the same way as any other malicious program [37]. An applet is a form of mobile code that can be placed in a HTML document. When a HTML document, such as a Web page, is downloaded, the malicious applet code is downloaded as well [37]. Denial of service is caused to a particular user surfing the Web when a malicious applet forces the user to 'kill' the browser, or even reboot the system [23].

The TCP/IP suite, which underpins today's Internet, was never intended to offer comprehensive, scalable security mechanisms [36]. This means that one of the fundamental protocols within the protocol suite can be subverted for resource starvation on the victim host or server: the Transmission Control Protocol (TCP). TCP SYN flooding specifically targets weaknesses in the TCP protocol to achieve its aim [12, 55, 57]. This attack method, which accounts for 94 per cent of denial-of-service attacks [52], is based on exploiting the three-way handshake in TCP. This handshake guarantees that both communicating parties, the source and destination machines, are ready to transfer data and allows both sides of the connection to agree initial sequence numbers [16]. The three-way handshake protocol works as illustrated in figure 5. *Host 1* chooses a sequence number, x, and sends a *connection request* transport protocol data unit containing x to *host 2*. *Host 2* replies with a *connection accepted* transport protocol data unit acknowledging x and announcing its own initial sequence number, y. Finally, *host 1* acknowledges *host 2*'s initial sequence number, y, within the first data unit that it sends [71].

Host 1   **Host 2**

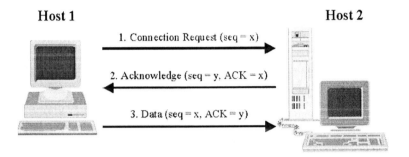

Figure 5. The TCP three-way handshake.

This handshake is necessary as the client and server numbers are not tied to a universally available clock, and the two hosts may have different mechanisms for picking authenticating numbers in the handshake [53]. SYN flooding subverts this handshake by not allowing it to take place correctly. In particular, the TCP ACK flag is never returned by host 1 causing host 2 to wait in a half-open state [36]. The attack packets originating from spoofed source IP addresses ensure this. In this way, the *Acknowledge* packet is in effect sent to the wrong address, and is never returned to host 2 for a connection to take place. Resources allocated to the bogus connection are tied up until the server times out and resets the connection request, thus preventing legitimate connection requests.

2.2   Bandwidth Consumption

The main aim of these attacks is to consume network bandwidth. By flooding the communications medium with messages, and possibly eliciting further responses from the victim, the attacker attempts to stop other traffic from reaching its destination [24, 26, 40]. A major problem with identifying and responding to bandwidth attacks is that attackers can release high volumes of seemingly legitimate packets on the Internet without being conspicuous or easily traceable [26]. These seemingly legitimate packets cause excessive amounts of endpoint, and possibly transit, network bandwidth to be consumed [39].

The User Datagram Protocol (UDP) can be easily subverted for the purposes of bandwidth consumption. Like TCP, this protocol is a transport layer protocol. However, unlike TCP, which is connection-oriented, UDP provides a connectionless communication among application programs and is therefore well suited for this type of attack. UDP uses the underlying IP to transport a message from one machine to another, and provides the same unreliable datagram delivery semantics as IP. However, UDP can be used as an effective tool to cause denial of service by flooding the target machine with forged packets that attempt to connect the UDP service to the echo UDP service [40, 54]. This situation has been further complicated with the emergence of distributed denial-of-service tools, which is discussed in greater detail later in this section. These tools enable an attacker to co-ordinate attack networks, sending a high rate of UDP packets in tandem to consume all the victim's available bandwidth [4].

Another example of a normal network protocol that can be subverted for bandwidth consumption is the Internet Control Message Protocol (ICMP). IP is not designed to be absolutely reliable and it therefore assumes that the network will experience problems in routing data from source to destination. The purpose of control messages is to provide feedback about problems in the communication environment, rather than make IP reliable [63]. ICMP messages are sent in certain situations. For example, a router may report that something unexpected has occurred, such as when a datagram is unable to reach its destination, or the gateway does not have the buffering capacity to forward a datagram [63].

The ICMP protocol therefore performs essential network functions. However, they can also cause problems in communications in certain circumstances. ICMP *destination unreachable, time to live exceeded, parameter problem*, and *source quench* messages can hinder or slow communications on a network if they are forged. For example, the *source quench* message may request the originating host to reduce transmission rate, or error messages may be returned [3].

ICMP messages can also be used for effective denial-of-service attacks [6, 28]. For example, a single packet can be sent to a broadcast network with the forged address of an intended victim. Many systems may respond to the *echo request*, causing a large amount of *echo responses* to be sent to the victim [24]. Other methods of ICMP exploitation include resetting existing connections by sending *destination unreachable* and *time to live exceeded* messages [3].

The Internet Group Membership Protocol (IGMP) can also be used in some conditions to cause denial of service to systems [3]. For example, a forged *membership query* from a machine with a lower IP address than the querier will cause querier duties to be assigned to the masquerader, which may result in denial of service for some members of the multicast group. A small amount of extra traffic on the LAN can be generated if a forged query message is sent to a group, causing member hosts to report their membership. Also, a forged *membership report* may cause multicast routers to think that members of a group exist on a subnet when there are none, generating unnecessary traffic [3]. In addition, a large amount of IGMP messages can be sent to the victim to consume network bandwidth.

2.3   Distributed Denial of Service

The denial-of-service problem is further complicated by the emergence of distributed denial-of-service tools, such as "trinoo", "Tribe Flood Network", "mstream", etc. [19-21]. These co-ordinated attacks are difficult to detect and effectively defend against [9]. Up to the emergence of these tools, denial-of-service techniques were focused on simple point-to-point attacks. Packets were sent from a single source to a single destination [39]. One factor that traditionally limited the attacker's ability to seriously degrade a victim system was that they were usually on much smaller, slower networks compared to the large organisations being targeted. The attacker was unable to provide the yield required to starve resources or consume bandwidth. However, by combining a number of attacking computers in a single attack, the attacker is able to direct more traffic at the victim than available in a simple point-to-point attack. This situation has arisen due to the success of the Internet where rapid, high-bandwidth connections are available for people who have little or no security, giving the advantage to the attacker [54]. These tools infiltrate legitimate systems to form attack networks for the purpose of overwhelming victims' resources. The philosophy of these attack tools is that by utilising several smaller networks, the largest ISPs can be saturated and their bandwidth consumed.

Distributed denial-of-service tools utilise distributed technology to create large networks of hosts capable of launching large co-ordinated packet flooding against target systems. Typically, an attacker will first seek out vulnerable machines to use in the attack against the final victim. Vulnerable machines are those that have little or no security mechanisms, and preferably, a high-speed connection to the Internet such as home users with broadband Internet access. The vulnerable machines are compromised by the attacker, who installs and conceals attack "masters" and "daemons" to form attack drones. Drones have been discovered on a variety of operating systems with varying levels of security and system management [11]. It is suggested that there are tens of thousands of unprotected Internet nodes that can be utilised in such an attack [11].

The installed software creates its own network of compromised machines in order to be employed in an attack, as illustrated in figure 6. At the head of the network is the attacker(s). A number of "masters" co-ordinate the attack from compromised machines. They send and receive communications from a larger number of "drones" utilised to attack the target machine.[1] Typically, in a distributed denial-of-service attack, the attacker runs a single command to all the compromised machines instructing them to begin sending data packets to the target. The drones then generate the specified type of attack and begin sending data. Within some of these tools, such as "Tribe Flood Network", the source IP address and source ports can be randomised and packet sizes can be altered [11]. This makes IP address trace back and firewall filtering based on pattern recognition techniques problematic. When the attacker decides to halt the attack, another single command is sent instructing them to stop.

---

[1] The terms "masters" and "daemons" differ between attack tools. For example, in TFN2K, the terms "masters" and "agents" are used.

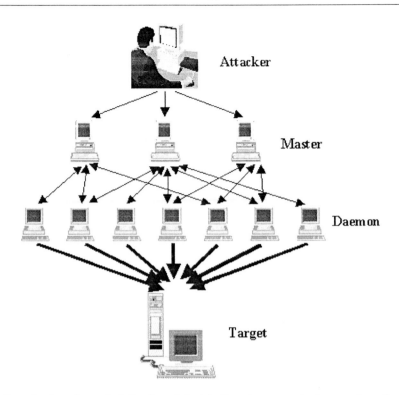

Figure 6. Organisation of a typical distributed denial of service network. Arrows show the direction of communications between network levels.

Not only do these attacks concentrate a large amount of co-ordinated traffic towards their victim, but they can also switch between attack types [20, 21]. For example, unlike the early distributed denial-of-service tools such as "trinoo" which used UDP flooding to overwhelm victim resources, "Tribe Flood Network" is capable of using a mixture of ICMP flood, TCP SYN flood, UDP flood, and Smurf[2] style attacks [20]. A network may be defended against trinoo by closing down services to UDP ports and monitoring UDP traffic. However, with Tribe Flood Network, there are more methods available to the attacker in addition to just using a UDP-based attack. The combination of both yield of traffic and multiplicity of attack methods make these tools dangerous. For example, in April 2000, the traffic from a system compromised with "mstream" at a major university caused a router serving 18 sub-networks to become non-responsive. This is despite the university employing egress filtering to prevent such situations [18].

As we can see, distributed denial-of-service tools do not cause denial of service in a new way. However, they have evolved to reflect the needs of their objective, being the requirement for old point-to-point denial-of-service methods to be delivered with greater power to their victim. The amount of traffic that these attacks can deliver was highlighted by the attack on Yahoo in February 2000. The attack directed approximately 630 Gb of data to the site in a 3-hour period. The amount of data sent in this attack is equivalent to enough printed pages to fill up 630 pick-up trucks being delivered physically to the Yahoo head office during this time period [25].

---

[2] An attacker sends ping requests to a broadcast address with the source address of the victim. The nodes receiving these requests send replies. The large number of ping packets sent to the victim causes denial of service.

3   Current Approaches to Denial of Service

Current approaches to denial-of-service attacks fall into two categories: *application-based* approaches and *protocol-based* approaches. Both approaches attempt to provide solutions to these attacks. Application-based approaches focus on protecting applications, such as operating systems, e-mail, or routers, from both being the victim of, or the attacker in, denial of service. These approaches are characterised by their short-term outlook, and traditionally provide advice on how to secure organisational critical applications 'now'. Protocol-based approaches are more diverse and attempt to enhance existing protocols to provide an effective defence against denial-of-service attacks. These approaches focus on longer-term issues of the inherent lack of security in the TCP/IP architecture, and often focus on how to prevent protocols from being subverted and used in an attack. These approaches suggest enhancements to the existing networking infrastructure required to counter denial of service.

3.1   Application-Based Defence Measures

Application-based approaches to denial of service attacks can be divided into two types. First, are those that provide *general advice* as to how to protect systems from these attacks. These are mainly aimed at system and security administrators who require an implementable and 'quick' solution. Second, are approaches that deal with specific applications used in networking. These focus on *protecting servers, e-mail*, and *malicious mobile code.*

The proposed countermeasures falling into the category of *general advice* attempt to prevent both being a victim of an attack, and being used as a drone in a distributed denial-of-service attack.

One strategy is to maintain the integrity of the organisational systems [54]. This is achieved by ensuring that the organisation has a security policy. A security policy outlines the security goals, responsibility for security, and commitment to security by the organisation. The security policy should set out that those responsible for the protection of the system remain current with security advisories and system patches from software vendors [74]. Another strategy is that unused network services should be disabled so that they cannot be used as a target of an attack [46]. For example, by disabling the facility for IP broadcasts on a network, host computers cannot be used as amplifiers in ICMP flood or 'Smurf' attacks [46].

A number of other countermeasures to protect systems from being the victim of an attack are also suggested. For example, filtering routers that are capable of ingress and egress filtering are placed on key entry and exit points for network traffic [11, 54]. Firewalls and intrusion detection systems are also recommended [61]. Good load balancing of network traffic is also recommended [74]. This attempts to ensure that unusual fluctuations in network traffic are detected, which may indicate that an attack is underway. Other measures include: checking the organisational Web site to ensure it is accessible [74], testing and monitoring of systems for signs of an attack [74], imposing rate limits on ICMP and UDP traffic [54], keeping connected servers in separate domains, ensuring distributed daemon software is not placed on systems [61], and ensuring back-up plans and responses are in place [11].

As discussed in the previous section, servers and routers can be effectively subverted for successful denial-of-service attacks through design or error [7]. These represent attractive targets for an attacker as they are able to disrupt communications by dropping or misrouting packets [8] or disable entire networks [14]. This has led to the concern of securing the routing infrastructure due to the faster connections to the Internet available than the attacker generally has at their disposal [59]. Therefore, the protection of servers is an important defence against these attacks.

A number of router monitoring techniques exist, which include: hop-by-hop acknowledgments, protection from packet corruption, probing techniques, network management tools such as SNMP, and recording and tracing routes. However, these have proved inadequate for detecting 'bad' routers [8]. Therefore, a detection-response approach has been developed to protect networks from attack [14]. Within this approach, routers co-operatively diagnose each other to detect, locate and respond to misbehaving routers. A testing router, A, sends a packet to a tested router, B, and verifies B's actual behaviour against its expected behaviour [14]. This work has developed into the WATCHERS protocol, where each router checks incoming packets to verify that they are being routed correctly.

A number of issues have prevented wide-scale deployment of the WATCHER protocol. First, the protocol requires a single administrative authority. Within the context of the Internet, this cannot be achieved as organisations responsible for routing are unlikely to agree to a single authority. Second, the four conditions required by WATCHERS to work are restrictive. For example, it assumes that there must be a 'good neighbour condition', where every router must be directly connected to at least one 'good' router. The protocol fails if this is not achieved. Finally, all participants must adhere to the protocol or be excluded. This is not going to be acceptable to every party on a network that is involved in general transactions, but is more suited to a restricted environment.

As discussed previously, there are a number of ways that the e-mail infrastructure can be subverted. The countermeasures to these attacks, in addition to the general advice methods, are of two types, both focusing on different problems. First, countermeasures to 'spam', which is unsolicited receipt of e-mail. Second, countermeasures to e-mail bombs.

The main problem with 'spam' is that users receive large quantities of unwanted e-mails that cost time, money and attention to deal with [34]. The cost of sending bulk e-mail is cheap, whilst the cost of being a recipient can be considerable. This can easily be expanded for use in an attack, for example, by co-ercing people to send e-mail to an address under the pretences of a false offer, or by signing a victim up to a number of e-mail services. A major problem against attacks of this sort is determining legitimate from illegitimate messages.

The primary defence against 'spam'-based attacks is to maintain a number of e-mail addresses for different purposes, for example, separate e-mail addresses for home and work [35]. A number of technical approaches to 'spam' detection have been proposed. For example, filtering by duplicate detection (FDD) and collaborative spamming (CF) [35]. In FDD, two or more e-mail addresses are maintained and distributed, both forwarding to the same mailbox. Friends and legitimate contacts will send to one address, and other contacts to the other. An e-mail software agent then automatically deletes any messages that are received more than once. CF also detects duplicates. In this approach, a group of e-mail users utilise a central server that maintains a list of known 'spam' messages.

Requirements for e-mail bomb countermeasures have been nicknamed the 'black hole strategy' [5]. The following countermeasures are recommended. First, do not provide any feedback or error messages to the source of the attacks. Second, capture and minimise delivery of illegitimate mail using a rule-based filter. Third, copy suspect mail for future analysis while delivering legitimate mail robustly and quickly. Finally, keep all captured messages as potential forensic evidence. This is achieved by queuing all incoming messages, filtering the mail based on developed rule sets, and forwarding 'clean' mail. It is also recognised that firewalls are ineffective against this type of attack as the blocking of individual IP addresses is futile [5].

Mobile code is an exciting technology that has come into widespread use through the Internet. However, as discussed previously, it can also be used for malicious purposes, for example, to target the processor on a host [29]. With the wholescale adoption of the Internet, and its move towards mobile networked applications, a major threat is that of java applets as these are in widespread deployment [27]. A number of approaches are proposed to protect systems from malicious java applets. These include; turning off java, acceptance of only signed applets, filtering applets by static analysis for malicious code, address-based filtering that considers the origin of the code, playground architecture using a proxy and sacrificial 'playground' machine, and using applications such as Applet Watch-Dog [23].

3.2   Protocol-Based Defence Measures

Protocol-based approaches to denial-of-service attacks are more diverse than application-based approaches. These approaches recognise that there is an inherent lack of security in the TCP/IP architecture, and that protocols can be easily subverted for this type of attack. These approaches therefore focus on protocol behaviour, rather than applications, to provide a robust defence against an attack.

The solutions offered by proponents of the payment mechanism approach suggest that price is used as a tool of traffic management. To achieve this, network resources are partitioned into several logical networks and rely on the assumption that networks with higher prices would attract less traffic, ensuring that quality of service levels can be maintained. For example, Paris Metro Pricing (PMP) uses the analogy of the Paris Metro system with its first and second class service [58]. Whilst all passengers arrive at the same time if they take the same route, the passengers in first class get a better standard of service. PMP assigns each subnet a fixed fraction of the entire network and is primarily concerned with interactions inside the network. In Dynamic Resource Pricing, micro-payments are seen as providing a useful side benefit of providing a uniform means of resource accounting, pricing and arbitration which can be used to mitigate distributed attacks [48]. VIPnet proposes that 'e-merchants' pay ISPs to carry packets of the e-merchants' best clients, called VIPs, in a privileged class of service [9]. The VIP rights are term- and usage-limited. Each VIP must perform transactions to obtain new VIP rights. Therefore, no host can sustain indefinitely a bandwidth attack against the e-merchant's class of service.

The content distribution approach is used to help offload Web server request volumes during normal Web activity [43]. During unexpected rises in Web traffic, such as occur in 'flash crowds'[3], the original server can call on its additional resources to help offload the traffic. These additional resources serve a subset of resources such as static images [43]. In effect, the services provided are replicated amongst a number of servers. A variation of this approach, XenoService, attempts to address the problem of resource management in a dynamic environment [76, 77]. In the XenoService model, XenoServers monitor the quality

---

[3] A 'flash crowd' is when a large number of users simultaneously attempt to access a Web site [124].

of service on behalf of the ISP. If the quality of service deteriorates as a result of a surge in demand, the Web site is at once replicated to other XenoServers [76]. In this way, the victim has at hand more resources than the attacker is able to consume.

Authentication between an originator of traffic and the destination host has been posited as a countermeasure to denial-of-service attacks for a number of years. This takes the position that the problem can be countered by end-to-end defence measures, such as a handshake between communicating parties, or authenticating trusted domains. For example, one approach takes the position that the authentication method should reside on the destination server. In this approach, the concept of gradually strengthening authentication is employed; as its assurances of the client's identity and intentions increases, so does the level of trust. An authentication protocol should specify how many resources the server will allocate to the client as this trust increases [51]. Another approach suggests that the client should be authenticated before the server commits any resources to it. In this approach, 'client puzzles' are given before any authentication takes place to ensure that the cost of the protocol run to the client is greater than that to the server [42]. To achieve this, a client is asked to compute solutions to puzzles that are easy to generate and verify, but whose difficulty for the solver can be adjusted to various levels.

As discussed earlier, TCP SYN flooding remains a problem as it ties up resources on the victim host by subverting the underlying fundamentals of the TCP protocol. This makes this attack extremely problematic to defend against. Three principal approaches have been proposed to counter this specific problem; *syncache* and *syncookies*, firewalls, and detection in first and last mile routers. The *syncache* approach is similar to the existing TCP behaviour, but allocates a much smaller state structure to record the initial connection request. Once the connection is completed, all the resources are then allocated to it [47]. The *syncookie* approach does not store any state on the machine, but keeps all states regarding initial connections in the network, therefore treating connections as an infinitely deep queue [47]. Various types of cookie have been posited, such as *Berkeley cookie*, *Linux cookie*, and *Reset cookie* [65].

Firewall approaches suggest that with some improvements to existing configurations, a defence against these attacks can be provided [68]. The first approach is the *relay* mechanism, where a packet for an internal host is received and the firewall answers on its behalf. Second, the *gateway* mechanism, where the firewall generates an ACK packet to the server that appears to come from the client. Finally, the *passive gateway* mechanism, where the firewall waits for an ACK message to come from the client before sending an ACK to the server [68].

The final approach is the first and last mile router approach. This approach relies on the protocol behaviour of TCP SYN-FIN (RST) pairs, which is observed at either the first router that packets encounter on their way to their victim, or the last router. In normal connections, a SYN packet results in the return of a FIN packet so that connections can be established. The first or last router monitors traffic behaviour to ensure that this exchange takes place [75].

Traffic filtering (ingress and egress) as a solution to denial-of-service attacks attempts to detect forged, or spoofed addresses and not allow them to reach their target by employing ingress and egress packet filters. This is primarily a defence against TCP SYN flood attacks, which require that attack packets are spoofed to realise the attack. Ingress filtering configures routers to block packets that arrive at the edge of a network with illegitimate source addresses, typically by the backbone provider [22]. Egress filtering ensures that only legitimate source-address traffic leaves the network, and is typically performed by the originating site or network [44]. At the routing level, filtering is achieved by employing route-based distributed packet filtering, which analyses routing information to determine if a packet arriving at a router is valid with respect to inscribed source or destination address. Alternatively, at the ISP level, the first hop router has the ability to determine the source address of each incoming packet [45].

Traceback attempts to trace attack packets back to their source, despite the source IP address being spoofed by the attacker [2]. In this way, the physical source of denial-of-service traffic can be identified and eliminated [60]. A number of methods have been proposed for traceback of attack packets, and are either *proactive* or *reactive*. Proactive tracing prepares information for tracing when the packets are in transit, and can either involve *packet marking* or *messaging*. In deterministic packet marking, information about the true source of the message is added to the packet. In probabilistic packet marking, each router along the path that the packet traverses adds information so that the route can be reconstructed by the victim of an attack. In messaging approaches, routers create and send messages containing information about the forwarding nodes a packet travels through, for example with ICMP traceback messages [2]. Reactive methods start tracing once an attack is detected. These methods include techniques such as hop-by-hop tracing, hop-by-hop tracing with an overlay network, hop-by-hop from centre, IPSec authentication, traffic pattern matching, reflector attack tracing, and traffic flow measurement on edge adjacencies.

Traffic monitoring and throttling analyses network behaviour, and in particular traffic patterns on a network, and if an attack is detected, some form of remedial action is taken. This approach attempts to identify malicious packets in the public Internet, and then filter out those packets *prior* to their reaching their target [40]. Once an attack is detected, network connections can be 'throttled' or the bandwidth limited. Two approaches exist to achieve effective traffic monitoring. First, networks are monitored using statistical measures for unusual upsurges in traffic. Once detected, a defence mechanism may be put in place. Second, congestion techniques are used to detect an attack within the routing infrastucture.

Statistical monitoring of networks for detection of denial-of-service attacks contains four categories: *network management information*, *traffic characteristics*, *threshold implementation*, and the *application of statistical techniques*. Network management approaches provide information, often to network administrators, about the state of the network that is being monitored. For example, the network may be monitored for upsurges in traffic of a particular type or for system compromise [17]. State transitions may also be used to indicate that an attack is underway [69]. System monitoring is taken to a further level of sophistication by identifying characteristics within traffic traversing the network. This may achieved in a variety of ways, including specific packet characteristics, keeping track of connections, and monitoring attacker communications in distributed denial-of-service attacks. Threshold implementation monitors traffic volumes and when a particular threshold is met, denial of service traffic is inferred [70]. Finally are approaches that apply statistical techniques to monitor deviations in conditions from that expected [10].

Congestion algorithms have long been used to react to large upsurges of traffic within the routing infrastructure to mitigate the network's performance. A number of approaches have attempted to enhance these algorithms to filter out denial-of-service attacks at the router by monitoring for packet characteristics, thus thwarting the attack. For example, in a congestion-triggered packet sampling/packet filtering architecture (CTPS/PF), if a CTPS/PF router notices a large volume of packets of a particular type, it assumes the presence of an attack. If a large volume of ICMP echo-reply packets are observed, the CTPS/PF router assumes the presence of a 'Smurf' attack and temporarily blocks those packets [40]. In the case of a TCP attack, a surge in TCP SYNs or TCP RSTs may indicate an attack [49]. In Pushback, functionality is added to each router to detect and drop malicious packets. It then informs routers upstream to drop packets that belong to the attack [41].

These approaches do not provide a total solution. For example, authentication, whilst attempting to prevent denial of service, leaves itself open to such an attack due to the computational load required for the defence. Payment approaches assume that a consumer is willing to pay for different levels of service, and also consumers could be forced to pay heavy financial penalties (refusing the payment itself may lead to denial of service to these consumers) if their computers are compromised and abused by an attacker. Often poor software development practices due to the pressure of getting a product to market lead to the release of server applications that could be subverted. Statistical approaches require human intervention to monitor the networks for upsurges, so they are both labour intensive and inefficient. Congestion adaptation approaches may only apply simplistic signatures so as to not impede on the throughput of traffic. In addition, many approaches require that state information be held on routers. This information is too computationally exhaustive to be effective within the routing infrastructure.

Therefore, a new and complementary approach is required that can provide early detection of denial-of-service attacks by combining and making use of the advantages of both the statistical and adaptation of congestion algorithm approaches. In this way, the following benefits may be achieved: computational load on networks is reduced by analysing fewer packets; no state information is required about the systems/services under protection; alerts may span many attack packets; and the defence may be placed within the routing infrastructure.

4   DiDDeM System Overview

If denial-of-service attacks are allowed to reach their intended target, the attack is able to succeed in its objective of denying resources to legitimate users. The objective of the DiDDeM system is to provide early detection and response to denial-of-service attacks before they denigrate the services and resources of the target. The DiDDeM design goals provide the requirements of the system to meet this objective. The two principal goals are as follows:

- *Scalability.* Scalability of the system can be measured in two ways. First, in terms of the ability to be deployed within the routing infrastructure, the system must meet the demands of both large LANs and the Internet itself. Second, scalability is measured in terms of the volume of network traffic processed by the system.
- *High-speed, large-volume monitoring.* A large amount of traffic must be considered within very tight temporal constraints within the routing infrastructure. The filtering of a large volume of traffic is achieved by identifying patterns in the TCP/IP headers, which greatly reduces the processing load of monitoring.

Other requirements met by DiDDeM include: acceptable performance degradation, inference of stateful information in a stateless environment, and real-time notification and response. These requirements form the focus of the DiDDeM system and are addressed in the remainder of this section.

The DiDDeM system integrates co-operative DiDDeM domains. The domain is comprised of two types of element, a C^2 and a number of *PFs*. The C^2 acts as a server to a number of PFs located within the domain. The services that the C^2 provides are attack analysis through collation of PF reported events, management of the domain, attack response, and authentication of PFs within a domain. It is also responsible for intra- and inter-DiDDeM domain communications. A PF is responsible for attack detection through stateful and stateless signatures and is located within the routing infrastructure. Figure 7 provides an overview of the DiDDeM domain.

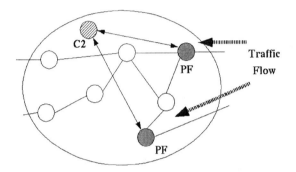

Figure 7. The DiDDeM domain with the direction of traffic flow right-to-left.

The domain allows a two-stage detection and analysis process. The first stage of detection is via traffic analysis. First, PFs detect surges in network traffic that indicate that a possible denial-of-service attack is under way. A selection of packets are inspected to determine whether the packets form part of an attack. If so, a message is sent to the C^2 server with details of the attack. Second, the C^2 compares this message with its posessed information and that received from C^2s in other relevant domains, and then issues a response as required.

There are two cases for the domain to consider. First, to detect an attack that occurs outside the domain and crosses the domain border, as illustrated above. In this case, an inter-domain PF detects the upsurge in traffic, alerts the C^2, and if an attack is determined, a response can be issued. Second, where an attack is contained within a domain and traffic does not cross domain borders. In this case, an intra-domain PF is located on routers directly linked to local networks to provide a "last defence" approach. A router checks to see if it is the last router before the traffic is passed onto local networks. If it is, and an upsurge in traffic is detected, it alerts the C^2 as any PF does, and receives a response. In this way, attacks that originate within the same DiDDeM domain as the PF may be detected. As all routers within the domain can be PF enabled, the attack can be traced back within the domain. It should be noted that trace back is not the aim of DiDDeM, however, it remains a benefit of the inter-domain co-operation.

Message authentication is required in DiDDeM to ensure that the message comes from who it purports to come from, i.e. message authenticity, non-repudiation, and integrity. In the case where a secret key $K_{x,y}$ is shared between two communicating hosts X and Y, a cryptographic one-way hash function $H(z)$ (e.g. [67]) can be applied to ensure this aim. The one-way hash function serves as a check for the authenticity and integrity of a message from one host, e.g. X, to the other in the following way. A hash result of the message denoted as M_x is computed using shared key $K_{x,y}$ by message sender X, which is expressed as $H(K_{x,y}, M_x)$ where '$K_{x,y}, M_x$' means the concatenation of $K_{x,y}$ and M_x. X sends both the message and hash result to message recipient Y. The same way is used by Y to compute another hash result from the shared key and message received to compare the two hash results. If they are different, then a change has occurred. One-way hash functions must be made easy to compute from input to output, but not in the opposite direction. An advantage of using hash functions for authentication is that they are computationally faster than public-key-based signature schemes [62].

In the case of a key not being shared between the two communicating hosts, X and Y, a one-way hash function in conjunction with a public-key cryptographic scheme such as RSA [67] can be applied to generate digital signatures for message authentication. Suppose that RSA is applied for signature generation, X has a pair of private/secret and public keys, SK_x and PK_x, and public key PK_x has been certified by a CA and known by Y. The message in figure 8 consists of X's identity, ID_x, its message, M_x, a timestamp, t_x, and X's signature. The signature is the encryption of the hash result with X's private key.

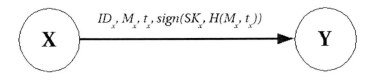

Figure 8. Authentication with no shared secret key.

Y receives the message, and using X's public key, PK_x, decrypts the signature to recover the hash result. Y then computes its own hash result from the message and timestamp received. If the recovered and computed hash results match, the authenticity and integrity of the message are assured as no other host could forge X's signature without knowing its private key. To ensure that the message is not part of a replay attack, a timestamp is included. In any dispute, the message signature will be used to resolve the dispute.

The use of public-key cryptographic schemes adds computational overhead. Therefore, symmetric encryption schemes may be used to reduce this overhead. Figure 9 illustrates a communication protocol using symmetric encryption such as DES [67]. Suppose that the confidentiality of host X's message content needs to be protected, and a key, $K_{x,y}$, is shared between hosts X and Y. X sends its identity, ID_x, and encrypts its identity, message, M_x, and timestamp, t_x using this shared key, which is denoted as $SE(K_{x,y}, ID_x, M_x, t_x)$.

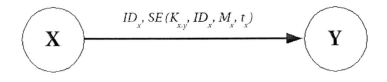

Figure 9. Authentication with shared secret key.

Y decrypts the encrypted part of the message it has received from *X* using the shared key. If the decryption is successful, the message has been sent by *X* as only *X* and *Y* know the key. This is verified by comparison of the two ID_x to ensure that they are the same. To ensure that the message is not part of a replay attack, a timestamp is included.

The domain is formed with the aid of a relevant ISP administrator. That is, the administrator appoints a router to act as a C^2 server, and assigns the other routers in the domain and their topology to the C^2. Based on the topology, the C^2 can determine which routers should run as PFs, and dispatch the PF code to these routers. An advantage addressed by this approach is that PFs and C^2 servers can be authenticated, thus reducing the risk of malicious attackers masquerading as legitimate DiDDeM nodes.

Within the network infrastructure, the domain is not a rigid structure as PFs will need to be allocated dynamically, if for example, a PF becomes unavailable due to networking problems. The C^2 server maintains information about the topology of the domain. In order to achieve this, the C^2 server periodically transmits to its subordinate PFs ensuring that they are still part of the domain. This is required as subordinate PFs may only contact their C^2 server when an attack is underway. The PF responds that it still is acting as a PF. If a PF is no longer available, the server selects the PFs adjacent router(s) to act as PF(s) based on the domain topology.

The location of servers has a direct impact on the networking cost associated with requests and replies between client and server. These costs include bandwidth and processing power costs for each request made of the server. A badly placed set of servers may result in excessive bandwidth wastage by request and response packets that have to be routed over more links than necessary [1]. To avoid such overheads, a placement strategy, such as [1], is used to place C^2 servers within the network.

The domain size is restricted in two ways; a lower limit and an upper limit. At the lower limit, the domain may only consist of two nodes, a PF and C^2 server. The upper limit is directly influenced and controlled by the C^2 server's bandwidth capacity to reduce the domain's susceptibility to denial-of-service attack. If a domain was of infinite size, all PFs reporting attacks at the same time would cause the unavailability of the C^2 server as the bandwidth would be consumed. Therefore, to counter this problem, the server only allows connection of PFs up to the maximum amount of connections it can receive if all PFs were to send reports of attack at the same time. To achieve this, the domain size needs to meet the following condition:

$$2 \times (r_i + a_i + d_i) \times p_i \leq m_i$$

Here, m_i is the server's maximum bandwidth, p_i is the packet size constant to all packets, r_i is the number of inter-PFs, a_i is the number of intra-PFs, d_i is the number of adjacent domains, and *2* is for both reporting and responding communications.

The first stage is the detection of possible attacks by the PFs. The objective of a PF is to identify the stateful signatures of denial-of-service attacks in stateless way, which indicate the possibility that an attack is under way against a particular host, domain, or network. Thus, they detect rises in traffic passing through the router heading in a particular direction, i.e. the target of an attack. If an attack is detected, the alert is then confirmed or discarded by applying stateless signatures to the packets in question [30].

The stateful detection of attack traffic flows is achieved by interacting with the congestion algorithm used by the router [32]. This algorithm already detects and responds to upsurges in traffic. During periods of heavy traffic, traffic is first queued by the router to control the traffic load on the network. By queuing the traffic, the router is able to implement a volume threshold. Once the threshold is surpassed, it drops packets rather than relay them across an already congested link. Rather than merely drop packets when a queue threshold is surpassed, a PF located on a domain ingress router picks packets to be dropped and inspects a statistical sample of those dropped packets to ascertain the direction of traffic flow. If the destination address of all the packets in the statistical sample match, it is likely that they are part of a large flow of traffic towards a destination, providing a stateful signature of a denial-of-service attack. In this way, we can infer unusual rises in traffic against a particular host, domain, or network without holding any state information on those networks.

Once a stateful signature of a denial-of-service attack is inferred, stateless signatures are then applied to a sample of packets to confirm the attack. If an attack is confirmed through the stateless signature, an alert is generated and forwarded to the controlling C^2. This alert contains details of the reporting PF, the destination of the traffic, and the attack signature matched.

Employing a PF approach enables the reduction of computational overheads in three ways. First, the PF utilises the already existing congestion algorithm for detection. The stateful signature can be inferred by the upsurge in traffic volumes that cause the congestion algorithm to drop packets. Second, only a small number of packets, i.e. those that are dropped, need be inspected by the PF. The number of packets during a denial-of-service attack may be high, and to perform signature analysis on each and every packet adds computational overheads. Therefore, the packets are inspected to ascertain direction of flow. Finally, a message reporting the alert is sent to the C^2 rather than redirecting the packets themselves. In traditional IDSs, each packet on the network is compared to a database of signatures, and as many as 300 signatures are applied to each and every packet traversing the network [15]. Every time a signature is matched with that in the IDS database, an alert is generated. By using a statistical sample of packets, the ratio of packets to alerts can be further enhanced to reduce computational load.

The second stage of detection occurs at the C^2 server overseeing the DiDDeM domain. The C^2 receives the alert message from a subordinate PF. If the attack is confirmed, a response directive, such as blocking all traffic matching a particular signature, is passed to the PF from the C^2.

To provide holistic security, the C^2 passes information about the attack to other DiDDeM domains. The C^2 identifies adjacent domains joined via ingress filter PFs. Once an alert is received from the PF, the server analyses the information. If an attack is confirmed, the C^2 passes an alert to the C^2s of adjacent domains. Each such adjacent C^2 is identified by the ingress link of the reporting PFs.

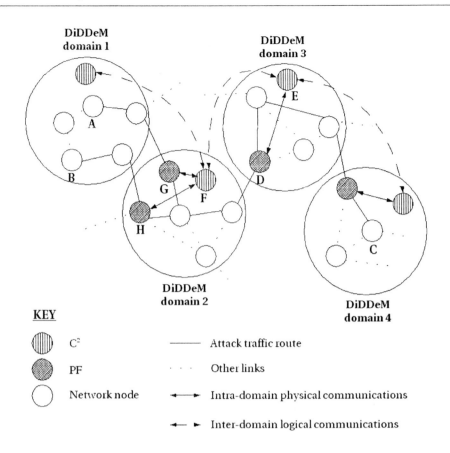

DiDDeM domain 1

DiDDeM domain 3

DiDDeM domain 2

DiDDeM domain 4

KEY

▨	C²	——	Attack traffic route
▣	PF	· · ·	Other links
◯	Network node	◄——►	Intra-domain physical communications
		◄— ►	Inter-domain logical communications

Figure 10. DiDDeM domain co-operation.

Figure 10 demonstrates the co-operative process among domains during a denial-of-service attack.

Nodes A and B in DiDDeM domain 1 launch a TCP SYN flood as part of a distributed denial-of-service attack against node C in DiDDeM domain 4. Due to the network topology, traffic passes through DiDDeM domain 2 undetected as congestion does not occur.

As traffic passes into DiDDeM domain 3, a PF, D, detects the upsurge in network traffic against one destination.

The PF issues an alert to the domain C^2, E. E determines the attack and issues a message alerting adjacent DiDDeM domains 2 and 4. A response is also passed to the reporting PF, D.

The message is received by the C^2 in DiDDeM domain 2, F. F compares this information with that received from its own PFs. If an attack is detected within the domain, F issues a response to PFs, G and H, and alerts its adjacent domains. If an attack is not detected, the alert times out after a set time period.

Thus, the attack is traced back to the originating domain of the attack, DiDDeM domain 1, and the attack is contained. It should be noted that trace back is not the aim of DiDDeM, however, it remains a benefit of the inter-domain co-operation.

The DiDDeM design has a number of advantages. First, PFs filter out a large number of packets to be inspected compared to traditional IDS that apply numerous signatures to each packet traversing the network. Second, by using the filtering process, signature analysis and stateful information are achieved statelessly, thus reducing the computational overheads placed on the system, particularly during a denial-of-service attack. Any stateful information required is held on a dedicated server, the C^2. Third, by utilising congestion algorithms currently employed by the router, packet inspection only occurs during periods of high traffic volume, which is a signature of an attack. Fourth, only one message per signature application is issued by a PF. Due to the statistical sample used, this alert covers a number of attack packets rather than re-directing each and every attack packet inspected to the C^2, ensuring efficiency of network resources. Fifth, domains co-operate to provide a holistic approach to ensure trace back and containment of the attack source. Further and more detailed discussions on the DiDDeM system design may be found in [33].

5   Early Detection Signatures

In order to achieve early detection, both *stateful* and *stateless* signatures must be utilised. Stateful signatures alert us to unusual traffic loads towards a target host or network, whereas stateless signatures verify that an attack is indeed taking place. Stateless signatures also reduce the number of false positives reported by the DiDDeM system. In traditional IDS, there are no combinations of the two types of signature. Systems are either one type or the other, i.e. misuse-based or anomaly-based IDS. These systems have knowledge of the network under protection: the perimeter is well-defined, security policies are applied, legitimate operations are determined, audit logs are maintained, and there is user accountability. Within the routing infrastructure, we have no such demarcations. Therefore, DiDDeM proposes a novel approach to counter these issues to provide a defence against denial-of-service attacks.

5.1   Stateful Signatures

Traditional stateful signature analysis applies statistical methods to collected data within the system over a period of time. This data is then analysed to generate some system-specific values: for example, traffic thresholds or user profiles to define normal or abnormal behaviour [72]. By allowing a system to keep state information of the system, detection signatures can be designed to match a complex series of events. A number of techniques are employed in this area and include:

- *Collection of events.* In any system, a number of events may be observed in conjunction to indicate that an attack is under way.
- *Threshold enforcement.* A certain threshold of acceptable events is determined for the system based on prior experience or threats. Once events in the system surpass this threshold, an alert is generated to indicate that an attack is under way.
- *Frequency threshold.* This is a variation on threshold enforcement and is widely used in authentication. If one or more events are observed, then an alert is raised or services halted until a time limit is reached.

Other approaches that fall into this category include analysis of mean and standard deviation information, the multivariate model, Markov process model, and clustering analysis [72].

These approaches are widely used in anomaly intrusion detection where misuse against known but ill-defined variables is being matched. Despite the requirement for state information to be held by these approaches, statistical monitoring is effective in detecting large volumes of traffic being directed at a victim host.

These approaches require state information to be held about the systems under protection but this is too computationally exhaustive to be used in the routing infrastructure.

Within the *stateful signature detection* module, congestion algorithms are adapted for use in the detection of denial-of-service attacks. During these attacks, large volumes of traffic are observed. Rather than purely dropping packets when the router threshold is met, packets that are to be dropped from the queue are inspected by the PF. This enables inference of stateful information about traffic flows and whether these unusual flows are attributable to a particular destination. It is the random inspection that allows the state inference. If two (or more) sampled dropped packets are heading to one destination, they are passed for stateless signature inspection as it indicates the possibility of a large flow of traffic in one direction.

To demonstrate the way in which this is achieved in the DiDDeM architecture, a *first-in, first-out* (FIFO) queue is used. The available space within the DiDDeM FIFO queue is divided into two sub-queues to allow comparison of packets whilst in the queue. An incoming packet to the router is placed in a queue, if due to bandwidth restrictions the packet cannot be immediately forwarded to the next router. These packets are placed in either the first or second sub-queue at the router based on a first-come, first-served basis.

Packets placed in the queue, and its sub-queues, are dequeued and forwarded to their destination. If the threshold of the total queue limit is exceeded the router begins to drop packets to ensure that packets already in the queue are forwarded and that new incoming packets can be placed in the queue. In this way, no stateful information is held about the queue apart from whether the queue limit has been exceeded, thereby reducing the computational overhead placed on the router.

At periods where congestion occurs, packets are dropped. By meeting the threshold of the particular router which invokes packet dropping, an upsurge in traffic can be inferred. However, this may or may not be due to large amounts of traffic, such as would occur during a denial-of-service attack, directed at a particular victim host or domain. Therefore, prior to packets being dropped, the IP header is accessed and the destination address obtained. This IP destination address is compared to the previous packet's IP destination address. If they are the same, then the IP destination address is stored for comparison with the next packet and the packet is passed to for stateless signature analysis. If the destination addresses are not the same, the destination IP address is still stored for comparison with the next packet, but the packet is dropped. The DiDDeM prototype algorithm is illustrated in figure 11.

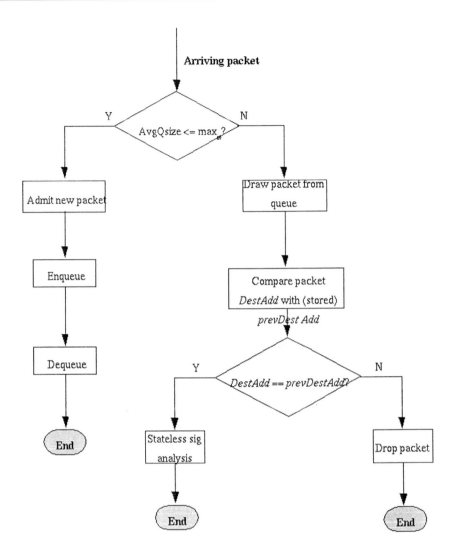

Figure 11. PF algorithm using FIFO queue.

5.2 Stateless Signatures

The *stateless signature detection* module receives a sample of packets from the stateful signature detection module.

Stateless signature analysis is widely used in intrusion detection, and in particular, network intrusion detection. This method defines a set of rules, based on the organisational security policy, and applies them to the traffic being analysed. The signatures used by this approach are more simplistic and therefore have less of an effect on run time performance compared to stateful signatures. A detection application compares an event to a list of known signatures, rather than having to hold information between events. In addition, signature verification is simple and may improve false positive reports. This is achieved by using a single event, for example, a packet or datagram, with which to compare against previously recorded events to determine whether the information represents normal or malicious traffic.

Due to their simplicity, widespread applicability, and reduction in false positive reports, stateless signatures are in widespread deployment by perimeter model devices. Attack signatures, often called *filters*, can be quickly developed in the face of new attack threats and vulnerabilities using application-specific formats. These rules can then be quickly disseminated amongst the application user community to provide contemporary defence against these attacks.

Within DiDDeM, string-matching techniques are used to match the attack signatures. Not all the information in the header is actually relevant for the detection of a denial-of-service attack; only certain fields are of interest. To search all elements of the stream adds overheads with the search of redundant information. Therefore, the signature detection jumps from one element of interest to the next within the stream to ensure that only the relevant parts of a packet header are read and compared.

As the variables in attacks are not constant, expressions of signatures must be made using formal language techniques rather than presenting specific values present in malicious packets. This technique is employed by traditional intrusion detection systems. Expressing specific variable values is not flexible or powerful enough in the case of denial-of-service attacks as relationships between packets cannot be represented. In DiDDeM, signatures are expressed by adopting set theory approach. This language has its roots in mathematics and allows for a concise, unambiguous statement which often needs many lines of carefully selected natural language to be expressed with the same degree of correctness.

The use of such operands allows us to attribute values to variables whilst still maintaining the clarity of the variable. For example, when discussing an IP sequence number, we are able to see the relationship of this variable to other variables that form the signature, as well as assign this variable a value. This provides greater flexibility to explore the relationships between variables than is offered by filter rule-set approaches. When events that satisfy the pattern of an attack are detected, an alert can be created.

Using this format encourages a precise, unambiguous model of a signature. The purpose of this is twofold. First, an unambiguous model of signatures will be interpreted by people in the same way, irrespective of the detection system used. Second, design, implementation, and testing teams will have an accurate single reference point.

In DiDDeM, stateless signatures for denial-of-service attacks are presented using the following general syntactic form:

$$attack\_by\_protocol = (attack, \{\})$$

In the above, *attack_by_protocol* refers to the set of denial-of-service attacks defined by the protocol used. For example, this set may represent all ICMP-based attacks (*ICMPDoSattacks*), or alternatively, all TCP-based attacks (*TCPDoSattacks*). The element *attack* refers to the specific denial-of-service attack. For example, Smurf attack or TCP SYN flood. The corresponding variables that constitute this attack are contained within the inner (curly) brackets.

As an example, a signature for an ICMP-based Smurf attack will take the following form:

$$ICMPDoSattacks = (smurf, \{IP\_seq\_nr, ICMP\_type, source\_IP, TTL\})$$

ICMPDoSattacks is the set of all denial-of-service attacks that utilise the ICMP protocol, and is a sub-set of all denial-of-service attacks. The attack itself is a *smurf* attack. The variables used to detect the attack are; IP sequence number (*IP_seq_nr*), the type of ICMP message (*ICMP_type*), the source IP address (*source_IP*), and the time-to-live value of the packet or packets (*TTL*).

Another example attack is one that utilises UDP and targets sequential ports from spoofed addresses. The attacker, using a spoofed source IP address, sends a large amount of UDP traffic to sequential ports in order to flood the network bandwidth with traffic and disrupt vulnerable services. In this attack, the attacker will want to hide their true identity and target as many vulnerable services as possible. Thus, the variables for such an attack are:

$$UDP\_sequential\_port\_flood\_attacks = (sequential\_spoof, \{IP\_seq\_nr, source\_IP,$$
$$TTL, dest\_port, rest\_port\})$$

The datagram is searched for the following variable relationships:

$$(sequential\_spoof, \{IP\_seq\_nr1_n = IP\_seq\_nr2_{n+1}, source\_IP1_n \neq source\_IP2_n,$$
$$TTL1_1 = TTL2_n, dest\_port1_n = dest\_port2_{n+1}, rest\_port = YES\}).$$

$IP\_seq\_nr1_n = IP\_seq\_nr2_{n+1}$; as the traffic is from a single host, the IP sequence number will be sequential despite the IP source address being spoofed. $source\_IP1_n \neq source\_IP2_n$; as the traffic is spoofed, source IP addresses will not be equal. $TTL1_1 = TTL2_n$; as the traffic is from a single host despite the packet source being spoofed, the messages are likely to have found the same route through the Internet, and the intermediate routers will have decremented the fields by one on the way. $dest\_port1_n = dest\_port2_{n+1}$; as the destination ports are sequential in order to target a range of services on the target host, the destination port will be incremental. *rest_port* = *YES*; as the attack targets sequential ports, it is likely that ports that are not normally associated with large traffic volumes will be targeted.

Another example is that of a TCP SYN flood attack. An attacker, using spoofed source IP addresses, sends a large amount of TCP connection requests to their target. The variables for such an attack are:

$$TCP\_SYN\_flood = (SYN\_flood, \{IP\_seq\_nr, SYN\_flag, ACK\_flag, source\_IP,$$
$$TTL, RST, imp\_add\})$$

The packet is searched for the following variable relationships:

$$(SYN\_flood, \{IP\_seq\_nr1_n = IP\_seq\_nr2_{n+1}, SYN\_flag = 1, source\_IP1_n \neq source\_IP2_n,$$
$$TTL1_1 = TTL2_n, ACK\_flag = 0, imp\_add = YES\}).$$

$IP\_seq\_nr1_n = IP\_seq\_nr2_{n+1}$; as the traffic is from a single host, the IP sequence number will be sequential despite the IP source address being spoofed. *SYN_flag* = *1*; the traffic is attempting to make a connection, therefore will be SYN traffic. $source\_IP1_n \neq source\_IP2_n$; as the traffic is spoofed, source IP addresses will not be equal. $TTL1_1 = TTL2_n$; as the traffic is from a single host despite the packet source being spoofed, the messages are likely to have found the same route through the Internet, and the intermediate routers will have decremented the fields by one on the way. *ACK_flag* = *0*; as no connections will be made, there will be no packets with both SYN and ACK flags set to 1. *imp_add_port = YES*; as the spoofed addresses are randomly generated, it is likely that they will containing source IP addresses belonging to internal networks.

6   Results

Both elements are implemented using the Linux operating system, SuSE 8.1. Two systems were chosen to test the prototypes: a laptop with a PII 400 MHz processor and 128 Mb RAM, and a desktop with a 2 GHz AMD Athlon processor and 256 Mb RAM. This division provides a minimum level with which to test issues such as memory usage and processor load of the system. The comparison of the two allows us to assess the impact of running the system on faster architectures.

6.1   Stateful Signature Detection Findings

Stateful signature detection, as implemented in the simulation software *ns2*, is tested in the following ways: the processor load on the router, packet detection, impact on the router links, and the impact on the router efficiency itself. As will be demonstrated by the results, stateful signature detection has no significant detrimental impact on the operation of the network and the router itself, whilst still effectively detecting denial-of-service attack packets. In addition, it is able to effectively determine stateful information about the network environment in a stateless way.

6.1.1   Processor Load

The stateful signature prototype is tested on two systems to measure the impact of the DiDDeM system on the router. The methodology used is to measure the impact of the simulation on the processor by using the *top* program. This program measures the load by applications on the processor in the UNIX/Linux operating system. To provide a comparison with current network standards, the memory and processor usage were tested for DiDDeM and three routing algorithms; FIFO, DropTail, and RED. This comparison allows us to see the impact on router efficiency in implementing DiDDeM and is presented in table 1.

Table 1. Impact on memory and processor of DiDDeM PF versus RED and DropTail algorithms.

Algorithm	PII 400 MHz 128 Mb RAM		AMD 2 GHz 256 Mb RAM	
	Memory usage	Processor load	Memory usage	Processor load
DiDDeM	4.70%	95.50%	2.30%	41.10%
FIFO	4.60%	97.00%	2.20%	61.70%
RED	4.70%	96.70%	2.30%	60.00%
DropTail	4.60%	96.20%	2.20%	51.80%

As demonstrated by table 1, the impact of the simulation routing algorithm affected the memory usage of both computers. The DropTail routing algorithm required less memory usage, an improvement of 2.13% (PII processor) and 4.34% (AMD Athlon) compared to both

DiDDeM and RED. A similar improvement was observed in the FIFO queue. However, DiDDeM was actively detecting denial-of-service attacks whilst the RED algorithm merely detected congestion at the router. In terms of processor load, DiDDeM proved to be more efficient. However, these figures are representative snapshots of the processor loads provided by the *top* program. Therefore, these figures cannot be used conclusively other than the four algorithms are comparable that the faster the processor used, the less load is placed on the processor itself.

6.1.2   Detection Efficiency

During the simulation, approximately 19,500 UDP attack datagrams are directed at the victim node by the two attacking nodes. This represents an attack consisting of approximately 1,000 datagrams per second. Once the congestion algorithm is invoked by the router, 798 attack datagrams and legitimate packets are to be dropped. Of this number, 742 datagrams are actual attack datagrams whilst the remainder are legitimate traffic. Therefore, out of a total of 19,500 attack datagrams, only 4.09% of this volume is inspected. This figure excludes legitimate traffic and compared to the inefficiency of the Snort approach where each packet traversing the network is inspected 315 times, is very efficient. DiDDeM detected 697 datagrams using the comparison algorithm described in the previous chapter. The enhancement of the FIFO queue in DiDDeM ensures that the minimum complexity of the congestion algorithm provides a maximum worst-case scenario. The 697 datagrams detected out of the 742 inspected ensures a 93.93% detection rate. In addition, only two legitimate packets were falsely detected as attack packets, showing a false positive rate versus actual attack packets of 4%. The above case study demonstrates that DiDDeM can successfully detect large-volume denial-of-service attacks at the router effectively and efficiently.

6.1.3   Network Performance

One key measure for DiDDeM is its performance within the network environment. In particular, the DiDDeM algorithm should not have an adverse affect on the network, thereby requiring a trade off between usability and effectiveness. In order to measure the performance of the DiDDeM PF in the network it is compared to three existing routing algorithms; RED and DropTail. Unlike RED, DiDDeM, FIFO and DropTail do not require any information about the state of the queue. However, to test the impact of DiDDeM on the queue and the network, the number of datagrams and packets that are passed from a router within the attack domain to the second router is measured. This impact is illustrated in figures 12, 13, 14 and 15 showing DiDDeM, FIFO, DropTail and RED.

Figures 12, 13, 14 and 15 show the number of packets sent by router 1 at 0.1 second intervals. As discussed previously, the attack is launched just before 5 seconds. Prior to the attack, all three approaches steadily send the packets comparably, although one slight dip in the number of packets sent is seen in RED at just after 4 seconds. At 5 seconds, the attack is launched causing a large upsurge in traffic observed in all three graphs. Although all four approaches maintain a queue, they are also able to comparably send packets. In fact, there is very little difference in the number of packets sent between the two routers. However, whilst in FIFO, DropTail and RED, those packets not sent are dropped, DiDDeM is comparing these packets for early detection of denial-of-service attacks. As these figures demonstrate, DiDDeM has little effect on the number of packets sent, and therefore network performance.

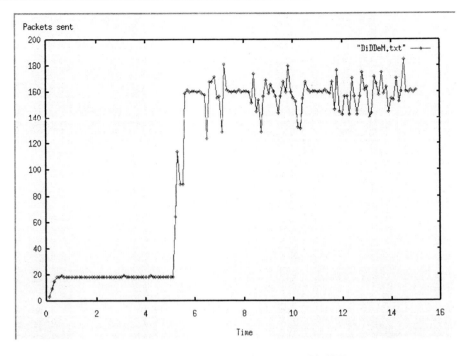

Figure 12. Packets sent by the DiDDeM-enabled PF router.

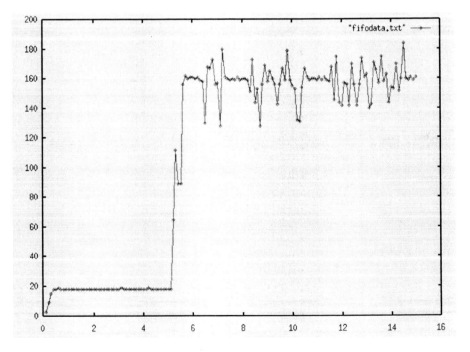

Figure 13. Packets sent by the FIFO-enabled router.

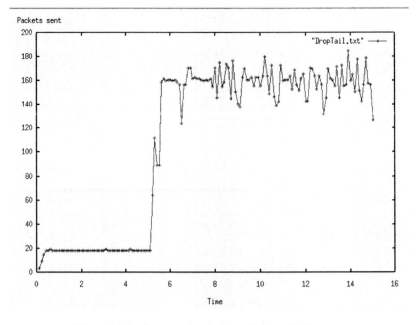

Figure 14. Packets sent by the DropTail-enabled router.

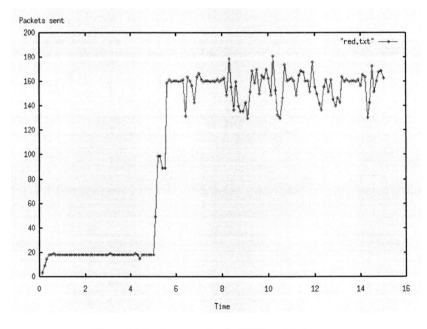

Figure 15. Packets sent by the RED-enabled router.

6.1.4   Router-to-Router Bandwidth Consumption

The *ns2* application has a built-in bandwidth generation tool available in NAM. Whilst the number of packets sent by the first router to the second router are comparable, it is useful to see the bandwidth usage of the link. Figures 16, 17, 18, and 19 show the bandwidth usage between router 1 and router 2. Each line point above represents a 0.1 second interval with 1 second intervals represented by the larger line. The bandwidth compared to the time is illustrated below.

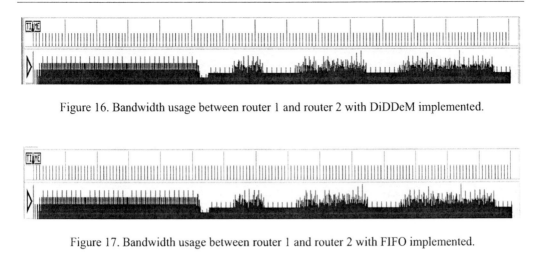

Figure 16. Bandwidth usage between router 1 and router 2 with DiDDeM implemented.

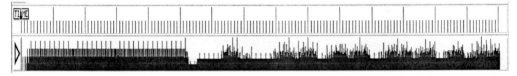

Figure 17. Bandwidth usage between router 1 and router 2 with FIFO implemented.

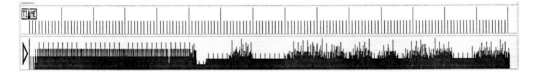

Figure 18. Bandwidth usage between router 1 and router 2 with DropTail implemented.

Figure 19. Bandwidth usage between router 1 and router 2 with RED implemented.

As can be seen by the four figures, DiDDeM is comparable with FIFO, DropTail and RED. Just as the attack is launched at 5 seconds, there is a slight dip in bandwidth used between the two routers. This is due to all four approaches having a 2 millisecond delay built into the queuing algorithms. However, all four approaches successfully send packets and during the attack, maintain periods of low bandwidth consumption. However, as can be seen in figure 16 with DiDDeM, the consumption of bandwidth is less than the DropTail and RED approaches due to the congestion algorithm used.

The stateful signature simulation demonstrates that the design requirements presented in chapter six are met by the system. By enhancing existing congestion algorithms at the router, stateful signature detection provides an efficient means of filtering attack traffic with little bandwidth overhead. The efficiency of the system is comparable to that of existing congestion techniques despite the additional programming costs required of the DiDDeM-enabled router. In addition, stateful signature detection is also able to effectively detect denial-of-service attacks despite reducing the number of packets observed by the system compared to traditional IDS.

6.2   Stateless Signature Detection Findings

As discussed in the previous section, the stateless prototype consists of a C program for matching signatures of attack traffic. These signatures are based on those presented in chapter eight. Three types of attack are considered for evaluation; TCP SYN flood, UDP flood, and ICMP flood. For clarity of testing, each attack signature has an associated matching program, although in reality, these signatures would be combined into one program. These programs take formatted data from programs such as *Ethereal* or *TCPDump*, in text format as illustrated in figure 20. This data is then stripped to provide a single string of TCP/IP headers, which is searched used the jumping window technique described in the previous chapter. Finally, once the data has been searched, the analysis results are printed to the shell, as illustrated in figure 21.

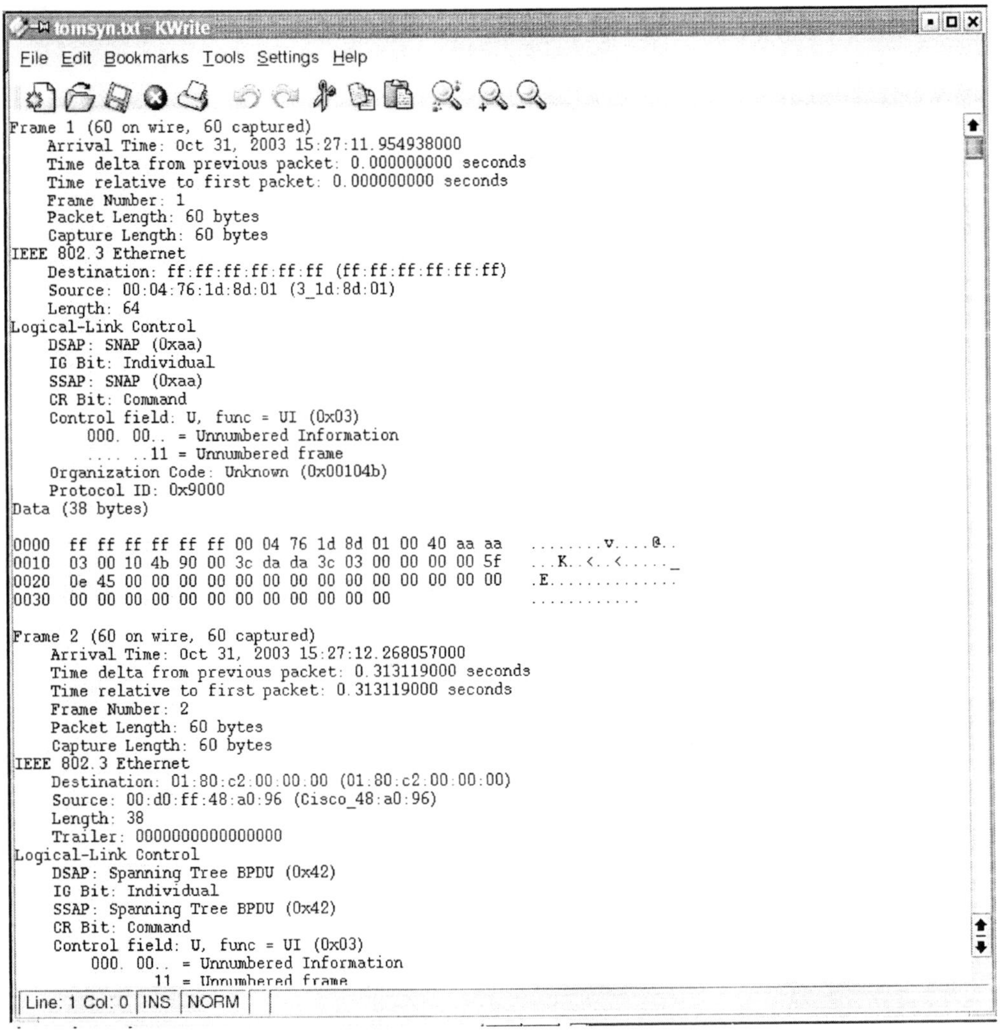

Figure 20. Raw data pior to search.

```
┌─────────────────────────────────────────────────────────────────┐
│ ▣-◪ Shell - Konsole                                    ▪ □ ✕     │
├─────────────────────────────────────────────────────────────────┤
│ Session  Edit  View  Settings  Help                              │
├─────────────────────────────────────────────────────────────────┤
│ packet 2 matches 47 times                                    ⬆  │
│ time to live: 128                                               │
│ dest. port: 32768                                               │
│ source port: 53                                                 │
│ destination IP: 150.204.48.217                                  │
│                                                                 │
│ packet 37 matches 21 times                                      │
│ time to live: 1                                                 │
│ dest. port: 48                                                  │
│ source port: 513                                                │
│ destination IP: 224.0.0.5                                       │
│                                                                 │
│ packet 49 matches 21 times                                      │
│ time to live: 128                                               │
│ dest. port: 138                                                 │
│ source port: 138                                                │
│ destination IP: 150.204.51.255                                  │
│                                                                 │
│ packet 200 matches 72 times                                     │
│ time to live: 64                                                │
│ dest. port: 53                                                  │
│ source port: 32769                                              │
│ destination IP: 150.204.48.55                                   │
│                                                                 │
│ packet 201 matches 72 times                                     │
│ time to live: 128                                               │
│ dest. port: 32769                                               │
│ source port: 53                                                 │
│ destination IP: 150.204.48.217                              ▤  │
│                                                             ▤  │
│ packet 263 matches 99 times                                 ▤  │
│ time to live: 128                                           ▤  │
│ dest. port: 4000                                               │
│ source port: 1030                                           ⬆  │
│ destination IP: 150.204.49.238                              ⬇  │
│ ⬛ New   ▣ Shell                                                 │
└─────────────────────────────────────────────────────────────────┘
```

Figure 21. Output of the stateless signature file search on UDP traffic.

6.2.1   Detection

The command and control server is able to detect all three attacks. A total of 1,000 packets are searched, of which 100 packets are attack packets. As can be seen in table 2, all three attacks were detected by their appropriate signatures presented in chapter eight. In total, the source data contained 195 UDP non-attack datagrams, 126 TCP non-attack packets, and 116 non-attack ICMP packets. UDP attacks return some false positives. This is due to three reasons. First, the TCP SYN flood has a robust signature in that the SYN flag must be set, whereas very little other traffic has this flag set. Second, the UDP protocol headers are less complex than TCP, with less information to search on. Third, the search sample is larger.

Table 2. Results of signature matching detection.

Attack	Detected Y/N	False +
TCP SYN flood	Y	0
UDP flood	Y	7
ICMP flood	Y	0

6.2.2   Detection Time

The placement of the command and control server within the routing infrastructure means that high-speed signature matching is an overarching requirement. In the prototype, some overhead is added to the system as the signature matching programs first must strip the text files of irrelevant data prior to any search made on relevant information. However, run on a

300MHz Pentium II 128Mb SuSE 8.2 system, this signature process takes approximately 0.06 seconds to complete for a 1,000 packet file 2Mb in size. In addition, the programs are very efficient in that very little processor load or memory usage takes place. Therefore, the signature matching system is able to search at approximately 40 Mb per second, or 320 Mbits per second. This rate is faster than that of many large networks. In addition, this is after packets have already been filtered at the router. Therefore, DiDDeM is able to scan network traffic at an extremely high speed.

7   Conclusion

Technological advances have shaped the twentieth century and will continue to shape life in the twenty-first. Just as the development of the aircraft in the first-half of the last century drastically changed the size of the world, so the development of networks has continued this resizing. With the development of flight, the world appeared a much smaller place, enabling trans-Atlantic and global operations in much shorter timescales. The development of the Internet and network technologies has shortened this timescale even further. This technology allows real-time data transfer at minimal cost, making information the most important commodity for business today. The exchange of information through technologies such as e-mail or the World Wide Web has become crititcally important to business. Assets unquantifiable in physical terms such as reputation or intellect are those valued most highly by large and small organisations alike.

Underpinning this flow of information are networking technologies. These technologies are the means by which the information economy is realised. Whilst there are heterogeneous networks and systems, there must be a means by which information is able to flow from one system to another without the disruption of the data. The TCP/IP model provides this functionality. This model encompasses a variety of protocols that combined, enable data to be sent from one host on one network, to another host on a different network transparently to the user. However, this use of the TCP/IP model is not without its problems. The primary issue is that it was not designed with security in mind; it was designed to ensure that packets reached their destination irrespective of the route taken. This design priority has left its legacy.

One of the greatest threats to the information economy is that the services provided are not available when needed. The cost due to unavailability of services on the Internet is difficult to quantify in economic terms. However, unavailability of services has a major impact on the business for three reasons. First, many businesses now integrate on-line strategies into their marketing and business plans. These strategies form a key component of future market and business growth. Second, organisations are relying on networking as a key technology for the flow of information, their most valuable commodity, both within and beyond their traditional organisational boundaries. Third, networks are set to become more pervasive with the rise of wireless networking and ubiquitous systems. Combined, such a traditionally unquantifiable cost such as unavailability of services is a major concern.

A lack of effectiveness of perimeter model defences has led to a number of approaches to be posited to counter the issue of denial of service. For example, payment approaches suggest that if network availability was paid for, the attacker could not afford to launch an attack. Alternatively, some argue for stronger authentication. However, the most effective approach is that of traffic monitoring and throttling. Traffic can be monitored for signs of an attack, and once that attack is detected, some remedial action may be put in place to prevent the attack from succeeding. However, many approaches lack the scalability or flexibility with which to detect and defend against denial-of-service attacks. Therefore, there is a requirement for a new approach for defence against denial-of-service attacks which is met by DiDDeM.

This requirement has motivated us to propose the novel distributed mechanism, DiDDeM, for effective early detection and prevention of DoS attacks. In this chapter, we have demonstrated that the DiDDeM makes use of stateful and stateless signatures in conjunction for attack detection, which differs from the other related work that mainly employs one of the two signature approaches. The main benefit from the combination of the two approaches is that not all malicious packets have to be inspected in order to ascertain the presence of an attack, thus improving detection efficiency and making attack detection feasible within the routing infrastructure. Moreover, as demonstrated by this chapter, the DiDDeM offers a novel, distributed and scalable approach to provide early detection for denial-of-service attacks.

References

[1] Al-Fawzan, M.A.H., Fahad Placement of network servers in a wide-area network. *Computer Networks*, **34**. 355-361.

[2] Baba, T.M., Shigeyuki Tracing Network Attacks to their Sources. *IEEE Internet Computing*, **6** (2). 20-26.

[3] Baltatu, M., Lioy, Antonio, Maino, Fabio & Mazzocchi, Daniele 'Security Issues in Control, Management and Routing Protocols'. *Computer Networks*, **34** (6). 881-894.

[4] Barlow, J.T., W. 'TFN2K - An Analysis', 2000.

[5] Bass, T., Freyre, A., Gruber, D. & Watt, G. 'E-Mail Bombs and Countermeasures: Cyber Attacks and Brand Integrity'. *IEEE Network*, **12** (2). 10-17.

[6] Bellovin, S.M. 'Security Problems in the TCP/IP Protocol Suite'. *Computer Communications Review*, **19** (2). 32-48.

[7] Bishop, M., Cheung, S. & Wee, C. 'The Threat from the Net'. *IEEE Spectrum*, **34** (8). 56-63.

[8] Bradley, K.A., Cheung, Steven, Pucketza, Nick, Mukherjee, Baswanath, & Olsson, Ronald A., 'Detecting Disruptive Routers: A Distributed Network Monitoring Approach'. in *Proceedings of the 1998 IEEE Symposium on Security and Privacy*, (Oakland, CA, 1998), 115-124.

[9] Brustoloni, J.C., Protecting Electronic Commerce from Distributed Denial-of-Service Attacks. in *WWW2002*, (Honolulu, Hawaii, USA, 2001).

[10] Cabrera, J.B.D., Lewis, Lundy, Qin, Xinzhou, Lee, Wenke, Prasanth, ravi K., Ravichandran, B. & Mehra, Raman K., Proactive Detection of Distributed Denial of Service Attacks using MIB Traffic Variables - A Feasibility Study. in *IEEE/IFID International Symposium on Integrated Network Management*, (Seattle, WA, USA, 2001), IEEE/IFIP, 609-622.

[11] CERT. 'Results of the Distributed Systems Intruder Tools Workshop, Pittsburgh, Pennsylvania USA November 2-4, 1999', CERT Coordination Center, 1999.

[12] Chen, Z.L., Moon-Chuen, An IP Traceback Technique Against Denial-of-Service Attacks. in *Annual Computer Security Applications Conference (ACSAC)*, (Las Vegas, NA, USA, 2003).

[13] Cheswick, W.R.B., S. M. *Firewalls and Internet Security - Repelling the Wily Hacker*. Addison-Wesley, Reading, MA, 1994.

[14] Cheung, S.L., Karl N., 'Protecting Routing Infrastructures from Denial of Service Using Cooperative Intrusion Detection'. in *New Security Paradigms Workshop*, (Cumbria, UK, 1997).

[15] Coit, C.J.S., Stuart, & McAleney, Joseph, Towards Faster String Matching for Intrusion Detection or Exceeding the Speed of Snort. in *DARPA Information Survivability Conference and Exposition II (DISCEX 01)*, (Anaheim, CA, USA, 2001), 367-373.

[16] Comer, D.E. *Internetworking with TCP/IP Volume I: Principles, Protocols, and Architecture*. Prentice Hall International, USA, 1995.

[17] Deri, L.S., Stefano 'Practical Network Security: Experiences with ntop'. *Computer Networks*, **34**. 873-880.

[18] Dietrich, S., Long, Neil, & Dittrich, David, 'Analyzing Distributed Denial of Service Tools: The Shaft Case'. in *14th Systems Administration Conference (LISA 2000)*, (New Orleans, Louisiana, 2000), 329-339.

[19] Dittrich, D. 'The DoS Project's "trinoo" Distributed Denial of Service Attack Tool', Ditrich, D., 1999.

[20] Dittrich, D. 'The "Tribe Flood Network" Distributed Denial of Service Attack Tool', Ditrich, D., 1999.

[21] Dittrich, D.W., G., Dietrich, S. & Long, N. 'The "mstream" Distributed Denial of Service Attack Tool', 2000.

[22] Ferguson, P.S., D. 'Network Ingress Filtering: Defeating Denial of Service Attacks Which Employ IP Source Address Spoofing', The Internet Society, 1998.

[23] Florio, M., Gorrieri, R, & Marchetti, G. 'Coping with denial of service due to malicious Java applets'. *Computer Communications*, **23**. 1645-1654.

[24] Gil, T.M., & Poletto, Massimiliano, "MULTOPS: a data-structure for bandwidth attack detection". in *Proceedings of USENIX Security Symposium*, (Washington, DC, USA, 2001).

[25]   Gonzalez, G. 'Congressional Statement on Cybercrime by the Federal Bureau of Investigation', FBI/US Govt, 2000.

[26]   Gorinsky, S., Jain, Sugat, Vin, Harrick & Zhang, Yongguang, Robustness of Inflated Subscription in Multicast Congestion Control. in *SIGCOMM '03*, (Karlesruhe, Germany, 2003), ACM, 87-98.

[27] Gorrieri, R.M., I., Applet Watch-Dog: A monitor Controlling the Execution of Java Applets. in *14th IFIP*, (Vienna, Austria, 1998), Chapman-Hall.

[28] Gouda, M.G.E., EN (Mootaz); Huang, Chin-Tser; & McGuire, Tommy M. Hop Integrity in Computer Networks. *IEEE Transactions on Networking*, **10** (3). 308 - 319.

[29] Grunwald, D.G., Soraya, Microarchitectural Denial of Service: Insuring Microarchitectural Fairness. in *35th Annual IEEE/ACM International Symposium in Microarchitecture (MICRO-35)*, (Istanbul, Turkey, 2002), IEEE/ACM.

[30] Haggerty, J., Berry, T., Shi, Q. & Merabti, M., DiDDeM: A System for Early Detection of TCP SYN Flood Attacks. in *Globecom 2004*, (Dallas, TX, USA, 2004), IEEE.

[31] Haggerty, J., Shi, Q. & Merabti, M., 'Defending Against Denial of Service: A Network Filtering Based Approach'. in *2nd Annual Post-Graduate Symposium on the Convergence of Telecommunications, Networking & Broadcasting*, (Liverpool, 2001), Liverpool John Moores University, 119-124.

[32] Haggerty, J., Shi, Q. & Merabti, M., Statistical Signatures for Early Detection of Flooding Denial-of-Service Attacks. in *IFIP SEC 2005*, (Chiba, Japan, 2005), IFIP.

[33] Haggerty, J., Shi, Qi & Merabti, Madjid Early Detection and Prevention of Denial-of-Service Attacks: A Novel Mechanism with Propagated Traced-Back Attack Blocking. *Journal on Selected Areas of Communications* (Q4).

[34] Hall, R.J. 'Channels: Avoiding Unwanted Electronic Mail'. *Communications of the ACM*, **41** (3 March 1998). 88-95.

[35] Hall, R.J. 'A Countermeasure to Duplicate-detecting Anti-spam Techniques', AT&T Labs, 1999.

[36] Harris, B.H., R. 'TCP/IP Security Threats and Attack Methods'. *Computer Communications* (22). 885-897.

[37] Hassler, V. *Security Fundamentals for E-Commerce.* Artech House, Norwood, MA, 2001.

[38] Heberlein, L.T.B., M. 'Attack Class: Address Spoofing'. in Denning, D.E.D., P. J. ed. *Internet Besieged*, ACM Press, New York, 1998, 147-157.

[39] Houle, K.J., Weaver, George M. in collaboration with Long, Neil & Thomas, Rob. 'Trends in Denial of Service Attack Technology', CERT Coordination Center, 2001.

[40] Huang, Y.P., J. Mark, Countering Denial-of-Service Attacks Using Congestion Triggered Packet Sampling and Filtering. in *Proceedings of the 10th International Conference on Computer Communication and Networks*, (Scottsdale, AZ, USA, 2001), IEEE, Piscataway, NJ, USA, 490-494.

[41] Ioannidis, J.B., Steven M., Implementing Pushback: Router-based Defense Against DDoS Attacks. in *Network and Distributed Systems Security Symposium*, (San Diego, CA, USA, 2002).

[42] Juels, A.B., John, Client Puzzles: A Cryptographic Countermeasure Agaianst Connection Depletion Attacks. in *Proceedings of the 1999 Network and Distributed Systems Security Symposium (NDSS)*, (San Diego, CA, USA, 1999), Internet Society, 151-165.

[43] Jung, J.K., Balachander; & Rabinovich, Michael, Flash Crowds and Denial of Service Attacks: Characterization and Implications for CDNs and Web Sites. in WWW2002, (Honolulu Hawaii USA, 2002).

[44] Kim, G.a.B., Tony, Active Ingress Monitoring (AIM): An Intrusion Isolation Scheme in Active Networks. in *Proceedings of the IEEE International Conference on Communications (ICC)*, (Helsinki, Finland, 2001), IEEE, Piscataway, NJ, USA, 194-198.

[45] Kim, G.B., Tony; and Chee, Dana, ACtive edge-Tagging (ACT): An Intruder Identification & Isolation Scheme in Active Networks. in *Proceedings of the 6th IEEE Symposium on Computers and Communications* 2001, (Hammamet, Tunisia, 2001), IEEE Comp Soc, Los Alamites, CA USA, 29-34.

[46] Lau, F., Rubin, Stuart H., Smith, Michael H., & Trajkovic, Ljiljana, 'Distributed Denial of Service Attacks'. in *Proceedings of the 2000 IEEE International Conference on Systems, Man, and Cybernetics*, (Nashville, TN, USA, 2000), 2275-2280.

[47] Lemon, J., "Resisting SYN floods DoS attacks with a SYN cache". in *BSDCon* 2002, (Berkeley, CA, USA, 2002), Usenix Association, 89-97.

[48] Mankins, D., Krishnan, Rajesh, Boyd, Ceilyn, Zao, John & Frentz, Michael, 'Mitigating Distributed Denial of Service Attacks with Dynamic Resource Pricing'. in *Proceedings of the Annual Computer Security Applications Conference (ACSAC)* 2001, (New Orleans, Louisana, USA, 2001), ACSAC.

[49] Mansfield, G., Ohta, K., Takei, Y., Kato, N., & Nemoto, Y. 'Towards trapping wily intruders in the large'. *Computer Networks*, **34** (4). 659-670.

[50] May, J.P., Jim & Bauman, John, Attack Detection in Large Networks. in *DARPA Information Survivability Conference & Exposition (DISCEX)* 2001, (Anaheim, CA, USA, 2001), 15-21.

[51] Meadows, C. 'A cost-based framework for analysis of denial of service in networks'. *Journal of Computer Security*, **9** (1-2). 143-164.

[52] Moore, D., Voelker, Geoffrey M., & Savage, Stefan, 'Inferring Internet Denial-of-Service Activity'. in *10th Usenix Security Symposium*, (Washington, DC, 2001).

[53] Mutaf, P. 'Defending Against a Denial-of-Service Attack on TCP', RAID Conference 1999, 1999.

[54] Narayanaswamy, K. ISPs and Denial of Service Attacks. *Information Systems Security*, **11** (2). 38-46.

[55] Ning, P.C., Yun & Reeves, Douglas S., Analyzing Intensive Intrusion Alerts Via Correlation. in *Proceedings of the 5th International Symposium on Recent Advances in Intrusion Detection (RAID 2002)*, (Zurich, Switzerland, 2002), LNCS, 74-94.

[56] Northcutt, S. *Network Intrusion An Analyst's Handbook*. New Rider Publishing, 1999.

[57] Northcutt, S.C., Mark; Fearnow, Matt; & Frederick, Karen *Intrusion Signatures and Analysis*. New Riders Publishing, Indianapolis, Indiana, USA, 2001.

[58] Odlyzko, A. 'A modest proposal for preventing Internet congestion', AT&T Research Labs, 1997.

[59] Papadimitratos, P.H., Zygmunt J. Securing the Internet Routing Infrastructure. *IEEE Communications Magazine* (Octoiber 2002).

[60] Park, K.L., Heejo, 'On the effectiveness of route-based packet filtering for Distributed DoS attack prevention in power-law internets'. in *SIGCOMM'01*, (San Diego, CA, 2001).

[61] Pethia, R.P., Alan; & Spafford, Gene. Concensus Roadmap for Defeating Distributed Denial of Service Attacks, SANS.org & Partnership for Critical Infrastructure Security, 2000.

[62] Pfleeger, C.P.P., Shari Lawrence *Security in Computing 3rd ed.* Prentice-Hall, Upper Saddle River, NJ, USA, 2003.

[63] Postel, J. 'RFC792 Internet Control Message Protocol, The Internet Society, 1981.

[64] Proctor, P.E. *The Practical Intrusion Detection Handbook*. Prentice Hall, Saddle River, NJ, 2001.

[65] Ricciulli, L., Lincoln, Patrick & Kakkar, Pankaj, 'TCP SYN flooding defense'. in *CNDS 1999*, (1999).

[66] Richardson, R. The Eighth Annual CSI/FBI Computer Crime and Security Survey 2003, Computer Security Institute/Federal Bureau of Investigation, 2003.

[67] Rivest, R.L., Shamir, A. & Adelman, L.M. A Method for Obtaining Digital Signatures and Public-Key Cryptosystems. *Communications of the ACM*, **21** (2). 120-126.

[68] Schuba, C.L., Krsul, I. V., Kuhn, M. G., Spafford, E. H., Sundaram, A., & Zamboni, D., 'Analysis of a Denial of Service Attack on TCP'. in *IEEE Symposium on Security and Privacy*, (Oakland, CA, 1997).

[69] Shan, Z.C., Peng; Xu, Ying; & Xu, Ke, A Network State Based Intrusion Detection Model. in *Computer Networks and Mobile Computing 2001 (ICCNMC)*, (Beijing, China, 2001), IEEE, 481-486.

[70] Sterne, D., Djahandari, Kelly, Balupari, Ravindra, La Cholter, William, Babson, Bill, Wilson, Brett, Narasimhan, Priya & Purtell, Andrew, Active Network Based DDoS Defense. in *DARPA Active Networks Conference and Exposition (DANCE '02)*, (San Fransisco, CA, USA, 2002), IEEE.

[71] Tanenbaum, A.S. *Computer Networks*. Pearson Education International, Upper Saddle River, NJ, USA, 2003.

[72] Verwoerd, T.H., Ray Intrusion detection techniques and approaches. *Computer Communications*, **25**. 1356-1365.

[73] Vijayan, J. Full Cause of Massive Internet Redirection Still Unclear, Computer-world, 2001.

[74] Walters, R. Top 10 Ways to Prevent Denial of Service Attacks. *Information Systems Security*, **10** (3). 71-72.

[75] Wang, H., Zhang, Danlu, & Shin, Kang G., "Detecting SYN Flooding Attacks". in *INFOCOM 2002*, (Hilton, New York, USA, 2002), IEEE.

[76] Yan, J., Early, S. & Anderson, R. 'The XenoService - A Distributed Defeat for Distributed Denial of Service', Computer Labs, Cambridge University, 2000.

[77] Yan, J.J. 'Denial of Service: Another Example'. in Ghonaimy, M.A., El-Hadidi, M. T., & Aslan, H. K. ed. *Security in the Information Society Visions and Perspectives*, Kluwer Academic Publishers, Dordecht, Netherlands, 2002, 161-169.

In: Computer Networking and Networks
Editor: Susan Shannon, pp. 41-62

ISBN 1-59454-830-7
© 2006 Nova Science Publishers, Inc.

Chapter 2

AUTOMATIC CREATION OF AGREEMENTS IN A SERVICE-ORIENTED SCENARIO

Pablo Fernandez, Manuel Resinas and Rafael Corchuelo
Universidad de Sevilla, Dpto. de Lenguajes y Sistemas Informaticos
Avda. de la Reina Mercedes, s/n. Sevilla 41.012 (Spain)

Abstract

New trends in Network Computing, such as SOA (Service Oriented Architecture), allow an easy integration of heterogeneous systems. Among other benefits, these advances make it possible to outsource several parts of the business process as services. Moreover, as a next step in that direction, we foresee an automatic outsourcing that allows the customer to choose at run-time the best provider according to its business rules. However, a significant gap still has to be solved: there is a need of an automated handling of the agreement process. Although several specifications and architectures have been proposed, no one covers, as far as we know, the agreement creation process completely because they focus on a one-to-one scenario and do not tackle the problem of searching and choosing the provider that better fits customer's needs and vice versa. In this article we make an introduction to the state of the art in the automatic creation of agreements in a service-oriented scenario. In addition, we present a novel standards-based proposal that solves the above mentioned problems with a many-to-many architecture. It deals with the whole process of creating agreements automatically taking three major concerns into account: non-functional requirements, dynamic business policies and automated negotiation.

1 Introduction

SOA [35] has irrupted into software development world as a new approach to deal with complexity of systems. This architecture is the result of a widely accepted web service framework [14] composed of a set of standards that is continuously extended forming an integrated stack of technologies.

Within SOA, complex systems can be seen as a collaborative environment of services. Each of those services interacts with each others through a standard-base expression of its capabilities. Furthermore, the aim of this infrastructure would make possible not only a discovery and use of services but also composition (workflow of services) and quality of service assurance mechanisms.

There are mainly two scenarios where SOA shows its benefits, intra-organisationals and cross-organisationals scenarios [11]: (i) On the one hand SOA provides a flexible way to integrate different systems in the enterprise; regarding this scenario it has been proposed [35] the idea of an enterprise service bus [1] as the next generation of integration middleware that would act as a central infrastructure of the whole organization (ii) On the other hand, interoperability among companies has been the holy grail pursuit by different technologies that have appeared in the last decades. At this point, web services initiatives can be seen as a step forward in that direction with a set of open standards that make possible a high degree of interaction between loosely coupled systems.

Though service orientation has appeared as a new concept in the software, this approach has been widely adopted in other industries. Among other consequences, service orientation boosts an special kind of collaboration between corporations: the so called, outsourcing [37] of services. Through this mechanism, a given enterprise would delegate some part of its business process to an external one. In order to understand the motivation and benefits of outsourcing, we can briefly analyse a classical industry: the supply chain management.

A supply chain is a network of facilities and distribution options that performs the functions of procurement of materials; transformation of this material into intermediate and finished products; and distribution of these finished products to customers. In this kind of scenario, enterprises based its business in the outsourcing of different parts of the chain. From a customer point of view, these companies appear as a black box that serves products; however, the main source of profit comes from the integration and management of the whole chain instead of the product building itself.

In the software industry, the idea of outsourcing has been adopted in last decades. There have been some specific studies of these techniques in IT companies and major benefits have been identified [47]: Reduction of risks, quick adoption of new technologies, optimisation of resource exploitation and cost saving. Traditionally, this outsourcing has been related to long term relationship between corporations where a given enterprise subcontracts a part of the system for a certain period of time (and, in some cases, forever).

However, with the arrival of SOA, we can foresee a new approach to this idea: the dynamic outsourcing. Service orientation in software development provides the perfect scenario for a short term outsourcing that can be dynamically created to fit the business needs of each moment. This would mean, a next step to an automatic procurement of services that will allow the customer to choose the best provider according to its business rules at run time.

Nevertheless, in order to achieve a high level of dynamism in the outsourcing phase, we should move toward an automated process that can reduce the cost and time of creating the business partnership among organisations involved. In fact, in the heart of the outsourcing process we can find the agreement concept. Concretely, an agreement that would regulate the responsibilities and guarantees of every party in the business relationship.

Following these ideas, one of the biggest trends of automated outsourcing nowadays is to solve a significant gap [21]: there is a need of an automated handling of the agreement

---

[1] More info in W. Chappel, Enterprise Service Bus, O'Reilly 2004

process [31]. This typically covers two steps namely: (i) The first step is to have a machine processable way to express the agreement. In our context, these agreements consist of a set of terms that the parties that sign the agreement are supposed to observe. If they do not, different sanctions can be imposed to them. These terms can be referred to both functional and non-functional requirements. (ii) The second step is the definition of the agreement process itself. Two different phases have been identified on it [31]: On the one hand, the agreement creation phase, which can include a negotiation process, in which both customer and provider try to get an agreement that maximises their benefits based on their business information and, on the other hand, a track of the service consumption in order to check the agreement fulfilment.

The motivation of an automated agreement (and therefore outsourcing) process is based on the business benefits achieved by the parties involved, service consumers and providers: The service consumer could dynamically change a service provider depending on the current market status. Furthermore, this would boost an environment where service providers would compete to make better service offers to satisfy consumer demands. In the service provider side, an automation of the agreement process would mean a highly adaptable offer creation based on the current provider capabilities and resource status. Finally, in general for both consumers and providers, the possibility of avoiding the human factor of agreement search and negotiation would potentially bring an important reduction in the time and cost of the partnership establishment.

In this chapter we discuss and analyse the issues and problems to be solved in order to achieve an effective automated agreement creation in a real-world scenario where multiple service consumers and services providers interact with each other. Their goal would be to look for the best business relationships that would maximise their profit. In Section 2 we introduce a conceptual background of the scenario addressed. Later on, in Section 3 we propose an abstract architecture for the construction of an infrastructure that supports the scenario described above. The description is done in two levels of abstraction: First we analyse the general scenario outlining roles and protocols that would form up the architecture. Second, in a refinement stage, we focus on negotiation issues and address a general framework of negotiation as we believe it is a key part of the agreement creation process. Next, in Section 4, the related work is analysed. Finally, our conclusions are detailed in Section 5.

2   Automated Agreement Creation

Several phases have been identified on the contracting process [29] as it is shown in figure 1. Next, we describe all those phases.

The first step that appears in the figure is outside the contracting process and it has been called *preparation phase*. This step consists in the creation of the offer by the provider of the service and the analysis of functional and non-functional requirements of the service by the consumer.

Next step in the process is the searching phase. The goal of this phase is to match service providers with potential consumers and vice versa. This may be done in several ways. For instance, service providers may publish their offer in some central place to make them available to potential consumers. Another option is that service consumers announce

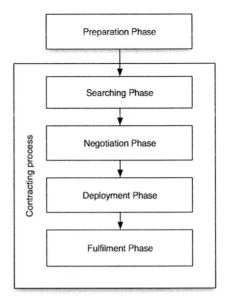

Figure 1: Contracting process

their needs so that service providers contact them to offer their services. The result of this phase is that both service provider and consumer get a list of potential service consumers or providers respectively. In the next phase, they may start a negotiation with those consumers or providers to find a mutually acceptable agreement.

The third step is the negotiation phase. In this phase, both participants (service provider and service consumer) carry out a negotiation process to reach an agreement about the conditions and terms of the execution of the service. This negotiation process may be carried out with several parties at the same time to find the provider or consumer that best fits its needs. The result at the end of this phase is the creation of an agreement about the execution of a service between a provider and a consumer.

In the next phase, both service provider and service consumer set up a deployment plan to make it possible to follow all terms established in the agreement settled in the previous phase. Thanks to the existence of the agreement, the deployment plan can be generated in an automated way, allowing a more accurate plan that optimises the resources in both the service provider and the consumer.

The last phase in the contracting process is the fulfilment phase. This phase consists in the fulfilment of the obligations established in the agreement and in the monitoring of the whole process (in order to assure that both parties observe the agreement correctly). This monitoring may be carried out by the involved parties or by a third party.

The first three phases (preparation, searching and negotiation) belong to the agreement creation process, where the goal is to get an agreement between a service provider and a service consumer that maximises their benefits based on their business information. In the remainder of the article we focus on this agreement creation process.

2.1 Offers and Demands

In order to reach an agreement, enterprises should previously express clearly their business goals. In this subsection we focus on the different types of information that can be involved in the agreement establishment among organizations. The main aim of this analysis is to reach a comprehensive definition of every kind of information involved in the process.

In general, a first classification of this information can be done depending on if it is public or private to the enterprise:

- **Public:** This would include all information that would be published by the corporation in order to look for potential partners. Traditionally, this set of public information has been called *offer* or *demand* regarding if it is announced by service provider or service consumer respectively.

- **Private:** In this group, we can find the necessary information to feed the decision making system. In general, this information is closely linked to the business strategy of corporation.

If we look down to a lower level of abstraction, we can create another classification based on the goal of information as follows:

- **Functional Requirements:** This information usually covers a set of descriptions about the functionality of the service. Formally, a functional requirement can be defined as a statement about what the service will or should do. In the case of the service consumer, a functional requirement will express a desire and, in the case of service provider, will express a capability. A first approach to this idea in the software industry has been the concept of interface; however, in order to achieve a comprehensive way of expression, we should take into account semantic information such as operational semantics [33]. In web services framework, main approach to the concept of interface (and, therefore, functional requirement) is WSDL [9]; this specification enables an extensible way of description that can be composed with other languages. In the last years web semantic initiative [5] has pushed the idea of semantic web services [15] forward.

- **Non-Functional Requirements:** This information is usually related with the quality of service. A formal definition of what is and what is not a non-functional requirement is not possible due it depends on a particular context and problem domain; a functional requirement in a given situation can be classified as non-functional in another. In the field of software engineering, quality has been extensively studied [32] [40] [10], and some catalogues of quality attributes have been developed. Based on these catalogues, a formal approach to the concept of non-functional requirement can be done in terms of acceptable domains of a given attribute.

- **Utility Functions:** Closely linked to non-functional requirements, utility functions are the information needed to express the preferences among different values of non-functional requirements. In fact, each non-functional requirement should usually have an utility function associated; this function would allow a given decision-making system to evaluate or rank different agreement proposals.

- **Negotiation Clauses:** When organisations specify their requirements (on both offers and demands) there is usually a degree of flexibility that would allow some changes over initial requirements. This is normally expressed in terms of relationships amongst non-functional requirements. The information where a corporation details that flexibility degree amongst requirements is known as negotiation clauses. Later on in this section, we analyse a conceptual background of agreement negotiation.

2.2   Agreement Structure

Generally, an agreement can be defined as a decision or arrangement between two or more parties. In the case of outsourcing, arrangements are related to rights and obligations of every corporation that participate in the service development.

Main parts of an agreement can be classified as following:

- A first part describing parties involved in the agreement. In this part also could be necessary to specify possible third parties or mediators between parties.

- The second part should have a description of responsibilities of every party such as cost, service level or reliability guarantees.

- A third part would clarify the terms used in every part of the agreement. This part is extremely necessary to achieve a good understanding by all parties about the exact meaning of every concept of the agreement.

In order to express these contents, we can select different approaches. The more flexible way would be usually achieved with natural languages while a formal language could facilitate a high grade of automation and integration amongst parties.

2.3   Agreement Negotiation

The automated negotiation process can be understood as a search, in the space of possible agreements, of a mutually acceptable agreement by the parties that are carrying out the negotiation, trying to maximise the common outcome. Different categories of kinds of automated negotiation can be established based on the characteristics of the parties involved in the negotiation and their relationship.

In this work, we focus on the so called service-oriented negotiations [41]. The goal of this negotiation is to reach an agreement between a service provider and a service consumer about the terms and guarantees of the service consumption. This scenario defines the characteristics of the negotiation that shall be carried out. It is a non-cooperative negotiation because the parties involved in it are selfish and, therefore, they just try to maximise their own benefit. It is also a negotiation with partial information because if a party have access to the private information of other parties, it may use it in its own benefit to get a more profitable agreement. Finally, the negotiation has hard computational constraints, because we are interested in negotiating a real scenario.

Three different parts must be taken into consideration in an automated negotiation process: the negotiation object (what is being negotiated), the negotiation protocol (which are the rules of the negotiation and how the parties communicate each other) and the decision-making model or strategy that are followed by the parties involved in the negotiation. These three parts are not independent but strongly related: depending on the negotiation object, it is better to use one negotiation protocol over another one, and, depending on the negotiation protocol, a specific decision-making model must be followed. Next, we detail these three parts.

2.3.1   Negotiation Object

In a service-oriented negotiation, the negotiation object is an agreement establishing the terms of the service consumption. Therefore, the goal of the negotiation is to find the values or ranges of those terms so that the agreement is optimum or, at least, acceptable to the parties involved in the negotiation.

Several proposals have been presented about the format of these agreements [45], but the most significant is WS-Agreement [2], that probably shall become the standard of agreement definitions.

2.3.2   Negotiation Protocol

The negotiation protocol establishes the rules that govern the negotiation and the way the communication between the different parties involved in the negotiation is carried out. The most common negotiation protocols can be categorised into [22] auctions and bilateral negotiations.

Auctions consist of one or more parties called auctioneers, that start the auction and other parties called bidders that bid following a protocol that may allow one or several rounds. There are a lot of kinds of auctions [43], but the most popular are [4]: English auction (auctioneer starts with the minimum acceptable price and bidders raise their bids until either nobody bid higher or a time limit is reached), Dutch auction (auctioneer starts with the maximum price and then lowers it while no offers are made, the first one that bids wins the auction), Vickrey auction (bidders don't know what the other bidders are offering, the highest bid wins the auction, but the price paid is the price of the second higher bid) and the first-price sealed-bid auction (like the Vickrey but the price paid is the higher bid price).

Bilateral negotiations involve the exchange of offers and counteroffers between the service provider and service consumer. This negotiation may be without restrictions on the content of the offer and counteroffer[41]; with restrictions like *the range of values of, at least, a term in the counteroffer must be narrower than in the offer* [23]. They may use a system of votes to avoid local minima in the negotiation of complex contracts [25]. The terms of the agreement may be negotiated one-by-one following an established agenda [18]. It may be possible to commit and decommit an agreement depending on the needs of the parties [34] or to argument why an offer is good to persuade the other party to accept it [38]. Another example of this kind of protocol is the FIPA Contract Net [13]. Obviously, a concrete negotiation protocol may present several of these characteristics or introduce small variations to them.

2.3.3 Decision Making Models

The decision making model determines the way different parties involved in the negotiation process shall behave. That is, what is being considered as an acceptable offer, what it is not, how the counteroffer is built or how the bid is carried out. Two parts are distinguished in the decision making model: the offer evaluation and the construction of a counteroffer to that offer.

The most common way of evaluating offers is through the definition of utility functions to each term of the agreement. Depending on the value of the term, it have a certain utility to the party [16]. The total utility of the agreement is usually calculated as the weighted sum of the utilities of each term of the agreement [39].

After evaluating the offer, it is decided whether it is acceptable to us and, if it is not, a counteroffer is built. A wide variety of techniques have been developed to generate counteroffers. The most significant are: those that use time-dependant functions, resource-dependant functions, etcetera to obtain the counteroffer by modifying the values of the terms of the offer [16]; those that try to make the counteroffer more appealing to the opponent by sending the counteroffer with the highest similarity to the received offer [17]; those that use constraint resolution techniques [27] or that are based on fuzzy constraints [26], and those that interpret the negotiation as if it were a game and use techniques similar to those used in chess games [24]. Genetic algorithms have also been used to calculate off-line which is the best strategy to use depending on the conditions of the negotiation in a certain instant [4, 19].

Finally, it is useful to model our opponent in the negotiation and to know its preferences in order to build better counteroffers. Bayesian learning [49] and kernel density estimation techniques [12] have been proposed to build such model.

2.4 WS-Agreement

To make the automated agreement creation process a reality, there is a need to standardise the way the agreements are created as well as the format of the agreement document. This standardisation effort is being made in the GRAAP work group of the Grid Global Forum (GGF). The name of the specification is WS-Agreement and currently it is being revised by the members of the group before its public presentation.

The goals that have been established in WS-Agreement are threefold: to define a document format for the agreements, to establish a concrete agreement creation process and to describe the communication interfaces that must be implemented by the parties involved in the agreement creation process.

The agreement document is defined in an XML format. It is composed of three sections: the name of the agreement, which is used to identify it, the context of the agreement, and its terms. The context of the agreement establishes the parties that are involved in the agreement, the expiration time and the name of the template which the agreement is based on. The terms of an agreement may be either service description terms or guarantee terms. Service description terms specify the functional characteristics that shall present the service during its consumption such as the endpoint reference or the WSDL interface if the service is a web service. Guarantee terms establish the non-functional characteristics of the service that the parties are agreeing to such as response time or cost of the service.

WS-Agreement is domain independent and just specifies the structure of the agreement document. Therefore, to build actual agreements WS-Agreement must be used in conjunction with one or several domain-specific vocabularies to give the appropriate semantic to both service description terms and guarantee terms.

Concerning the agreement creation process, WS-Agreement distinguishes four different roles that take part in it: agreement initiator, agreement provider, service consumer and service provider. These roles are distributed in two layers: the service layer composed of the service consumer and service provider, and the agreement layer composed of the agreement initiator and agreement provider. This separation in roles allows that both service consumer and service provider could be the agreement initiator or the agreement provider, depending on what is more valuable to them in each moment.

The agreement creation process in WS-Agreement is very simple. More complex scenarios shall be covered in the future by other specifications such as WS-Agreement Negotiation. However, those specifications are now in an early stage of development. Keeping the agreement creation process simple but extendable by other specifications allows to reduce the overhead in simple agreement creation processes while keeping the ability of covering more complex scenarios.

The process of creating an agreement is the following. The agreement provider publishes agreement templates. An agreement template is very similar to an agreement document but it has some gaps that must be filled and some rules specifying restrictions on how to fill them. These rules are called creation constraints. The agreement initiator must contact to an agreement provider, download its templates, analyse them and select the template that best fits its needs, fill it following the creation constraints of the template and submit it back to the agreement provider. The template with the gaps filled is called agreement offer. After receiving the agreement offer, the agreement provider decide between accepting the offer or rejecting it. If the offer is accepted, a new agreement is created.

Finally, WS-Agreement also specifies the interfaces that must implement both the agreement initiator and the agreement provider as well as the mechanisms used to manage the agreement, which are based on the WS-Resource specification.

However, this standard covers only a part of the infrastructure that is needed to make the automatic outsourcing a reality. Specifically, WS-Agreement is just focused in two-party interactions, i.e. there is no specification about how an agreement initiator looks for different possible providers or makes a decision about which is the best offer of a set of several offers from different providers. Other aspect that it is not covered by the specification, as it is mentioned above, is the negotiation process between the parties, the only possible negotiation is the provider to reject the agreement offer and the agreement initiator to fill the template again. Finally, the monitoring and tracking of agreements are not treated in WS-Agreement either.

Therefore, although WS-Agreement is a good starting point, much work must be done in an infrastructure that allows the search of agreement providers and a decision making model to select the one that fits better with its needs.

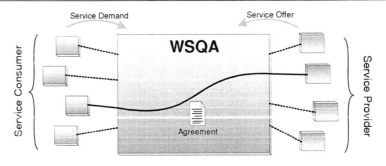

Figure 2: Global overview

3 An Abstract Architecture

In this section, we outline the elements of an abstract architecture (WSQA) that builds upon WS-Agreement and fills the gaps pointed out at the end of the previous section, enabling the automated agreement creation in a scenario with multiple providers and consumers.

We define the roles and interaction protocols needed to perform the first three phases described in section 2 and then we detail a framework for automated negotiations, which is an important part of this architecture and it is complex enough to examine it separately.

3.1 WSQA

In this section we describe WSQA in different levels. First, we start with a high level picture of the whole scenario with a black-box point of view. Then, we make a progressive looking into interactions and elements that compound our system.

Our starting point is a scenario as shown in Figure 2 where multiple service customers and providers interact with WSQA in order to look for optimal business links between them. From this point of view WSQA can be seen as an infrastructure that facilitate searching and creation of agreements between services and providers in a way that optimise business benefits of the organizations that take part.

It is important to remark that this scenario has a strong relationship with classical service industries in the real world. We can think in supply industries or communications where several customers look for services that can be served by multiple providers. In such a complex situations, an important figure appears: the service trader.

The idea of a service trader is a cornerstone in our proposal. Within it, customers and providers would have a trusty organization on which they would rely to obtain good agreements. This trader would take into account information about several customers and providers and, for each of them, would search the counterparty that best could fit maximizing mutual interests.

In order to facilitate the reading and have an unified notation, from now on, we would refer to customers and providers as clients of a trader. In fact, Traders act in a similar way with all its clients despite they are service customers or providers.

Focusing on the information exchange, clients would pass an agreement demand to their trusty traders in the terms described in Section 2.2: functional requirements, non-functional requirements, utility functions and negotiation clauses. As a result, trader's obligation would be to obtain an agreement that, being compatible with its demands, maximise their

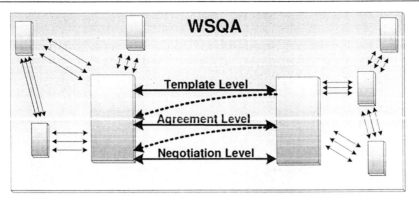

Figure 3: Trader interactions

profit. It is important to remark that is not mandatory that agreements link parties from the same trader. In any case, an agreement shall always establish a relationship where one of the parties would act as the service consumer and the other as the service provider.

In a closer look into WSQA (Figure 3), we can see a trader network that would be responsible for the agreement construction mentioned. The interaction between two traders can be structured in three levels: Template level, Agreement level and Negotiation level.

In the first one, traders will search for promising counterparties. This level is highly based on the idea of Agreement Template.

Traders advertise the types of offers it is willing to accept by means of agreement templates. The structure of an agreement template is similar to an agreement, but an agreement template would contain a creation constraint section, i.e. a section with constraints on possible values of terms for creating an agreement. Amongst other possibilities, the constraints make it possible to specify the valid ranges or distinct values that the terms may take. At this level, we have two trader roles: A Template Consumer and a Template Provider. The former would look for agreement templates in the trader network while the latter would expose the templates. When a Template Consumer finds a suitable Template Provider, it requests the template and uses it to create an agreement offer.

In the agreement level, traders receive potential offers that are collected. In a progressive process, offers are ranked and studied in order to create a negotiation plan that would improve them. After this process, the best agreement is selected and communicated to the client.

Finally The negotiation level is carried out by traders when they want to reach better offers or adjust some terms of the agreement that do not satisfy completely the demands of its clients.

Looking into a trader (Figure 4), we outline several roles that perform the functionality described above. Our proposal describes these roles in terms of interactions and behaviour. Before making a complete description of every element of the trader, we describe a typical scenario of agreement creation.

In this scenario, the process starts when a Client contacts its trusted Trader and specifies its agreement demand to the Policy Manager role. After that, in a certain moment, this role decides to start the agreement search and creates a Policy Manager Worker to coordinate the

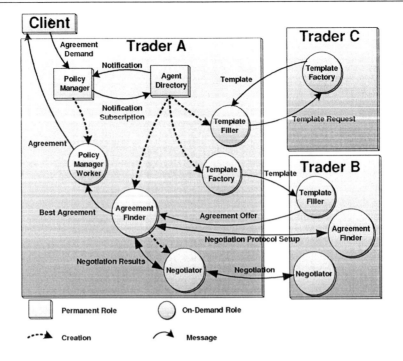

Figure 4: Trader decomposition

search. Its activity will start by requesting the Agent Directory to create the roles used in the search: Template Factory, Template Filler and Agreement Finder. The first two ones would handle templates in a different manner, Template Factory would distribute templates and Template Filler would search and fill templates. As a result of these activities, Agreement Finder would start to receive agreement offers from other Traders (or even itself acting on behalf of another client) and its main responsibility would be to select the most promising agreement offers. With these offers, a separate negotiation process could be done in order to achieve better agreements. Once Agreement Finder has enough good offers, a match-making process is carried out and the best agreement offer is selected and communicated to the client. If this process is not successful, Agreement Finder would repeat its behaviour until Policy Manager Worker decides to cancel the search. As we can see, the activity of the Trader is performed by different roles that collaborate actively. We can distinguish two kinds of elements namely: (i) Permanent Roles. These roles will be implemented by the same agents always. The roles that belong to this category are: Agent Directory and Policy Manager (ii) On-Demand Roles. These roles would be mapped to different agents depending on different factors (Workload, Service level agreed with client, etc...). In fact, these agents could be created and destroyed for a specific amount of time. Normally, their live would be linked to an agreement search. In this category we can find: Policy Manager Worker, Template Factory, Template Filler, Agreement Finder and Negotiator.

Next, we describe roles of our proposal with a higher level of detail:

- Policy Manager. This role receives and manages all of the agreements demands of clients. Its main goal is to decide when an agreement search should be started. Two aspects should be taken into account: time lapsed since the last search and number of new possible counterparties suitable for a certain demand. The latter concern is tackled in terms of notifications from the Agent Directory.

- Policy Manager Worker. This role is a delegate of Policy Manager for a single agreement search. It coordinates the process by deciding when the search has to finish and when it is successful. It is also responsible for communicating the result agreement to the client.

- Template Factory. This role appears in traders that behave as Template Providers; its goals are to generate appropriate templates according to business information provided and to distribute them to the Template Fillers that request a Template. As a result of this distribution, several agreement offers may be sent back to the Agreement Finder.

- Template Filler. In the Template Consumer side, Template Filler role obtains different templates and fills them according to the information provided to it in the creation phase. After that process, it sends the offer back to Template Provider and a notification to its Agreement Finder in order to have a negotiation phase driven by this one.

- Agreement Finder. Its purpose is to reach the agreement that best fits the business requirements given and send this agreement to the Policy Manager Worker. Its behaviour can be divided into three different stages. First, it receives different agreement offers, filters them and makes a decision on the possible negotiation that can be made with each one. Second, it gives instructions to different negotiators in order to improve each agreement offer to maximize the benefits. Finally, it makes a matchmaking process to decide if an agreement offer is good enough to promote it.

- Negotiator. Following the negotiation guidelines given by Agreement Finder, it will try to refine agreement offers. The scenario where this role act is, fundamentally, two-party although in some negotiation schemes a 1-N situation could appear; it is focused on the improvement of a single agreement offer based on the goals specified by Agreement Finder.

- Agent Directory. This role is a cornerstone of the system. It will have the information about the Temporal Roles of the system. It will be the responsible for the creation and registry of their capabilities. Also, it maintains a registry of other Agent Directories (from different Traders). This registry is used to communicate the creation of new Template Factories. Moreover, when a Template Filler wants to search for Template Factories, the Agent Directory acts as a mediator expanding the search among other Agents Directories. Registry coherence in Agents Directory and incremental agreement search are problems that can be tackled with temporal coherence protocol based on local timestamps [28].

3.2   Framework for Automated Negotiations

In section 2.3 we enumerated several proposals about negotiation protocols and decision making models for automated negotiation. However, any proposal seems to be better than the others, but the goodness of a proposal depends on the negotiation context (object which is being negotiated, time constraints of the parties, number of parties participating in the negotiation). Hence, several negotiators implementing different negotiation techniques could be required in a real world environment. Therefore, there is a need for a common framework to unify them and to make the development of automated negotiators easier. In our framework we solve this problem through:

- Identify the communication primitives of the negotiation protocols to get the highest independence between negotiation protocol and decision making model.

- Define the different parts that constitutes an automated negotiator.

- Describe the information that an automated negotiator must handle.

- Establish the phases of the decision making process.

The framework supports and allows the integration of the most significant negotiation protocols and decision making models. Specifically, all decision making models mentioned in section 2.3.3 and all protocols but [25, 18, 38].

3.2.1 Negotiation Protocols

One main goal of the framework is to establish a neat distinction between the negotiation protocol and the decision making model and to make them as independent as possible. This cannot be done completely because, for instance, the decision making model for an auction is different than the decision making model for a bilateral negotiation. However, the same decision making model might be used for two similar bilateral negotiation protocols.

Six communication primitives have been identified in the negotiation protocols. Specifically: *accept* (accept a proposal), *rejectNegotiation* (cancel the whole negotiation process), *rejectProposal* (reject the proposal but the negotiation goes on), *propose* (make a proposal), *commit* (commit to a given proposal) and *inform* (additional information about the negotiation, for instance, a new bid has been done). These primitives make it possible to build decision making models, with independence of the specific negotiation protocols. [2]

Therefore, two aspects must be defined for each negotiation protocol supported by the framework: a mapping from the specific messages of the protocol to the communication primitives and a set of rules specifying when and how these primitives can be used in a particular state of the negotiation. Hence, adding a new negotiation protocol to the framework is as easy as defining these two aspects for the protocol.

The management of the messages received from the opponent are shown in figure 5. First, they are checked against the protocol rules to validate it and they are transformed into the negotiation primitives. Next, they are sent to the decision making system together with the set of possible answers, which are generated by using the protocol rules and the current state of the negotiation. Finally, the answer produced by the decision-making system is converted into a message in the negotiation protocol that is being used and it is sent to the opponent.

---

[2]Note that FIPA's ACL is just an implementation of these communication primitives

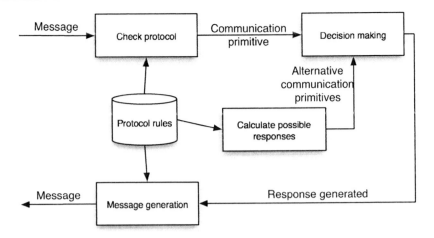

Figure 5: Negotiation protocol management

3.2.2   Decision Making

As shown in figure 5, the decision making process has as entry the received communication primitive and a set of possible answers depending on the current state of the negotiation. The result of that process is usually a message that shall be sent to the opponent, but occasionally, the decision may be to send no answer and wait for the opponent to send more information.

The decision making process have five phases: history update, evaluation and modelling, response type selection, strategy selection and counteroffer generation.

The first step after receiving a message is to add it to the negotiation history. This is carried out in the *history update* phase. We must keep this history because some heuristics that can be used to generate a counteroffer or to model the opponent may require this information like in [12].

Next, the offer is evaluated and the model of the opponent is updated. This is performed in the *evaluation and modelling* phase. Evaluation consists in calculating how good is the received offer. This evaluation is usually carried out by using utility functions [16]. However, other evaluation mechanisms may be used like in [6]. On the other hand, it is useful to know the opponent's preferences (what agreement is willing to get) and characteristics (how the opponent try to achieve that agreement, for instance, whether it is a hard or soft negotiator) to make a more effective negotiation. To do so, bayesian learning or kernel density estimation mechanisms may be used as mentioned in Section 2.3.3.

In the *response type selection* phase, it is decided what response is to be sent to the opponent. That is, we decide if the proposal is accepted, rejected or if a counteroffer shall be generated.

If it is decided to generate a counteroffer, the *strategy selection* phase take place. The negotiation strategy determines the guidelines that are going to be followed to build the counteroffer. For instance, if we are going to concede [16], to make a trade-off based on similarity with the offer received [17] or to use any other strategy that had been proposed in the literature. In this phase, first we decide whether a change of negotiation strategy is

Table 1: Comparative of Web Service Selection Frameworks

Proposal	a	b	c	d	e	f	g	h	i	j	k
Cremona	F				N	F	F	P	F		N
WS-QoS				F		P		F			
QCWS		F		F			F	F			
GlueQoS	N	P			F	N		F	F		
Panda	F	F			F	F				P	N
Meteor-S				F		F	F	F	F		F
G-QoSM	P	P		F		F	F	F			
EWSF	N			P			F	F			
WSQA	F	F	F	F	F	F	F	F	F	F	P

necessary and if it is so, then we determine which other strategy must be used to generate the counteroffer. This decision shall be made based on the negotiation history, the opponent model, our own preferences and our previous negotiations experience.

Finally, in the *counteroffer generation* phase, the counteroffer is built following the strategy selected.

4   Related Work

In this section we present a comparative analysis of the set of relevant proposals related to automated outsourcing. We divide the different works into two groups: In the first comparison we can find proposals that deal with web services selection based on non-functional requirements. In the second group, a collection of negotiation frameworks is studied.

Proposals in table 1 introduce different approaches to the problem of web services selection based on non-functional requirements. As presented in previous sections, this issue is the cornerstone for an automated outsourcing of services. However, each work studied has a different way to deal with the problem.

In order to analyse different proposals, we have selected following attributes:

a) There is a document that expresses the agreement or service level.

b) A negotiation process is supported.

c) Multiple negotiation protocols can be used.

d) There is an element that acts as a Mediator, Trader or Broker of services.

e) Behaviour of system can be parameterised (e. g. with the use of policies)

f) Language of offers, demands (and agreement if supported) can be extended to support different service domains.

g) Language vocabulary can be distributed. There is no need of a centralized vocabulary.

Table 2: Proposals comparison

	Several protocols	DM support	Protocol/ DM separation	Evaluation indep. of strategy	Dynamic change of strategy	DM phases
[3]	No	No	N/A	N/A	N/A	N/A
[13]	No	No	N/A	N/A	N/A	N/A
[8]	Y	No	N/A	N/A	N/A	N/A
[46]	Y	Y	Y	No	No	No
[20]	Y	Y	Y	Y	Y^3	No
Ours	Y	Y	Y	Y	Y	Y

h) 1-N focus. A customer can select between multiples providers.

i) Symmetric search. Either customer or provider can select between multiples counterparties.

j) Incremental refinement of searches

k) Semantic technologies support.

Table Caption:

F: Full support.

P: Simple/Partial support.

N: Non Applicable.

We can observe that none of the analysed proposals satisfy all attributes. In fact, we can outline some high level attributes such as *Expressivity* (which correspond with e, f, g and k attributes), *Industry-orientation* (a, b, c, h, i and j) and *Flexibility* (c, e, f and k). Based on these high level attributes we can see that the more expressive proposals usually have an important lack of industry-orientation. In the case of flexibility, there is no proposal that reach a good level. The main goal of abstract proposal presented (WSQA) in 3.1 is to reach an architectural framework that successfully deals with all exposed attributes, particularly with a balanced amount of Expressivity, Flexibility and Industry-orientation.

A comprehensive information about each of the previously mentioned proposals can be found in: Cremona [30], Panda [20], WS-QoS [44], QCWS [7], GlueQoS [48], EWSF [42], Meteor-S [36] and G-QoSM [1].

In table 2 we show a comparison of works that present different negotiation frameworks. WS-AgreementNegotiation [3] is a draft of a specification that is being developed by GRAAP-WG and that extends WS-Agreement [2] with negotiation capabilities. However, it only specifies the protocol and the communication mechanism between the different parties. It does not deal with the decision making process. This is also the case of FIPA Contract Net Protocol [13], where it is only defined the communication between parties. In fact, both protocols may be supported by our framework if the mapping to communication primitives is done and the protocol rules are defined.

In Bartolini et al. [8], a framework for automated negotiation is developed but it is only focused on negotiation protocols. It defines a rules taxonomy and several messages protocols to specify how parties may start a negotiation, how the messages are validated, when it is finished the negotiation, and how the final agreement is built. However, it does not cover the decision making process. Hence, this work is complementary to ours because it describes the rules and the elements that may be included as part of the elements mentioned in section 3.2.1.

The work developed in [46] is closer to ours because a neat distinction between negotiation protocol and decision making model is done and they use a plug-ins mechanism to support new protocols and strategies. Nevertheless, it is not possible to change dynamically the negotiation strategy depending on the state of the negotiation; it does not distinguish several phases in the decision making process (everything appears in the same module), and it does not define how the protocol plug-in interacts with the strategy plug-in.

In PANDA [20] a framework is proposed that mixes utility functions and rules to carry out the decision making process. A set of communication primitives is used to make independent the decision making of the negotiation protocol as well as in our framework. The decision making component is composed of rules, utility functions and an object pool with several estimation libraries, negotiation history and the current offer. However, this component is vaguely defined and it establishes neither the interface of the estimation libraries objects nor the process that must be followed in the decision making. Another problem is that the strategy selection is done through rules created manually. Nevertheless, the global architecture includes some elements that may be future extensions of our framework such as a negotiation coordinator or an utility updater.

5   Conclusions

In an automatic outsourcing scenario where a service consumer uses a service from a service provider, there is a need for an agreement between parties. In this chapter we discuss and analyse the issues and problems to be solved in order to achieve an effective automated agreement creation in a real-world scenario where multiple service consumers and services providers interact between each other. Regarding this concern, we propose an abstract architecture for the construction of an infrastructure based on the emerging standard WS-Agreement that covers the different parts of the agreement creation process. We do so by defining a mechanism to publish templates and to search for agreement providers through the use of service traders.

The negotiation of agreements plays an important role in the architecture because as providers preferences are usually opposed to consumers ones, both parties must negotiate in order to reach a mutually acceptable agreement. Negotiation protocols and decision-making techniques developed during last years can be used but as no one has proven to be better than the others but it depends on the negotiation context, there is a need for a system that integrate them all and select the best option to use in every moment. In this work we

---

[3] Guided by rules created manually

outline such a framework. Its main features are that it gives support to the most significant negotiation protocols and strategies, allows to add easily new ones, defines the negotiation capabilities of the negotiator in a modular way, makes possible to reuse strategies, offers evaluation mechanisms and negotiation protocols in several negotiators, and, unlike other works, the communication between negotiation protocol and decision making is clearly defined as well as the phases of the decision making process.

Finally, proposed architecture unveils new business opportunities in this scenario through the development of service traders and agreement negotiators. Service traders are used by service providers and consumers as entities that deal with all aspects related to agreement creation process. Therefore, a service trader can have several customers in the form of service providers or service customers and its task is to try to achieve the best agreements for them but always taking in consideration its own profit. In this way, service providers and consumers become customers of service traders so that they do not need to be extended to support that agreement creation process and just focus in doing what they are supposed to do, that is, providing or consuming the service. On the other hand, negotiators can either be integrated in service traders or be first level entities specialized in, given a set of policies, negotiating the best agreement with the other party for their customers.

References

[1] R. J. Al-Ali, K. Amin, G. von Laszewski, O. F. Rana, and D. W. Walker. An OGSA-based Quality of Service Framework. In *Proceedings. Grid and Cooperative Computing, Second International Workshop, GCC 2003*, pages 529–540, 2003.

[2] A. Andrieux, K. Czajkowski, A. Dan, K. Keahey, H. Ludwig, J. Pruyne, J. Rofrano, S. Tuecke, and M. Xu. WS-Agreement Specification, 2004.

[3] A. Andrieux, K. Czajkowski, A. Dan, K. Keahey, H. Ludwig, J. Pruyne, J. Rofrano, S. Tuecke, and M. Xu. WS-AgreementNegotiation specification, draft, 2004.

[4] P. Anthony and N. R. Jennings. Developing a bidding agent for multiple heterogeneous auctions. *ACM Trans. Internet Technology*, 3(3):185–217, 2003.

[5] T. Berners-Lee, J. Hendler, and O. Lassila. Semantic web, The. *Scientific American*, 5 2001.

[6] R. Bordley and M. LiCalzy. Decision analysis using targets instead of utility functions. *Decisions in Economics and Finance*, 23(1):53–74, 5 2000.

[7] H. Chen, T. Yu, and K.-J. Lin. QCWS: An implementation of QoS-capable multimedia web services. In *Proceedings. Fifth International Symposium on Multimedia Software Engineering, 2003.*, pages 38–45, 2003.

[8] R. Choren, A. Garcia, C. Lucena, and A. Ramonovsky, editors. *A Software Framework For Automated Negotiation*. Springer Verlag, 2005.

[9] E. Christiensen, F. Curbera, G. Meredith, and S. Weerawarana. Web services description language (WSDL) specification, 2001.

[10] L. Chung, B. . Nixon, E. Yu, and J. Mylopoulos. *Non Functional Requirements in Software Engineering.* Kluwer Academic Publishers, 2000.

[11] S. Chung, L. H. Tang, and S. Davalos. A web service oriented integration approach for enterprise and business-to-business applications. In *Web Information Systems - WISE 2004, 5th International Conference on Web Information Systems Engineering*, pages 510–515, 2004.

[12] R. M. Coehoorn and N. R. Jennings. Learning on opponent's preferences to make effective multi-issue negotiation trade-offs. In *ICEC '04: Proc. of the 6th Intern. Conf. On Electronic Commerce*, pages 59–68, New York, NY, USA, 2004. ACM Press.

[13] FIPA. FIPA Contract Net Interaction Protocol specification. *FIPA TC Communication*, http://www.fipa.org/specs/pesspecs.tar.gz.

[14] F. Curbera, R. Khalaf, N. Mukhi, S. Tai, and S. Weerawarana. The next step in web services. *Commun. ACM*, **46**(10):29–34, 2003.

[15] N. J. Davies, D. Fensel, and M. Richardson. The future of web services. *BT Technology Journal*, **22**(1):118 – 130, 2004.

[16] P. Faratin, C. Sierra, and N. R. Jennings. Negotiation decision functions for autonomous agents. *Int. Journal of Robotics and Autonomous Systems*, **24**(3-4): 159–182, 1998.

[17] P. Faratin, C. Sierra, and N. R. Jennings. Using similarity criteria to make trade-offs in automated negotiations. *Artificial Intelligence*, **142**:205–237, 12 2002.

[18] S. S. Fatima, M. Wooldridge, and N. R. Jennings. An agenda-based framework for multi-issue negotiation. *Artificial Intelligence*, **152**(1):1–45, 1 2004.

[19] S. S. Fatima, M. Wooldridge, and N. R. Jennings. A comparative study of game theoretic and evolutionary models of bargaining for software agents. *Artificial Intelligence Rev.*, **23**(2):187–205, 2005.

[20] H. Gimpel, H. Ludwig, A. Dan, and B. Kearney. PANDA: Specifying policies for automated negotiations of service contracts. In *Service-Oriented Computing - ICSOC 2003*, pages 287–302. Springer-Verlag, 2003.

[21] N. Gold, A. Mohan, C. Knight, and M. Munro. Understanding service-oriented software. *IEEE Software*, **21**(2):71–77, 3 2004.

[22] M. He, N. R. Jennings, and H.-F. Leung. On agent-mediated electronic commerce. *IEEE Trans. On Knowledge and Data Engineering*, **15**(4):985–1003, 7 2003.

[23] A. H. Karp. Rules of engagement for automated negotiation. *Technical Report HPL-2003-152, HP Laboratories,* **7** 2003.

[24] A. H. Karp, R. Wu, K.-Y. Chen, and A. Zhang. A game tree strategy for automated negotiation. In *ACM Conference On Electronic Commerce*, pages 228–229, 2004.

[25] M. Klein, P. Faratin, H. Sayama, and Y. Bar-Yam. Protocols for negotiating complex contracts. *IEEE Intelligent Systems*, **18**(6):32–38, 2003.

[26] R. Kowalczyk. Fuzzy e-negotiation agents. *Soft Computing*, **6**(5):337–347, 2002.

[27] R. Kowalczyk and V. Bui. On constraint-based reasoning in e-negotiation agents. In *Agent-Mediated Electronic Commerce III*, pages 31–46. Springer-Verlag, 2001.

[28] L. Lamport. Time, clocks, and the ordering of events in a distributed system. *Commun. ACM*, **21**(7):558–565, 1978.

[29] H. Ludwig. A conceptual framework for building e-contracting infraestructure. In R. Corchuelo, R. Wrembel, and A. Ruiz-Cortes, editors, *Technologies Supporting Business Solutions*, chapter 1. Nova Publishing, 2003.

[30] H. Ludwig, A. Dan, and R. Kearney. CREMONA: An architecture and library for creation and monitoring of WS-Agreements. In *Proc. of the 2nd International Conference On Service Oriented Computing*. ACM Press, 2004.

[31] H. Ludwig, A. Keller, A. Dan, R. P. King, and R. Franck. A service level agreement language for dynamic electronic services. *Electronic Commerce Research*, **3**(1-2): 43–59, 2003.

[32] J. McCall, P. Richards, and G. Walters. *Factors in software quality, volume III: Preliminary handbook on software quality for an acquisition manager*. Department of Defense of the USA, 1977.

[33] E. Moggi. Notions of computation and monads. *Information and Computation*, **93**(1):55 – 92, 1991.

[34] T. D. Nguyen and N. R. Jennings. Reasoning about commitments in multiple concurrent negotiations. In *Proc. 6th Int. Conf. On E-Commerce*, pages 77–84, 2004.

[35] M. P. Papazoglou and D. Georgakopoulos. Introduction to Service-Oriented Computing. *Communications of the ACM*, **46**(10): 24–28, 2003.

[36] A. Patil, S. Oundhakar, A. Sheth, and K. Verma. Meteor-s web service annotation framework. In *Proc. of the 13th Int. World Wide Conference (WWW 2004)*. ACM Press, 2004.

[37] J. B. Quinn and F. G. Hilmer. Strategic outsourcing. *MIT Sloan Management review*, **35**(4):43–55, 1994.

[38] S. D. Ramchurn, N. R. Jennings, and C. Sierra. Persuasive negotiation for autonomous agents: A rhetorical approach. In *Proc. IJCAI Workshop On Computational Models of Natural Argument*, pages 9–17, 2003.

[39] A. Ruiz-Cortés. *Una Aproximación Semicualitativa Al Tratamiento Automático de Requisitos de Calidad*. PhD thesis, Universidad de Sevilla, 2002.

[40] L. G. Kahn, R. B Pannara, and S.E. Keller. Specifying software quality requirements with metrics. In *Systems and Software Requirements Engineering*, pages 145–163, Washington, DC, USA, 1990. IEEE Computer Society.

[41] C. Sierra, P. Faratin, and N. R. Jennings. A service-oriented negotiation model between autonomous agents. In *Proc. of the 8th European Workshop On Modelling Auton. Agents in a Multi-Agent World*, pages 17–35. Springer-Verlag, 1997.

[42] Z. U. Singhera. Extended web services framework to meet non-functional requirements. In *Proceedings. Symposium on Applications and the Internet Workshops (SAINT 2004 Workshops)*, pages 334–341, 2004.

[43] M. Ströbel and C. Weinhardt. Montreal taxonomy for electronic negotiation, The. *Group Decision and Negotiation*, **12**(2):143–164, 3 2003.

[44] M. Tian, A. Gramm, H. Ritter, and J. H. Schiller. Efficient selection and monitoring of QoS-aware web services with the WS-QoS framework. In *IEEE/WIC/ACM International Conference on Web Intelligence (WI 2004)*, pages 152–158, 2004.

[45] D. Trastour, C. Bartolini, and C. Preist. Semantic web support for the business-to-business e-commerce pre-contractual lifecycle. *Comput. Networks*, **42**(5): 661–673, 2003.

[46] M. T. Tu, F. Griffel, M. Merz, and W. Lamersdorf. A plug-in architecture providing dynamic negotiation capabilities for mobile agents. In *Mobile Agents: Second International Workshop. Proceedings.*, volume 1477. Springer-Verlag, 9 2003.

[47] O. Williams. *Outsourcing*. CRC Press, 1998.

[48] E. Wohlstadter, S. Tai, T. Mikalsen, I. Rouvellou, and P. Devanbu. Glueqos: Middleware to sweeten quality-of-service policy interactions. In *ICSE '04: Proceedings of the 26th International Conference on Software Engineering*, pages 189–199, Washington, DC, USA, 2004. IEEE Computer Society.

[49] D. Zeng and K. Sycara. Bayesian learning in negotiation. *Int. J. Hum.-Comput. Stud.*, **48**(1):125–141, 1998.

In: Computer Networking and Networks
Editor: Susan Shannon, pp. 63-97

ISBN: 1-59454-830-7
© 2006 Nova Science Publishers, Inc.

Chapter 3

BROADBAND RESIDENTIAL MULTISERVICES ACCESS NETWORKS

S.W. Song[1]

Senior Member, IEEE, Department of Physics and Computer Science, Wilfrid Laurier
University, Waterloo, Ontario, Canada N2L 3C5

W.B. Gardner[2]

Member, IEEE, Department of Computing and Information Science, University of
Guelph, Guelph, Ontario, Canada N1G 2W1

Abstract

This chapter presents a thorough discussion of broadband residential multiservices, also
known as integrated access networks. Section X.1 provides an overview of broadband
residential multiservices. Network architectures based on different network protocols,
including the B-ISDN (Broadband Integrated Services Digital Network), the Ethernet, the
SONET/SDH (Synchronous Optical Network/Digital Hierarchy), and the IP (Internet
Protocol), are all introduced in Section X.1. In the following sections, X.2 to X.5, we discuss
each of these network models in turn. Finally, a summary of these possible broadband
residential access networks is presented in Section X.6.

X.1 Broadband Residential Multiservices Overview

An overriding belief existed even in the early 1970's that optical fiber would one day make its
way into the subscriber loop and be used to connect individual homes [1]. As we all know,
this day is not quite here yet. Although information technologies, from computers to the
Internet, have advanced enormously during the past thirty years, the dream of fiber-to-the-
home (FTTH) broadband integrated services to every residence has not materialized.

Anticipating the forthcoming optical fiber network access technologies, and also due to
the low cost of optical fibers today, a trend of pre-laying fiber cables to residential areas in the

---

[1] E-mail address: ssong@wlu.ca
[2] E-mail address: wgardner@cis.uoguelph.ca

development phase has started. Although most of these pre-laid optical fibers in residential areas have not been fully utilized, the trend continues, since it costs far less to lay cables in the development phase than having to add them to existing residential developments in the future. On the other hand, there has not been any commercially available residential integrated access system to utilize these pre-laid optical fibers or to deliver broadband residential multiservices. One current use of these pre-laid fibers is connecting homes to a local Ethernet network.

The Broadband Integrated Services Data Network (B-ISDN) based on ATM (Asynchronous Transfer Mode) had been the dominant potential network architecture for broadband services to homes for more than twenty years. Unfortunately, it has lost its strength due mainly to its complexity and cost. The last attempt to deploy the B-ISDN was the Full Service Access Networks (FSAN) initiative organized by a group of telephone companies throughout the world in the mid 90's [2-7]. Efforts were made to combine all available technologies, such as ISDN over ADSL and ATM over Passive Optical Network (ATM-PON), into one working system in order to break the cost barrier. In the end, the cost remained to be the major obstacle for bringing the technology to the marketplace. The B-ISDN area has been quiet since then.

Recent advancement of Dense Wavelength Division Multiplexing (DWDM) technology has prompted focus on wavelength channels. Researchers had been studying network architectures to allow the usage of wavelength channels to deliver broadband integrated services to homes with or without Time Domain Multiplexing (TDM) within each wavelength channel. The passive optical access network [8-10] is one of the models that does not employ TDM. It uses one wavelength channel to transmit one service. Although DWDM can create 80 or even 160 wavelength channels today, it is still not economical to use one wavelength channel to carry only one service, since several services, such as telephones, TVs, and computers, are required at each residential premise. The amount of fiber required in this type of network is still unmanageable, since each fiber can only serve a dozen or so residences. In the meantime, the vast bandwidth capacity of each wavelength channel is wasted, since only one service is carried by one wavelength channel at a given time even if dynamic wavelengths allocations are employed. ATM over DWDM with ATM providing the TDM scheme within wavelength channels, which is referred to as the Broadband PON (B-PON), has been proposed as a solution to the problem [11], but the complexity and cost of ATM equipment required in the network again becomes an obstacle. In other words, ATM over DWDM will further increase the transmission capacity, but it will not reduce the cost of the ATM system.

In recent years, the research community and the telecommunication industry have been studying and developing residential multiservices networks based on existing network protocols which include the Internet Protocol (IP), the Ethernet, and the Synchronous Optical Network (SONET) also known as the Synchronous Digital Hierarchy (SDH).

IP is a best effort protocol that does not guarantee Quality of Service (QoS) for real-time applications. Although narrowband real-time applications, such as IP phones, have been deployed in many cases, full-blown broadband integrated residential services based on IP can be challenging. It requires upgrading the IP routing mechanism and much higher routing power. However, it is attractive to system developers in the short term, as it requires less investment and time to have a product. But from the long term system development point of view it might not be the best choice, as the cost and complexity will increase significantly when the Quality of Services (QoS) requirement increases. It may end up at an even higher cost than ATM, if the same QoS as of ATM is implemented on IP. The Cable TV industry is currently moving toward IP based multiservices, such as PACKETCable based on a DOCSIS (Data Over Cable Service Interface Specification) modem platform. It is obvious that the IP based system can provide selected multiservices, such as video conferencing, within relatively short development time. In return it generates near term profits. But, whether it can eventually be developed into a full-blown broadband residential integrated services network system remains to be seen.

The Ethernet protocol, switched Ethernet in particular, has become a front runner for future broadband residential multiservices in terms of technology development. One of the important reasons for this is the market continuity for the Ethernet switch manufacturers, such as Nortel Networks, as they are selling products continuously in LAN (local area network), MAN (metro area network), and enterprise network markets, and in the meantime constantly improving the switches. When the intelligence of the products becomes sufficient, they will be marketed for broadband residential integrated service. From a technical point of view, the Ethernet switches are hardware based systems which provide higher packet switching speed and capacity. In comparison with the software based IP routers, the packet switching speed can be significantly higher and the per-bit switching cost can be much lower. By adding intelligence to the Ethernet switches, such as priorities and follow controls, future generations of Ethernet switches will eventually become simple versions of ATM switches, but with less overhead and higher flexibility. However, one potential long-term obstacle for this system is the same one that has already been faced by ATM—the cost and complexity—as ATM was originally designed for broadband integrated service with hardware based switching mechanisms. However, this obstacle may or may not emerge, due again to the market continuity of Ethernet products and continuous decrease in hardware costs.

SONET/SDH was primarily designed for voice communications. It uses a fixed slot time domain multiplexing mechanism to share the bandwidth among voices transmitted in each link, with each service being assigned a fixed bandwidth. SONET/SDH provides guaranteed services which can be used to build a fixed bandwidth allocation system to provide reliable multiservices to residential users [12]. It may also cost less in the long term. But the problem is that SONET/SDH components usually involve high prices due mainly to the market size of SONET/SDH products. It does not enjoy the market continuity and short term benefits as do the Ethernet and IP protocols. This leads to an awkward dilemma of long term versus short term, which actually delays the development of the all-in-one integrated services to homes. From a technical point of view, the SONET/SDH based system can be considered as the long-term solution for the broadband metro network, for both residential and business broadband integrated communications.

In this chapter we provide an overview of the technologies developed in the past, namely the B-ISDN and PON. We then delve into the technologies presently under development, which are the Ethernet, the SONET, and the IP based broadband residential multiservices systems, in that order. We will discuss the potential architectures, protocols, and devices for these three possible systems, with particular attention to designs for Ethernet and SONET based systems that stem from our own current research.

X.2   The Broadband Integrated Services Digital Network (B-ISDN)

Broadband integrated services digital network (B-ISDN) was once the leading technology being advocated for integrated residential services for more than two decades. The core underlying technology of the system is the ATM [13, 14]. Although it will unlikely be deployed as originally proposed, the integrated services concepts and the technologies that have been accumulated in the field will influence future development of residential communications for a long time to come. In many ways, B-ISDN will serve as a datum for future systems, in terms of capacity, performance, and cost. In this section we provide an overview of the B-ISDN, which includes a brief review of its history, its core technology, the ATM, its network architecture, and its protocols.

X.2.1   B-ISDN History

B-ISDN is a further development of the narrowband integrated services digital network (N-ISDN or simply ISDN) concept [15]. The first ISDN standard was published in 1970, under the title "G.705 Integrated Services Digital Network (ISDN)." The data rate of ISDN was originally designed from 64 Kbps to 1.544 Mbps, using the telephone networks. Three types of ISDN services were defined within the ISDN Recommendation (I.200), which are Bearer services, Tele-services, and Supplementary services. Bearer services (I.140) provide the mechanisms to convey information in the form of speech, data, video, etc., between users. There is a common transport rate for bearer services, which is the 64 Kbps rate of digital telephony. Various bearer services are defined as multiples of this basic 64 Kbps data rate, for example 64, 2x64, 384, 1536, and 1920 Kbps. Tele-services cover user applications and are specified in I.241 as telephony, teletex, telefax, mixed mode, videotex, and telex. Supplementary services are defined in I.250. These services are related to number identification (e.g., calling line identification), call offering (e.g., call transfer, call forwarding, and call deflection), call completion (e.g., call waiting and call hold), multiparty (e.g., conference or three-party calling), community of interest (e.g., a closed user group), charging (e.g., credit card charging), and additional information transfer (e.g., the use of the ISDN signaling channel for user-to-user data transfer).

ISDN was never deployed at a commercial scale in North America, although it was deployed in some regions of Europe. The reasons for this can be summarized as: 1) high cost for making the subscriber loop digital; 2) lack of compelling push from consumer demands, as ISDN does not provide revolutionary services; 3) emerging technologies, such as the Internet and modems, filling in the gaps between ISDN and the telephone system at the beginning, and then quickly surpassing ISDN; and 4) the extension to B-ISDN due to the bandwidth needs for video services thereby making ISDN unnecessary.

In 1988, CCITT issued a set of Recommendations for ISDN under the general name of "Broadband Aspects of ISDN" (I.113: Vocabulary of Terms for Broadband Aspects of ISDN, and I.121: Broadband Aspects of ISDN). These documents represented the level of consensus reached among the participants concerning the nature of the then future B-ISDN. They provided a preliminary description and a basis for the standardization and development work.

Since then, seventeen Recommendations in the I series that specifically related to B-ISDN have been published by CCITT (now ITU-T).

Around that time, there was increased activity in video coding within the contexts of HDTV (High Definition Television) and MPEG (video coding specification by Moving Picture Experts Group), voice compression was beginning to achieve acceptable voice quality at rates around 8 Kbps, and the first residential data access applications were appearing in the context of accessing office computers and electronic bulletin boards. Consequently, telecommunications industry representatives came to the conclusion that a need for broadband services in the telecommunication network was imminent. Since ISDN was not capable of answering high-speed and packet-based service needs of such services, the concept of B-ISDN was deemed necessary. Aiding in this process was the availability of high-speed transmission, switching, and signal processing technologies. It became clear that even higher processing speeds were going to become available in the near future (e.g., the fact that the speed of processing doubles every 1.5 years, also known as Moore's Law). CCITT considered these signs so important that the usual 4-year cycle of a study group to issue Recommendations was considered too long and an intermediate set of Broadband ISDN (B-ISDN) Recommendations were first issued in 1990.

By 1993, ITU-U had published more than twenty Recommendations, most of them in I and Q series, marking the maturation of the technology. The effort of deploying the B-ISDN was started in 1995 by the FSAN (Full Service Access Network) Initiative group organized by seven major telephone companies throughout the world [16]. The goal of FSAN at the beginning was to break the cost barrier by putting all available technologies together, so that the B-ISDN could be deployed. The first FSAN workshop was held in London in June 1996. Two more important workshops followed in 1997 and 1998, in Atlanta and Venice, respectively. Several task groups were formed to study issues and subsystems of the network infrastructure. There was no activity in 1999, which indicates that the confidence in the ATM based B-ISDN had somehow been weakened by the reality of its complexity and cost of the system by that time. After a period of absence of activities, the FSAN initiative group (now also referred to as the FSAN consortium) has broadened its scope beyond the initial focus of deploying B-ISDN. Today, the members of FSAN have grown to about twenty companies. One of the major discussions is the B-PON (Broadband Passive Optical Networks) which is independent from signal formats and protocol (e.g., SONET/SDH, Internet, and Ethernet). Ethernet based broadband residential access network is also under discussion by FSAN.

In short, access technology has come a long way and has accumulated significant knowledge and products; however, with the fading of the ATM based B-ISDN, it does have a flavor of "back-to-square-one." The future of the broadband integrated residential service network is not certain at this time, whether it will be based on IP, Ethernet, SONET/SDH, or perhaps even on all of them. Starting from section X.3, we discuss each of these mechanisms. A comparison of these systems will be presented at the end of the chapter. However, we focus on the B-ISDN in this section.

X.2.2 Asynchronous Transfer Mode (ATM)

Asynchronous Transfer Mode (ATM) is the core technology of B-ISDN. Therefore, we will briefly review the fundamentals of ATM before discussing the B-ISDN itself.

Design Goals

ATM is a cell based packet network protocol designed by the ATM Forum and adopted by the ITU-T for the B-ISDN as the core of the system [17]. The design goal of ATM was to transmit mixed traffic, including both datagram and time-critical data, in one network. A series of mechanisms were introduced to meet the challenges of handling the mixed traffic and to provide a certain level of quality of service (QoS) guarantees for real-time applications. Key mechanisms can be summarized as: 1) smaller and equal sized packets, called cells, to reduce the blocking of real-time packets at a switching point; 2) hardware switching fabrics to allow fast cell switching; 3) switching control mechanisms to handle mixed traffic for better QoS; 4) virtual circuit options to allow real-time applications to reserve the path and bandwidth for achieving QoS guarantees; and 5) flow control mechanisms to reduce congestion and blocking. These aspects are discussed below.

ATM Cells and Multiplexing

Many of the problems associated with packet internetworking, especially when mixed data are involved, can be solved by adopting a concept called cells. A cell is a small data unit, a special packet, with fixed size in terms of bits. Fig. 1 shows the ATM cell format. It consists of 53 bytes, with 5 bytes being the header. The cell header format is also shown in the same figure.

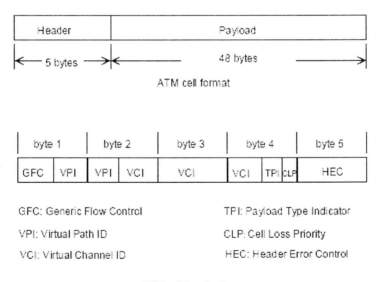

Fig. 1 ATM cell format

The first advantage of cell networking is that it can reduce the average delay for the services, which is important to real-time applications. The second advantage is that it reduces the jitter of the network for real-time services, since it eliminates the situation of a real-time packet being blocked by a long packet at a switching point. The third advantage is that it makes switching simpler and therefore faster. However, small cells do come with one severe disadvantage, which is a high overhead ratio. As shown in Fig. 1, the overhead payload ratio in an ATM cell is over 10%, which significantly reduces the efficiency of the network. This disadvantage has become one of the factors that make ATM an unlikely choice for future broadband access networks.

ATM cells are multiplexed in the time domain by the switches in the network. The mechanisms of cell multiplexing are according to the ATM traffic management, flow control, and virtual circuits.

Virtual Path and Virtual Circuit

Two important mechanisms introduced in ATM networks are Virtual Paths (VPs) and Virtual Circuits (VCs). A VP provides a connection or a set of connections between two nodes in an ATM network. Thinking of a virtual path as a highway that connects two cities, virtual circuits are the lanes of the highway. When a virtual path is selected in the network, it is similar to a highway or a set of highways from city A to city B having been decided. When a virtual circuit has been established, it is similar to the lanes connecting the two cities having been determined. Virtual paths and virtual circuits provide the network with the capability of fast switching and bandwidth reservations, which are important to real-time applications. The identifiers of a virtual path and virtual circuits for the cell are in the cell header, as shown in Fig. 1.

ATM Switches

ATM uses switches to route the cells from a source end point to the destination end point. The architecture for an ATM switch is not part of any standard. All that matters is forwarding the cells along their path to the destination with absolute minimum delays. An ATM switch normally consists of two major components: the switching fabric and the control unit. The switching fabric allows the user cells to "switch themselves" from the input ports to the destination output ports. Another kind of cells, network cells, are absorbed by the control unit, which executes the requested network control functions.

There are three main architectures of ATM switching fabrics: 1) Multiple high-speed backplane switching; 2) Distributed matrix switching, and 3) Electrically controlled optical switching. These three types of switches have been built for different market needs.

To make the switch more efficient, it normally uses two types of switching mechanisms: VP and VPC. A VP switch routes the cell using only the Virtual Path ID. However, a VPC switch routes the cell using both the Virtual Path and the Virtual Circuit IDs.

ATM Traffic Management: Traffic Control and Congestion Control

The ATM network must be able to adapt to unforeseen traffic conditions. In doing so, the network must be able to enforce an allowable peak cell rate for each VPI/VCI connection. This means that when an application tries to send the burst rate beyond a maximum peak rate, it may be discarded. In addition to these bit rate controls, the network must also be able to monitor traffic, detect problems, and trigger alarms when certain troubling events are encountered. These functions of the network are referred to as traffic control and congestion control.

To meet the objectives of traffic control and congestion control, the ATM network must perform the following functions:

(1) Connection admission control (CAC) during a call setup, to determine if a user connection will be accepted or rejected. These actions may include acquiring routes for the connection.

(2) Usage parameter control, to establish controls to monitor and regulate traffic at the User Network Interface (UNI).

(3) Accept user input to establish priorities for different types of traffic, through the use of the cell loss priority (CLP) bit.

(4) Establish traffic shaping mechanisms to obtain a stated goal for managing all traffic (with differing characteristics) at the UNI.

X.2.3 B-ISDN Architecture

B-ISDN Protocol Reference Model
As shown in Fig. 2, the B-ISDN model conceptually divides three categories of network functions into three "planes": the user plane (U-plane), the control plane (C-plane), and the management plane (M-plane). The user plane is responsible for providing user information transfer, flow control, and recovery operations. The control plane is responsible for setting up a network connection and managing the connections. It is also responsible for connection release. The control plane is not needed for permanent virtual circuits. The user and control planes accomplish their functions by means of a layered architecture. The management plane, which straddles the other planes' layers, is described below.

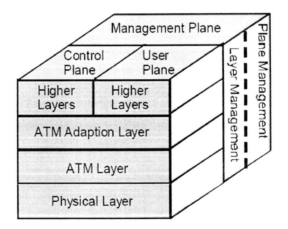

Fig. 2 The B-ISDN protocol reference model

B-ISDN Functional Architecture
The functional architecture of B-ISDN is shown in Fig. 3. The management plane has two functions: plane management and layer management. Plane management has no layered structure. It is responsible for coordinating all the planes. Layer management is responsible for managing the entities in the layers and performing operations, administration, and maintenance services (OAM). The layer structure and the functions of each layer are summarized in Fig. 3.

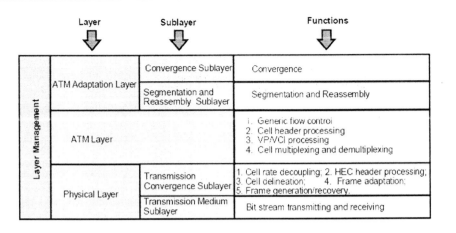

Layer		Sublayer	Functions
Layer Management	ATM Adaptation Layer	Convergence Sublayer	Convergence
		Segmentation and Reassembly Sublayer	Segmentation and Reassembly
	ATM Layer		1. Generic flow control 2. Cell header processing 3. VP/VCI processing 4. Cell multiplexing and demultiplexing
	Physical Layer	Transmission Convergence Sublayer	1. Cell rate decoupling; 2. HEC header processing; 3. Cell delineation; 4. Frame adaptation; 5. Frame generation/recovery.
		Transmission Medium Sublayer	Bit stream transmitting and receiving

Fig. 3 The functions of the B-ISDN layers

X.2.4   B-ISDN Implementation and FSAN Architecture

The goal of the FSAN (Full Services Access Network) was to deploy B-ISDN. The mechanism developed by the FSAN group was to put together all available access technologies, which range from FTTH (Fiber to the Home), through to FTTB/C (Fiber to the Building/Curb) and FTTcab (Fiber to the Cabinet), all into one system in order to overcome the cost barrier of B-ISDN. Fig. 4 depicts the network architecture of FSAN proposed by the FSAN initiative group [18]. The optical section of a local access network system could be a point-to-point, active, or passive point-to-multipoint architecture. The OAN (Optical Access Network) is common to all architectures as shown in Fig. 4, hence commonality in this system has the potential to generate large volume product demand worldwide, thereby reducing the cost of the system. The FTTB/C and FTTCab network options differ in implementation, but not in architecture.

Although the architecture proposed by the FSAN Initiative group did not reach the market place, it nonetheless represents a realistic model for the B-ISDN.

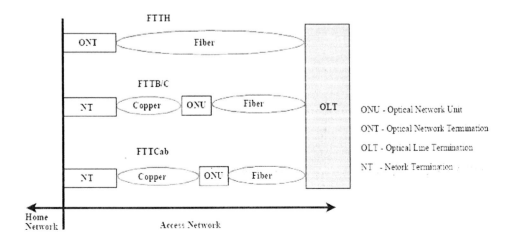

Fig. 4 The FSAN Architecture

We now leave behind the hopeful model of the '80s and '90s, and turn to the technologies that are presently vying for practical deployment. Ethernet and SONET could be good long-term solutions, while IP will be exploited in the short run.

X.3   Ethernet Based Integrated Residential Access Network

Ethernet was developed for Local Area Network (LAN) applications. However, it has been extended to enterprise networks to connect offices in different cities by using optic fiber transmissions. Currently, the industry keeps adding intelligence into the Ethernet switches, such as prioritized services for real-time and non-real-time applications. With such continuous development, Ethernet switches will one day be close to the functionality of ATM switches. This allows a residential multiservices network to be built based on the Ethernet protocol.

In comparison with the IP based multiservices network, an Ethernet based system has the advantage of faster packet switching, since Ethernet switches are based on hardware versus software based IP routers. One important issue faced by the Ethernet based multiservices network is the QoS, the same problem that was addressed by the ATM protocol. However, this problem might be solved by setting the application bandwidth below the capacity of the system, as the cost of the hardware decreases due to the size of the market. This remains to be seen.

In this section, we introduce a potential residential multiservices network system based on the Ethernet protocol. Although a fiber-to-the-home (FTTH) Ethernet based residential network is simpler in terms of architecture, a hybrid fiber-coax network is more practical for the market. Therefore, a hybrid fiber-coax network architecture is described in this section.

X.3.1 Network Architecture

From a network architecture point of view, an Ethernet [19] based residential access network or Metropolitan Area Network (MAN) can be implemented as a Fiber-To-The-Home (FTTH) or a hybrid fiber and coax network. Practically, it would be advantageous to have a combination of both FTTH and coax to home: a network provides fiber to the home and business and at the same time it allows optic fiber to be terminated at access nodes which can be located at curb or residential areas. In this section, we discuss this combined metro network architecture as it represents a general case.

The network can be viewed as two levels of networks, the metro-backbone network and the local distribution networks. The metro-backbone network, shown in Fig. 5, provides links among the lower-level local distribution networks, and between the central office and the local distribution networks, through the local switches. The topology of the metro backbone network can be configured as a simple mesh (shown on the left in Fig. 5) or a self-healing recovery ring (right of Fig. 5) [20], or a mixture of both. DWDM is applied in the fiber links.

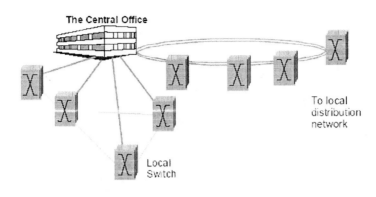

Fig. 5 Metro-backbone network

As shown in Fig. 6, each local distribution network fans out from a local switch in a hybrid structure of optical fiber and coaxial cables, in which optical fiber cables are used to connect each local switch with its nearest fiber-to-coax nodes. Residential users are connected to the network through coaxial cables via the nearest fiber-to-coax node. The topology of the local distribution network is a tree with the fiber cables forming the trunk and major branches. The coaxial cables form the two lowest branches. A pair of fibers are used for each branch, with one for upstream and the other for downstream transmissions. Only one single coaxial cable is used for the two lowest branches, as both the upstream and downstream transmissions are carried by the same cable through FDM. This design can be updated to a coaxial pair configuration with one cable for upstream and the other for downstream transmissions. This is suited for the network installations in new residential areas. The fiber drop nodes in the local distribution networks are simply points where fiber pairs are dropped from the fiber bundle, although wavelength channels can be dropped by employing add/drop multiplexers/demultiplexers.

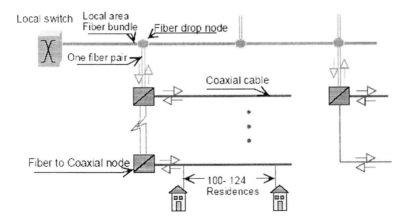

Fig. 6 Local distribution network

The switched Ethernet protocol is used to transmit the applications in the network. A residential gateway (RG) is required at each residential premise to pack and unpack Ethernet frames in order to provide multiservices. Details of the RG are provided in section X.3.3.

Each residential user is assigned an Ethernet address in order to communicate through the network. A name service system, similar to the Domain Name System (DNS), is used to map telephone numbers and video services to the Ethernet address of the user. Video applications may use the same telephone number of the residence or individual numbers can be assigned.

The other key components of the proposed hybrid network are the central office switch, the local switches, and the fiber-to-coax nodes. These components are all based on Ethernet switches, which will be discussed, along with the cabling of the network, in the following sections.

The proposed multi-residential-service network not only provides the existing telephone and cable TV services, but also provides new broadband services to homes, such as 10Base-T Ethernet, video conferencing, and video-on-demand. New services, such as security monitoring and utility billing, can be added to the network in the future.

The current proposed Ethernet metro network [21] allows computer communications over the IP protocol, in the same manner as IP over LANs and MANs. Real-time services over IP can also be carried with the same or even better quality of service (QoS), since Ethernet switches can implement different levels of QoS. This opens new opportunities for real-time services over IP networks. In other words, the proposed Ethernet metro area network allows both Ethernet based and IP based integrated residential and business services, which can be called metro services, at the same time.

The feature of this network is that it utilizes the existing Ethernet technology and the infrastructure of the cable TV networks or pre-laid fiber systems. It provides a transparent layer between the service providers and the residential/business applications, and this layer does not require modifications of existing user devices and provider systems. Also, this architecture utilizes the existing technology of Ethernet over DWDM and FDM channels to achieve a low cost implementation. The proposed multiservices network can be launched by extending the existing cable TV network. By adding extra fibers and the required network components into the cable TV network, the proposed multiservices access network can be achieved. The cost could be tremendously reduced in comparison with other architectures.

X.3.2   Cabling, DWDM, and FDM

As shown in Fig. 5, the metro backbone network is a fiber optical network, which can be configured as a mesh or a self-healing protection ring, or a combination of both. DWDM is used in the fiber to increase the bandwidth capacities of the links. The number of wavelength channels in the DWDM system is mainly determined by the bit rate and cost ratio, which is a changing factor at this time. Currently, 4- to 16-channel DWDM systems seem suited for the proposed network architecture, based on the estimated cost of the system. However, we anticipate that 80-channel DWDM systems may become favorable in the near future.

As shown in Fig. 6, the trunk and the major branches of the tree structure of the local distribution network are optical fiber cables. We use a pair of fibers for each link, with one for upstream and one for downstream communications. Different fiber-count cables can be selected according to the needs of the area. Fiber pairs are dropped at the fiber drop nodes to serve the designated areas. DWDM is also employed within these fiber links. The wavelength channels are extracted at the fiber-to-coax nodes, in order to connect with the coaxial cables.

Also shown in Fig. 6, the bottom two levels of the tree branches are formed by coaxial cables. FDM is used in these coaxial cables. Although the same 75Ω cables are used for both levels, the lowest level branches carry only one downstream channel and upstream channel in each branch. The second level branches from the bottom carry 100-124 frequency channels for downstream and 100-124 narrowband channels. This indicates that each coaxial branch can serve up to 100-124 residences.

Fig. 7 shows our proposed frequency division scheme. The frequency band between 150 MHz and 750 MHz is divided into 100 channels with bandwidth of 6 MHz, which are used for downstream transmissions. The frequency band between 5 MHz to 145 MHz is divided into 1.4 MHz channels for a total of 100 upstream channels. Each residential user is assigned one upstream and one downstream channel, which is built into the cable modem used. This frequency division coincides with today's cable TV system, except the upstream region. Commercially available cable modems, such as the RCA DCM315C, already have the capability of transmitting 38 Mbps using a 6 MHz frequency channel. As for the upstream region, we allocated 1.4 MHz for each channel, which is aimed for transmitting 4 Mbps. Although there may not be identical modems commercially available at this time, the MHz/Mbps ratio is very close to the technology available today. For example, the RCA DCM3150C modem can transmit 5.12 Mbps by using a 1.6 MHz channel.

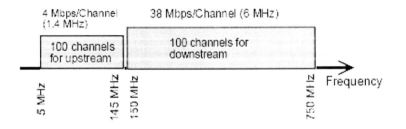

Fig. 7 Frequency channel spacing for single cable to home

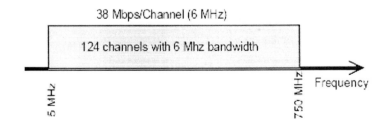

Fig. 8 Frequency channel spacing for cable pair to home

With the 38 Mbps downstream bandwidth, multiple broadcasting TVs along with other applications can be carried at the same time, noticing that the TV channels are sent from the head-end individually to each user in the form of Ethernet frames which share the 38 Mbps bandwidth. With the 4Mbps upstream bandwidth, telephones and video conferencing types of applications can be carried. The RG may also be implemented with bandwidth reservation and virtual circuit capacities in order to guarantee the bandwidth for certain real-time applications.

The above discussed frequency channel spacing is for one single coaxial cable carrying both upstream and downstream traffic, which is suited to the situation where an existing cable TV network is extended to the current proposed multiservices network. For new residential areas, it is more advantageous to lay a coaxial pair instead of one single coaxial cable. With the coaxial pair, we can provide the same bandwidth for upstream as for downstream, which will lead to better services. It also utilizes the fiber pair in the distribution network for upstream communications. With a pair of coaxial cables between the residences and the fiber-to-coax node, the number of users on one coaxial branch can be increased to 124. Fig. 8 shows the frequency channel distribution for the FDM within each coaxial cable in the coaxial pair. The frequency distributions in the upstream and downstream cables are identical.

The utilization of the bandwidth above 750MHz in the 75Ω coaxial cable is currently evolving. As the technology advances, extra frequency channels will be added to the system to serve more residences in one coaxial subnet.

X.3.3   The Residential Gateway

An important element of the proposed network is the residential gateway (RG) which packs and unpacks Ethernet frames on behalf of the user devices, such as TVs and telephones. Each RG is assigned an Ethernet address as the identity of the user to communicate with the metro-network [22]. The RG distributes the payload of the received Ethernet frames to the intended users for downstream communications, and packs the upstream data into Ethernet frames with the Ethernet address of the gateway. Each home device on the RG is given an ID which is inserted at the beginning of the Ethernet payload to be used by the receiving side to distribute the data accordingly. No modification of the Ethernet protocol is needed using this mechanism.

Fig. 9 shows the architecture of the RG, in which a cable modem is used to transmit and receive data streams from the network. A specific frequency filter is required in the modem at each residential premise to use one channel for downstream and one channel for upstream among the available frequency channels.

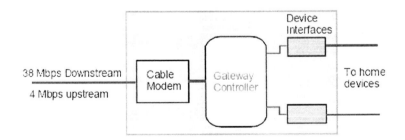

Fig. 9 The architecture of the residential gateway

The core part of the RG is the gateway controller which performs all necessary functions of the RG, including data buffering, framing/deframing, distributing the services, and frame packaging. Another important function of the gateway controller is to provide the services according to the priority of the services, such as real-time and non-real-time. The RG controller gives high priorities to real-time applications, such as telephones and videos. Real-time applications can also be carried by the home computer port, which is a 10-BaseT Ethernet connection, as the Ethernet frames are marked with their own priority. This allows real-time computer communications, which supports the real-time IP applications. The RG communicates with each home device through a gateway-device interface. The interface "talks" with the home device using the "native language" of the device, while communicating with the RG controller through simple binary streams. This eliminates any home device modifications and set-top boxes at the user level.

X.3.4   Fiber-to-Coax Node

Fig. 10 depicts the structure of the fiber-to-coax node. A modem pool is employed to communicate with the modems at the user side. A frequency domain multiplexer combines the frequency channels in front of the modem pool. The upper side of each modem in the pool is connected to one input port of an Ethernet switch. The other side of the Ethernet switch is connected to the DWDM MUX/DEMUX via optical transmitters and receivers.

The Ethernet switch is the key element of the fiber-to-coax node. It not only achieves the interconnection between the frequency channels in the coaxial cable and the lightwave channel in the optical fiber, but also provides the switching function within the local distribution network, and between the neighboring local switch nodes and the local distribution network. Since the aggregated output can be made equal to the aggregated input at the fiber-to-coax node, the QoS is not an issue in the Ethernet frame switching process. A cut-through switch with the capacity of handling the peak traffic could be a good choice in this case. One of the most important features of this design is that it employs existing technology of switched Ethernet, which leads to low cost of the network.

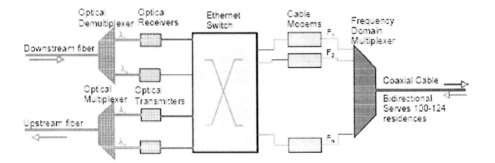

Fig. 10 The fiber-to-coax node

X.3.5 Local Switches

The local switches provide the interconnections between the metro backbone network and the distribution networks. Each local switch is responsible for traffic within the same local distribution network and the traffic in-and-out of the local distribution network to the metro backbone network. Fig. 11 illustrates the architecture of the local switches, which consists of a layer 3 Ethernet switch, optical-electrical interface, and DWDM MUX/DEMUXs.

A name server is installed at this level to store the database for mapping the telephone numbers and video user numbers with the gateway Ethernet address. The name server will periodically broadcast the database of the local subnet to the RGs on the same subnet to inform them of the mapping within the same subnet. Therefore, the communications within the same subnet are based on the Ethernet address inserted by the RG's. The name server at this level will resolve the destination Ethernet addresses for those frames going out of the local subnet using the telephone/video numbers in the payload. The RG inserts the local switches Ethernet address for those frames designated for outside of the local distribution subnet. For the frames going to the outside of the metro network, the mapping between the numbers and the Ethernet address will be performed at the central office level. One of the Ethernet addresses of the central office is inserted by the local switch in this case.

The level of intelligence of the Ethernet switch defines the performance and quality of services of the network. In order to provide QoS, the Ethernet switch is required to switch the frames according to their priorities. The Ethernet switch may also have the ability of bandwidth reservations for virtual circuits. Many layer 3 Ethernet switches that incorporate these functions are available at the current time.

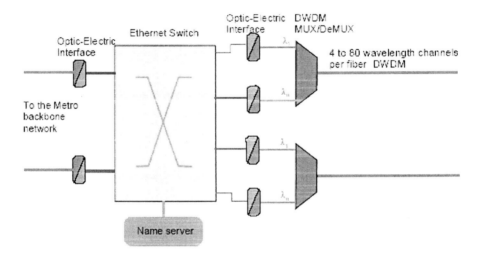

Fig. 11 The architecture of the local switch

X.3.6 Central Office

The configuration of the central office is shown in Fig. 12. A powerful Ethernet or a cluster of Ethernet switches is responsible for forwarding the Ethernet frames to the designated links. In order to connect with the current three existing backbone networks, namely the telephone network (or SONET), the Internet, and the cable TV network, an interface for each network is placed in between each of these networks and the central office Ethernet switch, as shown in Fig. 12. Local service providers, such as a video-on-demand store, can be directly connected to the central Ethernet switch system to provide services to the residential users. Future new services can also be added to the network, as long as the data are packed in Ethernet frames. A name-resolving server is also attached to the central office switching system to match the user numbers to the designated Ethernet addresses.

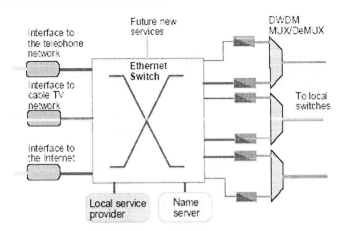

Fig. 12 The central office configuration

The proposed configuration offers transparency between user and the current major existing communication systems, namely the telephone, the Internet and the cable TV networks. The central office system can also be configured to allow the sharing of the three backbone networks, such as IP over SONET or voice IP, by implementing the corresponding interfaces between the central office and the three existing backbone networks. This opens a new era for future telecommunications.

X.3.7 Summary

We presented a broadband residential multiservices network architecture that is based on Ethernet over a hybrid fiber-coaxial framework with DWDM applied in the fiber links and FDM used in the coaxial cables. An RG is employed at each residential premise to deliver multiservices through receiving and sending Ethernet frames. Cable modems are used to transmit and receive data through two FDM channels, with downstream bit rates of 38 Mbps and upstream bit rates of 4 Mbps. The network can provide service guarantees through bandwidth reservation in virtual circuits. IP packets are transmitted in the proposed network in the same manner as IP over LANs and MANs. Real-time application over IP can also be made transparent to the Ethernet switches in the proposed network to provide QoS for real-time IP packets. The key advantages of the network include flexibility and low cost, drawn from the nature of switched Ethernet and the market size of Ethernet components. The implementation of the proposed network can be achieved by extending the current cable TV networks.

X.4   SONET/SDH Based Integrated Residential Access Network

The Synchronous Optical Network (SONET), which is also referred to as Synchronous Digital Hierarchy (SDH) in European standards, was developed specifically for voice transmissions [23]. It used fixed time slots to multiplex voices in optical links. It is now also upgraded to SONET over WDM (Wavelength Division Multiplexing), in which SONET data streams are transmitted through wavelength channels within optic fibers to increase the transmission capacity of optic fibers, as one fiber carries a number of wavelength channels. The current industry standard for SONET allows the transmission bit rate from 51.84 Mbps (STS-1) to 9,953.28 Mbps (OC192). The next generation of SONET will have the maximum line bit rate of 39,813.12 Mbps (OC768). The popular WDM systems used today in the telephone industry are from 4 to 16 wavelengths. However, 80 to 160 wavelength-channel DWDM (Dense WDM) are now available. The combination of high line bite rate and large number of wavelength channels brings enormous transmission capacity in SONET/SDH.

One of the key issues for utilizing the transmission capacity of SONET is packet over SONET, which is currently being researched in the telecommunication industry. Packet over SONET for point-to-point application has been deployed, such as the Cisco Internet routers that use SONET transceivers to achieve high bit rate transmissions between routers with low costs. However, there are many technical issues needing to be studied for packets over the entire telephone network, issues like how to manage the links for packets. On the other hand, a metro network can be implemented using the SONET without having to deal with these issues. In this section, we look into a metro network based on SONET for broadband residential and commercial communications. The key concept is to use fixed bandwidths for each type of service, and multiplex multiservices into SONET frames. At the central office, the services will be segregated and routed to the existing backbone networks, which are the SONET, the Internet and the cable TV networks.

The architecture of the network is based on the technology of SONET/SDH over DWDM. The network provides 50 Mbps downstream and 6 to 50 Mbps upstream bandwidths to each resident. These bandwidths can be upgraded to 300 Mbps, with 150 Mbps in each direction. A fixed bandwidth-sharing multiservice (FBM) protocol has been developed to allow residential services to be transported by SONET/SDH frames [24]. A Residential Gateway (RG) has been designed to implement the FBM protocol, which multiplexes upstream data into SONET/SDH STS-1 frames and de-multiplexes downstream data onto separate ports for each home device. The network also allows both enterprise and residential services to share a common network, which forms a broadband all-in-one multiservices metro-system. The bandwidths for enterprise users can range from 100 Mbps to 160 Gbps, depending on the demand of the user. It is bandwidth-on-demand for enterprises. This chapter emphasizes the issues of the residential services, in particular, the FBM protocol and the residential gateway, which enables integrated residential services through a SONET/SDH over DWDM framework.

In comparison with the Ethernet based system, the SONET/SDH based multiservices network provides guaranteed QoS. It also has the advantage of lower maintenance costs. However, the SONET/SDH based system does not enjoy the market continuity of the Ethernet based multiservices network system. The current proposed architecture of the network, the FBM protocol, and the RG design and implementation [24, 25] are presented next.

X.4.1 The Network Architecture

Fig. 13 shows the structure of the proposed broadband multiservices access network. As with the Ethernet based network proposed above, this network consists of optical fiber metro-backbones and local distribution sub-networks. The optical fiber metro-backbones connect the local distribution networks to the central office. The topology of a metro-backbone can be a tree or a self-healing protection ring, depending on the needs of the area. The local distribution networks can be configured according to the requirement of the users, which can be fiber-to-the-home, or coaxial-to-the-home. In the case of coaxial-to-the-home, it can be either a hybrid fiber-coaxial tree, or coaxial with frequency division multiplexing, as shown in Fig. 13. Cable modems are used in the case of coaxial-to-the-home configurations.

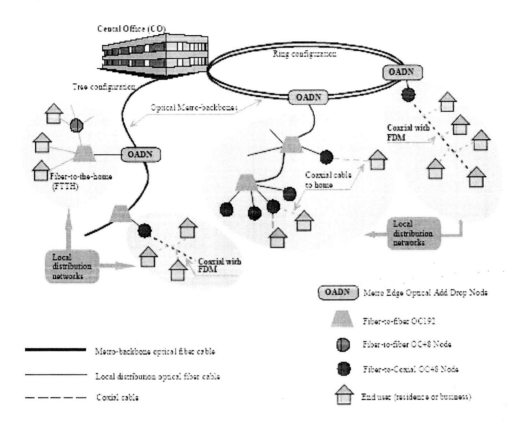

Fig. 13 The Structure of the proposed broadband residential multiservices access network

Normally, the STS-1 bandwidth of 51.84 Mbps for downstream and DS-2 with the bandwidth of 6.312 Mbps for upstream are provided for each residence. However, the network has the capacity of bandwidth-on-demand. STS-1 bandwidth for upstream and STS-3 (150Mbps) or higher for downstream can be provided to users if required. This configuration allows residential users, organizations, and businesses to share the same metro-network system. A residential gateway is employed at each user premise to distribute multiservices by receiving and sending SONET frames. The central office connects the proposed access network to the current backbone networks, namely the telephone, the Internet, and the cable TV networks. The multiservices carried by SONET frames are segregated at the central office and directed to one of the three existing backbone networks.

The feature of this network is that it does not require modifications from existing systems, including home devices and service provider systems. It provides a transparent layer between the service providers and the residential applications. Also, this architecture utilizes the existing technology of SONET/SDH and DWDM to achieve a low cost implementation.

The network not only provides the existing telephone and cable TV services, but also has the capacity of providing other broadband services to homes, such as 10Base-T Ethernet to home, video conferencing, and video-on-demand. Resources have also been reserved in the network design for future services, such as security monitoring and utility billing. The network provides enterprises with bandwidth-on-demand with a SONET end node, such as an STS-3 or an OC48. An enterprise gateway similar to the residential gateway can be implemented to provide multiservices to business users

The key components of the proposed network are the central office, the metro edge optical add/drop node (OADN), the fiber-to-fiber OC192 node, the fiber-to-fiber OC48 node, the fiber-to-coaxial OC48 node, and the residential gateway (RG). The RG and part of the central office equipment have been developed in our research and will be presented in section X.4.6 below, following section X.4.5 where the fixed bandwidth-sharing multiservice protocol is discussed. The metro edge optical add/drop node, the fiber-to-fiber node, and the fiber-to-coaxial node are mostly commercially available SONET/SDH and DWDM devices. Customizations of these devices and interfaces are required in some cases. In the following subsections we describe each of these elements.

X.4.2   The Metro Edge Optical Add/Drop Node

The metro edge optical add/drop node consists of a commercially available SONET/SDH based multiservice DWDM transport platform with a built-in optical add/drop multiplexers (OADM) to combine or extract a single wavelength to/from a metro-backbone fiber and distribute to/from the local distribution optical fiber, as shown in Fig.13. The OADM, with 100 GHz (ITU-T grid) spacing, is used in the architecture to drop one dedicated wavelength to each neighborhood offering multiservices to its customers. The metro edge node is connected in series with OC192 nodes and OC48 nodes, shown in Fig. 14.

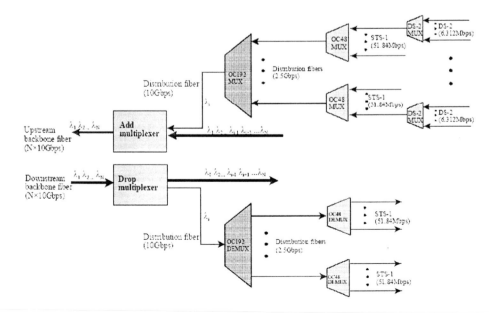

Fig. 14 The configuration of optical wavelength add/drop multiplexer and OC192/OC48

In the case of a self-healing protection ring backbone, optical protection switching is required at the metro edge node, to protect the metro access ring from fail-over, fiber cut, or any other damages. In this structure, the protection used is the Optical Unidirectional Path Switched Ring (O-UPSR), which is sometimes referred to as dedicated protection. This protection scheme is favorable in metro access rings due to their robustness, simplicity, cost and fast protection.

X.4.3 The Fiber-to-Fiber OC192 Node

The fiber-to-fiber OC192 node is a standard SONET/SDH MUX/DEMUX that multiplexes/demultiplexes, in the time domain, 4 OC48's or 192 STS-1's into/from one DWDM wavelength channel. The output bandwidth of the OC192 is 10 Gbps. Since we use one STS-1 bandwidth for each residence, one OC192 will serve 192 residents. If we use 16 wavelengths per fiber, the number of residents served by one optical fiber would be 3072 (16x192). If we use an 80-wavelength DWDM system, we would be able to serve 15360 (80x192) residents with each fiber link to the central office.

The proposed network architecture provides the flexibility for adopting the DWDM system. The larger the number of wavelength channels in the DWDM system, the smaller the number of optical fibers. The decision on the number of wavelength channels in the DWDM system to be used is purely based on cost, which is determined by the cost of the DWDM components and the cost of optical fiber cables. Our research, based on the current price trends, has shown that the DWDM with 4-16 wavelengths are the optimal DWDM systems at current time.

X.4.4 The Fiber-to-Fiber OC48 Node and Fiber-to-Coaxial OC48 Node

A fiber-to-fiber OC48 is used for the area of fiber-to-the-home (FTTH), where a dedicated fiber links each user to the OC48 node. Standard OC48 SONET MUX/DEMUX is employed in every OC48 node.

The fiber-to-coaxial OC48 node terminates optical fiber in the neighborhood of residential area. It may have two types of configurations: 1) single coaxial cable to each home, and 2) coaxial tree with FDM. In configuration-1, a dedicated coaxial provides the connection between the user and the OC48 node, as shown in Fig. 15. Two frequency channels are used by the modems, with one for upstream and one for downstream transmissions. In configuration-2, a tree topology of coaxial cables connects a group of users to the OC48 node. FDM is used to create one hundred channels for upstream and one hundred channels for downstream within the trunk of the tree, as shown in Fig. 16.

As shown in Fig.14, the OC48 nodes are linked to the nearest OC192 node through a pair of fibers. The bandwidth between an OC48 node and the OC192 node is 2.5 Gbps.

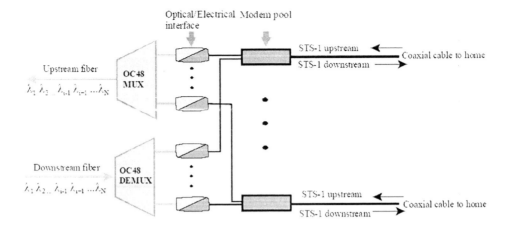

Fig. 15 Fiber-to-coaxial OC48 node (configuration-1: single coaxial to home)

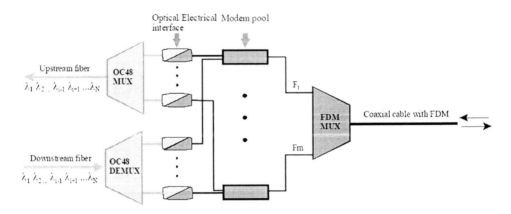

Fig. 16 Fiber-to-coaxial OC48 node (configuration-2: tree topology of coaxial cables)

X.4.5 The Fixed Bandwidth-Sharing Multiservice Protocol

The Transmission Protocol

The concept of fixed bandwidth sharing is to multiplex the data streams of residential services in the time domain by allocating a constant time slot for each intended service. The size of the time slot assigned to each service is determined by the bandwidth required to provide the service. In our design, we use the payload of STS-1 frames to transmit the combined downstream data of all the home services. The STS-1 transmits 8000 frames per second, with each frame containing 810 bytes. The bandwidth of the STS-1 is thus 810 (frames) x 8 (bits/byte) x 8000 (frames/second) = 51.84 Mbps. In each STS-1 frame, 27 bytes are used for SONET/SDH overhead, which leaves 783 bytes for payload. The payload bandwidth of STS-1 is therefore 783 (frames) x 8 (bits/byte) x 8000 (frames/second) = 50.112 Mbps.

In our Fixed Bandwidth-Sharing Multiservice (FBM) protocol, we divide the STS-1 payload into fixed time slots, with each slot dedicated for one home service. Fig. 17 shows the frame format of the FBM protocol. The calculation of the number bits for each service is listed in Table 1.

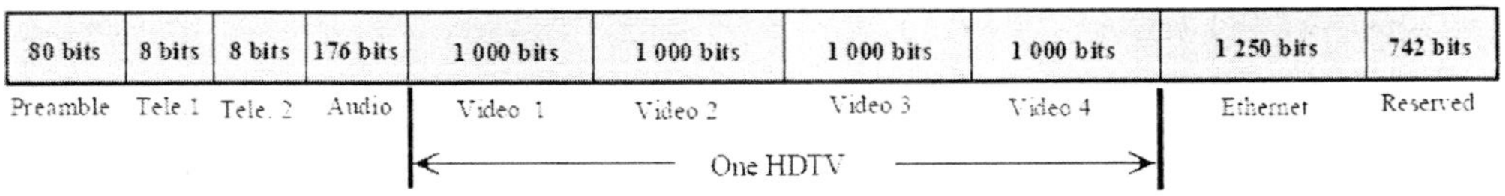

80 bits	8 bits	8 bits	176 bits	1 000 bits	1 000 bits	1 000 bits	1 000 bits	1 250 bits	742 bits
Preamble	Tele 1	Tele. 2	Audio	Video 1	Video 2	Video 3	Video 4	Ethernet	Reserved

One HDTV

Fig. 17 The frame format of the Fixed Bandwidth Sharing Residential Multiservice (FBSRM) protocol

Table-1. The required bandwidth and the frame slot size of home services

Service Type	Bandwidth Required (bits/Second)	Size of the Slot (bits/Frame)
10BaseT Ethernet	10 000 000	1 250
Telephone	64 000	8
Broadcast Audio	1 411 200	176
Video	8 000 000	1 000

The FBM frame shown in Fig. 17 consists of 6264 bits, which exactly equals the payload of one STS-1 frame. The preamble field in the frame is used by the RG and the central office switch to extract the data from the frame for each service. One of the major functions of the preamble bits is to indicate whether the corresponding data field is carrying the service or if it is currently idle. One byte in the preamble is responsible for one service field in the frame. Currently, 8 bytes are assigned respectively to each of the 8 services shown in Fig. 17, which are telephone 1, telephone 2, audio, video 1, video 2, video 3, video 4, and Ethernet. The remaining 2 bytes in the preamble field will be assigned to the 726 bits reserved field that will be used for future applications, such as security monitoring and utility billing.

In the current version of the FBM, we allocated two telephones and four video streams for each residence. The reserved field can be used for additional telephones if required. This has been considered in the design of the RG. Each video field has 1000 bits in the frame, which translates to a bit rate of 8 Mbps for broadcasting TVs and video-on-demand. When HDTV is used, the four broadcast TV fields are combined to offer 32 Mbps bandwidth. It is noted that there is some bandwidth waste in the case of broadcast TV applications, since it is unlikely all four video channels are used at the same time. However, as the trend of moving to HDTV's continues, HDTV's will soon become the dominant home service. This means that the whole STS-1 frame will be fully utilized.

The same principle is applied to upstream transmission. If STS-1 bandwidth is used for upstream, the same frame format described above is applied. When DS-2 bandwidth is used for upstream, we allocate two telephones and one video only. Also, the Ethernet connection shares the time slot of the video, which means that only one of them can be used at one time. The sharing mechanism is implemented in the residential gateway.

As was mentioned in Section X.4.1, the proposed architecture has the flexibility to provide varieties of bandwidths to residential and enterprise users. An STS-3 bandwidth of 155.25 Mbps can also be provided to homes if multiple HDTV's or high-speed Ethernets are required. It will follow the same scheme of fixed bandwidth time domain sharing as we used in the STS-1 case. It also requires an RG designed for STS-3 transmissions. This part is under development and will not be described here.

The Central Office Structure and the Control Protocol

There are a number of control issues needing to be dealt with in the network, which include channel selections of broadcasting video and audio, as well as the telephone connections. Unlike the cable TV system where the signals of all the channels are delivered to every user at the same time, the proposed multiservices network delivers only the signals of those channels selected by the user. The protocols for these control issues are related to the central office switch structure, which are discussed together in this section.

Fig. 18 shows the structure of the central office switch unit. The first function of the central office switch is to connect the users to the three traditional services, which are the telephone, the cable TV, and the Internet. The second function of the central office switch is to connect the users to new services, such as video-on-demand, security monitoring, and utility billing. By connecting the users to the current existing backbone networks of telephone, cable TV, and the Internet, it eliminates any changes to the existing systems. This is very important from an economical point of view.

As shown in Fig. 18, the central office switch consists of three elements, which are the DWDM wavelength MUX/DEMUX, SONET/SDH MUX/DEMUX, and user cards. The DWDM MUX/DEMUX and the SONET/SDH MUX/DEMUX are commercially available at the current time. The user card is a new device designed for the proposed network system. The transmission and framing function of the user card is the same as those of the residential gateway. The designs of these elements are also the same. However, the control protocol unit inside the user card is different from the one inside the residential gateway. A video/audio channel selection device is required in the user card.

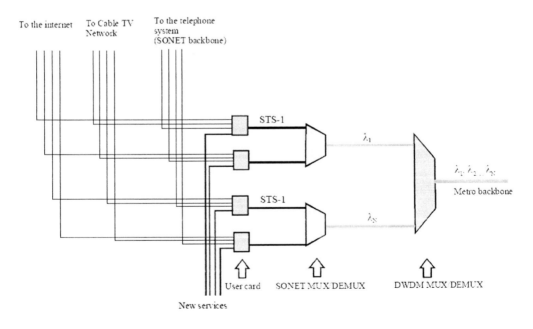

Fig. 18. The central office system

To select a channel, the channel selection protocol uses the upstream connection to transmit a special control frame, in which the information of the channel to be selected is inserted in the payload. The control unit of the user card uses the information to connect the requested channel to the corresponding downstream link. There will be a minor delay in this process, but it is not noticeable to the users.

X.4.6 The Residential Gateway Design

The overall architecture

The proposed Residential Gateway (RG) [24, 25], which is also called the Residential Multiservices Switch (RMS), described here is a key component in the network that allows home services to be carried by SONET/SDH frames. The RG multiplexes, according to the Fixed Bandwidth-Sharing Multiservice (FBM) Protocol, upstream data from home devices into STS-1 or DS-2 frames and transmits the combined signal through the coaxial cable or optical fiber that connects the user to the nearest OC48 node. The RG is also responsible for demultiplexing the downstream data from the STS-1 frames to each individual port that connects to a home device. In the case of fiber-to-the-home, a symmetrical bandwidth of STS-1 is used for upstream and downstream, shown in Fig. 19(a). Fig. 19(b) shows the layout of the RG for the case of coaxial cable to the home. A cable modem is used to transmit and receive data via one cable in which FDM is used to create two channels, one for upstream and the other for downstream communications. The bandwidth for upstream can be either DS-2 (6.312 Mbps) or STS-1 (51.84 Mbps) for this case.

As shown in Fig 19, the RG has both analog and digital connectors for videos and telephones, which allows both analog and digital devices to be directly connected to the RG. The RG provides separate ports for upstream and downstream video communications, which allows teleconferencing to be conducted by a video camera and a TV set. The 10Base-T twisted pair Ethernet cable is used to connect a home computer to the RG. An Ethernet hub can also be connected to the Ethernet port of the RG to allow multiple computers to share the 10 Mbps dedicated to Internet applications.

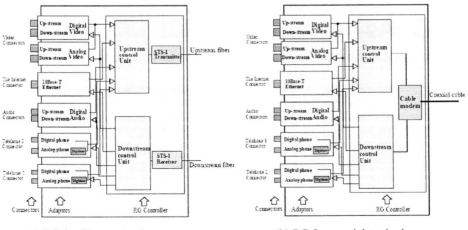

(a) RG for fiber-to-the-home   (b) RG for coaxial-to-the-home

Fig. 19. The layout of the residential gateway

The main function of the RG is to combine the data streams from the different home devices into SONET/SDH frames for upstream direction, and extract data for each home device from the downstream STS-1 frames. To achieve this function, the RG needs to comply with the SONET/SDH protocol in order to transmit/receive data to/from the multiservices access network. The RG also needs to communicate with each home device according to the protocol of each individual device, such as the Ethernet protocol for computers. To achieve all of these, we developed an RG design with implementation using the Altera FLEX10KE PLD in mind.

The block diagram of the RG is shown in Fig. 20. It consists of four blocks: Double Buffers, Address Generators, Control Logic, and Multiplexer. The double buffers are used to buffer multiple-channel input data and the output frames. The Address Generators generate the write and read addresses of the double-ported buffers, respectively. The Address Generators also create control inputs for Control Logic. Control Logic creates write enables and read enables that control the behavior of the Double Buffers. A Multiplexer is used to select the correct framed data to make up one output STS-1 frame. The "Select" signals are created by Control Logic. The details of these four blocks are discussed in the following Subsections.

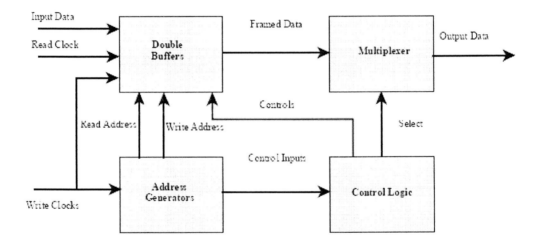

Fig. 20. The block diagram of the residential gateway

The Double Buffer Unit

In order to transmit the data streams of the home devices through SONET/SDH, we need to buffer the data for every port in 125 μS intervals, since SONET/SDH transmits one frame in each 125 μS. We use a double buffer mechanism to allow simultaneous receiving and transmitting. Fig. 21 shows the structure of the double buffer for the upstream direction, which consists of two identical buffers, A and B. Fig. 21(a) shows the case that Buffer A is receiving data from the home devices, while Buffer B is in the sending mode used by the STS-1 transmitter. In Fig. 21(b), Buffer A is in sending mode, and Buffer B is in the receiving modal. Each buffer is composed of 8 memory blocks, with each block responsible for one home device port. The size of each memory block is equal to the bit length allocated for that service in the STS-1 frame by the FBM protocol. A double buffer of the same configuration is used for the downstream direction.

The roles of receiving and sending data for buffers A and B are switched every 125 μS. The switching takes place at the half clock cycle at the end of each STS-1 framing, which guarantees the continuity of the incoming and outgoing data streams. When the buffer is in receiving mode, the memory is written as independent blocks by each home device. While the buffer is in sending mode, it becomes one single memory buffer which is read in serially from the beginning to the end. This is controlled by the address generator shown in Fig. 20 and described next.

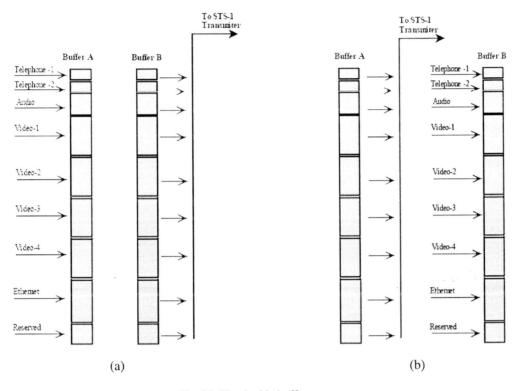

(a)   (b)

Fig. 21. The double buffer structure

The Address Generator Unit

Since the data framing is implemented by double buffering, logic is needed to generate addresses for each double buffer unit. The address generator generates both write addresses and read addresses. Write address generation is synchronized with the specific channel clock and outputs addresses in a cycling mode so that the A or B half of the double buffer unit is written from beginning to the end. Read address generation is synchronized with the STS-1 clock and also outputs addresses in a cycling mode, but the read process is faster than the write process. Because write processes for different signal channels are parallel, while read processes are in a serial mode. An appropriate analogy of this process is parallel to serial conversion, where the frequency of the serial clock is faster than that of the parallel clocks. Modulo N binary counters are used to implement the address generators.

The Control Unit

The control unit is responsible for all of the required control functions of the RG. The control functions can be divided into two types, transmission control and channel selection control. The transmission control includes the following RG internal functionalities:

- The alternation of writing or reading the two buffers in the double buffer unit
- Inserting/decoding the preamble bits in the FBM frame according to the applications
- Delay control of the memory blocks to accommodate the delayed output of the memory blocks

The channel selection control is used to select a memory block in a predefined order. Therefore, the STS-1 frame can be created. Since the write and read processes of the double buffers are always executed without interruption, it is the channel selection control's responsibility to ensure data from a specific channel to be output in a given time slot. In this design, the channel selection control is used to control the behavior of the multiplexer that makes a many-to-one selection.

The Multiplexer

The inputs of the multiplexer are the double buffers containing the framed data from all channels. The output is an STS-1 frame that complies with the payload specification. The multiplexer functions as a switch which connects the buffers of each home device to the output according to the time sequence. The control logic unit provides control signals that pick up a specific channel at a certain time.

X.4.7 Summary

This section presented a metro network based on SONET/SDH. The most important feature of the network is that it provides guaranteed QoS for all applications, which cannot be matched by other types of networks. Although the bandwidth utilization can be low in some cases, the cost for the services is not necessarily higher than other options, due to the low cost of optical fibers and the simplicity of the system. From a long term point of view, this network could be the best for metro and residential broadband communications.

One important aspect worth mentioning is that the long haul backbone networks are still the current existing networks, which themselves are mainly the SONET (for voice), the Internet (for data), and wireless/satellite networks. The proposed metro network uses the same SONET protocol for signals, but organizes data into packets. If those packets had to go out on the connection-based long haul SONET backbone, we would face the problem of establishing a connection for each packet, or at least for the duration of each application that is communicating packets, which would be wasteful. Instead, multiple applications are combined and separated at both the residential premises and the central office of the metro network. This mechanism avoids the requirement to send packets over SONET in the long haul backbone network.

X.5 IP Based Residential Multiservices Network System

The Internet is the most popular network on the surface of the earth. Virtually all known communications have been implemented on IP. However, there is one important thing that IP cannot provide, which is the Quality of Service (QoS) guarantee [26]. This "defect" roots back to the Internet networking protocol, which was designed for datagram communications from the very beginning. Aside from accommodation in the protocol, QoS also requires high routing speed of the network. In order to provide QoS for real-time applications, the packet forward speed needs to be fast enough to guarantee that the delay and jitter are in the tolerable range. It is very hard for software based IP routers to have the required packet forwarding speed, given especially the transmitting speed available of optic fibers. These deficiencies were, in fact, the reasons behind the development of the ATM in the first place. ATM was designed to maintain the benefits of packet networks while at the same time providing mechanisms for controlling the QoS. We saw from section X.3 that the complexity of ATM is significantly greater than IP, which in return has resulted in its high cost. The complexity and cost of ATM became the major barriers for the deployment of the ATM base B-ISDN, as we discussed earlier.

From long term point of view, QoS will become a major issue for IP based multiservices networks. The solution to it will go back down the route of ATM. However, the short term benefits of IP based residential services are so attractive to businesses that they cannot afford to lose the market opportunities. Cable TV networks are at the leading edge of IP based residential services and will continue to grow in this direction. It is very difficult to predict the future of this trend. However, whether IP will eventually be the protocol for broadband residential services is very questionable.

Owing to fact that IP based real-time applications, mainly voice and video, can easily be deployed by user programs, many software programs are now available for video and voice over IP. However, if QoS guarantee is demanded, the IP network itself, including protocols, routing mechanisms, and routing speed will all have be reexamined. In this section we look into the key elements of IP as related to real-time communications.

X.5.1   IPv6 and QoS

IPv6 has built-in provisions for real-time applications [27]. It improves the QoS, but without guarantees. This can be seen by examining the packet header format of IPv6, which is shown in Fig. 22. There are two fields in the packet header, namely the Priority Field and the Flow Label Field, that can be used by IPv6 routers to improve the QoS for real-time applications.

The 4-bit priority field can assume 16 different values. It enables the source node to differentiate packets it generates by associating different delivery priorities to them. These 16 possible values are further divided into two groups: from 0 through 7, and from 8 through 15. Values 0 through 7 are used to specify the priority of the traffic for which the source is providing traffic control. A typical example is the traffic of applications that use TCP and its congestion control mechanisms based on variable sizes of windows. Values 8 through 15 are used to specify the priority of traffic that does not back off in response to congestion. A typical example is represented by real-time packets like those of voice and video. Among the 8 levels of priority represented by values 8 through 15, 15 indicates the highest priority and 8 represents the lowest priority. Priority 8 is associated with those packets that the network will discard first under conditions of congestion (for example, high-fidelity video traffic), and priority 15 is associated with those packets that the sender will discard at the end, only if absolutely necessary (for example, low-quality telephone audio traffic).

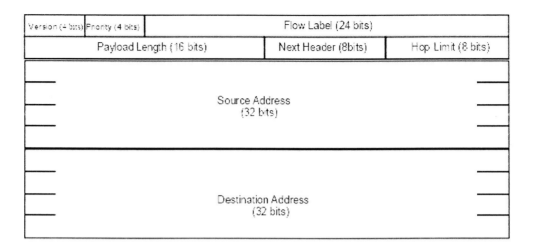

Version (4 bits)	Priority (4 bits)	Flow Label (24 bits)	
Payload Length (16 bits)		Next Header (8bits)	Hop Limit (8 bits)
Source Address (32 bits)			
Destination Address (32 bits)			

Fig. 22 IPv6 packet header format

By prioritizing the packets, the routers are able to forward higher priority packets first and let the lower priority packets wait, to achieve better QoS for higher priority (usually real-time) applications. However, this is not sufficient to guarantee the QoS. Bandwidth reservation and sufficient routing speed are also necessary in order to provide a certain level of QoS guarantee. In regards to bandwidth reservation, a reservation protocol (RSVP) [28] can be added into IP, provided that the provisions of using the reserved bandwidth are implemented. In regards to routing speed, it can be extremely challenging for software based IP routers to keep up the packet forward speed, considering the line bit rate at multi-gigabits level on each port of the router. Hardware based switching naturally becomes an alternative for high speed packet forwarding. These, in fact, were the key reasons for the development of a new network system called MPLS (Multi Protocol Label Switching) [23]. We devote the next section to discuss MPLS and its application in residential multiservices networks.

X.5.2 Switched IP Network and MPLS

MPLS is an Internet Engineering Task Force (IETF) specified framework that provides for the efficient designation, routing, forwarding, and switching of traffic flows through the network. MPLS performs the following functions:

- Manages traffic flows of various granularities, such as flows between different hardware and different machines, or flows between different applications
- Provides mechanisms to map IP addresses to simple, fixed-length labels used by different packet-forwarding and packet-switching technologies
- Interfaces to existing routing protocols such as resource reservation protocol (RSVP) and open shortest path first (OSPF) [23]
- Supports the IP, ATM, and frame-relay Layer-2 protocols

One of the major goals of MPLS is to achieve high-speed packet switching by hardware to allow broadband real-time applications in a packet network, IP in particular. The switching mechanism is similar to the one of ATM, except that labels are used as the identifier of the packet or cell in the switches. The labels, which are underlying protocol-specific identifiers, are distributed using label distribution protocol (LDP) [23] or RSVP, or piggybacked on routing protocols like border gateway protocol (BGP) [23] and OSPF. Each data packet encapsulates and carries the labels during their journey from source to destination. Data transmission occurs on a label-switched path (LSP). LSPs are a sequence of labels at each and every node along the path from the source to the destination. LSPs are established either prior to data transmission (control-driven) or upon detection of a certain flow of data (data-driven).

X.5.3 IP Based Multiservices on the Cable TV Networks

Background
With the widespread deployment of optical fibers, cable TV networks have been increasing their bandwidth capacity significantly over the past decade. As optic fibers are run closer and closer to residential areas, extra bandwidths are also carved out of the coaxial cables. The available bandwidth provides cable TV companies with the capacities to provide more channels on top of the traditional ones. It also provides the bandwidth for cable Internet and other services, such as pay-per-view. The available bandwidth also promotes IP telephony, and two way communications via IP on cable TV networks, which is on the horizon. As these different technologies are integrated into cable television networks we are seeing the term Broadband Television Network used more frequently.

One mechanism to utilize the available bandwidth to provide new services, including two-way communications, without needing to change the architecture of the cable TV networks is to deploy IP based services, such as IP telephony, over cable modems or set-top boxes. PacketCable based on DOCSIS (Data Over Cable Service Interface Specification) platform is the technology designed for this market, which is under continuous development and near to deployment stage.

Undoubtedly, there are good market potentials for IP based services over cable TV networks. Most importantly, the short term investment required for developing IP based services will be significantly less than any other type of technologies over the cable TV networks. However, from a long term point of view, IP based technology may not be the best one to convert the cable TV network into a full-blown broadband residential integrated service network, even though the cable TV networks have the bandwidth capacity. Nevertheless, the market for IP telephony, limited video-on-demand, and teleconferencing over cable TV networks is an opportunity that the cable TV providers cannot afford to miss.

In this section, we provide an overview of the two key elements of IP technology for cable TV networks, namely DOCSIS and PacketCable.

DOCSIS
Simply put, DOCSIS is a standardized set of specifications, determined by the CableLabs [29, 30] organization, to create a common benchmark for data transmission via high-speed cable modems over cable television networks. CableLabs, short for Cable Television Laboratories, Inc., is a research group for the cable telecommunications industry whose members are composed of cable operators and vendors. CableLabs' DOCSIS project and

standardization has become the next wave in cable Internet advances, offering benefits to service providers, equipment manufacturers, and consumers.

DOCSIS 1.0 was approved by the International Telecommunication Union (ITU) in March of 1998, since then many cable providers have integrated this platform into their cable Internet structure. Current DOCSIS implementations found in cable networks are either version 1.0 or 1.1. Assuming that the original equipment is capable of the higher platform, a provider can simply update the EEPROM memory in the modem to upgrade it. Each platform is also backwards compatible with its predecessor. The introduction of DOCSIS provided the industry with a common standard, offering more consistent and measurable performance for high-speed Internet access.

Moving to DOCSIS 1.1 provides further benefits, features, and advancements. We are introduced to voice, gaming and streaming multimedia over IP. This platform has become the basis for PacketCable and IP telephony because it introduces higher speeds and quality of service (QoS). DOCSIS 1.1 doubles the upstream speed of version 1.0 from 5 Mbps to 10 Mbps (assuming 16 QAM modulation is used rather than QPSK modulation). This platform also defines dynamic QoS for PacketCable which requires a level of quality that can meet or exceed the public switched telephone network (PSTN).

Integrating to DOCSIS certified modems is beneficial for the service providers, manufacturers, and consumers. Since DOCSIS was created by CableLabs, whose members consist of cable network providers and technologists, the requirements were based on the industry's needs and expectations. Therefore, those using or integrating DOCSIS within their networks play a large part in the decision process behind the specification requirements, including revisions and current advancements. DOCSIS provides an open standards process in both the ITU and the Society of Cable Telecommunications Engineers (SCTE) [31]. Following a path that one might consider similar to the Global Systems for Mobile (GSM) cellular technology, DOCSIS is a standard for global use stretching beyond the boundaries of North America. Since CableLabs does not manufacture the equipment, there are many different vendors developing DOCSIS modems, providing more choices and a competitive market which benefits the consumers by lowering equipment costs. Another benefit, as stated earlier, is the backward compatibility between DOCSIS platforms, which maximizes interoperability on the network. These are some of the major benefits to DOCSIS implementation in cable networks, and with the further progression of this technology we can expect the benefits to multiply.

The DOCSIS 2.0 platform is already being tested by some cable providers, but it has not yet been released to consumers. This platform provides even higher QoS and doubles upstream data transfer rates from 1.1; the higher transfer rates assume utilization of a larger 6.4 MHz channel bandwidth and 64 QAM. What does this mean for cable Internet subscribers? With the implementation of DOCSIS 2.0, we can expect improved upstream utilization, better spectral efficiency, and we will also see better noise immunity. The platform will also introduce enhanced modulation and improved error correction.

On November 10, 2004, CableLabs issued a press release, "CableLabs® Issues RFI for an Integrated DOCSIS® Access Device for Commercial Applications," inviting further expansion in device technology [29]. With the success of the DOCSIS platform, IP telephony trials being in place, and the industry's need for an "all-in-one" device, this request was launched to meet consumer needs. By again providing a common set of specifications for Integrated DOCSIS Access Devices (IDADs), CableLabs is hoping to receive submissions from numerous manufacturers. The benefit to consumers would be economical pricing, and for the industry we could potentially eliminate the need for separate devices to utilize Internet and IP telephony in the home. IDADs will be similar to those Multimedia Terminal Adapters (MTAs) currently in the market, since they will be PacketCable based for voice service. However, they will go a step beyond by integrating DS1 circuit emulation over IP with DOCSIS. It essentially combines IP telephony and standard IP networking capabilities into one device.

PacketCable

PacketCable [29] is another initiative led by CableLabs and its member companies to develop efficient and interoperable real-time two-way cable communications. The focus is to provide services such as IP telephony, video conferencing, gaming, and other multimedia over IP technology. Unlike DOCSIS, the idea behind PacketCable is not in assessing whether vendor equipment meets the set specifications for certification; but rather determining the interoperability and compatibility of devices with other PacketCable compliant devices and ability to comply with DOCSIS networks. PacketCable applies to most multimedia services that require two-way communications, often built or expanding on a DOCSIS device. MTA devices are currently being tested on numerous cable networks for IP telephony and with CableLabs request for IDADs we should expect to see these devices appearing residentially sometime within the next year.

Cisco Systems is one of the biggest contributors/developers of voice over IP (VoIP) and PacketCable implementations on DOCSIS 1.1 networks. Three of the most significant components of a telephony network are the MTA, cable modem termination system (CMTS), and the call management server (CMS)/media gateway controller (MGC). MTA devices used in telephony are PacketCable compliant DOCSIS modems with a built in voice digitizer. What Cisco focuses on are the larger scale network components that transport the packet streams produced by the MTA. The subscriber plugs their standard telephone into the MTA, and dials as usual. The cable provider would have a device such as Cisco's uBR7246VXR and uBR10012 universal broadband routers acting as the CMTS. The CMTS accepts the packet streams from the MTA by means of a hybrid fiber coax (HFC) access network. From the CMTS, the packet stream can be directly transmitted to another telephony subscriber and logged by the CMS, or directed through the MGC which acts as an interconnection between the telephony network and the public switched telephone network. Cisco Systems is currently producing the Cisco MGX® 8000 series MGCs. Full Cisco telephony implementation can be seen on Cisco's website [32], the Cisco PacketCable-Based VoIP solution primer white paper.

X.6 Summary and Conclusion

In the previous sections we have discussed four possible networks for broadband residential integrated or multiservices, which are B-ISDN, Ethernet based, SONET based, and IP based broadband access/metro networks. It is not clear at this time which model will eventually become the industry standard and be deployed commercially. As we have discussed earlier that the evolution depends not only on the technological aspects but also heavily on the commercial market. From a technical point of view, the SONET based metro network model provides stable QoS and minimal network management cost. But it does not have the advantage of market continuity. The IP based model, on the other hand, provides near term profits, but it has a very insecure future. The Ethernet based model is somewhere in between, and it will likely lead to the similar system as the ATM based B-ISDN, if it is adopted as the industrial standard.

References

[1]   D.B. Keck, Fellow, IEEE, A.J. Morrow, D.A. Nolan and D.A. Thompson, "Passive Components in the Subscriber Loop," (Invited Paper) in *Journal of Lightwave Technology*, Vol. 7, No. 11. November 1989.

[2]   K. Okada et al., "Overview of Full Services Optical Access Networks," *Full Service Access Network Conference*, London, June 1996.

[3]   Dan Spears et al., "FSAN FTTH Chapter Report," *Third Workshop on Full Service Access Networks*, Venice, 1998.

[4]   Jeff Stern et al., "Report on progress for the FTTCab Chapter," *Third Workshop on Full Service Access Networks*, Venice, 1998.

[5]   Don Clarke et al., "The FSAN VDSL Working Group – Update," *Third Workshop on Full Service Access Networks*, Venice, 1998.

[6]   K. Okada et al., "Full Service Optical Access Network Systems," FSAN OAN-WG Report. *Third Workshop on Full Service Access Networks*, Venice, 1998.

[7]   Y. Picault et al., "Full Service Access Networks - Group Customer Network Specification," *Third Workshop on Full service Access Network*, FSAN'98, Venice, 1998.

[8]   Eytan Modiano and Richard Barry, "Architectural considerations in the design of WDM-based optical access networks," in *Journal of Computer Networks*, **31** (1999), pp. 327-341.

[9]   Yih-kang Maurice Lin, and Dan R. Spears, "Passive Optical Subscriber Loops With Multiaccess," in *Journal of Lightwave Technology*, vol. 7. No. 11, Nov. 1989, pp. 1769-1777.

[10] I.P. Kaminow et al., "A wideband all-optical WDM network," *in IEEE Journal on Selected Areas in Communications*, Vol. 14, NO. 5, June 1996.

[11] John D. Angelopoulos, Nikos I. Lepidas, E.K. Fragoulopoulos and Iakovos S. Venieris, "TDMA Multiplexing ATM cells in a residential access superPON," in *IEEE Journal on Selected Areas in Communications*, Vol 16, No. 7, September 1998.

[12] Tianying Ji, Shaowen Song, Li Wei, "An Implementation of A Residential Gateway Controller For A Fixed Bandwidth-Sharing Multiservices Residential Access Network," *Proc. IEEE Canadian Conference on Electrical and Computer Engineering* (CCECE04), 2004, May 2-5, pp. 0023-0026.

[13] Uyless Black, ATM, Volume I – *Foundation for Broadband Networks*, Prentice Hall, 1995.

[14] Walter J. Goralski, *Introduction to ATM Networking*, McGraw-Hill, 1995.

[15] William Stallings, *ISDN and Broadband ISDN with Frame Relay and ATM*, Third Edition, Prentice Hall, 1992.

[16] http://www.fsanweb.org/default.asp

[17] Behrouz A. Forouzan, *Data Communications and Networking*, Second Edition update, McGraw-Hill, 2001.

[18] J.A. Quayle (Editor), "Full Services Access Network Requirements Specification".

[19] Charles E. Spurgeon, *Ethernet, The Definite Guide,* O'Reilly, 2000.

[20] http://tccomm.com/TC3720.htm

[21] Shaowen Song, Li Wei, and Tianying Ji, "A Broadband Residential Multiservices Network Based on Ethernet over a Hybrid Optical Fiber and Coaxial Infrastructure," *Proc. of The Fourth International Conference on Optical Internet (COIN05),* 2005, pp. 436-444.

[22] Larry Lindsay, Shaowen Song, and Li Wei, "A study on a Residential Gateway for an Ethernet Based Residential Multiservices Network," *Proc. IEEE Canadian Conference on Electrical and Computer Engineering (CCECE04),* 2004, May 2-5, pp. 617-620.

[23] Uyless Black, *Optical Networks, Third Generation Transport System,* Prentice Hall, 2002.

[24] Tianying Ji, Shaowen Song, and Li Wei, "An Implementation of a Residential Gateway Controller for A Fixed Bandwidth-Sharing Multiservices Residential Access Network," *Proc. IEEE Canadian Conference on Electrical and Computer Engineering (CCECE04),* 2004, May 2-5, pp. 0023-0026.

[25] Wei Zhang, Jiandong Zheng, and Shaowen Song, "The Interface Design for A Residential Gateway in A SONET over DWDM Broadband Access Network," *Proc. IEEE Canadian Conference on Electrical and Computer Engineering (CCECE04),* 2004, May 2-5, pp. 0269-0272.

[26] Behrouz A. Forouzan, *TCP/IP Protocol Suite,* McGraw-Hill, 2003.

[27] Silvano Gai, *Internetworking IPv6 with Cisco Routers,* McGraw-Hill, 1998.

[28] R. Barden, Ed., "Resource ReSerVation Protocol (RSVP)," http://www.ietf.org/rfc/rfc2205.txt

[29] ODCSIS Overview, http://www.cablelabs.com/, *Cable Television Laboratories.*

[30] Ralph W. Brown, "Convergence on the DOCSIS Platform," CableLabs 2005 Media Briefing, http://www.cablelabs.com/conferences_public/MB2005/.

[31] http://www.scte.org/home.cfm

[32] http://www.cisco.com/

In: Computer Networking and Networks
Editor: Susan Shannon, pp. 99-113

ISBN 1-59454-830-7
©2006 Nova Science Publishers, Inc.

Chapter 4

FLOW-BASED ANALYSIS OF INTERNET TRAFFIC

Andrei Sukhov[1]*, Warren Daly[2] †, Fedor Afanasiev[3‡] and Anton Petrov[3§]
[1] Laboratory of Network Technologies, Samara Academy of Transport
Engineering, 1st Bezymyanny per., 18, Samara, 443066, Russia
[2] HeaNet Ltd, Crampton Ave, Shelbourne Rd, Ballsbridge, Dublin 4, Ireland;
[3] JSC "SamaraTelecom", Aerodromnaya 45, Samara, Russia

Abstract

We propose the use of flow-based analysis to estimate the quality of an Internet connection. Using results from queueing theory we compare two expressions for backbone traffic that have different applications. We will demonstrate a curve that shows the dependence of link utilization and the number of active flows in it, to describe different states of the network. We propose a methodology for plotting such a curve using data received from a Cisco router from the NetFlow protocol, and use this curve to show the working area and the overload point of the given network. Our test demonstrates an easy way to identify when a backbone upgrade is required.

Keywords: Flow-based test of network quality, Cisco NetFlow, queueing models, Passive Monitoring System

1 Introduction

Modeling the traffic at the packet level has proven to be very difficult, since traffic on a link is the result of a high level of aggregation of numerous flows. Recently, a new trend has emerged for modelling Internet traffic at the flow level.

A flow here is a very generic concept. It can be a TCP connection or a UDP stream described by source and destination IP addresses, source and destination port numbers, or

---

*E-mail address: sukhov@ssau.ru(Corresponding author)

†E-mail address: warren.daly@heanet.ie

‡E-mail address: afv@smrtlc.ru

§E-mail address: apetrov@smrtlc.ru

the protocol number etc. It is possible to determine the response time and the distribution flows that are active at a certain time in the network. For simplicity, it is much easier to monitor flows than to monitor packets in a router.

Until recently network operators collected statistics at the packet level, which included source and destination addresses, ports, protocols, packet flags, size, start and end time of UDP and TCP sessions, duration of the sessions etc. Processing such huge volumes of data is difficult and requires powerful hardware, software and significant human resources. We note that this type of data collection does not produce the necessary information needed to provide useful recommendations for the network under consideration.

Typically, the following four values are used for the estimation of the network quality:

- Link utilization level

- Round trip time (comparable to 2*one way delay (OWD))

- Packet loss rate

- IP packet delay variation

The round trip time, packet loss rate and IP packet delay variation describe the quality of connectivity between two remote points or end-to-end connection. The link utilization is applied to the monitoring of a single hop between two routers.

Network operators need to know when their backbone or peering links must be upgraded. Boundary values of network parameters may serve as an indicator e.g. as the current values of the network parameters reach a defined limit, the links have to be upgraded. The problem with this method is that there is no standardized set of network parameters to monitor. Each provider has its own set of technical specifications aimed at avoiding overload. Big providers, like Sprint [8], rely on the results of their own research. Usually, network operators monitor peak and average link utilization levels and upgrade their links when the utilization level is in the range 30%-60%.

The main focus of this paper is to use flow-based analysis to monitor the backbone link and identify when an upgrad is needed. Previous work by Chuck Fraleigh et al [9] addressed a similar provisioning problem to reduce the 'per packet' end-to-end delay. Dina Papagiannaki et al [13], at Infocom 03, introduced a methodology on the basis of SNMP statistics to predict when and where link additions/upgrades should take place in an IP backbone network.

Traffic accounting mechanisms based on flows should be considered as passive measurement mechanisms. Information gathered by flows are useful for many purposes:

- Understanding the behaviour of existing networks

- Planning for network development and expansion

- Quantifying network performance

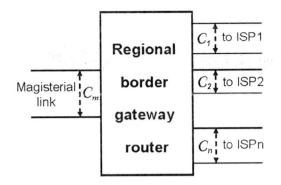

Figure 1: The scheme of interregional link

- Verifying the quality of network service

- Attribution of network usage to users

Unfortunately, at the present time there is no united view on how to estimate the connection quality, and find "narrow" places in the networks.

As mentioned above many ISPs such as Sprint use the 50% maximum utilization rule as a guideline for link upgrading. There are some cases when this approach is better and more precise than traditional tests. In Russia and in other countries where the links of national backbone are long and expensive, regional connectivity is provided by only two or three telecommunication operators. Often the capacity of interregional link C_m is less than the sum of the capacities C_i from the border gateway router to the Internet service providers (ISP), see Fig. 1.

$$C_m < \sum_{i=1}^{n} C_i \tag{1}$$

In this case the 50% utilization of link rule to the regional provider is fulfilled, but the quality of the connection is of a low level. If the staff of a regional ISP have no concept of higher networks, their capacity and connection quality, then, our model will allow them to estimate the quality of the above channel.

Barakat et al [2] propose a model that relies on flow-level information to compute the total (aggregate) rate of data observed on an IP backbone link. For modelling purposes, the traffic is viewed as the superposition (i.e., multiplexing) of a large number of flows that arrive at random times and that stay active for random periods.

This paper presents a technique for estimating the network behaviour based on the utilization curve that is the graphical correlation between link utilization and the number of active flows in it. We locate the threshold point at which the addition of new flows does not increase the link utilization. We implicitly argue that the number of active flows may be considered the "real" network state and is consequently, a better indication of utilization or desired operating point.

Our objective is to gather knowledge and plot the curve for network quality and related terms for utilization such as: length of working part, points of overload, etc., as well as formulating basic recommendations for identifying an instance for link upgrading. Traffic measurement and analysis is extended to consider the state of a single path (hop) between two routers on a high-speed backbone. This will help discover possible bottlenecks on network backbones such as GEANT.

In order to prove our hypothesis we took measurements from the border gateway routers of Russian ISP "SamaraTelecom" (ST) and from HEAnet - Ireland's National Research and Education Network. Both networks have several internal and external links.

"SamaraTelecom" is a commercial telecommunications operator in the Middle Volga Area of Russia. Beginning in 1995 ST has installed telephone stations, metropolitan SDH ring (STM16, 2.5 Gbps) inside Samara and Togliatti, as well as Internet services for end users: xDSL and dial-up access. The general bandwidth of ST's Internet connection is 8 Mbps. The utilization of these links varies widely from 5% to 60% with a clearly identifiable busy period. For the purposes of this paper a suspicion by the authors about an overload of the main connection from Samara to Moscow, provided by national Russian operators: GlobalOne, GoldenTelecom, Rostelecom, Transtelecom, etc. is investigated.

HEAnet, an academic and research network, has a number of connections, and measurements from 155 Mbps and 622 Mbps where taken. We use the results of the GEANT and TF-NGN working groups [7, 11], especially the Flow-based Monitoring and Analysis (FloMa) activity. The academic research community should play an important role in providing analytical generalizations and establishing common terminology for processes taking place in networks. HEAnet utilizes Netflow technology to provide wide ranging network management applications. This key set of applications include network traffic accounting, usage-based network monitoring, network planning, as well as Denial of Services monitoring capabilities and data mining capabilities for both HEAnet and its member institutions.

This paper describes a simple flow-based model to identify the quality of the connection and the instance when a backbone upgrade is required. We present our findings under the following headings:

- Section 2 - using queueing theory for flow-based analysis of a backbone

- Section 3 - discuss three states of a network with different performances

- Section 4 - a test for network quality

- Section 5 - results from experiments conducted in the real ISP's

2   The Model

In this paper we model traffic as a stationary process, using the results from the papers of Barakat et al [2] and Ben Fredj et al [3]. They proposed a traffic model for uncongested backbone links that is simple enough to be used in network operations and engineering. The model of Barakat et al relies on Poisson shot-noise. With only 3 parameters (λ, arrival rate of flows, $\mathbb{E}[S_n]$, average size of a flow, and $\mathbb{E}[S_n^2/D_n]$, average value for the ratio of the square of a flow size and its duration), the model provides approximations for the average of the total rate (the throughput) on a backbone link and for its variations at short timescales. The model is designed to be general so that it can be easily used without any constraints from the definition of flows, or on the application or the transport protocol. In summary, this model allows us to completely characterize the data rate on a backbone link based on the following inputs:

- Session arrivals in any period where the traffic intensity is approximately constant are accurately modelled by a homogeneous Poisson process of finite rate λ. The measurements of Barakat et al [2] showed that the arrival rate λ remains pretty constant for at least a 30 minute interval. In general, this assumption can be relaxed to more general processes such as MAPs (Markov Arrival Processes) [1], or non homogeneous Poisson processes, but we will keep working with it for simplicity of the analysis.

- The distribution of flow sizes $\{S_n\}$ and flow durations $\{D_n\}$. In this paper we denote T_n as the arrival time of the n-th flow, S_n as its size (e.g., in bits), and D_n as its duration (e.g., in seconds). Sequences $\{S_n\}$ and $\{D_n\}$ also form independently of each other and are identically distributed sequences.

  The precise distribution clearly depends on the type of document considered. A reasonable fit [6, 14] to the form of the heavy tail is provided by the Pareto distribution:

$$\Pr[\text{size} \leqslant x] = 1 - \frac{k}{x^\beta}, \quad \text{for } x \geqslant k \tag{2}$$

  with $1 < \beta \leqslant 2$, this distribution having a finite mean and infinite variance.

- The flow rate function (shot) is $X_n(\cdot)$. A flow is called active at time t when $T_n \leqslant t \leqslant T_n + D_n$. Define as $X_n(t - T_n)$ the rate of the n-th flow at time t (e.g., in bits/s), with $X_n(t - T_n)$ equal to zero for $t < T_n$ and for $t > T_n + D_n$.

Define $R(t)$ as the total rate of data (e.g., in bits/s) on the modeled link at time t. It is determined by adding the rates of the different flows. We can then write

$$R(t) = \sum_{n \in \mathbb{Z}} X_n(t - T_n) \tag{3}$$

The process from Eq. (3) can describe the number of active flows found at time t in an $M/G/\infty$ queue [10], if $X_n(t - T_n) = 1$ at $t \in [T_n, T_n + D_n]$.

The model presented by Barakat et al [2] can compute the average and the variation of traffic on the backbone. In summary:

- The average total rate of the traffic is given by the two parameters λ and $\mathbb{E}[S_n]$:

$$\mathbb{E}[R(t)] = \lambda\mathbb{E}[S_n] \tag{4}$$

- The variance of the total rate V_R (i.e., burstiness of the traffic) is given by the two parameters λ and $\mathbb{E}[S_n^2/D_n]$:

$$V_R = \lambda\mathbb{E}[S_n^2/D_n] \tag{5}$$

It should be mentioned that Eq. (4) is true only for the ideal case of a backbone link of unrestricted capacity, that can be applied to underloaded links. The main drawback of the ratio (4) is its lack of definite usage limits, due to the fact that variables λ, $\mathbb{E}[S_n]$ describing the system are in no way connected with its current state. The average flow size $\mathbb{E}[S_n]$ does not depend on a specific system, it is a universal value determined by the current distribution of file sizes found in the Internet, see Eq. (2).

The arrival rate of flows λ describes the user's behaviour and doesn't depend on the network state and utilization. The cumulative number of flows that arrive at a link will remain linear even if the network has problems and doesn't satisfy all the incoming demands.

In order to describe the real network state with arbitrary load we should use Little's law:

$$N = \lambda\mathbb{E}[D_n] \tag{6}$$

Here $\mathbb{E}[D_n]$ is the mean duration of flow and N is the mean number of active flows.

Formula (6) is true [10] for any flow duration and thus for an arbitrary flow size distribution and rate limit. This formula describes the network state more precisely than Eq. (4) as the average number of active flows on the bandwidth unit increases with the utilization. In other words, the average duration of flow $\mathbb{E}[D_n]$ enables us to judge the real network state in contrast to its average value $\mathbb{E}[S_n]$.

3   Performance States on Flow Level

Analyzing Eqs. (4) and (6) we compare the ideal and the real states of the network link under consideration. In order to analyze the connection quality to the backbone area or the link to the provider we are going to construct a graphical dependence between the link utilization and the number of active flows in it.

If the investigated link has unrestricted capacity then link load is directly proportional to the number of active flows. On Fig. 2 this dependence is described by a straight line. For real networks, a link capacity is restricted not only by the link capacity but also by the network topology (see Fig. 1).

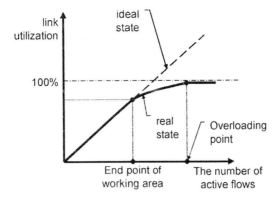

Figure 2: Link utilization vs the number of active flows

We will now examine a network state whereby, the capacity needed to provide a required quality of service is above that of the existing network capacity in accordance with Eq. (4). This Eq. (4) does not describe such a network state as well as Eq. (6). The corresponding point of network overload in the Fig. 2 lies bellow the ideal line, in the area restricted by network capacity.

The curve describing the network behaviour beyond a certain point will be convex. The linear part of the curve corresponding to the ideal network behaviour is defined as the working part. The working part ends at the threshold point which should be found experimentally. The dislocation of this point depends on many factors, such as, transport layer protocol, network topology, the amount of buffering at the link, etc. It may be interesting at some point to investigate further, these effects on the given curve.

On the curve shown in Fig. 2, three parts can be identified, corresponding to the different network states.

The first part of the curve describes the network state close to the ideal, which coincides with the definition of the equation (4). Considering the possibility for errors, the working network is defined by the straight line section as shown in Fig. 2.

The second part of the curve corresponds to the moderately loaded network. This part coincides with the scope of the less restrictive equation of state (6) (when the diversion from the ideal network state becomes obvious). There is an increase in the average duration of a flow compared to the working area, and therefore, a larger number of active flows on the bandwidth unit characteristic of this network state.

The third part of the curve corresponds to the totally disabled network with considerable packet loss evident. We propose some simple preliminary models for an overloaded link, accounting for user impatience and reattempt behaviour. In a real network, if demand exceeds capacity, the number of flows in progress does not increase indefinitely. As per-flow throughput decreases, some flows or sessions will be interrupted, due either to user impatience or to aborts by TCP or higher layer protocols.

In the end of this section we would like to estimate a confidence interval for the working part of our curve (see Fig. 2). Since the total rate is the result of multiplexing of $N(t)$ flows of independent rates, the Central Limit Theorem [10] tells us that the distribution of $R(t)$ tends to Gaussian at high loads, which is typical of backbone links. The variance of the total rate requires two parameters: the arrival rate of flows λ and the expectation of the ratio between the square of the size of a flow duration $\mathbb{E}[S_n^2/D_n]$ (see Eq. (5)). It tells us that the total rate should lie between $\mathbb{E}[R] - A(\epsilon)\sqrt{V_R}$ and $\mathbb{E}[R] + A(\epsilon)\sqrt{V_R}$ in order to provide a required quality of service. When we talked about the required quality of service we implied the accordance of network behavior to Eq. (4). Here $A(\epsilon)$ is the normal quantile function that could be found experimentally.

Suppose we want to choose the bandwidth of the link L in such a way that the breaking of the required quality of service, including congestion occurs in less than $100 * \epsilon\%$ of time. The Gaussian approximation tells us that L has to be set outside the interval:

$$L \notin \left[\mathbb{E}[R] - A(\epsilon)\sqrt{V_R}, \mathbb{E}[R] + A(\epsilon)\sqrt{V_R} \right] \tag{7}$$

The value $\lambda \mathbb{E}[S_n] * \mathbb{E}[S_n/D_n]$ should be estimated as an upper bound on the variance of the traffic in case of weak correlation between $\{S_n\}$ and $\{D_n\}$. Here ϑ_N

$$\vartheta_N = \mathbb{E}[S_n/D_n] = \mathbb{E}[R]/N \tag{8}$$

is average flow' performance that may be expressed via the average total rate of the traffic and the number of active flows. Then, the confidence interval of the bandwidth L on a working part of our curve is

$$L = k(N \pm A(\epsilon)\sqrt{N}), \tag{9}$$

where the values of k and $A(\epsilon)$ will be calculated in Section 5.

4   Test for Network Quality

In order to prove our hypothesis we took measurements on border gateway routers from HEAnet - Ireland's National Research and Education Network, and also from the Russian ISP "SamaraTelecom". Both networks have several internal and external links. SamaraTelecom's basic load lies on one channel to the Internet, whereas HEAnet relies on a number of connections. Measurements from 155 Mbps and 622 Mbps where taken for HEANet and 8 Mbps for SamaraTelecom. The utilization of these links varies widely from 5% to 60% with a clearly identifiable busy period.

A passive monitoring system based on Cisco's NetFlow [5] technology was used to collect link utilization values and active flow numbers in real-time. In Samara we measured on a Cisco 7206 router with NetFlow switched on. In HEAnet a Cisco 12008 was utilized. A detailed description of Cisco NetFlow can be found in the Cisco documentation [5].

It should be mentioned that exporting of flows needs to be switched on on all interfaces from which data is to be collected. Otherwise, the data obtained will not be complete. As

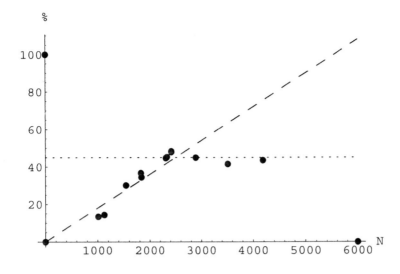

Figure 3: Link U utilization vs the number of active flows N for SamaraTelecom network

mentioned above SamaraTelecom (ST) is a commercial provider and its billing system has been based on NetFlow data. This fact does allow us to get precise results, but, any change to the system tuning as well as the organization of additional measurements are difficult to achieve. The research network gives more freedom but it does not include the usual traffic accounting mechanism and the installation and verification of NetFlow software is a complicated process.

Usually, a network has only one or a few heavily loaded external links, while internal connections remain considerably less loaded. This allows us to construct the dependency of the number of all active flows on the boundary router from the general loading of the external links. This is achieved using the following commands on the Cisco 7206:

- *sh ip cache flow* - gives information about the number of active and inactive flows, about the parameters of the flows in the real time.

- *sh int* [a name for the external interface] - gives information about the current link utilization.

On a GSR Router these commands are:

- *enable*

- *attach* slot-number

- *show ip cache flow*

The ST' data obtained (see Fig. 3) contains all the necessary values for the construction of a curve similar to the one drawn in Fig. 2. The values were recorded at 30-minute

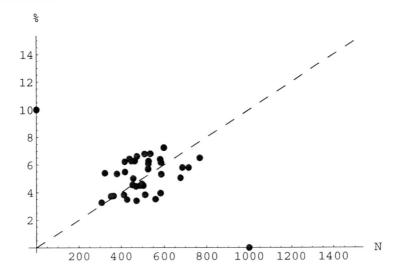

Figure 4: Link utilization vs the number of active flows N for 155 Mbps, HeaNet

intervals, twenty-four hours a day for a week to discover network behaviour with different loading levels. The HEAnet data (see Fig. 4) was obtained using scripts running every 5 minutes for a period of 72 hours. It is quite easy to write a script, which will collect the data from the router to the management server.

5   Experimental Validation

It has already been mentioned that such a test has been conducted on the boundary router of the ST Company. As four external $E1$ links (4 x 2.048 Mbit/s) to different ISPs were used. We have taken a number of points for different network loading states. The results of these measurements are represented on Fig. 3. The X axis shows the number of active flows and the Y axis shows the network loading percentage from its maximal value.

The separate points on Fig. 3 and Fig. 4 correspond to the real network states, and the discrete straight line depicts the ideal network behaviour (corresponding to the Eq. (4)). The slope angle of this straight line is found as the average of the U/N ratio taken from the states when the network loading was below 40%.

The working area of ST network is limited from the top by a straight dotted line. This is close to the description of the network when the loading is heavy. The crossing of the two straight lines defines the length of the working area (45%). When the number of flows is more than 2500, the network experiences overload, which leads to a reduction in flow performance. The overall link loading does not increase with the number of requests, and the connection quality becomes almost twice as bad.

It should be mentioned that the rule of 50% utilization does not work for regional links to the backbone router in Samara. Our test gives a more objective picture and allows us to reveal the critical point of the network. This experiment proves that providers do not always guarantee quality within the working network area which is especially important for applications requiring high network quality, for example, IP telephony and videoconferencing. At the times when the network loading was the heaviest the actual network capacity proved to be nearly twice as low as stated.

After these measurements the national providers like ROSTELECOM, TransTeleCom, ColdenTelecom are obliged to expand their main links to Moscow up to 155 Mbps instead of several E1 connections. At the present time ST are installing a new 10 Mbps link and we are going to conduct repeated measurements.

The angle of inclination of the working line gives the average flow' performance in 1400 bits/sec for the ST network. This value is unacceptable for the majority of internet applications except http and ftp protocols. In Russia ISPs use the special links for IP telephony with low loading, i.e. public internet network divorces from IP based network for special applications. The flow' performance of HEAnet differs by more than one order and equals 15000 bit/sec that allows them to provide not only IP telephony through public network but also video applications.

A significant question concerns the numerical value for the normal quantile function $A(\epsilon)$ from Eq. (9). As mentioned above we calculate coefficient k as mean value of flow' performances from Figures 4 and 3. The separate dots from Figures 4 and 3 correspond the real network states with link bandwidth L_i, number of active flows N_i and flow' performance $k_i = L_i/N_i$. The distribution of flow' performances k_i may be considered as Gaussian in the view of reasons from Section 3. Our data both from ST and HEAnet allows to calculate the numerical value $A(0.01)$ from the expression (9)

$$A(0.01) = 10, \tag{10}$$

It means that only one percent of real network states L_i, N_i has been displayed within the confidence interval of L

$$L = k(N \pm 10\sqrt{N}) \tag{11}$$

We restrict this interval by upper and lower curves on Figs. 5, 6, which consists of dashes of larger length.

The expression (11) allows to formulate the easy rule how to display the network defects. If two consistent measurements running every 5(30) minutes gives the departure of real network states L_i, N_i from the confidence field then we must say about network problems. Unfortunately, coefficient k_i as well as the values L_i, N_i may be found only as result of data processing and we do not yet write the corresponding software.

6   Conclusion

In this paper some methods are described that allow us to evaluate Internet link quality based on flow technology, and give an indication as to when capacity needs to be increased. At the moment we are working on developing utilities, which will make it possible to construct

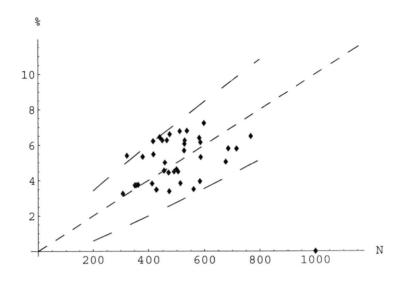

Figure 5: HEAnet confidence interval

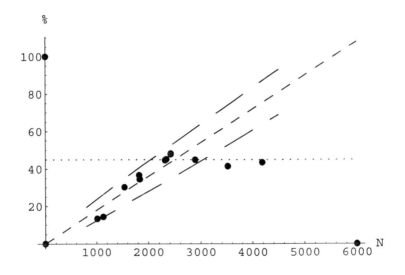

Figure 6: ST confidence interval

the dependence of link loading on the number of active flows automatically, and calculate the length of the working area.

We also plan further research work, evaluating flow parameters and different speeds of data transfer. We propose to derive an analytical dependence of flow speed, *i.e.* to evaluate the time of transfer of a file of a certain size between two remote IP addresses (end-to-end), the packet delivery time and percentage loss. In other words, to theoretically evaluate the connection quality according to ping data and its analogue for TCP packets.

Unfortunately, low-speed Russian Internet links are only available for our research work. Our attempts to collect the necessary data from high-speed international links with preferable speeds of 622 Mbps and 2.4 Gbps failed initially. HEAnet Ltd will provide data sets for 622Mbps, 1Gbps and 2.5Gbps connections in the future. As we know from our own experience one can get the data in the necessary format only through personal communication with the staff of the research network. That's why we need continuing assistance and joint projects for financing future research.

This paper has demonstrated that it is possible to easily determine the working area and the overload point of a network connection, utilizing low cost commodity hardware and simple software. This allows us to identify when a backbone upgrade is required. Further experiments are necessary in order to develop software utilities for this purpose. Thus, providing analytical generalizations and establishing common terminology for processes taking place in networks.

References

[1] Altman, E.; Avratchenkov, K.; Barakat, C. A stochastic model for TCP/IP with stationary random losses, *ACM SIGCOMM* , September 2000

[2] Barakat C.; Thiran P.; Iannaccone G.; Diot C.; Owezarski P. A flow-based model for Internet backbone traffic, *IEEE Transactions on Signal Processing - Special Issue on Signal Processing in Networking*, 2003, vol. 51, no. 8, pp. 2111-2124

[3] Ben Fredj S.; Bonald T.; Proutiere A.; Regnie G.; *Roberts J. Statistical Bandwidth Sharing: A Study of Congestion at Flow Level*, ACM SIGCOMM, August 2001

[4] Brownlee N.; Mills C.; Ruth G. *Traffic Flow Measurement: Architecture (RFC 2722)*, October 1999

[5] Cisco IOS NetFlow site, Cisco Systems, http://www.cisco.com/go/netflow/

[6] Crovella M.;& A.Bestravos A. Self-similarity in world wide web trafic: Evidence and possible cause. In *Proceedings of ACM SIGMETRICS'96*, 1996

[7] Deri L. nProbe: an *Open Source NetFlow Probe for Gigabit Networks*, TERENA 2003

[8] Fraleigh C.; Moon S.; Diot C.; Lyles B.; Tobagi F. *Packet-Level Traffic Measurements from a Tier-1 IP Backbone*, Sprint ATL Technical Report TR01-ATL-110101, November 2001

[9] Fraleigh C.; Tobagi F.; Diot C. *Provisioning IP Backbone Networks to Support Latency Sensitive Traffic*, INFOCOM 2003

[10] Kleinrock L. *Queueing Systems*, Wiley, NY, 1975, Vol. I: Theory

[11] Leinen S.; Przybylski M.; Reijs V.; Trocha S. *Testing of Traffic Measurement Tools*, GEANT Report GEA-01-113, October 2001

[12] Padhye J.; Firoiu V.; Towsley D.; Kurose *J. Modeling TCP Throughput: A Simple Model and its Empirical Validation*, ACM SIGCOMM, September 1998

[13] Papagiannaki K.; Taft N.; Zhang Z.-L.; Christophe Diot C. *Long-Term Forecasting of Internet Backbone Traffic: Observations and Initial Models*, INFOCOM 2003

[14] Paxson V.;& Floyd S. Wide-area trafic: The failure of poisson modeling, *IEEE/ACM Trans. Networking*, 1995, Vol.3, no. 3, pp. 226-255

Andrei Sukhov is an Associate Professor, Head of Laboratory of Network Technologies, Samara State Academy of Transport Engineering, Russia and was awarded a PhD in Moscow, in Physics and Mathematics in 1993. Over the last 10 years he has been involved in acting as an investigator for more then 10 telecommunication projects supported by the Russian government, INTAS, NATO, ESA, US Information Agency, etc. These are the construction of Samara Regional Network for Science and Education - the first Russian provincial network providing a digital connection to Moscow, the regional transport network at level STM16, etc. He is a founder of the biggest Regional ISP and an expert in the area of telecommunication investments in Russia.

Warren Daly works as a Network Security Expert for HEAnet Ltd. He has been an IT professional for 8 years and holds a BSc in Business and Information Technology from Trinity College Dublin and a Diploma in Electronic Systems from Dublin Institute of Technology. He has successfully deployed a PKI infrastructure for the Irish Academic&Research community and has extensive knowledge in Information Security Management Systems (ISO17799). He is also a member of the EU National Research Networks Policy Committee Review panel.

 **Fedor V. Afanasiev** (Year of birth: 1976). Has completed Radio Technician Engineer in 1999 and post-graduate course Elements&Equipment of Automated Systems&Management System in 2002 in Samara State Aerospace University. From 1999 till now he works in Samara Telecom JSC located in Samara, Russia. He is currently Technical Development Manager. Science interests cover network analysis, statistical simulation of wide area networks.

 **Anton V. Petrov**, (Year of birth: 1978). Has completed Multichannel Telecommuncation Systems Engineer in 2000 in Volga State Academy of Telecommunications and Informatics. In 2004 he received a PhD in Networking and Telecommunication Systems. Now he holds lectures on Networking Concepts there as associate professor. From 1999 till 2004 he was working as system/network administrator at Samara Telecom JSC - big ISP located in Samara, Russia. From 2004 till now he works there as Head of Networking Department. Science interests cover UNIX programming, network analysis, statistical simulation of wide area networks.

In: Computer Networking and Networks
Editor: Susan Shannon, pp. 115-140

ISBN: 1-59454-830-7
© 2006 Nova Science Publishers, Inc.

Chapter 5

DYNAMIC MAINTENANCE OF A GIVEN PROXY CACHE HIT RATIO BY LEVERAGING THE RELATIVE DATA OBJECT POPULARITY PROFILE

Allan K. Y. Wong[1a], Richard S. L. Wu[1b] and Tharam S. Dillon[2c]

[1]Department of Computing, Hong Kong Polytechnic University, Hung Hom, Hong Kong,
[2]Faculty of Information Technology, University of Technology,
Sydney Broadway, N.S.W. 2000

Abstract

Without caching support the Internet can easily become terribly congested, slow and lose its appeal. The danger of congestion is aggravated by the fact that the WWW (*World Wide Web*) volume of pages has a monthly growth rate of around 15% but the Internet backbone capacity increases only by 60% yearly. The massive amount of information needed to be transferred across the network in browsing and information retrieval can quickly deplete the amount of sharable bandwidth. This situation worsens if retransmissions are involved as a means to recover the information lost owing to different kinds of network faults, which are inevitable due to the sheer size and heterogeneous nature of the Internet. Caching alleviates network congestion and speeds up WWW information retrieval by providing two advantages. The explicit advantage is the shortening of the service roundtrip time (*RTT*) for WWW information retrieval. The service *RTT* is the time interval between sending a request by the client and getting the corresponding result from the server correctly. The service RTT in this client/server relationship conceptually consists of two legs. The first leg is for the roundtrip between the client and the proxy server, and the second leg is between the proxy server and the remote data source or web server. If the proxy server finds the data object in its cache, then the second leg is automatically obviated. The hit ratio is the probability of finding the required data locally in the proxy's cache. It fluctuates with the clients' shift of preference for certain data items. For a set of data objects this shift changes the relative popularity profile. If ψ is the cache hit ratio, and RTT_{leg1} and RTT_{leg2} as the average roundtrip times respectively for the first and second legs, then the retrieval speedup is

---

[a] E-mail address: csalwong@comp.polyu.edu.hk
[b] E-mail address: csslwu@comp.polyu.edu.hk Fax: (852) 2774 0842
[c] E-mail address: tharam@it.uts.edu.au

$$S_{cache} = \left.(RTT_{leg1} + RTT_{leg2})\middle/(RTT_{leg1} + [1-\psi]*RTT_{leg2})\right., \text{ where } [1-\psi] \text{ is the miss ratio}$$

of the proxy cache. With hit ratio $\psi = 0.5$, $RTT_{leg1} = 10$ and $RTT_{leg2} = 40$ the speedup is

$$S_{cache} = \left.(10+40)\middle/(10+0.5*40)\right. = \left.50\middle/30\right. \text{ or } 1.67.$$ It is advantageous to have a high proxy

cache hit ratio because RTT_{leg2}, which involves the Domain Name Server (DNS), is usually very much longer than RTT_{leg1}. The DNS helps the proxy locate the required data objects in the right remote data source. The implicit advantage from S_{cache} is less data needed to be transferred across the network. This means more backbone bandwidth available for sharing and a reduction in the chance of network congestion. The explicit and implicit advantages from caching motivate different areas of relevant research. The most popular topic is how to design replacement strategies to effectively keep as many hot data objects in the cache as possible. Almost all the known replacement strategies work with a static cache size. They aim at yielding a high cache hit ratio but not necessarily maintaining it. For this reason the cache hit ratio fluctuates with respect to the system dynamics and the current data object popularity profile. Maintaining a given cache hit ratio needs dynamic cache size tuning. In this article the novel MACSC (*Model for Adaptive Cache Size Control*) framework, which leverages the relative data object popularity profile as the sole parameter for this purpose, is proposed. It represents an important departure from previous work which always postulated static cache size. This new approach leads to significant improvements in cache hit ratios or allows one to maintain a prescribed hit ratio. It computes the tuning solution in a short time to avoid possible deleterious effects by the tuning process. Three different versions of the framework, namely, MACSC(PE), MACSC(M³RT), and MACSC(F-PE) are presented.

Keywords: MACSC, dynamic cache size tuning, relative data object popularity profile, maintenance of a given proxy cache hit ratio, IAT traffic, Internet

1   Introduction

The Internet and the worldwide web (WWW) have provided different new opportunities for people to extend their horizon of knowledge, to communicate quickly and effectively, and to set up e-business. In fact, in this era Internet based distributed systems are a key factor in the achievement of economic gains for many companies. Firstly, it is common for company employees to interact with buyers and suppliers via the Internet in field operations. Secondly, business transactions such as buying a birthday present in Hong Kong and having it sent to the receiver in Canada can be conducted quickly and accurately in an electronic manner (i.e. e-business). Thirdly, up-to-date background information can be obtained immediately to back up a time-critical decision such as trading stocks right at the airport minutes before boarding a plane via an electronic small-form-factor (SFF) device (e.g. PDA) [27]. Fourthly, opportunistic data acquisitions can be conducted in a pervasive manner to prevent disasters proactively [16]. For example, a pedestrian has encountered the beginning of a terrorist act and videoed the scene with her mobile phone (a SFF device). Then, the short video is immediately transmitted to the police so that the latter can assess the situation quickly to save the hostage. The examples above involve nomadic users in a pervasive computing environment, in which the client (a SFF device of a nomadic user) communicates through a wireless cell with the wired part of the Internet based PCI (pervasive computing infrastructure). Actually, examples such as those mentioned above, involve many different cutting edge technologies for support, including location-aware means to determine the whereabouts of the SFF clients, time-critical communication and information retrieval techniques, trustworthy wireless and wired operations, and advanced SFF devices with a reasonable battery life. The novel MACSC (*Model for Adaptive Cache Size Control*) proposed in this article addresses the issue of time-critical information retrieval. It improves the serviceability of the server in a client/server interaction or asymmetric rendezvous [22]. All the *pervasive* "wireless-wired" (or simply W&W) computing setups, however complex, are *mobile distributed systems* (MDS). The main obstacle today that prevents confident MDS deployments is the *dependability* problem [5], [21] that includes many attributes such as reliability, availability, maintainability, and serviceability. The serviceability attribute is only loosely defined in [20] as the "*ability of a service to be obtained*". For the MACSC research it is redefined as the "*ability to obtain the required service at the appropriate quality-of-service (QoS) level within a defined period*". For example, obtaining a service within a deadline is a *QoS* requirement.

Figure 1 illustrates the information retrieval actions in a MDS, which has a wireless smart space [15], [31] and a supporting wired PCI. The nomadic users follow the transient mass transit and pass through the wireless smart space of the W&W system. In the light of information retrieval "on the run", they use their SFF devices to make requests. Therefore, the number of retrieval requests is tied to the mass transit traffic pattern [23]. The SFF device interacts with the assigned surrogate node in the PCI. The surrogate, which is temporarily assigned to provide assistance, is a gateway to other PCI nodes. It houses different logical servers or agents. If a surrogate can enlist help from the other PCI nodes, the result is *cyber foraging* [15]. For example, if an agent, which is a proxy server, cannot find a data object requested by a SFF client locally, it may ask for help from other PCI nodes through its surrogate. This is easily achieved if the PCI operates with the peer-to-peer content distribution concept [2], [30], as demonstrated by the Gnutella framework [42]. This framework allows direct sharing of computer resources without a central server. The peer-to-peer architecture scales and self-organizes freely in response to sudden increases in the number of network nodes and partial failures.

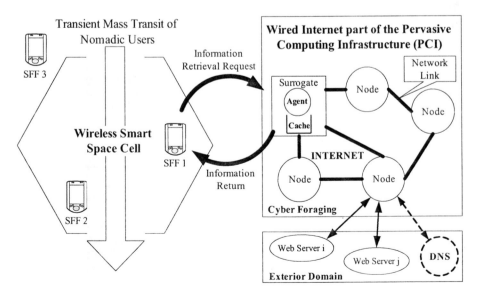

Figure 1. Information retrieval by a SFF client in the W&W architecture

If the data object to be retrieved is not in the PCI domain, then the latter enlists the DNS (*Domain Name Server*) to help locate it in one of the remote data sources (web servers). Therefore, data retrieval in the W&W architecture has two "*legs*" in the information retrieval process. The first leg is the average RTT delay between the SFF client and the agent server, which finds the information locally. The second is the average RTT required to find the information object involving other PCI nodes and possibly the DNS. The importance for the agent server to have a local cache is shown by the speedup calculation by equation (2.1).

$$S_{cache} = \left. (RTT_{leg1} + RTT_{leg2}) \middle/ (RTT_{leg1} + [1 - \psi] * RTT_{leg2}) \right. \qquad (2.1)$$

In this equation, the average RTT for the first leg is RTT_{leg1} and that for the second leg is RTT_{leg2}. If the average hit ratio ψ of the agent's cache is 60% or 0.6 (i.e. miss ratio is $(1 - \psi$ or 40%), $RTT_{leg1=1}$, *and* $RTT_{leg2}=10$, then the speedup for the retrieval operation is 2.2 fold. The agent's 60% cache hit ratio is the chance of obviating RTT_{leg2} to produce this speedup. The calculation of S_{cache} in this case is as follows:

$$S_{cache} = \left. (1 + 10) \middle/ (1 + [1 - 0.6] * 10) \right. = 11 \middle/ 5 = 2.2$$

The S_{cache} speedup benefit provided by caching is essential for sharing WWW information and data efficiently. The empirical evaluation in [9], [14] indicates that the volume of static web pages in total increases by 15% monthly, but the Internet backbone bandwidth improves by only 60% yearly. If this continues, the Internet backbone bandwidth will not be able to sustain the large number of web pages to be transferred across the Internet. The result would be massive network congestion, which would make the Internet lose its appeal. The congestion problem is real because of the following reasons: a) WWW is relatively inexpensive and faster than other means, and b) WWW provides a wide range of popular information such as daily news, entertainment programs, weather report, transportation schedules, financial news, and e-shopping.

The S_{cache} speedup benefit has inspired different areas of research in caching. All the strategies and algorithms from the literature are aimed at producing a high S_{cache} value but not necessarily maintaining it. These approaches use a fixed/static cache size and leverage different parameters. In fact, too many parameters could be counterproductive because heavy parameterization leads to long execution time and deleterious effects. A long execution implies that by the time the caching solution is computed the actual problem may have already passed. The solution ends up correcting a spurious problem and leads to undesirable or deleterious consequences. Maintaining a given hit ratio requires dynamic cache size tuning and the novel MACSC dynamic cache tuner proposed in this article is for this purpose. It has fast execution and thus little chance of deleterious effects because of its light parameterization. It leverages the relative data object popularity profile as the sole parameter.

2 Related Work

The S_{cache} speedup benefits have motivated different areas of active caching research. The aim of these areas include [30]: a) fast information retrieval of a reasonable S_{cache} for a proxy server, b) system robustness for fail-soft operations, c) caching operation transparency, d) system scalability, e) caching adaptivity in response to changing user demands and network environment, and f) stable collaborative caching by avoiding naive cache routing that introduces Internet perturbations. A summary of the different research areas are as follows:

a) *Replacement strategies*: The aim is to enhance a proxy server's S_{cache} by efficaciously pushing out the aged data in a fixed-size cache to make room for the new "hot" ones [3], [32]. There are basically two approaches: LRU (least recently used – recency based) and LFU (least frequently use – frequency based). The recency concept associates with *temporal locality*, which states that the chance η of getting a data object is inversely proportional to the elapsed time t since its last access (i.e. $\eta \propto \frac{1}{t}$) [17]. The frequency of access of a data object indicates its relative popularity. The log-log plot of access frequencies versus the corresponding ranked data objects is the Zipf-like behaviour [9], [41]. For the same set of data objects the Zipf-like behaviour from the proxy point of view is different from that of the web server (data source). The difference is due to the fact that more hot data in the cache means less remote access to these objects in the data source (i.e. they are relatively cold). A replacement strategy leverages the chosen parameters to compute the cost/index that determines which cold data objects should be evicted first from the cache.

b) *Filtration of One-timers*: One-timers are those objects that are rarely accessed [8], and their removal is necessary to make the hot data objects in the proxy cache more concentrated for a higher hit ratio [1].

c) *Collaborative caching*: The concept is to make different caching systems work together in a hierarchy so that the chance of lowering RTT_{leg2} is enhanced [11], [33]. These systems can work in a confined environment or in a distributed manner such as the CARP (*Cache Array Routing Protocol* [29]). The problem with hierarchy caching is that the higher level caches would incur long queuing time and easily become the operational bottlenecks. If it is distributed, naive routing from one cache system to another based on dynamic network statistics can cause serious oscillations in the whole system.

d) *Prefetching*: The aim is to proactively put potential hot data objects into the proxy cache, but so far this approach has yielded only limited benefits [19].

e) *Cache data coherency*: Empirically a bigger cache usually yields a higher hit ratio, but it is a source of data incoherence because the stale data in the proxy cache is not flushed frequently enough [13].

f) *Dynamic data*: This is a significant and yet one of the least explored areas. Dynamic data are basically non-cacheable unless first manipulated (e.g. data generated dynamically by the server) by special techniques such as active cache and server accelerator [30].

g) *Web traffic*: For caching, web traffic has two components: a) clients' data objects access patterns determined by preferences at the time [7], and b) the information retrieval inter-arrival times (IAT) that intrinsically follow the power law [25]. In fact, clients usually shift their preferences towards certain data objects as time goes by. The IAT distribution can be LRD (*long range dependence* such as self-similar) or SRD (*short range dependence* such as Markovian) and switches to cause caching system instability [39].

h) *Adaptive caching*: The strategies in this area fulfil different *adaptivity* requirements [30]. From the literature two main streams can be identified: adaptive replacement and dynamic cache size tuning. The adaptive replacement stream, which is still very rudimentary, addresses the following: 1) adaptive replacement strategies that can timely activate/deactivate some parameters to achieve a more efficient replacement process [18], and 2) selective application of different replacement strategies in a dynamic manner so that specific conditions such as workload and traffic pattern can be dealt with [4]. The known algorithms for the two approaches mentioned above, however, work with a fixed-size cache. Therefore, they do have the capability to maintain a given hit ratio. The dynamic cache size tuning approach not only yields a high hit ratio but also maintains it consistently on the fly. The adjustment process will automatically compensate for any changes that bring down the hit ratio. These changes include swift shift of user preference for certain data objects over time and the ill effects caused by different traffic patterns on the caching system's stability [39]. The novel MACSC strategy proposed in this article is for dynamic cache size tuning over the Internet. It is simple in that it leverages only a single parameter to carry out the tuning process, namely, the *relative object popularity*. The MACSC power and accuracy are independent of the web traffic because it utilizes results statistically computed on the fly by the IEPM (Internet End-to-End Performance Measurement [12]) support, namely, the Convergence Algorithm (CA), which is based on the *Central Limit Theorem* [6], [34], [35], [36] to adaptively adjust the cache size.

3   The MACSC Framework

The MACSC consists of a few fundamental elements as follows:

1) *Popularity distribution (PD)*: It is derived from the Zipf-like behavior of the cached objects from the proxy server's point of view.

2) *Popularity ratio*: It is the ratio of the current PD standard deviation measurement over the last one. The cache size adjustment in the dynamic tuning process is computed from this ratio. It is the sole parameter leveraged by the tuning process and this makes the MACSC computation simple and free of deleterious effects.

3) *PD standard deviation computation*: The computation is dynamic and should be independent of web traffic patterns, which have widely dispersed *inter-arrival times* (IAT). The IAT pattern at any time may be heavy-tailed, multi-fractal, self-similar, or Poisson, and change without warning [28]. This can affect the PE accuracy in different ways. The *Central Limit Theorem*, however, provides the necessary traffic pattern independence solution.

The two basic techniques adopted for computing the PD standard deviation statistically on the fly are: the "*point estimate* (PE)" method, and the *Convergence Algorithm* (CA) [35]. The CA is the basis to the stable *macro* IEPM M^{2}RT tool [34] from which the *micro* M^{3}RT version is developed [36]. A *macro* tool must be installed in the nodes that represent the two ends of a logical channel and user intervention is required in the measurement process, for example, prediction of the mean for a TCP's RTT time series by the M^{2}RT. A *micro* tool differs in that it exists as an independent logical entity (i.e. object or agent), which can be invoked by message passing for a prediction service. The MACSC adopts the *micro* M^{3}RT as a component, which always runs as an object in parallel with the MACSC main body. In this way it does not incur extra execution time for the MACSC operation.

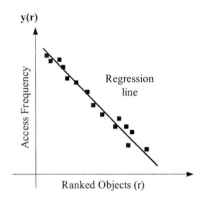

Figure 2a. Zipf-like distribution (log-log)

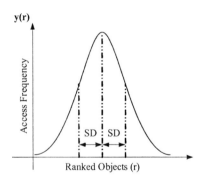

Figure 2b. Bell-shape distribution

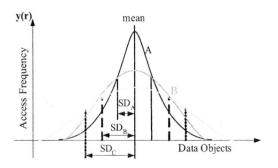

Figure 2c. Popularity Distribution (PD) changes over time and reflects the change in user preference

3.1   Popularity Ratio

The MACSC framework leverages the *relative object popularity* of data objects as the sole parameter to achieve dynamic cache size tuning. This is relatively a recent parameter leveraging concept for caching operations. For example, *relative object popularity* is leveraged as an additional parameter in the "*Popularity-Aware Greedy Dual-Size Web Proxy Caching Algorithms*" [17]. Leveraging this parameter alone to attain a higher cache hit ratio was never tried before the MACSC proposal. Using *relative object popularity* only as an additional parameter easily offsets its benefits because of heavy parameterization that prolongs the execution time of the replacement algorithm. The MACSC framework is derived directly from the Zipf-like behaviour intrinsic to any caching systems [9], [41]. This behaviour is represented by the log-log plot in Figure 2a, which shows that the chance for the jth popular object in the *sorted/ranked list* (X-axis) to be accessed is proportional to $(1/j)^{-\beta}$, for $0 < \beta \leq 1$.

The original plot of the raw scattered data shown in Figure 2a can be approximated by the linear regression: $y(r) = f_{highest} - \gamma(r - 1)$, where γ is a curve fitting parameter, r the ranked position of the object, and $f_{highest}$ the highest access frequency for the "*ranked-first*" object in the set. This regression is then mapped into the bell curve in Figure 2b, which is known as the *popularity distribution* (PD). The PD represents the current profile of the relative popularity of the objects. The central region of this curve includes the more popular objects, and $f_{highest}$ is the therefore considered as "*mean of the PD distribution*" in the MACSC context [37]. The shape of the PD changes over time due to changes in the user preference towards specific data objects. The change is immediately reflected by the current standard deviation. For example, the three curves: A, B and C in Figure 2c mimic the different PD shapes of three different time points. The running MACSC tuner traces all the PD changes continually and uses them to adjust the cache size adaptively. This tuning process maintains the prescribed minimum hit ratio consistently, and the *adjusted cache size* (ACS) is based on one of the following two equations:

$$ACS^j_{SR} = CacheSize_{j-1} * \left(\frac{SD_j}{SD_{j-1}} \right) \tag{3.1}$$

$$ACS^j_{VR} = CacheSize_{j-1} * \left(\frac{SD_j}{SD_{j-1}} \right)^2 \tag{3.2}$$

The popularity ratios for equation (3.1) and equation (3.2) are the *standard deviation ratio* (SR) and the *variance ratio* (VR) respectively. SD_j is the measured standard deviation at j^{th} cycle. The MACSC efficacy depends on the accurate measurement of the PD's current standard deviation. Two approaches are proposed for making the measurements accurate and traffic pattern independent: PE and M³RT.

The basic concept embedded in equation (3.1) is that the current cache size should change with respect to the (SD_j/SD_{j-1}) ratio. The main point is to adjust the cache size by using standard deviations of two consecutive tuning cycles (i.e. $(j-1)^{th}$ and j^{th} cycles). The correct implementation of equation (3.1), however, depends on the accurate estimation of the initial cache size before the MACSC starts to run. Any initialization error will propagate throughout the whole dynamic cache size tuning process. To tackle this error propagation problem the implementation of the concept by equation (3.1) is changed to the form shown by equation (3.3). The ∇ symbol is the number of standard deviations that represent the prescribed hit ratio to be maintained (e.g. $\nabla = 1$ for 68.3% and $\nabla = 2$ for 95%). It is actually part of the numerator as well of the denominator (but cancelled out) in the (SD_j/SD_{j-1}) expression. The $OS_{average}$ value in equation (3.3) is the mean object size that MACSC deals with. Before MACSC runs (i.e. at time $t=0$ and $j=1$) the cache size is initialized by $ACS_{SR_{t=0}}^{j=1} = 2*\nabla*SD_{t=0}^{j=1}*OS_{average}$. The $SD_{t=0}^{j=1}$ value is the standard deviation computed from the past performance data. Equation (3.3) clearly indicates that for $j > 1$ the cache size tuning process does not depend on $SD_{t=0}^{j=1}$ but the current SD_j value of the jth cycle.

To implement the concept of equation (3.2) the equation should be changed to the form in equation (3.4). The MACSC cache size initialization is considered as the 0th cycle or $j=0$. The initial cache $ACS_{VR_{t=0}}^{j=0} = 2*\nabla*SD_{t=0}^{j=0}*OS_{average}$ becomes the "$seed\ value$" of $CacheSizeSeed_{j-1}$ for $j \geq 1$. In the subsequent dynamic cache tuning cycles this seed value is replaced by $2*\nabla*SD_j*OS_{average}$ and the factor "2" means one ∇ on both sides of the mean. This scheme stops the propagation of the initialization error due to inaccurate $ACS_{VR_{t=0}}^{j=0}$ estimation. The VR based tuning process is, hence, tied to the latest computed SD_j value for $j \geq 1$. The focus of the MACSC is mainly on how equation (3.1) or its alternative (3.3) can effectively support small caching systems for $j=1,2,...n$. These inexpensive systems have limited memory but are substantial in number in the field.

$$ACS_{SR}^j = 2*\nabla*SD_j*OS_{average} \qquad (3.3)$$

$$ACS_{VR}^j = 2*\nabla*(SD_j)^2*OS_{average} \qquad (3.4)$$

3.1.1   The MACSC(PE) Approach

The original MACSC framework adopts the *point-estimate* (PE) approach to estimate the SD_j value, and this is called the MACSC(PE) version. This approach is represented by the statistical equation (3.5) which is based on the *Central Limit Theorem*. The parameters: $\bar{x}$ and s_x are the measured mean and standard deviation of the n data samples. Statistically, s_x and $\bar{x}$ are the estimators to predict the N value that satisfies the given E and k tolerances [6]. Although the VR-based tuner (equation (3.2)) is more effective in maintaining the given hit ratio, it consumes too much memory, making it impractical for small caching systems with limited memory resources [38].

$$E\lambda = k\delta_{\bar{x}} = k\left(\delta_x \middle/ \sqrt{N}\right) \qquad (3.5)$$

$$N = \left({k\delta_x} \Big/ {E\lambda} \right)^2 \qquad\qquad (3.6)$$

$$N = \left({ks_x} \Big/ {E\bar{x}} \right)^2 \qquad\qquad (3.7)$$

The PE approach is based on equation (3.5), which is sometimes called the $\sqrt{N} - equation$. The MACSC version that works with this approach is called the MACSC(PE) approach. The $\sqrt{N} - equation$ involves the following parameters:

a) *Fractional error tolerance (E)*: It is the percentage error between λ (ideal/population mean value) and m (the mean estimated from a series of *sample means* $\bar{x}$ of sample size $n \geq 10$ on the fly, based on the *Central Limit Theorem*).

b) *SD tolerance (k)*: It is the number of standard deviations (SD) that m is away from the *true mean* λ but is still tolerated (same tolerance connotation as E).

c) *Predicted standard deviation ($\delta_{\bar{x}}$)*: It is estimated from the same series of sample means $\bar{x}$ of sample size $n \geq 10$. By the *Central Limit Theorem* $\delta_{\bar{x}} = {\delta_x} \Big/ {\sqrt{n}}$ holds, where δ_x is the population's (or true) SD.

d) *Minimum N value*: From $E\lambda = k\delta_{\bar{x}} = k\left({\delta_x} \Big/ {\sqrt{N}} \right)$ relationship the *minimum sample size N* is needed to estimate λ and δ_x for the given k and E values. In practice λ and δ_x should be substituted by $\bar{x}$ and s_x, and this substitution converts equation (3.6) to equation (3.7). s_x is the standard deviation for the sample with mean $\bar{x}$. The estimation for the value of N is repetitive. In the first trial a data sample of size n is used, and in every repetition a new sample of size n is added. That is, the number of samples used in the current repetition is $n = n + R*n$, where R is the number of repetitions for $R = 0,1,2,\ldots$. The repetition stops when the $n \geq N$ criterion is satisfied. In every repetition the PE computes $\bar{x}$ statistically from the n samples first and then computes $s_x = \sqrt{\dfrac{\sum_{i=1}^{N}(x_i - \bar{x})^2}{N-1}}$, where x_i marks the ith data item in the sample.

The following example demonstrates how the $\sqrt{N} - equation$ can satisfy the $n \geq N$ criterion:

a) It is assumed that the initial 60 data samples (i.e. sample size is $n = 60$) have yielded 15 and 9 for $\bar{x}$ and s_x respectively.

b) The given SD tolerance is 2 (i.e. $k = 2$ or 95.4%), and the fractional tolerance E is therefore equal to 4.6% ($E=0.046$); both E and k connote the same error.

c) The N value then should be $N = (\dfrac{2*9}{0.046*15})^2 \approx 680$.

The value of $N \approx 680$ indicates that the initial sample size $n = 60$ is incorrect. To rectify the problem one of the following two methods can be used:

a) The first is to collect ($680 - 60$) or 620 more data samples and re-calculate $\bar{x}$ and s_x. There is no guarantee, however, the new estimation by this approach would converge to $n \geq N$ and the same process therefore has to be repeated.

b) The second, which is adopted by the MACSC, is to collect another 60 data samples and re-calculate $\bar{x}$ and s_x from the total of 120 data samples (i.e. $n = 120$ for the 2nd trial). The PE is actually the $n = n + R * n$ repetitive process, which stops when the $n \geq N$ criterion is satisfied.

The MACSC adopts the second method because practical experience confirms that it converges much faster. Usually $\bar{x}$ and s_x stabilize in the second or third trial. The above example, however, has not illustrated the IAT delay between data items to be sampled for the $n=n+R*n$ process. For example, sampling the 680 data items may take days, hours or merely seconds. This kind of sampling time unpredictability reduces the cache size tuning precision of the MASCSC and makes the hit ratio oscillate in the steady state [38]. The key measure to resolve the unpredictable PE execution time problem is to make the $n=n+R*n$ process non-repetitive or $n=F$, where F is the fixed number of data items to be sampled. It implicitly imposes the following "*PE replacement criteria*": a) the replacement should have comparable computation time to PE, b) the accuracy of the replacement should be traffic independent, c) the replacement should have comparable sensitivity to the PD changes to the PE, and d) the replacement should work with only F number of data items to make the sampling time predictable. These criteria lead to the *Convergence Algorithm* (CA) adoption as a support for better MACSC performance.

3.1.2   Convergence Algorithm (CA)

The CA technique in its basic form is represented by the equations (3.8) and (3.9) [34], where the parameters are defined as follows: a) M_i is the distribution mean estimated for the time window in which the chosen F (*flush limit*) number of data items is to be collected, b) M_{i-1} is the feedback of the last estimated mean to the current i^{th} estimation cycle, c) m_j^i is the jth sample in the ith M_i estimation cycle for $j=1,2...(F-1)$, and c) M_0 is the first data sample when the M³RT first started. The simulated results indicate that the F (*flush limit*) range of $9 \leq F \leq 16$ yields faster convergence to M_i and $F=14$ is the fastest. Subsequently the CA concept was refined and implemented into the M²RT (Mean Message Response Time) tool. The M²RT version is a *macro* IEPM (*Internet End-to-End Performance Measurement* [12]) tool. The M³RT (*Micro Mean Message Response Time*) [36] is its micro version, which runs as an object in parallel with the MACSC main body and other components. The CA form in equation (3.10) is used instead because proportional (P) control is needed to prevent too much oscillation in the M_i convergence process. The f parameter in equation (3.10) indicates the number of samples (i.e. m_j^i) used in the M_i prediction cycle.

$$M_0 = m_{j=0}^{i=1} \tag{3.8}$$

$$M_i = \frac{M_{i-1} + \sum_{j=1}^{j=F-1} m_j^i}{F} \; ; i > 1 \tag{3.9}$$

$$M_i = \frac{P * M_{i-1} + \sum_{j=1}^{j=f} m_j^i}{P + f} \; ; i > 1 \tag{3.10}$$

Using M^3RT for MACSC support provides the following potential advantages:

1. It runs in parallel with the MACSC main body, which requires a much longer time to execute. As a result the M^3RT does not prolong the MACSC execution time.
2. The M^3RT always settles to the mean of the distribution in the time window of interest. For example, Figure 3 shows how M^3RT has correctly estimated the mean for a RTT trace of a TCP (*Transmission Control Protocol*) channel. This trace [34] can be approximated by the gamma function in Figure 4 with parameters: $\alpha = 2$ and $\beta = 5$. The symbols in Figure 3 are as follows: *RawIAT* for IAT samples, *CA_EstMean* for "*the mean estimated by* M^3RT", *Raw Mean* for the mathematical average of all the IAT samples in the trace, and *Typical Mean* is the *mode* (i.e. typical value) in the trace.

Figure 3 shows that the convergence to the distribution mean "M_i" by M^3RT is much smoother than the raw IAT waveform. This convergence smoothness of M_i, however, could be a liability for the MACSC operation because it also requires high sensitivity to the PD changes for accurate estimation of its current standard deviation. The MACSC framework adopts the M^3RT essence in two different ways for support:

a) MACSC(M^3RT): In this case the PE method is completely replaced by a novel M^3RT based approach and yields equation (3.15) . It is essential to synchronize the SD_j computation with the M_i prediction cycle.
b) MACSC(F-PE): "*F-PE*" stands for *fine-tuned point estimate*, and it uses the feedback concept in MACSC(M^3RT) as shown by equations (3.13) and (3.14). The power of the feedback depends on the proper use of the α and β parameters (to be explained later).

Repeated timing analyses of the M^3RT [34] by using the *Intel's VTune Performance Analyzer* [40] confirms that intrinsically it requires an average of 250 clock cycles (T cycles) to execute. The physical time for the 250 clock cycles depends on the actual platform that the M^3RT entity is running on. For example, on a platform of 100 Mega hertz (MH) speed (SP) the physical time (PT) is $PT = T/SP$ or $PT = 250/(100*10^6) \approx 2.5$ micro seconds. The intrinsic execution time is the raw computation time that does not include the actual IAT delays. In real-time applications, however, the actual M^3RT time depends on the average IAT for the F (*flush limit*) or f number of samples to be collected. Yet, F and f are known values and this reduces the chance for M^3RT to cause deleterious effects.

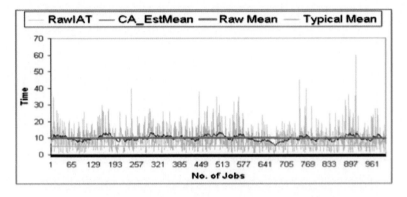

Figure 3. Example of actual M^3RT application for a TCP channel

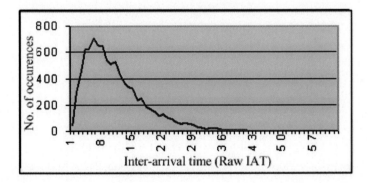

Figure 4. Approximated gamma distribution for the trace in Figure 3 ($\alpha = 2$, $\beta = 5$)

3.1.3   The MACSC(M^3RT) Approach

For gaining more sensitivity in the process of calculating the PD standard deviations on the fly, the M^3RT application is enhanced. The enhancement based on equation (3.10), is summarized by the equations from (3.10) to (3.16), which use f data items (i.e. sample size of $n = f$). Equation (3.10) can be rearranged easily into equation (3.11) and then (3.12). By assuming $\alpha = \dfrac{p}{p+f}$ and $(1-\alpha) = \dfrac{f}{p+f}$, equation (3.12) can be rearranged into equation (3.13) for $\dfrac{p}{p+f} + \dfrac{f}{p+f} = 1$. The physical meaning of equation (3.13) is that the M_i

convergence speed and accuracy depends on p for $p > 0$; a large p makes M_i depend more on the past performance (i.e. M_{i-1}).

$$M_i = \frac{p}{p+f} * M_{i-1} + \frac{1}{p+f} \left(\sum_{j=1}^{j=f} m_i^j \right) \tag{3.11}$$

$$M_i = \frac{p}{p+f} * M_{i-1} + \frac{1}{p+f} (f) \left(\frac{1}{f} \right) \left(\sum_{j=1}^{j=f} m_i^j \right) \tag{3.12}$$

$$\because \frac{p}{p+f} + \frac{f}{p+f} = 1$$

$$M_i = \alpha * M_{i-1} + (1 - \alpha) * \left(\frac{\sum_{j=1}^{j=f} m_i^j}{f} \right) \tag{3.13}$$

Based on the philosophy of equation (3.13), the equation (3.14) which calculates the instantaneous PD standard deviation SD_j can be synchronized with the ith M_i prediction cycle. That is, $SD_j = \sigma_i$ is estimated with a sample size of $n = (f - 1)$. The trick is to find the right β value for fast, smooth and accurate σ_i convergence. The aim is to set $\alpha = \beta = \frac{\rho}{(\rho + f)}$ so that M_i and σ_i are predicted with the same basis. The user, however, can choose to set a different value for β for whatever valid reasons. With equation (3.14) the dynamic cache size tuning mechanism is now represented by equation (3.15), where $CacheSize_i$ is the ACS in the ith cycle. To stop propagation of the error in the initialized cache size for MACSC operation, equation (3.15) should be rewritten into equation (3.16) for implementation. Equation (3.16) is different in that it uses the latest PD standard deviation σ_i to compute the new adjusted cache size.

$$\sigma_i = \beta * \sigma_{i-1} + (1 - \beta) * \sqrt{\frac{\sum_{j=1}^{j=f} \left(m_i^j - M_i \right)^2}{f - 1}} \tag{3.14}$$

$$CacheSize_i = CacheSize_{i-1} * \left(\frac{\sigma_i}{\sigma_{i-1}} \right) \tag{3.15}$$

$$CacheSize_i = 2 * \nabla * \sigma_i * OS_{average} \tag{3.16}$$

3.1.4   The MACSC(F-PE) Approach

It is based on the successful MACSC(M^3RT) empirical experience of using feedback. The feedback in this case makes use of α and β in equations (3.13) and (3.14) respectively. It involves the following steps: 1) compute $\overline{x}$ from the $n \geq N$ samples by using the PE approach, namely, the $\sqrt{N} - equation$, and 2) the standard deviation s_x. These values are then fined-tuned by equations (3.17) and (3.18), where z is the operation cycle. The adjusted cache size or ACS is conceptually determined by equation (3.19) and its implementation is represented by equation (3.20) to avoid propagation of any cache size initialization error.

$$\overline{x}_z = \alpha \overline{x}_{z-1} + (1 - \alpha)\overline{x}_z \tag{3.17}$$

$$s_x^z = \beta s_x^{z-1} + (1 - \beta)s_x^z \tag{3.18}$$

$$CacheSize_z = CacheSize_{z-1} * \left(\frac{s_x^z}{s_x^{z-1}} \right) \tag{3.19}$$

$$CacheSize_z = 2 * \nabla * s_x^z * OS_{average} \tag{3.20}$$

4   Experimental Results

Experiments with different object retrieval datasets with embedded IAT traffic were carried out for the three different MACSC prototypes in Java. The goal was to verify the following:

a)   The MACSC(PE), MACSC(M^3RT) and MACSC(F-PE) versions indeed maintain the given hit ratio consistently. The MACSC(PE) should yield a worse performance than MACSC(M^3RT), which is also known as the *Enhanced* MACSC (or E-MACSC), due to its lack of the necessary capability to track the PD changes accurately.
b)   The accuracy of these dynamic cache size tuners is independent of IAT traffic patterns.

The experiments made use of known distributions to set the references for comparison with those results obtained from using pre-collected Internet traffic traces. The platform for the experiments is the Java-based Aglets mobile agent platform [26]. It is chosen for its stability, rich user experience, and scalability. The Aglets platform is designed for Internet applications, and this should make the experimental results scalable for the open Internet environment. The replacement algorithm used in all the simulations is the traditional basic LRU (*Least Recently Used*) approach supported by the "*twin cache system* (TCS)" [1]. The TCS was used successfully in the verification of the original MACSC(PE) framework. It actively filters out the "*one-timers*", which is caching "*noise*", to make the hot data in the proxy cache concentrated for more meaningful results [38]. One-timers are infrequently accessed data objects.

The set up for the experiments is shown in Figure 5, in which the three different MACSC tuners run with the same request traffic in parallel to the *"fixed cache size* (FCS)" system and maintain their own TCS for comparison. The FCS was present for control and comparison purposes. The driver and the tuners are *aglets* (*agile applets*) that interact in a client/server relationship. The driver generates the IAT as *input traffic* to the tuners. The IAT traffic patterns are either chosen known waveforms or pre-collected traces that embed different traffic patterns over time (e.g. heavy-tailed, self-similar, Poisson, and multi-fractal). Every IAT is paired with the requested data object. That is, every request has two attributes: the IAT and the corresponding unique data object to be retrieved. These attributes are generated in three steps: a) in the first step the IAT waveform drives the interrupt timer, b) in the second step the timer interrupts the driver, and c) in the third step the driver wakes up and generates a random number P(x) and uses it to interpolate the unique *object identifier* (OI) from the X-axis of the *Cv* curve. The *Cv* curve represents the chosen popularity distribution for the simulation. It correlates the access probabilities/frequencies and the corresponding data objects. The OI is an integer (1,2,3…) that uniquely identifies the specific data object. The OI is sent as the request to the proxy server for data retrieval. Conceptually, if the proxy cannot find the requested data in its local cache, it will search for it from one of the remote data sources with help from the Internet DNS (*Domain Name Server*). In Figure 5 the control system for comparison purposes is the *"LRU + a fixed size cache"* system or simply FCS.

There is a background mechanism in the MACSC framework that continually maps the OI with the physical data objects. This is necessary because the position of the OI in the current PD curve depends on its relative popularity to the rest of OI values that represent different data objects in the set. For example, an OI, which was ranked 10th before may have become 1000th in the current cycle. Although the creation of the PD is based on OI, the mapping enables correct data object retrievals.

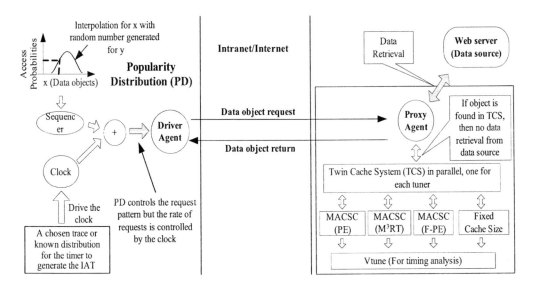

Figure 5. The set up for the experiments for verification and comparison

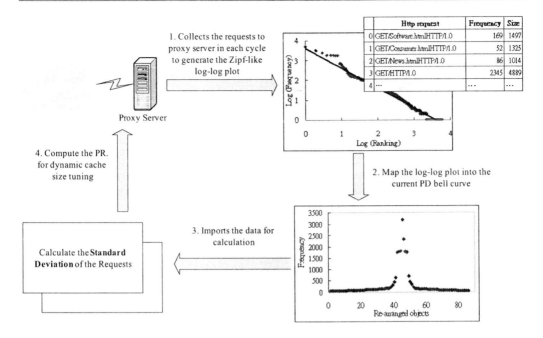

Figure 6. Mapping of the http objects into the bell-shape PD curve

Figure 6 summarises the four basic operation steps in each dynamic buffer size tuning cycle in the MACSC framework: 1) to collect the OI (paired with an IAT) to create the log-log plot or Zipf-like behaviour, 2) map the log-log plot into the bell-shaped PD, 3) import the PD data to calculate the popularity ratio (PR), and 4) adjust the cache size for the current PR ratio.

For the experimental results presented in this article the average data object size is 5k bytes. The number of retrievals generated by the driver is 1 million. The cache size is first initialised to meet the prescribed hit ratio. For example, a given hit ratio of 68.3% (confidence level of one standard deviation or one ∇) means that the cache size should be initialized to $5k * 0.683 * 40,000$ bytes (or 136.6MB). The basic LRU replacement algorithm deletes aged objects in the cache to accommodate the hot newcomers. The simulation results in this article are SR (*standard deviation ratio*) based (equation (3.1)). The primary goal of the MACSC tuner is to provide more effective dynamic cache size tuning for the substantial number of small caching systems in the field. These inexpensive systems usually cost less than US$1000.

In the experiments, different http traces are used to verify the performance of the different MACSC dynamic cache size tuning models. The 1st dataset is generated by a simulator that interleaves different bell distributions. The 2nd and the 3rd are real http traces from ACM SIGCOMM. The experiments with these two http datasets can demonstrate if the tuners indeed work for the real environments. The 2nd http dataset, namely EPA-HTTP, is the trace of a day's worth of http requests to the EPA WWW server in the Research Triangle Park of USA. It has logged the 24-hours http traffic from 23:53:25 EDT on Tuesday of August 29 1995 through 23:53:07 EDT in August 30 1995. There are 47,748 total requests logged, 46,014 GET requests, 1,622 POST requests, 107 HEAD requests, and 6 invalid requests. The logging process operated with the one-second precision. The 3rd http trace, namely the

Calgary-HTTP, contains roughly one year's worth of http requests to the WWW server located in the Department of Computer Science in University of Calgary of Alberta Canada. There are 722,982 requests time-stamped with one-second resolution. Table 1 summarizes the characteristics of the three traffic distributions that were used to obtain the results presented in this article.

Table 1. Summary of the three traces that yielded the experimental results presented

Table 1a. The simulated distribution

Simulated dataset(bell-shape distribution)	
No. of transactions	400000
No. of objects	10000
Combination of S.D.	1k->3k->2k->5k

Table 1b. The Calgary-HTTP trace

Calgary-HTTP (real http dataset)	
No. of transactions	722982
No. of objects	11799
Duration	353 days

Table 1c. The EPA-HTTP trace

EPA-HTTP (real http dataset)	
No. of transactions	42438
No. of objects	5584
Duration	24 hours

For the experimental results presented in this article the given hit ratio to be maintained is 68.3%. Figure 7 compares the results by FCS and MACSC(PE) with the 1st dataset. The MACSC(PE) consistently produces a higher hit ratio than the FCS. For the EPA-HTTP and Calgary-HTTP traces, the tuner consistently maintains at least the given hit ratio for the TCS.

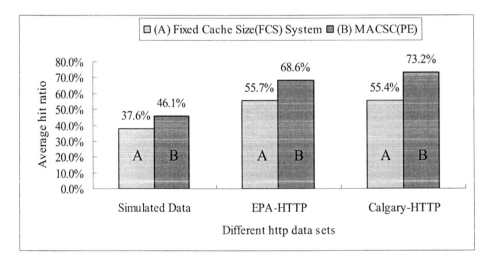

Figure 7. Average hit ratios by MACSC(PE) and Fixed Cache Size(FCS) System

Figure 8 compares the FCS and MACSC(M^{3}RT) performance for the three traces. The MACSC(M^{3}RT) tuner which is also known as the E-MACSC has no problem of maintaining the given hit ratio consistently for the EPA-HTTP and Calgary-HTTP datasets. Figure 9 compares the FCS and MACSC(F-PE) performance with the datasets. The MACSC(F-PE) dynamic buffer size tuner consistently yields and maintains the given hit ratio for the EPA-HTTP and Calgary-HTTP traces. All three dynamic buffer size tuners, however, fail to maintain the given hit ratio for the simulated dataset, which is formed by interleaving different bell distributions characterized by their standard deviations. Our analysis shows that the failure is caused by the rapid changes in the IAT traffic pattern over time due to the interleaving operations. This indicates that some kind of compensation is needed to counteract the possible traffic ill effects, which could impede the dynamic cache size tuning efficiency. Figure 10 compares the performance by the four caching systems. It is obvious that the MACSC(F-PE) always yields the best result for hit-ratio maintenance followed by the MACSC(M^{3}RT).

Figure 11, 14 and 16 show the changes in hit ratios in the control processes by the four caching systems with respect to the three datasets: simulated, EPA-HTTP and Calgary-HTTP. The FCS hit ratio suddenly drops steeply when the standard deviation or SD increases. It is the result of lacking cache space to store enough hot data objects that are equivalent to the given hit ratio. The three MACSC dynamic cache size tuner versions, however, are still able to upkeep higher hit ratios.

Figure 13, 15 and 18 show the corresponding changes in memory usage for the cache tuning processes for the simulated, EPA-HTTP and Calgary-HTTP datasets. These plots also show that the dynamic cache size adjustment process by the MACSC(F-PE) fluctuates much less than the MACSC(PE). Therefore, with the same amount of memory usage the MACSC(F-PE) can yield and maintain a much higher hit ratio. The MACSC(F-PE) consistently uses the same memory as the MACSC(PE) but it still can produce and maintain a much higher hit ratio. For example, in Figure 10 with the Calgary-HTTP trace the MACSC(F-PE) yields a hit ratio of 90.2%, which is 17% higher than the MACSC(PE). Empirically the MACSC(F-PE) uses around 20% less memory than the MACSC(M^{3}RT) in a consistent manner as observed in all the experiments conducted. It can be concluded that the MACSC(F-PE) performs the best.

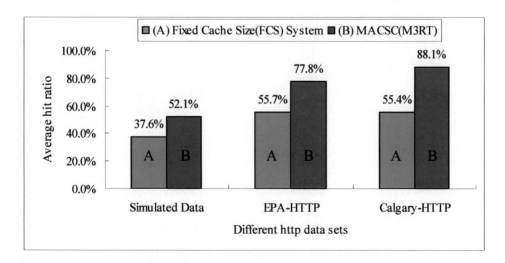

Figure 8. Average hit ratios by MACSC(M^{3}RT) and FCS

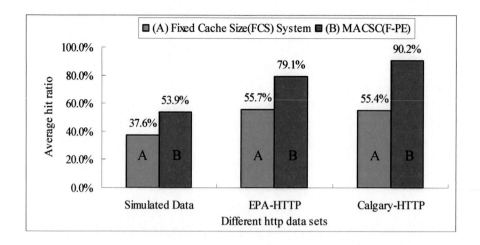

Figure 9. Average hit ratios by MACSC(F-PE) and FCS

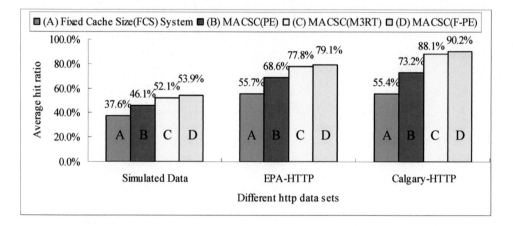

Figure 10. Performance comparison of four systems with the three datasets

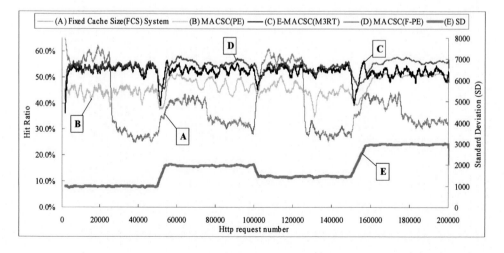

Figure 11. Changes of hit ratios by different caching systems with the simulated data

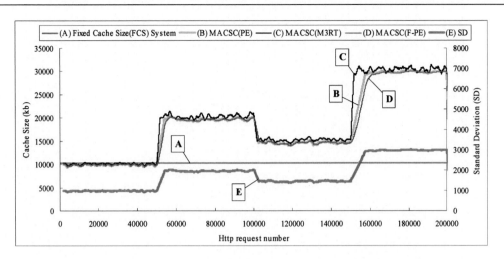

Figure 12. Changes of memory usage by different caching systems with the simulated data

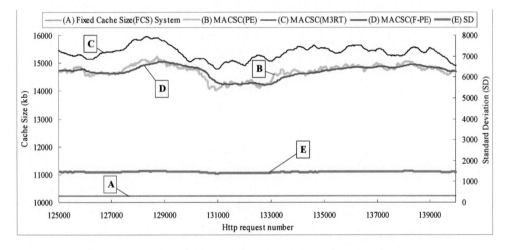

Figure 13. Magnified view of changes in memory usage in Figure 12

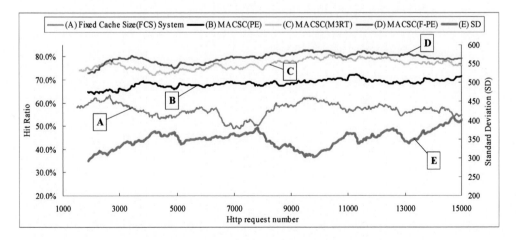

Figure 14. Changes of hit ratios by different caching systems with the EPA-HTTP dataset

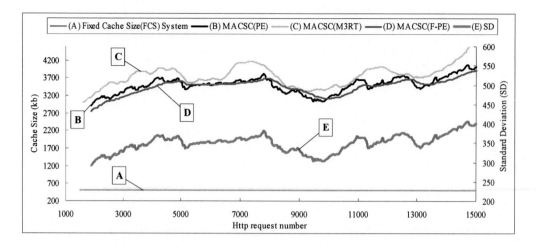

Figure 15 Changes in memory usage by different caching systems with EPA-HTTP dataset

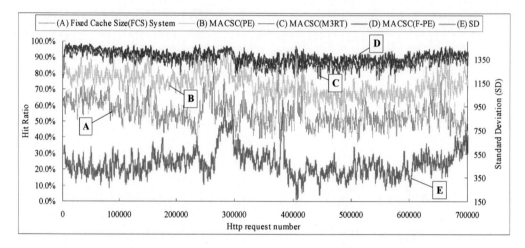

Figure 16. Changes in hit ratios by different caching systems with Calgary-HTTP dataset

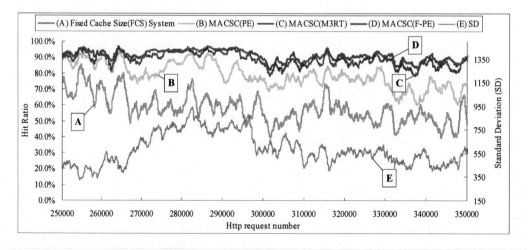

Figure 17. Magnified view of changes in hit ratios in Figure 16

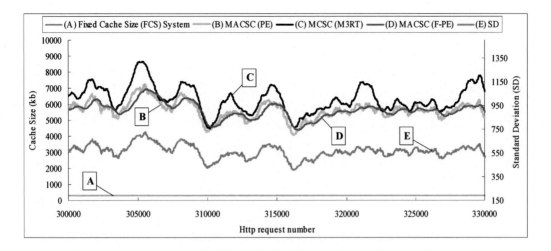

Figure 18. Magnified view of changes in memory usage for Figure 16

5 Conclusion

In this article the novel MACSC (*Model for Adaptive Cache Size Tuning*) framework is proposed. It maintains the given proxy cache hit ratio by leveraging the relative data object popularity as the sole parameter. By doing so it shortens the roundtrip time for information retrieval over the Internet. The present MACSC research focuses on how to make the framework applicable to small caching systems, which are inexpensive and therefore substantial in number in the field. These systems have limited recyclable memory and cost less than US$1,000. The following equation represents the present research focus:

$$ACS_{SR}^{j} = CacheSize_{j-1} * \left(\frac{SD_j}{SD_{j-1}} \right)$$

It uses the two most current successive standard deviations (SD) that represent changes in the popularity distribution to compute the adjusted cache size (ACS). ACS_{SR}^{j} is the ACS computed at the jth dynamic cache size tuning cycle with the standard deviation ratio (SR). The SR or (SD_j / SD_{j-1}) is one of the two forms of the popularity ratio (PR), as shown by equations (3.1) and (3.1.2). The VR (variance ratio) represented by $(SD_j / SD_{j-1})^2$ is the other form. The key issue in realizing MACSC is to compute SD_j quickly, accurately and independent of the IAT traffic patterns. For this reason a lot of research effort is focused on finding suitable tools that are based on the *Central Limit Theorem*. At first the point-estimate or PE approach that works with the $\sqrt{N} - equation$ was proposed. This led to the development of the original MACSC(PE) framework. The problem with the PE approach is the difficulty experienced in controlling real-time computation delay because enough samples must be collected for proper SD_j computation. This leads to the M³RT adoption as a more efficient alternative. The M³RT is a *micro* version of the *Convergence Algorithm* that is based on the *Central Limit Theorem*. When the PE computation is replaced by the M^3RT mechanism, it is the brand new MACSC(M^3RT) model, which is also known as the *Enhanced MACSC* or simply E-MACSC. The E-MACSC always yields higher hit ratios than the MACSC(PE). The empirical E-MACSC experience also indicates that it is possible to further improve the proxy cache hit ratio by using proper feedback. This led to the proposal of the MACSC(F-PE) version. "*F-PE*" stands for *fine-tuned point estimate*, which involves two feedback parameters, namely, α and β in equations (3.17) and (3.18) respectively. The vigorous experiments verify that the three different Java MACSC implementations, namely, MACSC(PE), MACSC(M^3RT) and MACSC(F-PE) have no problem in maintaining the given hit ratio. The MACSC(F-PE) consistently yields a higher hit ratio than the MACSC(M^3RT), which in turn performs better than the MACSC(PE). In the experiments it was observed that the IAT traffic can produce ill effects that drops the cache hit ratio. Therefore these ill effects should be neutralized for even better performance by the MACSC framework. As a result the logical next step in the research is to find a way whereby the IAT traffic pattern (e.g. short-range dependence (SRD) such as Markovain and long-range dependence (LRD) such as self-similar and heavy-tailed) can be detected on the fly. If this can be achieved, then the MACSC mechanism can be compensated accordingly in a dynamic fashion to neutralize possible traffic ill effects so that high cache hit ratio can be consistently maintained.

Acknowledgement

The authors thank the Hong Kong Polytechnic University and the Department of Computing for the H-ZJ91 and A-PG51 research grants.

References

[1] Aggarwal, C., Wolf, J. L., & Yu, P. S. (1999). Caching on the Word Wide Web, *IEEE Transaction on Knowledge and Data Engineering*, **11**(1), 94 – 107.

[2] Androutsellis-Theotokis & Spinnellis, D. (2004). A Survey of Peer-to-Peer Content Distribution Technologies, *ACM Computing Surveys*, **36**(4), 335 – 371.

[3] Arlitt, M., Cherkasova, L., Dilley, J., Friedrich, R., & Jin, T. (1999). Evaluating Content Management Techniques for Web Proxy Caches, *Proc. of the 2nd Workshop on Internet Service Performance*.

[4] Aguilar, J. & Leiss, E. L. (2001). A Web Proxy Cache Coherency and Replacement Approach, *Proc. of the 1st Asia-Pacific Conference on Web Intelligence: Research and Development*, **78** – 84.

[5] Avizienis, A., Laprie, J.-C., Randell, B. & Landwehr, C. (2004). Basic Concepts and Taxonomy of Dependable and Secure Computing, *IEEE Transactions on Dependable and Secure Computing*, **1**(1), 11-33.

[6] Chisman, J.A. (1992). *Introduction to Simulation and Modeling Using GPSS/PC*. New Jersey, Prentice Hall

[7] Barford, A., Bestavros, A., Bradley, A. & Crovella, M.E. (1999). Changes in the Web Client Access Patterns: Characteristics and Caching Implications, *World Wide Web (Special Issue on Characterization and Performance Evaluation)*.

[8] Belloum, A. & Hertzberger, L.O. (1998). Dealing with One-Timer-Documents in Web caching, *Proc. of the 24th Conference on EUROMICRO*, 2.

[9] Bjarat, K. & Broder A. (1998). Estimating the Relative Size and Overlap of Public Web Search Engines, *Proc. of the 7th International World Wide Web Conference (WWW7)*.

[10] Breslau, L., Cao, P., Fan, L., Phillips, G. & Shenker, S. (1999). Web Caching and Zipf-like Distributions: Evidence and Implications, *Proc. of IEEE INFOCOM'99*.

[11] Chankhunthod, A., Danzig, P. B., Neerdaels, C., Schwartz, M. F. & Worrell, K. J. (1996). A hierarchical Internet object cache, *Proc. of USENIX Annual Technical Conference*, **153** – 164.

[12] Cottrel, L., Zekauskas, M., Uijterwaal, H. & McGregor, T. (1999). Comparison of Some Internet Active End-to-End Performance Measurement Projects, http://www.slac.stanford.edu/comp/net/wan-mon/iepm-cf.html

[13] Dingle & T. Partl (1996). Web Cache Coherence, *Proc. of the 5th Word Wide Web Conference*, Paris.

[14] Duska, B.M., Marwood, David & Feeley, M. J. (1997). The Measured Access Characteristics of World-Wide-Web Client Proxy Caches, *Proc. of the USENIX Symposium on Internet Technology and Systems*.

[15] Garlan, D., Siewiorek, D.P., Smailagic, A. & Steenkiste, P. (2002). Project Aura: Toward Distraction-free Pervasive Computing, *IEEE Pervasive Computing*, **1**(2), 22 – 31.

[16] Hightower, J. & Borriello, G. (2001). *Location Systems for Ubiquitous Computing, IEEE Computer*, **33**(8), pp. 57-66.

[17] Jin, S. & Bestavros, A. (2000). Temporal Locality in Web Request Streams: Sources, Characteristics, and Caching Implications, *Proc. of the International Conference on Measurement and Modeling of Computer Systems*.

[18] Kelly, T. P., Jamin, S. & MacKie-Mason, J. K. (1999). Variable QoS from Shared Web Caches: User Centered Design and Value-Sensitive Replacement, *Proc. of the MIT Workshop on Internet Service Quality Economics*.

[19] Kroeger, T. M., Long D. D. E., & Jeffrey C. (1997). Exploring the Bounds of Web Latency Reduction from Caching and Prefetching, *Proc. of the USENIX Symposium on Internet Technology and System*.

[20] Laamanen, R.H., Alanko, T., T. & Raatikainen, K. (1999). Dependability issues in mobile distributed system, *Proc. of the Pacific Rim International Symposium on Dependable Computing*, **7** – 14.

[21] Laprie, J.-C. (1995). Dependable Computing: Concepts, Limits, Challenges, *Proc. of the IEEE 25th International Symposium on Fault-Tolerant Computing*.

[22] Lewandowski, S.M. (1998). Frameworks for Component-based Client/Server Computing, *ACM Computing Surveys*, **30**(1), 3 – 27.

[23] Malla, A., El-Kadi, M., Olariu & S., Todorova, P. (2003). A Fair Resource Allocation Protocol for Multimedia Wireless Networks, *IEEE Transactions on Parallel and Distributed Systems*, **14**(1), 63 – 71.

[24] Mahanti, A., Williamson, C. & Eager, D. (2000). Traffic analysis of a Web proxy caching hierarchy, *IEEE Network*, **14**(3).

[25] Medina, A., Matta, I. & Byers, J. (2000). On the Origin of Power Laws in Internet Topologies, *ACM SIGCOMM Computer Communication Review*, **30**(2), 18 – 28.

[26] Oshima, M., Karjoth, G. & Ono, K. (1998). Aglets Specification 1.1 Draft, IBM Corp., http://www.trl.ibm.com/aglets/spec11.htm

[27] Patterson, C.A., Muntz, R. R. & Pancake, C. M. (2003). Challenges in Location-Aware Computing, *IEEE Pervasive Computing*, **2**(2), 80 – 89.

[28] Paxson, V. & Floyd, S. (1995). Wide area traffic: The Failure of Poisson Modeling, *IEEE/ACM Transactions on Networking*, **3**(3), 226 – 244.

[29] Valloppillil, V. & Ross, K. (1998). Cache array routing protocol v1.0, Internet Draft, http://icp.ircache.net/carp.txt

[30] Wang, J. (1999). A Survey of Web Caching Schemes for the Internet, *ACM Computer Communication Review*, **29**(5), 36 – 46

[31] Weiser, M. (1991). The Computer for the Twenty-First Century, *Scientific American*, 94 – 104

[32] Abrams, M., Standridge, C. R., Abdulla, G., Fox, E. A. & Williams, S. (1996). Removal Policies in Network Caches for WWW Documents, *ACM SIGCOMM Computer Communication Review*, **26**(4)

[33] Wu, K. L. & Yu, P. S. (2000). Latency-Sensitive Hashing for Collaborative Web Caching, *Computer Networks*, **33**(1-6), 633 – 644.

[34] Wong, A. K. Y., Dillon, T. S., Lin, W. K. W. & Ip, M. T. W. (2001). M^2RT: A Tool Developed for Predicting the Mean Message Response Time for Internet Channels, *Computer Networks*, **36**(5/6), 557 – 577.

[35] Wong, A. K. Y. & Wong, J. H. C., (2001). A Convergence Algorithm for Enhancing the Performance of Distributed Applications Running on Sizeable Networks, *Computer Systems, Science & Engineering*, **16**(4), 229 – 236.

[36] Wong, A. K. Y., Ip, M. T. W. & Dillon, T. S. (2002). M^3RT: An Internet End-to-End Performance Measurement Approach for Real-Time Applications with Mobile Agents, *Proc. of the ISPAN*, 119 – 124.

[37] Wong, A. K. Y., Ip, M. T. W. & Wu, R. S. L. (2003). A Novel Dynamic Cache Size Adjustment Approach for better Retrieval Performance over the Internet, *Computer Communications*, **26**(14), 1709 – 1720.

[38] Wu, R. S. L., Ip, M. T. W. & Wong, A. K. Y. (2003). LDC-CM: A Novel Model for Dynamic Cache Size Adjustment, *Proc. of the International Conference on Internet Computing*, **2**, 753 – 758.

[39] Wu, R. S. L., Wong, A. K. Y. & Dillon, T. S. (2004). RDCT: A Novel Reconfigurable Dynamic Cache Size Tuner to Shorten Information Retrieval Time over the Internet *Computer Systems, Science & Engineering*, **19**(6) 363 – 372.

[40] Intel Vtune, http://developer.intel.com/software/products/vtune/

[41] Zipf Curves and Website Popularity, http://www.useit.com/alertbox/zipf.html

[42] The Gnutella web site: http://gnutella.wego.com

In: Computer Networking and Networks
Editor: Susan Shannon, pp. 141-155

ISBN: 1-59454-830-7
© 2006 Nova Science Publishers, Inc.

Chapter 6

VERTICAL HANDOFF SCHEMES FOR INTERWORKING OF 3G CELLULAR NETWORKS AND WIRELESS LAN

Maode Ma

School of Electrical and Electronic Engineering,
Nanyang Technological University, Singapore

Abstract

The combination of cellular wireless technology and wireless LAN technology offers great possibility of achieving anywhere, anytime Internet access. Wireless LAN technology can provide high bandwidth data transmission within a small coverage while cellular wireless network including 3G cellular wireless networks can serve relative low bandwidth data transmission in a wider area. The integration of these two wireless technologies will enhance the Internet access ability of mobile users to achieve "Always Best Connected". Loosely coupled architecture seems to be prospective to implement. One of the important issues in loosely coupled approach is the handoff between wireless LAN and 3G cellular networks. This chapter presents an overall view on various techniques to perform the vertical handoff. We describe several state-of-the-art schemes to implement the vertical handoff and seamless connection processes in quite detail. The objective of this review is to present a general picture on the topic and the relevant techniques for further research.

1 Introduction

Recent development on the wireless technologies has indicated that wireless local area networks, wireless LAN, based on IEEE 802.11.x standards and third-generation, 3G, cellular wireless networks such as CDMA2000 or UMTS (i.e. WCDMA) could be integrated together to offer Internet access to end users. The two technologies can offer functions that are complementary to each other. The 802.11.x standards based wireless LANs support data rates from 1 Mbps to 54 Mbps. However, by 802.11.x standard, one access point (AP) in a wireless LAN can only cover an area of a few thousand square meters. It is perfectly applied for enterprise networks and public hot-spots such as hotels and airports. On the contrary, wireless cellular networks built with 3G standards can only support peak data transmission rates from

64Kbps to nearly 2 Mbps with a much wider area of coverage that enables ubiquitous connectivity. It is reasonable and feasible to combine these two technologies to make Internet access much easier and more convenient. The implementation of the integration of 3G cellular wireless networks and 802.11.x standard based wireless LANs is a challenging task. Its difficulty lies in the objective of the integration, which is to achieve the seamless interoperation between the two types of the wireless networks with QoS level and other requirements maintained at the same time, from the perspectives of both the end-users and the operators. There are basically two proposals as the solutions to the architecture of the integration. One is the tight coupling. The other is the loose coupling. Although there is no final decision on whether the future integrated network would use either of these techniques or some other one, much focus of the research is currently on the loose coupling approach due to its feasibility.

The loose coupled architecture for the integration of 3G cellular networks and wireless LANs has shown a lot of advantages [1-3]. And it is the preferred architecture for the integration. However, to implement such architecture in order to realize the integration, there are a lot of issues to be addressed. One of the important issues is the mobility management in such heterogeneous wireless networks. In order to maintain the network connectivity, efficient and seamless handoff schemes are needed to handle two types of transfer. One of them is the switch between two different APs or base stations (BS) in a homogeneous wireless network, which is referred as horizontal handoff. The other is the switch between two different wireless networks, which is featured as vertical handoff. The horizontal handoff is the traditional handoff received a lot of discussions while the vertical handoff deserves extensive research due to its need of extra supports in both the terminal side and the network side. Vertical handoff is a critical issue to maintain the connectivity in a heterogeneous wireless network. There are a number of challenges in vertical handoff including the strategy to decide a vertical handoff, the scheme to keep connectivity during handoff, and the architecture to support the handoff scheme.

The rest of the chapter will be organized as follows. Section 2 will review the strategies on vertical handoff decision making. Section 3 will present various approaches and corresponding architectures to handle the mobility management during the vertical handoff. And the last section will conclude the paper with a summary.

2   Vertical Handoff Decision Strategies

The handoff decision is to decide whether a handoff should be performed, where a mobile user should be transferred to, and when to perform the handoff. The decision is going to be formed based on different metrics and strategies. Handoff metrics are the quantities to provide an indication to show whether a handoff is needed. Horizontal handoff needs only signal strength and channel availability for consideration. However, other new metrics should be considered when a vertical handoff decision is making. They could include QoS provided by the target wireless network, cost of the service in the target network, the target network system states (including the parameters like traffic load and bandwidth availability, which show medium access control (MAC) and upper layers states, and the physical layer states shown by the parameters like channel bit error rate and inter-channel interference, etc.), dynamic states and profile of mobile nodes, and the user preferences. The reason to include the new parameters in a vertical handoff decision lies in its differences from the traditional horizontal handoff. And it makes the vertical handoff decision making more complex.

We identify that a handoff decision process could be divided into three phases in general. The first one is the discovery phase, in which based on the two basic parameters, signal strength and channel availability, reachable wireless networks can be found. The second phase can be referred as evaluation phase, which is for the mobile nodes to evaluate all of other parameters to decide whether a handoff to one of reachable candidate networks is worthwhile. The handoff decision could be immediately made and got into the handoff execution phase if the handoff criteria could be met by all of the parameters. If all the real-time state independent parameters can meet the criteria, the decision could be delayed to execute the handoff until all of the real-time state dependent parameters meet the criteria. Otherwise, there will be no decision to make.

The strategies on horizontal handoff decision had received a lot of research focuses during the development of wireless cellular networks. Traditionally, the horizontal handoff decision algorithms employ thresholds to compare the values of basic metrics from different points of attachment and then decide whether to make the handoff after a stability period. Almost all of typical legacy algorithms make decisions with the major basic parameter of the strength or power of the received signals, which are reviewed in [4]. Recently, other techniques such as hypothesis testing, dynamic programming, and pattern recognition techniques based on neural networks or fuzzy logic systems have been taken into consideration to evaluate whether the parameters can meet the criteria in making handoff decision. These complicated algorithms are necessitated by the complexity of the handoff problem, especially, in the hybrid data or voice networks.

The vertical handoff decision making is more complicated than the horizontal handoff with more parameters and different scenarios to consider. It will experience every phase of general handoff decision making process. Moreover, the difficulty could come from the cases as following. When a mobile user moves from a cellular network into a wireless LAN, the vertical handoff may not be able to be triggered by signal decay of the current cellular system as in the process of horizontal handoff. Both the MAC layer sensing and traditional physical layer sensing for the wireless LAN are needed to perform to ensure smooth handoff and better QoS. On the other hand, when the mobile user moves out of a wireless LAN area, the connection will be lost if no handoff is operated so that prompt detection on the unavailability of the wireless LAN and quick switch the connection from the wireless LAN to the cellular network seamlessly is extremely important. The seamless vertical handoff should be able to not only avoid disconnections but also improve QoS whenever is possible or support user device independence (user can change their devices when continue their applications).

2.1   Simple Evaluation for Vertical Handoff

A solution to the vertical handoff with explicit two stages has been proposed in [5]. Its handoff decision stage is the evaluation phase, in which handoff target is chosen based on the predefined criteria. The decision on the handoff in both directions will be made based on two major parameters, which are signal level and the distance between mobile user and BS/AP. Moreover, the handoff decision scheme provides high priority to the handoff from UMTS network to the wireless LAN since wireless LAN can always provide high bandwidth service to the mobile users. Another solution proposed in [6] provides further differentiation on the vertical handoffs in different directions of vertical handoff with two different strategies. For a handoff from a cellular network to a wireless LAN, both MAC layer sensing and traditional physical layer sensing for the wireless LAN are performed to ensure better QoS. More specifically, physical layer sensing is used to detect the availability of the stable wireless LAN signal, while MAC layer sensing is used to detect the network conditions of the wireless LAN system such as access delay and available bandwidth. On the other hand, for a handoff from a wireless LAN to a cellular network, a fast Fourier transform based signal decay detection scheme and an adaptive threshold configuration approach are adopted.

The solution proposed in [7] utilizes context information as major parameter to make vertical handoff decisions in order to support required QoS during the handoff. The scheme operates above the transport layer to allow changes between networks with different protocol stacks. The vertical handoff decision scheme includes the context repository, which gathers and manages context information and the adaptability manager, which makes decision about adaptations to context changes including decisions about handoffs between different networks and responsibility for executing handoffs. Decisions can be made based on evaluation of context changes including user location changes and a selection of a new network to which the application's communication streams should be redirected. The evaluation of user location changes is performed with respect to the network grid map and the network coverage with the user device and network priorities. The evaluation is a rules-based process. The selection of a new network process selects a network that satisfies multiple objectives, which include satisfying the user's preference of devices, achieving the highest level of bandwidth for their respective applications while minimizing packet loss, delay, and jitter, and avoiding bandwidth fluctuations which may affect the applications.

The first two vertical handoff decision making solutions are similar to the traditional handoff schemes with simple consideration of the signal strength lever and distance. The only difference from traditional handoff is that different directions of vertical handoffs have been handled in different ways. The handoff from a cellular network to a wireless LAN has been given a higher priority to process in order to achieve better QoS service for the mobile users. The third scheme has employed more information on users as well as networks. The vertical handoff decision is based on a rules-based evaluation of context changes and a multiple-criteria selection of a new network. The handoff decision has considered maintaining QoS requirements of mobile users and real-time situation of the networks.

2.2   Quantitative Evaluation for Vertical Handoff

In order to make effective evaluation on the system parameters for the vertical handoff decision, a fuzzy logic based multiple criteria-decision scheme has been employed in [8]. This scheme takes multiple parameters such as signal quality, terminals available battery power, required bandwidth, and service priority as inputs of the fuzzy engine to find suitable candidate network and decide whether and when to execute the vertical handoff. The criteria used to make decision are the signal strength, network load, network cost, and bandwidth requirement. The fuzzy engine can make the vertical handoff decision based on the inputs and criteria in a reasonable processing time.

In [9], a utility function has been used to evaluate the system parameters for the vertical handoff decision. The utility function quantifies the QoS provided by the wireless network from the view of running applications on the mobile terminals. A virtue performance agent is assumed to periodically announce the available resources information at BSs. The utility function of wireless network j from the view of mobile users is composed of several normalized factors $f_{i,j}$ that are multiplied with their weights w_i of importance for application i. Different applications have different weight values for a particular factor. The maximum requirement and the minimum requirement for each factor should be defined by the corresponding application. And the application system parameters can be mapped to the factors. Those application system parameters may include effective bandwidth, charge model and cost, power consumption, moving speed and coverage, etc. The vertical handoff decision will be made relying on the utility ratios of the two wireless networks. After a reachable wireless network found for vertical handoff by signal strength, in the evaluation phase, the utility of the reachable wireless network will be evaluated. The network with higher utility than the current one will be considered as a target network. After a stability period, if it is consistently better than the current one, the vertical handoff will be executed. An improvement on this scheme can be found in [10], which is going to achieve the optimization for the vertical handoff decision when multiple reachable wireless networks and multiple services at each mobile user are present. A vertical handoff cost function is proposed to measure the benefit obtained for each application by handing off to a particular network. It is evaluated for each network n that covers the service area of a user. The network choice that results in the lowest calculated value of the cost function is the network that would provide the most benefit to the services of the user. The major element in the cost function is the QoS factor, which represents the QoS experienced by choosing to receive service s from network n. It is a multiplication of normalized value for the QoS parameter and a weight for the impact of the parameter on either the user or the network. The system parameters should be mapped to the QoS parameters and impact factors for different system parameters in order to use the cost function for the vertical handoff decision making. After multiple reachable wireless networks founded as target networks for vertical handoff in the discovery phase, in the evaluation phase of the vertical handoff decision process, for each service in a priority order at the mobile node, the cost function for each reachable network will be evaluated to find out the minimum value of the cost function. Then the service will be transferred to the target network with minimum value of the cost function. The evaluation continues until every service can find its desired target network.

The evaluation has become more complex due to the multiple metrics and criteria introduced into the vertical handoff process. In order to consider mores factors and objectives to get close optimal or optimal solution, complicated evaluation is necessary. The first approach can just provide a rough quantitative evaluation for the vertical handoff decision. The last two proposals can provide quite accurate evaluation based on the calculation of the utility function or the cost function. The last solution is the improvement to the second one in terms of that it can serve more complicated environment with multiple reachable networks and multiple services at one mobile user. There will be a tradeoff between accuracy and efficiency of the evaluation. If the evaluation algorithm is much complex to achieve high accurate outcomes resulting in longer execution time, it cannot keep the rapid pace of the system parameters' change. The high accurate evaluation results will always lag behind the real-time situation of the networks. Then any accurate results will be no use.

From this point of view, accurate evaluation algorithms with less complexity are necessary to develop for the vertical handoff decision making.

3 Mobility Management Schemes and Architectures

After a vertical handoff decision has been made, the mobility management scheme should maintain a connection's continuity after a vertical handoff. Mobile IP is the most widely studied approach for mobility handling. The mobile IP protocol is a network layer independent mobility protocol. It is a popular candidate to support smooth vertical handoff because vertical handoff involves changing the access interface, which typically results in changing the mobile nodes' IP address. Mobile IP provides IP layer mobility by enabling a mobile node that originates from its home network to be addressable by the same home IP address across different networks, in one of which that the mobile node is visiting, while maintaining a binding between the mobile node's home IP address and the care of address. Recently, there are some other proposals to support mobility at different layers including MAC, transport, and application layer. However, among them, the approaches at transport layer have shown much feasibility. In this section, the approaches at both network layer and transport layer will be presented in detail.

3.1 Approaches at Network Layer

IP is the default network layer protocol in the Internet. It routes packets from a source node to a destination node by allowing routers to forward packets from an incoming network interface to an outbound network interface based one a routing table. Mobile IP is designed to solve the problem of link disruption by allowing each mobile node to have two IP addresses with transparent maintaining the binding between them. One of the IP addresses is the static home address that is assigned at the home network and is used to identify communication endpoints. The other is a dynamic care-of address that represents the current location of the mobile node.

Mobility agents maintain the mobility binding. There are two types of them including home agents and foreign agents. A home agent, a designated router in the home network of the mobile node, maintains the mobility binding by a mobility-binding table, which maps a mobile node's home address with its care-of address in order to forward packets accordingly. A foreign agent is another specialized router in the foreign network that is the network the mobile node is currently visiting. The foreign agent maintains a visitor list, which contains information about the mobile nodes currently visiting that network.

In the following subsections, the solutions supported by the Mobile IPv4 will be presented. The first proposal is the initial proposal to support mobility in the interworking of 3G cellular network and wireless LAN. The subsequent three proposals can be considered as variants to improve the performance of the interworking networks in different ways based on Mobile IP technique.

3.1.1   Direct Mobile IP Solution

The goal of mobile IP service is to preserve user sessions when a user roams among heterogeneous networks of different providers. The system reported in [11] takes advantages of Mobile IPv4 to handle the vertical handoff in the interworking of CDMA2000 and wireless LAN networks. The system achieves this goal with the idea to implement Mobile IP at the wireless LAN gateway node.

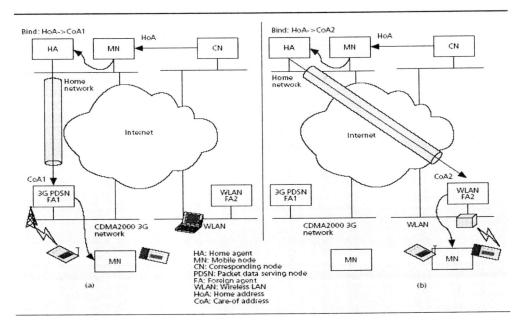

Figure 1. Vertical handoff by Mobile IP

The CDMA2000 standard has incorporated Mobile IP to achieve inter-packet data serving node (PDSN) handoff. The PDSN in the CDMA2000 network functions as a foreign agent. Therefore, a natural way to implement vertical handoff between CDMA2000 and wireless LAN networks is to implement Mobile IP functionality in the wireless LAN gateway and mobile node. The architecture of the system is depicted in Figure 1. A mobile node performs session handoffs in two cases: when it loses signal on the wireless link currently in use or when it finds a better wireless link that can provide better performance. For example, a MN will switch from 3G to wireless LAN when it acquires wireless LAN, and switch from wireless LAN to 3G when it loses wireless LAN signal. To avoid service disruption and packet loss during handoff, the mobile node can exploit any overlapped 3G and wireless LAN coverage. It can keep both network interfaces active. While using the current network link (e.g., 3G), it can use the non-current network link (e.g., wireless LAN) to prepare a handoff in the background.

3.1.2   Connectivity Manager Solution

To provide an efficient and seamless roaming service to mobile users, a systematic IP–centric scheme has been proposed in [7]. The architecture of this scheme is shown in Figure 2. The distinct feature of this scheme is that a connection manager (CM) and virtual connectivity manager (VC) have been introduced to intelligently detect the conditions of the different types of networks and manage the availability of multiple networks.

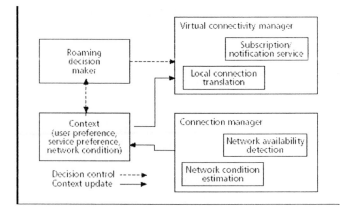

Figure 2. An architecture of seamless handoff between wireless LAN and cellular network

The CM can handle two directional handoffs between 3G networks and wireless LAN: from 3G to wireless LAN and from wireless LAN to 3G networks. Meanwhile, the proposed VC is to maintain connection's continuity using an end-to-end argument when handoff occurs. By utilizing the information provided by the CM, the VC can not only maintain the connection unbroken, but also always achieve the best possible communication quality. In the VC, a local connection translation (LCT) is designed to maintain a mapping relationship between the original connection information and the current connection information for each active connection, making the mobility solution transparent to upper applications.

A roaming decision maker and a context database are introduced to act as the interconnection between CM and VC. The purpose of this context database is to make roaming context-aware. The context may consist of user/service preferences and technical parameters such as access delay, available bandwidth, and capabilities of the terminal. The roaming decision maker makes the roaming decision after taking the entire related context into consideration. The collaboration among these four components accomplishes efficient end-to-end mobility management for vertical handoff.

3.1.3 Gateway Solution

Mobile IP approach is a reasonable way to maintain the connectivity while handoff. However, mobile IP introduces serious latency and packet lost for roaming users to move between two networks frequently. A new approach, called gateway approach, is introduced in [12-13] to interconnect UMTS and wireless LAN to handle vertical handoff. Figure 3 shows the protocol architecture of the gateway approach. In this approach, a mobile user uses standard UMTS session management (SM) and GPRS mobility management (GMM) to access the UMTS network and uses the standard IP to connect to the wireless LAN. In the wireless LAN, the mobile users can use mobile IP to handle the mobility within the wireless LAN. For users to have interworking services, the control signals and data packets will be routed through the gateway. The gateway approach aims to separate the operations of the two networks making them to handle their single mode subscribers independently. If the two network operators have a roaming agreement, the gateway enables the intersystem roaming of the two networks. The merits of this approach are that the two networks can be operated independently and mobile IP is not necessary.

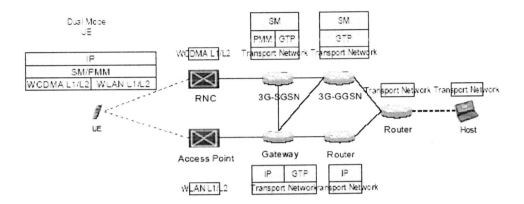

Figure 3. Protocol architecture of the gateway approach

Figure 4 shows the detailed UMTS to wireless LAN and wireless LAN to UMTS handoff procedures. It is assumed that a mobile user is registered in a UMTS network and the UMTS network has a roaming agreement with wireless LAN operators. The first scenario is the handoff from UMTS to wireless LAN. Initially, the mobile user is sending or receiving packets through a UMTS network. At the step 1, a mobile user decides to handoff to a wireless LAN. The mobile user performs L1/L2 handoff procedures. At the step 2, the mobile user tries to obtain a gateway address in order to perform the intersystem handoff procedure by dynamic host configuration protocol (DHCP). The mobile user sends a message of DHCPDISCOVER to ask a gateway address in the visited network. The gateway responds it with its IP address. Once the gateway address obtained, the mobile user sends routing area update (RA update) to the gateway using its original IP address of the UMTS network. Then, the gateway sends a standard Update PDP Contexts Request to a GGSN to ask a GGSN changing its SGSN address-in-use. Once the GGSN receives PDP Context Request from the gateway, it knows that the mobile user wants to move to a wireless LAN. The gateway becomes the SGSN temporally. Packets to the mobile user should go to the gateway instead of the old SGSN. The GGSN sends a PDP/MM context standby command to the old SGSN.

After above steps, the mobile user can send packets out using its original IP address of the UMTS network. For the packets from the mobile user to Internet, they can be sent through the wireless LAN if the wireless LAN does not perform ingress filtering on these UMTS IP address. If the wireless LAN applies the ingress filtering on non-wireless LAN IP addresses, packets should go to the gateway and then to the Internet. For the packets to the mobile user, they should go to the UMTS network based on IP routing. The GGSN recognizes that the mobile user moves to the wireless LAN and it tunnels the packets to the gateway.

The second handoff scenario is that a wireless LAN user performs a handoff to a UMTS network. It is assumed that a mobile user is registered in a wireless LAN network and the wireless LAN has a roaming agreement with a UMTS network. The mobile user is also a subscriber of the UMTS network. Initially, a mobile user is sending or receiving packets through a wireless LAN. Once the mobile user decides to move to the UMTS network, it performs UMTS standard procedures. If it has already attached to the UMTS network and in the same RA, it can just start the service. If it is the first time to attach to the network, it should perform attach and PDP context activation and then can start the service. In the attach procedure, a mobile user uses the gateway as its access point name (APN) to inform the SGSN that it wants to use wireless LAN IP. During the PDP context activation procedure, the UMTS user uses the wireless LAN IP to request the PDP context. Once the gateway detects the IP is a wireless LAN IP and the security process is passed, it responds the mobile user with the same wireless LAN IP. The mobile user can use the same IP address that was used in the wireless LAN. Here, the gateway simulates the GGSN in a UMTS network. The SGSN will send outgoing packets to the gateway and incoming packets go through the gateway to the SGSN.

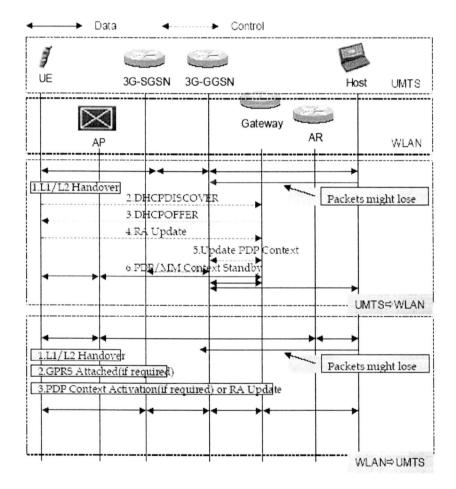

Figure 4. UMTS to wireless LAN and wireless LAN to UMTS handoff procedures

Both incoming and outgoing packets go through the same path. If Internet hosts send packets to the wireless LAN mobile user, the packets will go through the wireless LAN, received by the gateway, sent to the SGSN and ended at the mobile user. The merits of this approach are that (1) handoff is faster and packet lost is less than mobile IP approach since all signaling messages are routed within the internal network; (2) mobile IP may not be necessary.

3.1.4   Dormant Solution

Non-dormant inter-technology roaming can be supported between wireless LAN and UMTS through home agent by using mobile IP. The mobile user is responsible for mobile IPv4 registration when it roams to UMTS from wireless LAN. Mobile IPv4 registration is performed after the mobile user establishes the GPRS Tunneling Protocol (GTP) tunnel to the Gateway GPRS Support Node (GGSN). If the mobile user roams back to the wireless LAN, it is responsible for performing "paging registration request" to mobility anchor point and mobile IPv4 registration to the home agent. To support dormant roaming, a new set of extensions is required in both wireless LAN and UMTS. Using a GTP tunnel for each mobile IPv4 registration during roaming is not feasible, and it degrades the wireless core network performance. It is benefit to support dormant roaming with a new set of required extensions in both wireless LAN and UMTS as reported in [14].

When a mobile user roams from UMTS to wireless LAN, it can figure out that it has changed its network from the beacons transmitted by AP in the wireless LAN. Then, the mobile user associates with AP and informs the AP that a mobile user will be in Power-save mode (dormant). The mobile user enters again into dormant mode. From this point on, the AP is responsible for the following actions: 1) Sending mobile IPv4 Registration Request message to the home agent (HA). 2) Receiving mobile IPv4 Registration Reply message from the HA. 3) If Layer 3 paging is supported, sending Paging Registration Request message to the paging agent, e.g. Paging Mobility Anchor Point (PMAP). 4) Receive Paging Registration Reply message from the PMAP. The proposed procedures are given in Figure 5.

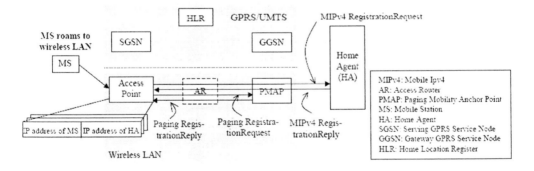

Figure 5. Dormant mode operation supports roaming from UMTS to wireless LAN

When a mobile user roams from wireless LAN to UMTS, the mobile user does not need disassociating from its AP in the wireless LAN. When it moves to UMTS, the mobile user performs the location update to SGSN, which is a GPRS attached procedure. Then SGSN activates the location information and Mobile Mobility (MM) context in the Home Location Register (HLR). Then, the mobile user can enter into dormant mode. It does not activate the GTP tunnel or perform any mobile IPv4 registration. The proposed procedures are given in Figure 6.

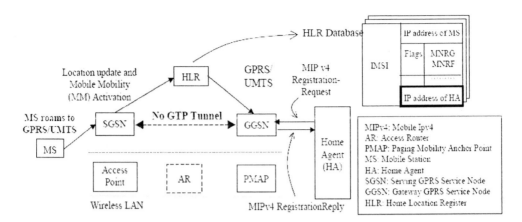

Figure 6. Dormant mode operation supports roaming from wireless LAN to UMTS

3.2   Approaches at Transport Layer

Although Mobile IPv4 based approaches are prevalent technologies to provide some levels of mobility management after vertical handoff in the interworking architectures, it is shown that there are difficulties to maintain the continuity of ongoing data sessions during vertical handoff due to long handoff latency. Mobile users may experience QoS degradation or session disruption/termination during vertical handoffs so that seamless connectivity, which referred as the connectivity with low latency and negligible loss of data, cannot be guaranteed. However, since the transport layer is the lowest end-to-end layer in the Internet protocol stack, it is a natural candidate to support mobility management after vertical handoff. In addition, by the transport layer approach, no modification or addition of network components is required, which makes this approach universally applicable to all present and future network architectures. Moreover, a transport layer approach for mobility management enables the end nodes to adapt the flow and congestion control parameters quickly, thus offering the potential for significant performance enhancements.

One proposal is to use TCP protocol to handle mobility management after vertical handoffs in [15]. The scheme of using TCP protocol for mobility management works based on the different bandwidths of the two heterogeneous networks in the interworking architecture. Since wireless LAN and 3G cellular networks can provide different bandwidths to a mobile user, a drastic change in data rate may occur when the mobile user is transferred to the target network. Based on this fact, during handoffs, the scheme will make a TCP sender temporarily halt its data transmission to avoid a timeout and packet losses. When the handoff is completed, the sender will restore the transmission in the slow start state. The implementation of the scheme needs to have a radio resource control (RRC) module and some operations at both receiver and sender sides. The physical layer at a mobile node measures strength of signal and its velocity to report to the RRC module. The RRC module determines the vertical handoff time and notifies the impending handoff to the TCP layer. The scheme uses an optional field in TCP header to identify the handoff situation. The TCP receiver sends an acknowledgement (ACK) with setting the handoff field to the proper value according to the handoff type when a handoff is impending. It sends another ACK with setting to indicate the handoff is over in the handoff field as soon as the handoff completed so that the sender can resume the data transmission without waiting for a timeout. This ACK message to inform the sender of an impending handoff can be delivered multiple times to improve reliability. The TCP sender monitors the handoff field and adjusts its congestion window size. If it detects a horizontal handoff, the TCP sender stops the timeout timer and suspends data transmission until the handoff is completed. When the handoff is completed, the TCP sender resumes data transmission at the congestion avoidance state with the same congestion window size as before. If a vertical handoff is detected, the TCP sender stops the timeout timer and holds data transmission until the handoff is completed. The TCP sender resumes data transmission at the slow start state to estimate the available bandwidth.

Another proposal in [16] introduce a new scheme to support mobility management after vertical handoff using transport layer protocol Mobile SCTP, referred as mSCTP, which offers a point-to-point connection- oriented reliable delivery service for applications communicating over an IP network. It inherits many TCP functions and at the same time incorporates two major attractive new features, which are partial reliability and multihoming. Mobile SCTP has a partial reliability mechanism, by which it can configure a reliability level. And it can benefit real-time traffic transferred during periods of poor QoS due to path failures or network congestion. Multihoming enables an mSCTP session to be established over multiple interfaces identified by multiple IP addresses. mSCTP normally sends packets to a destination IP address designated the primary address. However, it can reroute packets to an alternative secondary IP address if the primary IP address becomes unreachable. Accordingly, the path between two mSCTP hosts using the primary addresses is the primary path. And a path between two SCTP hosts involving a secondary address is a secondary path. With this powerful feature, mSCTP can provide a simple but powerful framework for mobility support over IP networks.

The rationale behind the proposed scheme is that, due to the multihoming feature of mSCTP, from the association point of view it does not matter whether an endpoint's network interfaces belong to the same network or not. As long as it is possible for an interface to establish a connection to the Internet via an IP address, the interface can be added into the current association. Particularly, mSCTP's capabilities to add, delete, and change the IP addresses dynamically during an active SCTP association provides an end-to-end UMTS/WLAN vertical handover solution. Using the multihoming feature of SCTP, an mobile node can have two IP addresses during vertical handoff, one from the UMTS and the other from the wireless LAN. Similarly, a fixed server can also be configured either for single-homing, the fixed server with only one IP address to support handoff, or dual-homing, the fixed server with more than one (usually two) IP addresses to support handoff. For each of these configurations, the handoff procedure has three basic steps: 1) add IP address, 2) vertical handover triggering, 3) delete IP address. Since no addition or modification of network components is required, the proposed scheme has a network architecture that is much simpler than those required by network layer solutions.

4   Conclusion

Integrated wireless LAN and 3G cellular wireless network services will benefit both service providers and users. A loosely coupled network architecture that allows independent deployment and growth of each network will emerge as a preferred way to implement such services. One of the important issues on the topic of interworking of 3G cellular wireless network and wireless LAN is the mobility management, which includes vertical handoff decision making and vertical handoff management. Several strategies on the vertical handoff decision making have been overviewed in the first part of this paper. By using mobile IP, vertical handoff management can be implemented at the network layer. There are several schemes and architectures proposed to directly take the benefits of Mobile IP in order to allow internetworking roaming as reviewed. Another two proposals to implement mobility management at transport layer have been also presented. With the support of TCP and mSCTP protocols, the mobility management can be easily provided without extra network components needed. It shows that they are the natural candidates for the solution of the mobility management although Mobile IP solutions are prevalent in the current research focus. In this paper, a general view on the current progresses of the research topic on vertical handoff schemes could be formed. It is expected that with help of this article, more efficient and effective solutions can be further developed.

The current solutions and the further research on better solutions on the topic are the steps towards one goal, which is getting to close to a proposed concept "Always Best Connected" [17]. The future wireless technology will make the mobile users in any parts of the world to be seamlessly connected by the Internet through any types of wireless access networks including wireless LAN, 3G cellular wireless networks, and other high bandwidth wireless networks.

References

[1]   H. Y. Lach, C. Janneteau, and A. Petrescu, "Network Mobility in Beyond-3G Systems", *IEEE Communications Magazine*, Vol. 41, Issue 7, July 2003, pg 52 – 57

[2]   D. Findlay, H. Flygare, R. Hancock, T. Haslestad, E. Hepworth, D. Higgins, and S. McCann, "3G Interworking with Wireless LANs", *Proceedings of IEEE Third International Conference on 3G Mobile Communication Technologies 2002*, May 2002, pg 394- 399

[3]   M. Buddhikot, G. Chandranmenon, S. Han, Y.W. Lee, S. Miller, and L. Salgarelli, "Integration of 802.11 and Third-generation Wireless Data Networks", *Proceedings of IEEE INFOCOM 2003*, Vol. 1, April 2003, pg 503 – 512

[4]   G. P. Ppllini, "Trends in Handover Design," *IEEE Communications Magazine*, Vol.34, Issue 3, March 1996, pg 82-90

[5]   H. Bing C. He, and L. Jiang, "Performance Analysis of Vertical Handover in a UMTS-wireless LAN Integrated Network", *Proceedings of the 14th IEEE International Symposium on Personal, Indoor and Mobile Radio communications 2003, PIMRC 2003*. Vol. 1, September 2003, pg 187 – 191

[6]   Q. Zhang, C. Guo, Z. Guo, and W. Zhu, "Efficient Mobility Management for Vertical Handoff between WWAN and wireless LAN", *IEEE Communications Magazine*, Vol. 41, Issue 11, November 2003, pg 102 – 108

[7]   S. Balasubramaniam and J. Indulska, "Handovers between Heterogeneous Networks in Pervasive Systems", *Proceedings of IEEE International Conference on Communication Technology 2003, ICCT2003*, Vol. 2, April 2003, pg 1056-1059

[8]   H. Bing, C. He, and L. Jiang, "Intelligent signal processing of mobility management for heterogeneous networks", *Proceedings of the 2003 International Conference on Neural Networks and Signal Processing 2003*, Vol. 2, December 2003, pg. 1578 - 1581

[9]   W. T. Chen, J. C. Liu, and H. K. Huang, "An adaptive scheme for vertical handoff in wireless overlay networks", *Proceedings of Tenth International Conference on Parallel and Distributed Systems 2004*, July 2004, pg 541 – 548

[10] F. Zhu, and J. McNair, "Optimizations for Vertical Handoff Decision Algorithms", *Proceedings of IEEE Conference of Wireless Communications and Networking*, Vol. 2, March 2004, pg 867 – 872

[11] M. Buddhikot, G. Chandranmenon, S. Han, Y. W. Lee, S. Miller, and L. Salgarelli, "Design and Implementation of a wireless LAN/cdma2000 Interworking Architecture", *IEEE Communications Magazine*, Vol. 41, Issue 11, November 2003, pg 90 – 100

[12] S. L. Tsao, and C. C. Lin, "VGSN: A Gateway Approach to Interconnect UMTS/wireless LAN Networks", *Proceeding of the 13th IEEE International Symposium on Personal, Indoor and Mobile Radio Communications 2002*, Vol. 1, September 2002, pg 275 - 279

[13] S. L. Tsao, and C. C. Lin, "Design and Evaluation of UMTS-wireless LAN Interworking Strategies", *Proceedings of of 56th IEEE Vehicular Technology Conference 2002,*. VTC 2002-Fall, Vol. 2, September 2002, pg 777 – 781

[14] B. Sarikaya, and T. Ozugur, "Dormant mode operation support for roaming from wireless LAN to UMTS",. *Proceedings of IEEE ICC 2003,* Vol. 2, May 2003, pg 1038 – 1042

[15] S. E. Kim, and J. A. Copeland, "TCP for Seamless Vertical Handoff in Hybrid Mobile Data Networks", *Proceedings of IEEE Globecom 2003,* Vol. 2, December 2003, pg 661-665

[16] L. Ma, F. Yu, V. C. M. Leung, and T. Randhawa, "A new method to support UMTS/WLAN vertical handover using SCTP", *IEEE Wireless Communications*, Vol. 11, Issue 4, August 2004, pg 44 – 51

[17] E. Gustafsson, and A. Jonsson, "Always Best Connected", *IEEE Wireless Communications*, Vol. 10, Issue 1, February 2003, pg 49 – 55

In: Computer Networking and Networks
Editor: Susan Shannon, pp. 157-187

ISBN: 1-59454-830-7
© 2006 Nova Science Publishers, Inc.

Chapter 7

INNOVATIVE NETWORK EMULATIONS USING THE NCTUNS TOOL

Shie-Yuan Wang[1] and Kuo-Chiang Liao

Department of Computer Science and Information Engineering,
National Chiao Tung University, Hsinchu, Taiwan

Abstract

Network emulation is an important research approach. It allows real-world traffic to interact with simulated traffic and experience various user-specified packet delaying, dropping, reordering, and duplication treatments. With emulation, one can test the function and performance of a real-world network device under various simulated network conditions without the need to get, know, or modify its internal protocol stack. Due to these capabilities, emulation is widely used to test network protocols and network devices. In this chapter, we introduce NCTUns, an innovative network simulator and emulator. We explain the novel simulation methodology used by it, present its design and implementation, and show its emulation capabilities and performance. Several examples are presented to illustrate its uses in wired and wireless network emulations.

1 Introduction

Network emulation refers to the ability to simulate the characteristics of a real-world network in real time and let real-world packets pass through the simulated network to receive various treatments such as packet dropping, delaying, reordering, duplication, etc. (For brevity, in the rest of this chapter we will simply use "the simulated network" to denote "the network simulated in real time," which is the emulated network.) By emulation, real-world network devices can exchange their packets under various network conditions simulated by just one machine. The cost, effort, and time involved in setting up a large network to do real experiments can thus be significantly saved. Using emulation, one can evaluate the performance of real-world network devices under various network conditions without the

---

[1] E-mail address: shieyuan@csie.nctu.edu.tw

need to get, know, or modify its internal protocol stack. This capability is important as sometimes it is impossible, difficult, or expensive to acquire the source code of the protocol stack used in a network device.

Traditional emulation tools operate by allowing real-world packets to pass through an emulated link that gives packets special treatments based on simple statistics distributions. NCTUns is an innovative network simulator and emulator tool with many unique advantages. In addition to supporting the above common usage, it supports innovative emulations in which real-world traffic passes through a simulated network to interact with simulated traffic. In NCTUns, a real-world network device can set up TCP connections with any host in the simulated network to exchange their information. In addition, packets generated from a simulated network can be directed to a router in the real world and then come back into the simulated network to test the functions and performance of a real-world router. These unique capabilities are difficult to achieve by traditional network emulators. In this chapter, we introduce NCTUns, explain the novel simulation methodology used by it, present its emulation design and implementation, and show its emulation capabilities and performance. We also use several examples to illustrate its uses in wired and wireless network emulations. In the following, we first introduce the NCTUns network simulator as it will be turned into an emulator for emulation purposes.

2   NCTUns Network Simulator

2.1   Development Status

Network simulators implemented in software are valuable tools for researchers to develop, test, and diagnose network protocols. Simulation is economical because it can carry out experiments without the actual hardware. It is flexible because it can, for example, simulate a link with any bandwidth and propagation delay. Simulation results are easier to analyze than experimental results because important information at critical points can be easily logged to help researchers diagnose network protocols.

Network simulators, however, have their limitations. A complete network simulator needs to simulate networking devices (e.g., hosts and routers) and application programs that generate network traffic. It also needs to provide network utility programs to configure, monitor, and gather statistics about a simulated network. Developing a complete network simulator is a large effort. Due to limited development resources, traditional network simulators usually have the following drawbacks:

First, simulation results are not as convincing as those produced by real hardware and software equipment. In order to constrain their complexity and development cost, most network simulators usually can only simulate real-world network protocol implementations with limited details, and this may lead to incorrect results.

Second, most traditional network simulators are not extensible in the sense that they lack the standard UNIX POSIX application program interface (API). As such, existing and to-be-developed real-world application programs cannot run normally to generate traffic for a simulated network, nor can their performance be evaluated under various simulated network conditions. Instead, they must be rewritten to use the internal API provided by the simulator (if there is any) and be compiled with the simulator to form a single, large, and complex program.

To overcome these problems, Wang invented a kernel re-entering simulation methodology [1, 2] and used it to implement the Harvard network simulator [3]. Later on, Wang further improved the methodology and used it to design and implement the NCTUns network simulator and emulator [4]. By using the novel kernel re-entering simulation methodology, NCTUns provides many unique advantages over traditional network simulators and emulators. Since its public release on November 1, 2002, as of May 15, 2005, more than 3,845 people from 81 countries in the world have registered at its web site (http://NSL.csie.nctu.edu.tw/nctuns.html) and downloaded it.

NCTUns is open-source and runs on the Linux operating system. It can simulate many different types of networks. After six years of development, it has become a high-quality and useful tool and has received many academic honors. For example, both ACM MobiCom 2002 [5] and MobiCom 2003 [6] international conferences select it as a research demonstration. The IEEE Network Magazine reports this tool in its July 2003 issue [7]. The IEEE MASCOTS 2004 international conference selects it as a tutorial [8]. The IEEE vehicular technology society selects it as a tutorial at its workshop [9]. The IEEE INFOCOM 2005 international conference selects it as a demonstration [10]. The SPECTS 2005 international conference selects it as a tutorial [11]. In addition, Wiley will publish a paper to present the capabilities of NCTUns on wireless resource management [12].

2.2 Kernel Re-entering Simulation Methodology

Tunnel network interface is the key facility in the kernel re-entering simulation methodology. A tunnel network interface, available on most UNIX machines, is a pseudo network interface that does not have a physical network attached to it. The functions of a tunnel network interface, from the kernel's point of view, are no different from those of an Ethernet network interface. A network application program can send or receive packets through a tunnel network interface, just as if these packets were sent to or received from a normal Ethernet interface.

Each tunnel interface has a corresponding device special file in the /dev directory. If an application program opens a tunnel interface's special file and writes a packet into it, the packet will enter the kernel. To the kernel, the packet appears to come from a real network and will go up through the kernel's TCP/IP protocol stack as an Ethernet packet would do. On the other hand, if the application program reads a packet from a tunnel interface's special file, the first packet in the tunnel interface's output queue in the kernel will be dequeued and copied to the application program. To the kernel, the packet appears to have been transmitted onto a real link and this pseudo transmission is no different from an Ethernet packet transmission.

Using tunnel network interfaces, one can easily simulate the single-hop TCP/IP network depicted in Figure 1 (a), where a TCP sender application program running on host 1 sends its TCP packets to a TCP receiver application program running on host 2. One sets up the simulated network with two operations. First one configures the kernel routing table of the simulation machine so that tunnel network interface 1 is chosen as the outgoing interface for the TCP packets sent from host 1 to host 2, and tunnel network interface 2 is chosen for the

TCP packets sent from host 2 to host 1. Second, the simulation engine process simulates the characteristics of these two links. For the link from host i to host j (i = 1 or 2 and j = 3 − i), the simulation engine opens tunnel network interface i's and j's special files in /dev and then executes a while loop. In each step of this loop, it simulates a packet's transmission on the link from host i to host j by reading a packet from the special file of tunnel interface i, waiting the link's propagation delay time plus the packet's transmission time on the link (in simulation time), and then writing this packet to the special file of tunnel interface j.

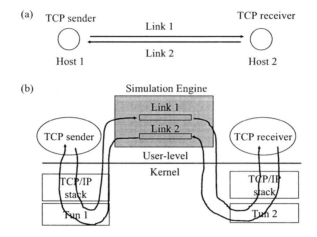

Figure 1. (a) A single-hop TCP/IP network to be simulated. (b) The single-hop TCP/IP network is simulated in NCTUns.

While the simulation engine process is running, the simulated network is constructed and alive. Figure 1 (b) depicts this simulation scheme. Since replacing a real link with a simulated link occurs outside the kernel, the kernels on both hosts do not know that their packets actually are exchanged on a virtual simulated network. The TCP sender and receiver programs, which run on top of the kernels, do not know the fact either. As a result, all existing real-world application programs can run on the simulated network, all existing real-world network utility programs can be applied to the simulated network, and the TCP/IP network protocol stack used in the simulation is the real-world working implementation. Note that in this methodology all nodes in a simulated network share the kernel of the simulation machine. Therefore, although two TCP/IP protocol stacks are depicted in Figure 1, actually they are the same one – the protocol stack of the simulation machine.

2.3   Features

The NCTUns network simulator has many useful and unique features. Here we describe each of them.

A. **It directly uses the real-world Linux's TCP/IP protocol stack to generate high-fidelity simulation results.** By using the novel kernel re-entering simulation methodology, the protocol stack of a real-world UNIX (e.g., FreeBSD or Linux) kernel is directly used to generate high-fidelity simulation results.

B. It can use any existing and to-be-developed UNIX application program as a traffic generator program without any modification. Any real-world program can be run on a simulated network to generate network traffic and be evaluated. This capability enables a researcher to test the functions and performance of a distributed application or system (e.g., an Internet on-line game or auction system) under various network conditions. Another important advantage of this feature is that application programs developed during simulation studies can be directly used and deployed on real-world UNIX machines after simulation studies are finished. This capability eliminates the time and effort required to port a simulation prototype to a real-world implementation if traditional network simulators were used.

C. It can use any real-world UNIX network configuration and monitoring tools. For example, the UNIX route, ifconfig, netstat, tcpdump, traceroute, commands can all be run on a simulated network to configure and monitor the simulated network.

D. The setup and usage of a simulated network and application programs are exactly the same as those used in real-world IP networks. For example, in NCTUns each layer-3 interface has an IP address assigned to it and application programs use these IP addresses to communicate with each other. A person who is familiar with real-world IP network configurations and operations can learn and operate NCTUns in a few minutes. NCTUns is a good educational tool by which students learn how to configure and operate a real-world IP network.

E. It simulates various networks. NCTUns currently supports fixed Internet (including IPv4 and IPv6), wireless LAN networks (including the ad hoc mode and infrastructure mode), wireless sensor networks, wireless mesh networks, military tactics mobile ad hoc networks, optical networks (including traditional circuit-switching mode and more advanced Optical Burst Switching mode), GPRS cellular networks, etc.

F. It simulates various network devices. For example, Ethernet hubs, switches, routers, hosts, IEEE 802.11(b) mobile stations and access points, WAN (Wide Area Network, for purposely delaying/dropping/reordering packets), Wall (wireless signal obstacle), GPRS base station, GPRS phone, GPRS GGSN, GPRS SGSN, optical circuit switch, optical burst switch, QoS DiffServ interior and boundary routers, wireless mesh routers, military agent nodes, etc.

G. It simulates various protocols. For example, IEEE 802.3 CSMA/CD MAC, IEEE 802.11(b) CSMA/CA MAC, IEEE 802.11(e) (MAC-layer QoS), learning bridge protocol, spanning tree protocol, IP, Mobile IP, Diffserv (IP-layer QoS), RIP, OSPF, UDP, TCP, RTP/RTCP/SDP, HTTP, FTP, Telnet, etc.

H. Its simulation speed is high. By combining the kernel re-entering simulation methodology with the discrete-event simulation methodology, a simulation job can be finished quickly.

I. Its simulation results are repeatable. NCTUns modifies the UNIX kernel to precisely control the scheduling order of the simulation engine process and application processes. As such, if the chosen random number seed for a simulation case is fixed, the simulation results of the case will be the same across different simulation runs even though some other activities (e.g., disk I/O) may occur on the simulation machine during simulation.

J. It provides a highly-integrated and professional GUI environment. The GUI can help a user (1) draw network topologies, (2) configure the protocol modules used inside a node, (3) specify the moving paths of mobile nodes, (4) plot network performance graphs, (5) play back the animation of a logged packet transfer trace, etc. All these operations can be easily and intuitively done with the GUI. Figure 2 shows the GUI environment of NCTUns.

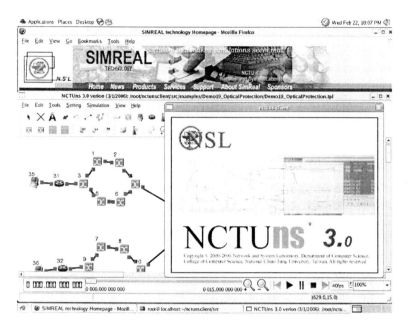

Figure 2. The GUI environment of NCTUns.

Its simulation engine adopts an open-system architecture and is open source. By using a set of module APIs provided by the simulation engine, one can easily implement a new protocol module and integrate it into the simulation engine. NCTUns uses a simple and effective syntax to describe the settings and configurations of a simulation job. These descriptions are generated by the GUI and stored in a suite of files. Normally the GUI will automatically transfer these files to the simulation engine for execution. However, if one wants to evaluate new types of networks that the GUI does not support, one can bypass the GUI and generate the suite of description files by himself/herself using any text editor (or by running a script program). The non-GUI-generated suite of files can be manually fed to the simulation engine for execution.

It supports more realistic wireless signal propagation models. In addition to providing the simple (transmission range = 250 m, interference range = 550 m) model that is commonly used in other network simulators, NCTUns provides a more realistic model in which a received bit's BER (Bit Error Rate) is calculated based on the used modulation scheme, the bit's received power level, and the noise power level around the receiver. Large-scale path loss and small-scale fading effects are also simulated.

Every node in a simulated network is equipped with a command console. One can launch application programs or execute UNIX commands during simulation in the command console of a simulated node. The operations are exactly the same as what one can operate in the command console of a real-world network device. For example, one may run the "netstat" command in the command console of a simulated node to obtain the packet transfer statistics of an interface used by that simulated node. As another example, one can use the "ping" and "traceroute" program to test whether the routing path between the local node and a remote node is properly set up in the simulated network. This capability allows researchers to flexibly issue commands during simulation based on the current needs.

It supports the tcpdump packet capturing and filtering tool. The tcpdump program is a user-level packet filtering and capturing tool. It passes filtering rules to the kernel and displays the information of captured packets. The Berkeley-Packet-Filter (BPF) module in the kernel performs packet-filtering operations. When a packet is sent or received at an interface, the device driver of the interface passes the packet to the BPF module for evaluation. If the BPF module accepts this packet, it associates a timestamp with the packet. The BPF module gives each captured incoming packet a timestamp to record when it is received by the interface. The module also gives each captured outgoing packet a timestamp to record when it is transmitted onto a link. The tcpdump program can display the header and payload of captured packets. In NCTUns, the tcpdump program can monitor any network interface in a simulated network to capture desired packets.

3   Emulator Architecture

NCTUns network simulator can be easily turned into a network emulator by performing the following operations. First, an as-fast-as-possible simulation should be turned into a real-time simulation by synchronizing the virtual clock with the real time. This is required because the simulated network should appear as a real network to real-world machines while they are exchanging their packets over the simulated network. Second, several routing entries need to be added to the system routing table on real-world machines so that their packets can be transmitted to the simulation machine. Third, several packet-filtering rules need to be installed and several routing entries need to be added to the system routing table on the simulation machine. Doing so will allow incoming real-world packets to be captured and then directed to the simulated network. Conversely, packets generated from the simulated network can be captured and then sent to real-world machines. Finally, the headers of the captured packets need to be translated so that they can be forwarded between the simulated network and the real-world machines.

Regarding the first operation of real-time synchronization, NCTUns periodically synchronizes its simulation clock with the wall clock so that they differ by at most 1 ms at any time. Regarding the second operation of setting relevant routing entries on real-world machines, NCTUns automatically computes and outputs them for the user's references. Regarding the third operation of setting relevant packet-filtering rules and routing entries on the simulation machine, NCTUns automatically computes and installs them when an emulation case starts. Thus, no human intervention is needed. Finally, regarding necessary packet header translations, NCTUns implements emulation daemons (user-level processes) to receive captured packets and perform header translations.

To conduct an emulation case, one needs to first construct the simulated network that real-world packets will pass through. Using the GUI of NCTUns can easily do this job. Second, one needs to specify how an external machine interfaces with the simulated network.

That is, when the packets generated by a real-world machine arrive at the simulation machine, to which part of the simulated network should they enter? To help a user easily specify this relationship, an external host/router icon is provided in the GUI of NCTUns. This node icon represents its corresponding external machine in the real world. By drawing a link between this node icon and a node icon in the simulated network in the GUI, one can clearly specify how the external machine in the real world connects to the simulated network. To avoid confusion, in the rest of this chapter, when we say "external host," we mean the one in the GUI. On the other hand, when we say "external machine," we mean the corresponding external machine in the real world.

3.1   User-Level Emulation Daemon

Packet header translations for emulation can be implemented as a user-level daemon or as a kernel module. Currently, NCTUns implements user-level emulation daemons to support emulation for two advantages. First, it is easier to implement a user-level daemon than a kernel module. Second, it is easier to port a user-level daemon across different UNIX systems than a kernel module. Because NCTUns network simulator can be run on FreeBSD and Linux operating systems, it is desirable that NCTUns can also support emulation on both systems. In the future, if performance becomes a concern, the emulation daemon can be easily re-implemented as a kernel module to improve its performance. One advantage of the kernel module approach is that the captured packets need not be diverted from the kernel level to the user level. This approach can reduce memory copy operation overhead.

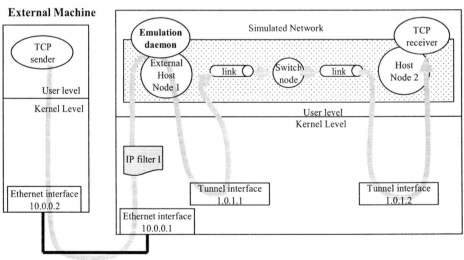

Figure 3. The emulation daemon serves the external host for the traffic direction from the external machine to the simulation machine.

In NCTUns, an emulation daemon serves an external machine in the real world. It is run on the corresponding external host in the simulated network. It performs header translations for all packets that are either originated from or destined to the external machine. It functions like a NAT (network address translator) to translate IP addresses between the simulated network and the real world. Figure 3 shows that an emulation daemon is running to serve the external machine (a host) in the real world. Packets generated by this external machine are transmitted through an Ethernet link to reach the simulation machine. These packets are intercepted, filtered, and then directed to the emulation daemon. After translating the headers of these packets, the emulation daemon injects them into the simulated network. These packets then are transmitted over one link, pass one switch, are transmitted over another link, and finally reach their destination host all by simulation. Figure 4 shows the operations for the opposite direction when the simulated host sends back a packet to the external machine in the real world.

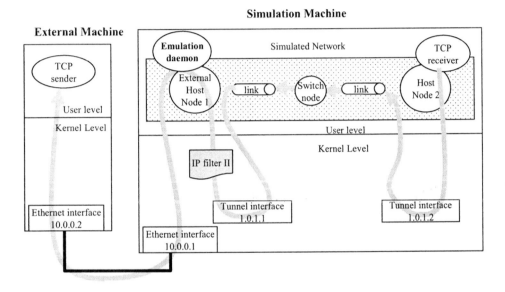

Figure 4. The emulation daemon serves the external host for the traffic direction from the simulation machine to the external machine.

3.2   Capturing Packets from the Kernel

Emulation daemons need a mechanism to filter and capture packets from the kernel. This is accomplished through the help of the kernel. Here, we describe how an emulation daemon filters and captures packets from the kernel under the Linux operating system.

I. The Original Filtering Mechanism

In Linux, the kernel does not support divert sockets provided by FreeBSD to divert certain packets from the kernel to a user-level process. Instead, the Linux kernel uses the *netfilter* [13] mechanism to filter and capture packets. Netfilter is a set of hooks inside the Linux kernel that allows kernel modules or functions to register their callback functions with the network stack. When a packet traverses a hook, the hook's associated callback function will be called. Based on netfilter, *iptables* is a generic hook that is used for applications that need to capture packets from the kernel.

Figure 5 shows the architecture of these modules. The netfilter module maintains a global structure that has five lists each of which is associated with a hook number. Every hook number corresponds to a packet filtering point inside the network stack. This figure shows the filtering scenario when a packet coming from network interface 1 is forwarded at the IP layer to network interface 2. On the forwarding path, the packet will pass through three filtering points, which are IP_PRE_ROUTING, IP_FORWARD, and IP_POST_ROUTING, respectively. When a packet passes through the IP_FORWARD filtering point, it means that the IP layer is being used to forward the packet. When a packet passes through IP_PRE_ROUTING, it means that the kernel is filtering the packet before routing it. When a packet passes through IP_POST_ROUTING, it means that the kernel is filtering the packet after routing it. In total, there are five filtering points in the IP network stack. In this figure, only three filtering points are shown. The other two filtering points are IP_LOCAL_IN and IP_LOCAL_OUT and their corresponding hook numbers are 1 and 3, respectively. IP_LOCAL_OUT represents the filtering point where the kernel sends out a packet generated by the local host. In contrast, IP_LOCAL_IN represents the filtering point where the kernel receives a packet whose destination is the local host.

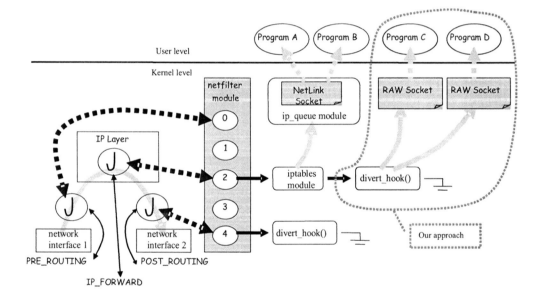

Figure 5. The packet filtering and capturing mechanism used in the Linux kernel.

When a packet passes through a filtering point, the kernel will send the packet to the netfilter module, which is depicted as a gray box in this figure. The netfilter module will relay this packet to those functions that have been registered in the corresponding filtering point (hook number). For example, when a packet passes through the IP_FORWARD filtering point, the kernel will send it to the netfilter module. The netfilter module will first relay the packet to the iptables module in the list of hook number 2. If the iptables module does not capture the packet, the packet will be sent back to the netfilter module. In this case, the netfilter module will continually relay the same packet to the next registered function, which is divert_hook() in this figure. Suppose that divert_hook() does not capture this packet, the packet will be sent back to the netfilter module again. At this time, the netfilter module will discover that no more registered function exists in the list of hook number 2. The netfilter module will then send the packet back to the network stack (the IP layer) and the packet will continually go through its original path.

In Linux with the 2.4.x kernel version, if one wants to send packets from the kernel to the user space, one needs to use the *ip_queue* kernel module and the *libipq* library. The ip_queue module uses a Netlink socket for kernel-user space communication. After netfilter and iptables match a packet, the packet is stored in the queue of the Netlink socket. A user-level program can use the API functions provided by libipq to retrieve and process packets stored in the Netlink socket. The following is an example showing how to specify a rule via iptables:

iptables -A OUTPUT -p icmp -j QUEUE

This rule indicates that any locally generated ICMP packets (e.g., ping output) should be sent to the ip_queue module. If no user-space application is waiting to retrieve these packets, these packets may be dropped due to queue overflow. Using ip_queue, a user-space program can get and modify these queued packets in the user space. Then the user-space program can specify what to do with these packets (e.g., ACCEPT or DROP) before re-injecting them back to the kernel.

II. The Enhanced Filtering Mechanism

The original Linux packet filtering and capturing mechanism does not support multiple packet queues, each storing a set of packets that match a particular filtering rule. In FreeBSD, every divert socket has one packet receive queue and each user-space program can create one or more divert sockets. Because each rule can specify its own divert port number, every program can get the packets that it wants. Therefore, when multiple programs create divert sockets with different port numbers, packets captured by the kernel can be sent to different divert sockets according to their port numbers. In Linux, however, there is only one packet queue available in the whole system. The ip_queue module only creates a Netlink socket to queue captured packets. In this design, every program needs to read matched packets from the same global queue and decides whether they are what it wants. Figure 5 illustrates a problem that program A may retrieve some packets from the global queue that program B wants. However, program A may not want these packets and therefore it may drop these packets. If this situation occurs, program B may never get the packets that it wants from the global queue.

Because NCTUns uses an emulation daemon to serve each external host, multiple emulation daemons may want to capture their packets from the kernel at the same time. In addition, other programs may also need this mechanism. For example, mobile-IP daemons or NAT daemons also need this mechanism. Obviously, the original Linux packet filtering and capturing mechanism does not meet this requirement.

To solve this problem, NCTUns modifies a RAW socket into a divert socket by adding user-defined system calls and modifying the kernel. First, the user-space program needs to create a RAW socket. Then it downloads its filtering rule and its RAW socket file descriptor into the kernel via a user-defined system call. The kernel maintains these rules in a rule table and every rule is associated with its RAW socket file descriptor. If any packet is matched by this rule, the kernel will insert the packet into the receive queue of the corresponding RAW socket. In the kernel, NCTUns implements a simple kernel function *divert_hook()* and registers it with the netfilter module. This function filters packets according the downloaded filtering rules to see if any rule would match the packet. Figure 5 shows the difference between the original approach and the enhanced approach.

4   Emulation Daemon Design

Besides capturing packets from the kernel, the emulation daemon needs to forward packets in the right direction. Here we describe how to forward packets between an external host in the real world and the simulated network. Due to space limitation, the emulation daemon design for supporting external routers is not presented.

4.1   Routing Entries Installation

In Figure 3, the external machine is equipped with a Fast Ethernet interface and this interface is configured with an IP address 10.0.0.2. The simulation machine's Fast Ethernet interface is configured with an IP address 10.0.0.1. In the simulated network, the external host (node 1) represents the external machine and has a tunnel interface with an assigned IP address 1.0.1.1. (In NCTUns, the IP address format is 1.0.subnetID.hostID [4].) If the TCP sender running on the external machine wants to communicate with the TCP receiver running on the simulated host (node 2), it should use 1.0.1.2 as the destination IP address of the packet. On the other hand, if the TCP sender running on the simulated host (node 2) wants to establish a TCP connection with the TCP receiver running on the external machine, it should use 1.0.1.1 as the destination IP address of the packet. That is, no matter whether the destination node of a packet is a simulated host or an external machine, the destination IP address used should be its assigned IP address in the simulated network.

Assume that the external machine wants to send packets to the simulated host and it is a Linux machine. One can execute the following command to add a routing entry on the external machine:

route add -net 1.0.0.0/16 gw 10.0.0.1

This command indicates that all outgoing packets whose destination IP addresses are 1.0.X.X should be sent to the gateway whose IP address is 10.0.0.1. Since the simulation machine is configured with the IP address 10.0.0.1, any packet that is generated by the external machine and destined to the simulated network will be sent to the simulation machine. These packets will be filtered and captured by IP filter I depicted in Figure 3 and directed to the emulation daemon.

4.2   IP Address Translation

In Figure 3, the TCP sender running on the external machine establishes a TCP connection with the TCP receiver running on the simulated host, which binds 1.0.1.2 as its source IP address in the simulated network. The TCP sender thinks that the TCP connection is established between 10.0.0.2 (its own IP address in the real world) and 1.0.1.2 (the destination node's IP address in the simulated network). When the TCP sender sends its packets to 1.0.1.2, these packets will be captured and delivered to the emulation daemon and their source IP addresses will be modified from 10.0.0.2 to 1.0.1.1. This is because the external host (node 1) represents the external machine and the IP address of node 1 is 1.0.1.1. All packets generated by the external machine should be treated as though they were generated and sent out from node 1. If the address translation is not performed, the simulated network will not know which node the 10.0.0.2 IP address belongs to. With this translation, the TCP receiver will think that the TCP connection is established between 1.0.1.1 and 1.0.1.2. The TCP receiver will return a TCP ACK packet with its destination IP address set to 1.0.1.1.

In Figure 4, when the TCP ACK packet comes back to the external host (node 1), the packet will be captured and delivered to the emulation daemon by IP filter II. Then, the daemon will change the destination IP address 1.0.1.1 to 10.0.0.2, which is the IP address of the external machine in the real world. In the mean time, the source IP address of the TCP ACK packet is still kept the same (1.0.1.2). With this design, the ACK packet can reach the external machine and the TCP sender on the external machine will not know that the IP addresses of its packets have been translated.

4.3   Port Number Translation

The emulation daemon needs to translate the port number inside the UDP/TCP header of a packet. This requirement is due to the design of NCTUns network simulator, which is explained below. Consider the following situation. Two Web servers are running on two different nodes in the simulated network and both of them want to use the default port number 80 as their listening port numbers. This situation is common and allowed in the real world. However, because they run on the same simulation machine (which uses only one TCP/IP protocol stack), only one of them can succeed in binding port number 80. To solve this problem, NCTUns performs port number mapping in the kernel. By the port-mapping approach, user-level programs can bind to the same port number on different nodes in a simulated network without any modification.

In NCTUns, the port number used by a user-level program is called a "virtual port number." For example, when a program executes the *bind()* system call to bind a INET socket into the per-protocol socket list, it should specify a port number. We call this port number a virtual port number. In the kernel, there are several kernel functions to service the bind() system call. When these kernel functions want to use the virtual port number to bind a socket, NCTUns instead finds an unused real port number to bind the socket and record this port-mapping relationship. The port number that is really used by the kernel is called the "real port number." As an example, a Web server A may be running on simulated node 1 and listening on the default port number 80. Another Web server B may be running on the simulated node 2 and also listening on port 80. Both the two port numbers (80) are virtual port numbers. The kernel may use the real port number 5000 to bind the socket that is created by A and the real port number 5001 for the socket created by B. In this case, 5000 and 5001 are called real port numbers. NCTUns records the real/virtual port-mapping relationship (80, 5000) in node 1 and (80, 5001) in node 2 for later uses.

Assume that in Figure 3, the TCP receiver's virtual port number is 8000 and the real port number used is 5000. Further assume that the TCP sender's port number is 4000. (Note that the TCP sender does not have a virtual port number because it is run on a real-world external machine.) When the TCP sender sends out a TCP data packet, the packet's destination port number should be 8000 and its source port number should be 4000. When this packet arrives at the simulated host (node 2), the destination port number should be modified to 5000. The source port number should still be 4000 because the kernel cannot find any virtual port corresponding to port number 4000 on the external host (node 1). Continuing with Figure 4, the kernel will automatically exchange the destination/source port number pair of the data packet for the TCP ACK packet. As such, the ACK packet's destination/source port number pair will be 4000/5000. If the emulation daemon does not modify the ACK packet's port numbers before sending it back to the external machine, the TCP sender on the external machine will think that the TCP receiver is bound on port number 5000. However, this is wrong as the TCP sender originally expects to establish a TCP connection with the foreign port number being 8000, rather than 5000. Therefore, this connection cannot be set up. For this reason, when the TCP ACK packet is captured by the emulation daemon, the emulation daemon should change its source port number from 5000 back to 8000.

The emulation daemon knows how to modify the returning ACK packet's source port number. When the data packet is first sent to the simulated network and captured by the emulation daemon, the emulation daemon saves the data packet's destination/source port number pair and destination/source IP address pair into a record. Later on, if any returning ACK packet is captured by the emulation daemon, the emulation daemon will use the packet's destination/source IP address and destination port number as keys to search the record table. If a record is matched, the emulation daemon will replace the packet's source port number with the destination port number stored in the found record.

4.4   Packet Filtering Rules Installation

In Figure 3, the IP filtering rule used by IP filter I is set as follows:

    # ipfw add divert 2000 ip from 10.0.0.2 to any in (FreeBSD version)

This rule says that all packets generated from 10.0.0.2 (the external machine in the real world) should be captured and directed to the divert socket with port number 2000. Here, the specified divert socket is used by the emulation daemon.

In Figure 4, the IP filtering rule used by IP filter II is set as follows:

    # ipfw add divert 2000 ip from any to 1.0.1.1 in (FreeBSD version)

This rule says that all packets whose destination IP addresses are 1.0.1.1 (the IP address assigned to the external host in the simulated network) should be captured and directed to the emulation daemon. That is, any packet that originates from the simulated network and intends to go to the external machine should be captured and directed to the emulation daemon. Note that due to the S.S.D.D IP address scheme used in NCTUns [4], before the ACK packet arrives at the external host in the simulated network, its destination IP address is 1.2.1.1. As such, it will not be immediately captured at the simulated host and thus its transmissions over the two simulated links can still be simulated. Only when the ACK packet reaches the tunnel interface 1.0.1.1, will its destination IP address be modified back to 1.0.1.1. At this time, the ACK packet will be matched by this filtering rule and directed to the emulation daemon. The emulation daemon will then transmit the packet to the external machine over the Fast Ethernet link.

NCTUns generates and installs the required filtering rules automatically. One just needs to provide relevant information in the GUI dialog box of the external host in the simulated network. From this example, we see that the information that needs to be provided for an external host are as follows: (1) the divert port number used by the emulation daemon, which is 2000 in this case, (2) the IP address assigned to the external host in the simulated network, which is 1.0.1.1 in this case, and (3) the IP address used by the external machine in the real world, which is 10.0.0.2 in this case.

5   Usage Examples

In the following, we illustrate how to use NCTUns to support emulations that involves real-world external hosts, external ad hoc mode mobile hosts, external infrastructure mode mobile hosts, and external routers, respectively.

5.1   External Host

External hosts can be connected to a simulated network in several ways. In the following, we present two emulation examples.

A. Example 1

Figure 6 shows the network topology used in the first example. In this figure, node 4 represents an external host in the real world (which is called an external machine interchangeably when there is no ambiguity) while all other nodes and links (inside the large dashed circle) are simulated in real time by another machine (which is called a simulation machine). This figure indicates that the external host (i.e., the external machine) is connected to the simulated network via the simulated switch (node 3). In this figure, the bandwidth and delay of the link between the external host (node 4) and the simulated switch is simulated. The bandwidth and delay of this simulated link need not be the same as those of the physical link that connects the simulation machine and the external machine. To let real-world packets be exchanged between the two machines as fast as possible, the bandwidth and delay of the used physical link should be as high as possible and as low as possible, respectively. After packets generated by the external machine arrive at the simulation machine, they will be injected to the simulated network from the external host in the simulated network (i.e., node 4). These packets will then be transmitted over the simulated link to reach the simulated switch.

Suppose that in the simulated network the IP address assigned to the simulated host on the left (node 1) is 1.0.1.1 and the IP address assigned to the external host on the right (node 4) is 1.0.2.1. Also suppose that in the real world the simulation machine's IP address is 192.168.1.1 and the external machine's IP address is 192.168.1.100. Figure 7 shows that the above information is provided to NCTUns through the GUI dialog box of the external host.

NCTUns will automatically set up relevant packet filtering rules and routing entries on the simulation machine. One only needs to set up a routing entry on the external machine to let its packets be directed to the simulation machine.

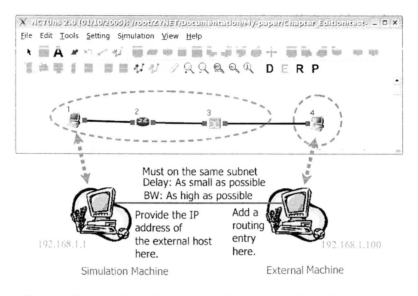

Figure 6. The network topology and physical setup used in the first example.

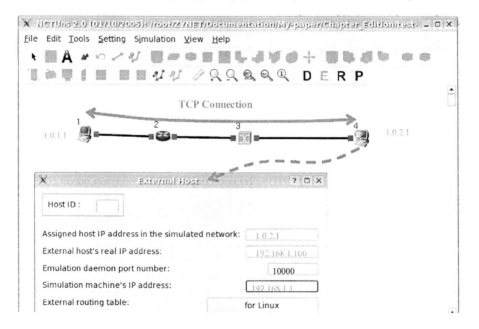

Figure 7. The GUI dialog box of the external host.

Suppose that the external machine wants to set up a greedy TCP connection to the simulated host. In such a case, the "rtcp -p 8000" command can be specified in the simulated host's GUI dialog box. This will cause NCTUns to run up a TCP receiver program that binds on port number 8000 on the simulated host during emulation. After starting the emulation, one can execute the "stcp -p 8000 1.0.1.1" command on the external machine to run up a TCP sender program. Doing so will set up a TCP connection between the external machine and the simulated host and user data will begin to be transferred from the external machine to the simulated host.

B. Example 2

The top of Figure 8 shows the second example, where two external machines (node 3 and node 4) are connected to the simulated network. The right external machine connects itself to the simulated switch (node 2) while the left one connects itself to the simulated router (node 1). The two external machines want to exchange their TCP packets through the simulated network. Suppose that the IP address assigned to the left external host is 1.0.1.1 and the IP address assigned to the right external host is 1.0.2.1 in the simulated network. Suppose that the three machines (i.e., the two external machines and the simulation machine) are physically connected together via a high-speed network (e.g., 100 Mbps Fast Ethernet) and each of them uses a different IP address in the 192.168.1.0/24 subnet. The bottom of Figure 8 shows this physical setup.

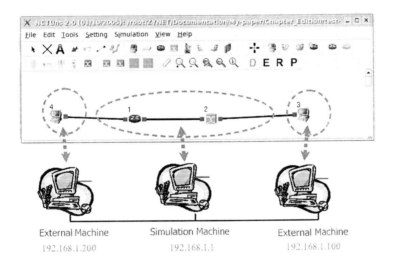

Figure 8. The network topology and physical setup used in the second example.

For this emulation case, one needs to provide NCTUns with information about the two external machines. The required information for this example is shown at the bottom of Figure 9. In this case, one should be careful about the setting of the emulation daemon port number. When an emulation case involves multiple external hosts, the emulation port numbers used by them should be different.

Suppose that one wants to set up a TCP connection between the two external machines and let their packets be exchanged over the simulated network. One can first start the emulation and keep it running. Then one executes the "rtcp -p 8000" command on the left external machine to run up a TCP receiver program. Then one executes "stcp –p 8000 1.0.1.1" on the right external machine to run up a TCP sender program. Doing so will set up a real-world TCP connection between the two external machines. User data will begin to be transferred from the right external machine to the left external machine over the simulated network.

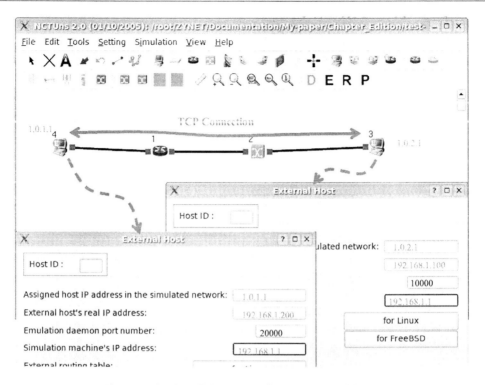

Figure 9. The GUI dialog boxes of the two external hosts.

5.2   External Ad Hoc Mode Mobile Host

An external ad hoc mode mobile host in the real world (called external mobile machine) can participate in a NCTUns emulation. In the simulated network one can specify the moving path of an external mobile host that represents an external mobile machine. However, the corresponding external mobile machine need not move in the real world. Actually, it can be a fixed host that uses an Ethernet link to connect to the simulated network (simulation machine).

The external mobile machine's IEEE 802.11 MAC protocol is simulated in the simulated network. It is not used to exchange packets between the external mobile machine and the simulation machine. When packets generated by the external mobile machine arrive at the simulation machine, they are directed to the emulation daemon running on the external ad hoc mode mobile host in the simulated network. The emulation daemon will then wirelessly transmit them to other nodes in the simulated network using IEEE 802.11 MAC protocol.

Since the external mobile host in the simulated network represents the external mobile machine, its mobility is simulated by NCTUns rather than by the user physically moving the external mobile machine around the simulation machine. With these capabilities, one can easily evaluate the performance of the applications and higher-layer protocols running on the external mobile machine under various simulated network and mobility conditions.

Figure 10 shows an emulation example in which one external ad hoc mode mobile host (node 3, which represents an external mobile machine in the real world) communicates with a simulated mobile host on the right (node 2) via another simulated mobile host in the middle (node 1). Initially, the external mobile host on the left can exchange packets with the simulated mobile host on the right via the middle mobile host. However, as time proceeds, the mobile host on the left begins to move away from the simulated mobile host (not in the real world but in the simulated network) and eventually it is out of the transmission range of the middle mobile host. At this time, it can no longer communicate with the simulated mobile host on the right via the middle mobile host. Later on, when the external mobile host moves into the transmission ranges of node 1 or node 2, it can communicate with node 2 again.

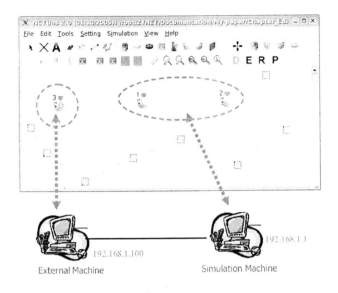

Figure 10. The network topology and physical setup used in the external ad hoc mode mobile host emulation example.

The physical setup for this emulation case is shown at the bottom of Figure 10. One simulation machine and one external mobile machine (need not be mobile) are used and they can be connected via an Ethernet link or an IEEE 802.11(b) wireless network. As stated above, it does not matter which type of network link is used between the simulation machine and the external mobile machine as long as their IP packets can be exchanged on the used network. As in the external host emulation example, the simulation machine and the external mobile machine should be on the same subnet. Assuming that the simulation machine's IP address is 192.168.1.1 and the external mobile machine's IP address is 192.168.1.100 and they are physically connected via a Fast Ethernet cable. Then on the external mobile machine, one can execute the following command to add the required routing entry to the system routing table.

route add 1.0/16 192.168.1.1 (FreeBSD version)

route add -net 1.0.0.0/16 gw 192.168.1.1 (Linux version)

After adding the required routing entry, the external mobile machine can begin to exchange packets with a simulated mobile host. If a node (either a simulated host or an external mobile machine) wants to send packets to another node (either a simulated host or an external mobile machine), it should use the IP address assigned to that node in the simulated network. Assume that in the simulated network node 1, node 2, and node 3 are assigned

1.0.1.1, 1.0.1.2, and 1.0.1.3 IP address, respectively. If the external mobile machine wants set up a greedy TCP connection to the simulated host on the right (node 2), the "rtcp –p 8000" command can be specified in the GUI dialog box of the simulated host and the "stcp –p 8000 1.0.1.2" command can be executed on the external mobile machine. On the other hand, if the simulated host wants to set up a greedy TCP connection to the external mobile machine, the "rtcp –p 8000" command can be executed on the external mobile machine and the "stcp –p 8000 1.0.1.3" command can be specified in the GUI dialog box of the simulated host. Figure 11 shows the information that needs to be specified in the GUI dialog box of the external mobile host for this example.

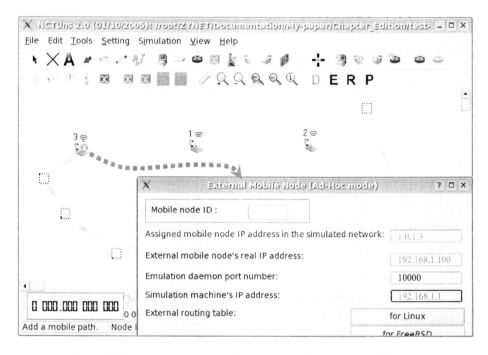

Figure 11. The GUI dialog box of the external ad hoc mode mobile host.

5.3   External Infrastructure Mode Mobile Host

An external infrastructure mode mobile host in the simulated network represents an external infrastructure mode mobile machine in the real world. The usage of external infrastructure mode mobile host is similar to that of external ad hoc mode mobile host. The only exception is that in the GUI dialog box of the external infrastructure mode mobile host, one needs to provide the gateway IP address for this mobile host in the simulated network. When the packets generated by the external mobile machine arrive at the simulation machine, they will be transmitted by the external mobile host that represents the external mobile machine and received by the simulated access points. With the gateway IP address information, the access point can correctly forward these packets to a simulated router (which is the gateway for these packets) for further forwarding.

Figure 12 shows an emulation example in which one external infrastructure mode mobile host (node 4) communicates with a simulated host (node 1) via a simulated wireless access point (node 3) and a simulated router (node 2). The mobile host is assigned 1.0.1.2 address in the simulated network and the gateway IP address specified for this mobile host is 1.0.1.254. Suppose that the simulated host on the right (node 1) wants to set up a TCP connection to the external mobile machine in the real world (represented by node 4), the "rtcp –p 8000" command can be executed on the external mobile machine and the "stcp –p 8000 1.0.1.2" command can be specified in the GUI dialog box of this simulated host. In the simulated network, initially the host (node 1) can communicate with the external infrastructure mode mobile host. However, as time proceeds, the external mobile host will eventually leave the coverage area (the dashed circle in red color) of the wireless access point and no longer can communicate with that host. Since the external mobile host represents an external mobile machine in the real world, the external mobile machine will experience the same condition as described above while exchanging data with the simulated host.

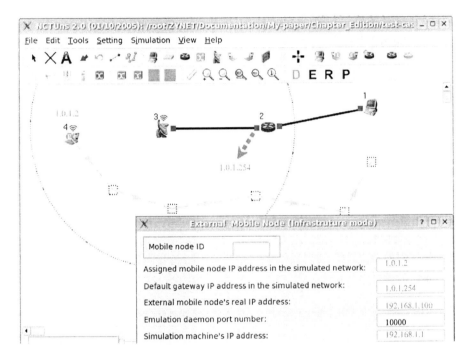

Figure 12. The GUI dialog box of the external infrastructure mode mobile host.

5.4 External Router

An external router machine in the real world can interact with a simulated network and it is represented by an external router in the simulated network. This is a useful function as traffic originated from the simulated network can be directed to the external router machine, experience the router machine's packet scheduling and buffer management processing, and then return back to the simulated network. With this capability, one can easily test the router machine's functionality (e.g., one can generate and send virus and network-attack packets from the simulated network to the external router machine to see whether it can detect them).

Figure 13 shows an emulation example where three simulated hosts (node 2, node 3, and node 4) are connected to an external router (node 1) in the simulated network. On top of this topology, two greedy TCP connections are set up. The first one originates at node 2 and ends at node 4 while the second one originates at node 3 and ends at node 4. The packets of these two TCP connections need to pass through the external router. For the packets generated by node 2, when they arrive at node 1, they need to leave the simulated network and enter the real world to reach the external router machine through one of its port. They will be routed by the external router machine and leave it through a different port. They will then reach the simulation machine and re-enter into the simulated network at node 1. Finally, node 1 will transmit them to node 4 on the simulated link between node 1 and node 4. The packets generated by node 3 experience a similar scenario.

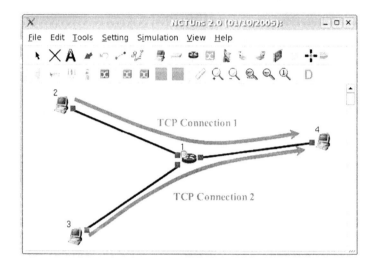

Figure 13. The network topology used in the external router emulation example.

The physical network setup for running this emulation is shown in Figure 14. The simulation machine simulates all hosts and links. It has three network interfaces each of which connects to one port of the external router machine via an Ethernet link. The bandwidth and delay of the links in the simulated network can be different from those of the three Ethernet links that physically connect the simulation machine and the external router machine.

The simulation machine needs some information about the external router machine. One needs to provide such information in the GUI dialog box of an external router in the simulated network, which is shown in Figure 15. For each port of the external router machine in the real world, one needs to provide the association among the following information entities: its assigned IP address in the simulated network (this information is automatically provided by the GUI in the second column of this association table after the port ID column), the real IP address of the network interface on the simulation machine that connects to this port via a link, the name (e.g., eth1) of the above interface (on the simulation machine), and the real IP address used by this port on the external router machine. Assume that the names of the interfaces configured with the 140.113.1.1, 140.113.2.1, and 140.113.3.1 addresses on the simulation machine are eth1, eth2, and eth3, respectively. Then the association table should contain the following entries: (1, 1.0.1.2, 140.113.1.1, eth1, 140.113.1.2) for port 1, (2,

1.0.2.2, 140.113.2.1, eth2, 140.113.2.2) for port 2, and (3, 1.0.3.2, 140.113.3.1, eth3, 140.113.3.2) for port 3. Figure 15 illustrates the settings.

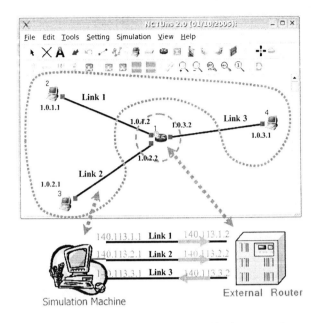

Figure 14. The network configuration and physical setup used in the external router emulation example.

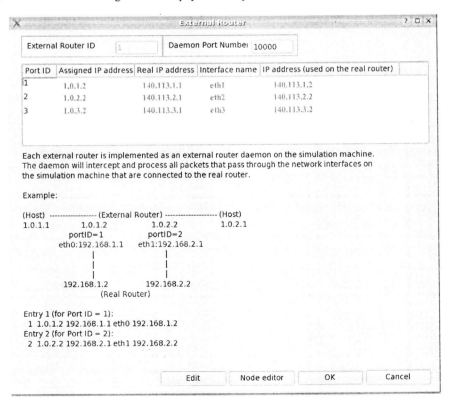

Figure 15. The GUI dialog box of the external router.

On the external router machine in the real world, some routing entries need to be added to the routing table so that packets originated from the simulated network can be redirected back to the simulated network. The rules for generating these routing entries are as follows. For every host with 1.0.X.Y as its assigned IP address in the simulated network, one can use the following routing commands (FreeBSD version) to add the needed routing entries: "route add 200.Z.X.Y -interface NICNAME" or "route add 200.Z.X.Y GatewayIPaddress." Here Z is a variable taken from the set of all subnet IDs used in the simulated network, NICNAME is the name of the interface on the external router machine (e.g., fxp0 or eth0), and GatewayIPaddress is the IP address of the interface on the simulation machine to which the external router machine would like to send these packets. Note that "200" should be used because the emulation daemon changes the first number of the destination IP address of every packet (e.g., Ss.Sh.Ds.Dh) going to the external router machine to 200 (200.Ss.Ds.Dh) so that it can come back to the simulated network correctly.

Using the above example to illustrate, assume that link 1 is subnet 1, link 2 is subnet 2, and link 3 is subnet 3 in the simulated network, and the IP address of node 2 is 1.0.1.1, the IP address of node 3 is 1.0.2.1, and the IP address of node 4 is 1.0.3.1, respectively. Further assume that the IP address of the external router on link 1 is 1.0.1.2, the IP address of the external router on link 2 is 1.0.2.2, and the IP address of the external router on link3 is 1.0.3.2. Suppose that in the real world the real IP address used by the external router port configured with 1.0.1.2 in the simulated network is 140.113.1.2, the real IP address used by the external router port configured with 1.0.2.2 in the simulated network is 140.113.2.2, and the real IP address used by the external router port configured with 1.0.3.2 in the simulated network is 140.113.3.2. Further suppose that on the simulation machine the IP address of the interface simulating link1 is 140.113.1.1 in the real world, the interface simulating link2 is 140.113.2.1, and the interface simulating link3 is 140.113.3.1. These address settings are best illustrated in Figure 14.

For this example, on the external router machine in the real world one can execute the following routing commands (FreeBSD version) to add the required routing entries.

```
route add 200.1.1.1 140.113.1.1
route add 200.2.1.1 140.113.1.1
route add 200.3.1.1 140.113.1.1

route add 200.1.2.1 140.113.2.1
route add 200.2.2.1 140.113.2.1
route add 200.3.2.1 140.113.2.1

route add 200.1.3.1 140.113.3.1
route add 200.2.3.1 140.113.3.1
route add 200.3.3.1 140.113.3.1
```

With these commands, all packets that originate from subnet 1, 2, or 3 and go to 1.0.1.1 will be sent back to 140.113.1.1 via link1. Similarly, all packets that originate from subnet 1, 2, or 3 and go to 1.0.2.1 will be sent back to 140.113.2.1 via link2, and all packets that originate from subnet 1, 2, or 3 and go to 1.0.3.1 will be sent back to 140.113.3.1 via link3.

If there are multiple hosts on a subnet in the simulated network, it is more efficient and convenient to use subnet routing rather than host routing to specify these routing entries. The following routing commands can be executed to add these subnet routing entries (FreeBSD version):

```
route add 200.1.1/24 140.113.1.1
route add 200.2.1/24 140.113.1.1
route add 200.3.1/24 140.113.1.1

route add 200.1.2/24 140.113.2.1
route add 200.2.2/24 140.113.2.1
route add 200.3.2/24 140.113.2.1

route add 200.1.3/24 140.113.3.1
route add 200.2.3/24 140.113.3.1
route add 200.3.3/24 140.113.3.1
```

6   Traffic Mix Capability

We use a case here to show that a real-world TCP connection can contend with a simulated TCP connection for bandwidth in the simulated network. The real-world TCP connection is set up between an external host in the real world and a host in the simulated network. The simulated TCP connection on the other hand is set up between two hosts in the simulated network.

I. Emulation Setup

Figure 16 shows the tested network topology. One machine (simulation machine) is used to simulate the portion of the network inside the dashed circle in real time while another machine (external machine) acts as the external host. These two machines are IBM A30 notebook computers with 1.5 GHZ CPU and 256 MB RAM. A 100 Mbps Fast Ethernet network physically connects them.

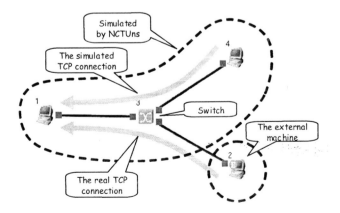

Figure 16. The network topology used in the traffic mix emulation test.

The link delay and bandwidth of all links in the simulated network are set to 1 ms and 10 Mbps, respectively. We set up two greedy TCP connections in this test. The first one is between node 1 and node 4. We call this connection a simulated TCP connection because both of these nodes are simulated by NCTUns. The other connection is between node 1 and the external machine. We call this connection a real TCP connection because one of its endpoints is an external machine in the real world. During emulation, the two TCP connections contend for the bandwidth of the bottleneck link from the switch (node 3) to node 1.

II. Performance Results

Figure 17 shows the contending behavior of the real and the simulated TCP connections. We see that they almost evenly share the bandwidth of the bottleneck link in the simulated network. This result shows that real-world and simulated traffic can dynamically mix and contend in a simulated network created by NCTUns. For comparison purpose, we run a similar simulation case where the two contending TCP connections are both simulated. Figure 18 shows the contending behavior of the two simulated TCP connections. By comparing Figure 17 and Figure 18, we see that both figures show the same behavior. This result shows that NCTUns does not bias against a real-world or a simulated TCP connection when they contend in a simulated network.

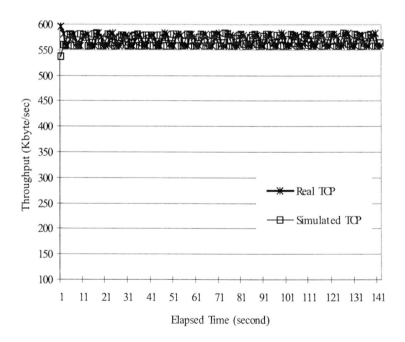

Figure 17: The contending behavior between a real TCP connection and a simulated TCP connection.

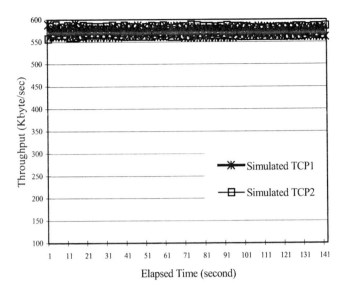

Figure 18: The contending behavior between two simulated TCP connections.

7   Performance Evaluation

We conduct the following emulation test to evaluate the accuracy performance of the NCTUns network emulator.

I. Emulation Setup

Figure 19 shows the network topology used in this test. The portion of the network inside the dashed circle is simulated in real time by one machine (simulation machine). The external host on the right (node 2) represents an external host in the real world (external machine). Each machine is an IBM A30 notebook computer with 1.5 GHZ CPU and 256 MB RAM. A 100 Mbps Fast Ethernet network physically connects them. In this test suite, the clock synchronization time interval used by NCTUns is varied to evaluate its effect on the accuracy of NCTUns in emulating an end-to-end delay.

The delay for every link in the simulated network is set to 0.5, 1, 5, 10, and 50 ms such that the expected RTT (Round-Trip Time) between the external host and node 1 on the left is 10 (0.5*20), 20 (1*20), 100 (5*20), 200 (10*20), and 1000 (50*20) ms, respectively, where 20 is the number of links that a packet needs to traverse from the external host to node 1 and then go back to the external host. The bandwidth of all these links is set to 10 Mbps.

On the external machine in the real world, a "ping" program is run to measure the RTTs between the external machine and node 1. The "ping" program measures a RTT by sending an ICMP request packet to the target host, receiving an ICMP reply packet generated by the target host, and then computing the time elapsed between these two events. The time interval between two successive ICMP request packet transmissions is set to 0.5 second and the packet length is set to 64 bytes. The clock synchronization time interval is set to 0.1, 1, and 10 ms. The variance of measured RTTs and the difference between the average of measured RTTs and the expected RTT are reported.

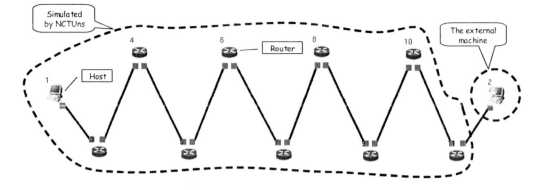

Figure 19. The network topology used in the performance evaluation emulation test.

II. Performance Results

Figure 20 shows the variance of the measured RTTs. We see that using a clock synchronization time interval of either 0.1 ms or 1 ms generates about the same level of accuracy, and using a clock synchronization time interval of 10 ms may result in a greater inaccuracy. This result suggests that using 1 ms as the clock synchronization time interval is a good choice considering both accuracy and time synchronization overhead.

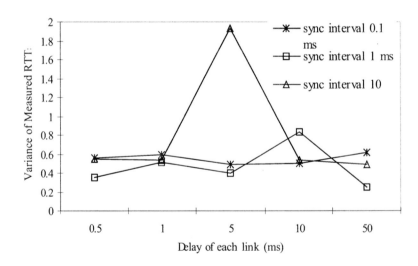

Figure 20: The variance of ping RTTs measured during the emulation test.

Figure 21 shows the difference between the average of measured RTTs and the expected RTT. The expected RTT should be 20 times the delay of each link because an ICMP request/reply packet needs to traverse 20 links in a round trip. In Figure 21, we see that using a clock synchronization time interval of 10 ms results in a large difference between the average and the expected RTT. However, the difference is small for the cases using 1 and 0.1 ms as the clock synchronization time interval. This result again suggests using 1 ms as the clock synchronization time interval.

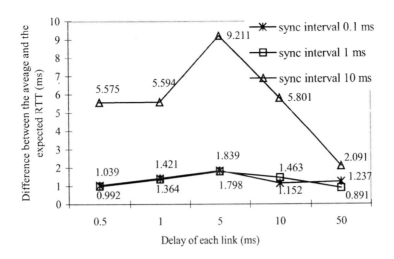

Figure 21: The difference between the average and the expected RTT under different clock synchronization time intervals.

The differences (about 1.4 ms extra delay) between the average of measured RTTs and the expected RTT are reasonable and can be explained. There are several reasons for the extra delay. First, an ICMP request packet generated by the external machine in the real world needs to be transmitted over the physical Fast Ethernet link to reach the simulation machine and its reply packet generated by node 1 needs to be transmitted over the same link to come back to the external machine. The transmission time of these two packet transmissions is 2 * 0.051 (64byte/10Mbps) = 0.102 ms. Second, the emulation daemon needs to capture an ICMP packet from the kernel, pass it to the user level, and then inject it into the simulated network. It also needs to perform reverse operations for the ICMP reply packet. These operations take about 0.3 ms. Third, in the simulated network an ICMP request packet needs to traverse 10 links to reach node 1 and its ICMP reply packet needs to traverse 10 links to come back to the external machine. Since the transmission time of an ICMP request/reply packet on each simulated link (10 Mbps) is about 0.051 ms, the total packet transmission time spent on these 20 links is about 1.02 (0.051*20) ms. In total, these delays sum up to 1.42 ms, which is close to the measured difference (1.4 ms).

Among the 1.42 ms delay, the 1.02 (0.051*20) ms delay is a natural result. This is because it will also occur in a real-world network whose network topology and link settings are the same as those of the simulated network. Regarding the 0.102 ms delay, using a higher-bandwidth link such as a Gbps Ethernet link will greatly reduce it. The real extra delay caused by NCTUns emulation daemons is only about 0.3 ms on the tested hardware platform. Using a higher-performance machine will further reduce this delay.

8   Related Work

The NIST Net [14] network emulator is a tool for evaluating the performance of the network protocol running on an IP host. It mainly operates at the IP layer. It can emulate the typical performance characteristics of a wide area network (e.g., congestion packet loss, congestion packet delay, and packet reordering, etc.). It can also emulate the characteristics of links built upon different underlying subnetwork technologies (e.g., the asymmetric bandwidth situations of xDSL and cable modems.). It is implemented as a Linux kernel module and users can install the module into a Linux system running on a PC-based machine. It allows users to specify several network conditions through which each packet needs to pass while it is forwarded by the PC-based router.

Ns-2 [15], although it is primarily used as a network simulator, can be used as a network emulator as well. Ns-2 is a traditional network simulator and is implemented as a user-level program. Ns-2 with emulation has two modes: the opaque mode and protocol mode. In the opaque mode, the simulator acts as a router allowing real-world traffic to pass through. In the protocol mode, ns-2 can be used as an endpoint to generate network traffic. Both of these two modes are naturally and correctly supported in NCTUns. Although according to the user manual ns-2 network simulator can be turned into a network emulator, from the current mailing list discussions, it seems that most people are still using it as a simulator rather than an emulator. The most recent ns-2 package downloaded from its web site cannot support emulation correctly. No one responded to the emulation bug reported in its mailing list. It seems that the emulation function of ns-2 is no longer maintained and supported.

The PacketStorm IP network emulator [16] and the Hammer PacketSphere network emulator [17] use special devices and hardware to perform emulations. These emulators are commercial products. Their advantage may be on the performance because they can be equipped with various network interfaces, high-speed processors, larger memory, and more efficient operating system, etc. A general-purpose PC-based emulation machine on the other hand may not provide the same level of emulation performance because a general-purpose operating system such as FreeBSD or Linux is not specially designed for the emulation purpose. Commercial hardware-based emulators, however, are expensive and thus are not widely used in the network research community.

9   Conclusion

In this chapter we present the NCTUns network simulator and emulator and illustrate how researchers may use it to conduct innovative network emulations. Network emulation refers to the ability to simulate the characteristics of a real-world network in real time and let real-world packets pass through the simulated network to experience various conditions such as packet dropping, delaying, reordering, duplication, etc. Network emulation is an important approach as one can test, diagnose, and evaluate the function and performance of real-world network devices without the need to get, know, or modify its internal protocol stack. Such capability is important as sometimes it is impossible, difficult, or expensive to acquire the source code of the protocol stack used in a network device.

NCTUns supports emulation by simulating a desired network in real time, intercepting real-world packets and redirecting them into the simulated network, and letting them leave the simulated network to reach their destination hosts in the real world. The simulated network used in emulation can be arbitrarily large and composed of various types of networks. While in the simulated network, real-world packets can receive special treatments simply based on statistics distributions or they can interact and compete with packets originated from simulated nodes to experience more realistic and dynamic traffic conditions. In addition, during emulation a real-world network device can set up real network connections with any node in the simulated network to exchange their packets. These innovative capabilities make NCTUns an ideal network emulation tool.

References

[1] S.Y. Wang and H.T. Kung, "A Simple Methodology for Constructing Extensible and High-Fidelity TCP/IP Network Simulators," *IEEE INFOCOM'99*, March 21 - 25, 1999, New York, USA.

[2] S.Y. Wang and H.T. Kung, "A New Methodology for Easily Constructing Extensible and High-Fidelity TCP/IP Network Simulators," *Computer Networks*, Vol. 40, Issue 2, October 2002, pp. 257 - 278.

[3] S.Y. Wang, Harvard TCP/IP network simulator 1.0, available at http://www.eecs.harvard.edu/networking/simulator.html.

[4] S.Y. Wang, C.L. Chou, C.H. Huang, C.C. Hwang, Z.M. Yang, C.C. Chiou, and C.C. Lin, "The Design and Implementation of the NCTUns Network Simulator," *Computer Networks*, Vol. 42, Issue 2, June 2003, pp. 175 – 197.

[5] *ACM MobiCom 2002 conference* (The Eighth Annual International Conference on Mobile Computing and Networking), September 23 - 28, 2002, Atlanta, USA.

[6] *ACM MobiCom 2003 conference*, (The Ninth Annual International Conference on Mobile Computing and Networking), September 14 - 19, 2003, San Diego, USA

[7] S.Y. Wang, "NCTUns," In the column "Software Tools for Networking," *IEEE Networks*, Vol. 17, No.4, July 2003.

[8] *IEEE MASCOTS 2004 conference* (12th Annual Meeting of the IEEE International Symposium on Modeling, Analysis, and Simulation of Computer and Telecommunication Systems), Volendam, The Netherlands, October 4 - 7, 2004. (available at http://www.mascots-conf.org/)

[9] The workshop on "Wireless Systems and Network Topologies," *IEEE Vehicular Technology Society*, September 1 - 3, 2004, Taipei, Taiwan.

[10] IEEE INFOCOM 2005 conference (24th international conference on computer communication), March 13 - 17, 2005, Miami, USA.

[11] *The Society for Modeling and Simulation International, 2005 International Symposium on Performance Evaluation of Computer and Telecommunication Systems*, July 24 – 28, 2005, Philadelphia, USA.

[12] S.Y. Wang and Y.B. Lin, "NCTUns Network Simulation and Emulation for Wireless Resource Management," *Wiley Wireless Communications and Mobile Computing* (to appear)

[13] The netfilter/iptables project, http://www.netfilter.org/

[14] Nist Net, http://snad.ncsl.nist.gov/itg/nistnet

[15] S. McCanne and S. Floyd, *ns-LBNL Network Simulator*, http://www.isi.edu/ nsnam/ns/

[16] *PacketStorm Communications*, Inc., http://www.PacketStorm.com

[17] Empirix Inc., http://www.empirix.com

In: Computer Networking and Networks
Editor: Susan Shannon, pp. 189-237

ISBN 1-59454-830-7
© 2006 Nova Science Publishers, Inc.

Chapter 8

QUALITY OF SERVICE PROVISION IN HIGH-SPEED PACKET SWITCHES

Qiang Duan
Computer Science Department,
University of Central Arkansas

Abstract

The wide range of emerging networking applications demand much stricter requirements on the quality of service (QoS) provided by computer networks. Packet switches play one of the most crucial roles in network QoS provision. Although the research community has achieved considerable results on both packet switch design and QoS support, these two aspects have not yet been neatly integrated together. Most research results for QoS provision assume a switch architecture with only output queueing, which is not practical for high-speed switches. Current research on switch design either mainly focuses on throughput and average performance that are not sufficient for QoS guarantee, or requires very complex control to support QoS that is not feasible in high-speed switches. Therefore, how to control traffic in high-speed packet switches to achieve QoS guarantees is an important issue; and this is the topic that we will discuss in this chapter.

First, we introduce a variety of typical switching fabric structures and queueing schemes, and discuss their influences on switch performance. We specifically describe the recently developed buffered crossbar architecture, which employs virtual output queueing scheme and a crossbar switching fabric with internal buffers. This switch architecture is expected to be widely applied in computer networks. Then we give a brief review about current research on high-speed switch design and network QoS provision, which shows that current available results are not sufficient in providing QoS in buffered crossbar switches. To tackle this problem, we develop a network calculus-based model and a set of analysis and design techniques for the traffic control system in buffered crossbar switches. Based on the model and techniques, we can evaluate the minimum bandwidth and maximum packet delay performance guaranteed by buffered crossbar switches, and can determine the amount of resources–service capacity and buffer space–that must be allocated in the switch for achieving given performance objectives. By applying this model, we show that buffered crossbar switches can provide very close bandwidth and delay guarantees to what can be achieved by the output-queueing switch. The developed model and techniques are also extended to study QoS provision in multistage buffered crossbar switches, which are constructed by interconnecting a set of single-stage switches. Traffic aggregation is typically employed in high-speed packet switches to simplify traffic control. We apply the network calculus-based model to examine the influence of traffic aggregation on resource utilization for QoS provision in buffered crossbar switches. Finally we investigate statistical QoS provision in buffered crossbar switches.

1   Introduction

A wide spectrum of emerging networking applications, especiallymultimedia and real-time applications, demand much stricterrequirements on computer network performance. Such performancerequirements include the minimum bandwidth and the maximum packetdelay guaranteed for certain classes of traffic. Achieving suchperformance guarantees in computer networks is typically referred toas Quality of Service (QoS) provision. However, the networkingtechnologies employed by the current Internet only support thebest-effort service model, which focuses on packet deliveryreachability instead of network performance optimization, thus lackQoS capability. Therefore, developing new technologies to provideQoS guarantees in computer networks becomes extremely important forimproving Internet performance to support a wide range of networkingapplications.Packet switches in computer networks are where traffic flowsgenerated from distinct sources merge together and compete witheach other to access available bandwidth at outgoing links. Mostnetwork control operations are performed at packet switches.Therefore, traffic control mechanisms in packet switches play oneof the most crucial roles in network QoS provision. Please noticethat the packet switches discussed in this chapter are generalnetworking devices that forward data packets from the arrivalinputs to the destined outputs. A packet switch could be an IProuter that forwards IP datagrams or an Ethernet switch thatforwards Ethernet frames.The switching fabric structure and the queueing scheme employed in apacket switch are two factors that have the most significantinfluence on switch performance. Typical switching fabric structuresinclude the shared transmission medium-based structure, the sharedmemory-based structure, and the crossbar-based structure. Amongthese structures, the crossbar-based structure is the mostattractive one for building high-speed packet switches due to itsparallel packet forwarding capability. Queueing schemes for packetswitches include output queueing (OQ), input queueing (IQ), virtualoutput queueing (VOQ), and combined input and output queueing (CIOQ). The CIOQ scheme has the potential for achieving not onlyhigh switch throughput but also QoS provision. The recentlydeveloped buffered crossbar switching architecture employs thecrossbar-based switching fabric structure and the CIOQ scheme. Sucha switching architecture inherits the properties of both thecrossbar-based structure and the CIOQ scheme for achieving highperformance, and it has some desirable features that significantlysimplify switch implementation. Therefore the buffered crossbarswitch architecture is expected to be widely deployed in high-speedcomputer networks [37].Although the research community has achieved considerable resultson both design techniques for high-speed packet switches andtraffic control technologies for QoS provision, these two aspectshave not yet been neatly integrated together. That is, the problemof how to control traffic inside a practical high-speed packetswitch to support QoS provision has not been completely solved.Most traffic control technologies for QoS provision assume theoutput queueing scheme, which is not practical for high-speedpacket switches. Current available results on switch design eitherfocus only on throughput and average delay performance, or requirespeeding up the switching fabric and applying very complex controlalgorithms to support QoS, which are not feasible in high-speedswitches. In this chapter, we will study the problem of supportingQoS provision in high-speed packet switches. Since bufferedcrossbar switches are expected to be widely applied in computernetworks, we will specifically investigate QoS provision inbuffered crossbar switches. Most networking applications with QoSrequirements are either bandwidth or delay sensitive, so theminimum bandwidth and the maximum packet delay for certain trafficclasses are the main QoS parameters discussed in this chapter.The remainder of this chapter is organized as follows. In Section2, we describe the general packet switchorganization, typical switching fabric structures and queueingschemes, and the buffered crossbar switching architecture. InSection 3, we briefly review the technologies forimproving switch throughput and the packet scheduling algorithms forQoS enforcing, then we discuss the output-queueing emulationapproach for supporting QoS in CIOQ switches. We also give anintroduction to the network calculus theory in this section, whichis the basis of the model and techniques that we develop infollowing sections. In Section 4, we applynetwork calculus to model traffic control in buffered crossbarswitches and develop techniques for bandwidth and delay performanceevaluation of buffered crossbar switches. In this section we alsoinvestigate resource allocation for providing QoS in bufferedcrossbar switches. In Section 5, we compare theachievable QoS guarantees in buffered crossbar switches with theoptimal QoS performance guaranteed by the ideal output-queueingswitch. We show that it is possible for a buffered crossbar switchto achieve identical worst-case delay and bandwidth performance asan output queueing switch without speeding up the switching fabric.In Section 6, we extend the model andtechniques developed in Section 4 to studyQoS provision in the multistage buffered crossbar switchingarchitecture, which is constructed by interconnecting a set ofsingle-stage buffered crossbar switches. To improve switchscalability and resource utilization, in Section7 we analyze the traffic control and resourceallocation in buffered crossbar switches with traffic aggregation.In Section 8, we study the problem ofstatistical QoS provision in buffered crossbar switches and showthat probabilistic bandwidth and delay guarantees require lessamount of resources than deterministic performance guarantees. Wesummarize this chapter and draw conclusions in Section9.

2 High-Speed Packet Switching Systems

2.1 Packet Switch General Organization

The organization of a generic packet switch with N inputs and$N$ outputs (referred to as an $N \times N$ switch) is illustratedin Figure 1. This packet switch consists of a setof ingress port modules X_i ($i = 1, 2, \ldots, N$), a set of egressport modules Y_j ($j = 1, 2, \ldots, N$), and a switching fabric. Weassume that all traffic in the network consists of streams ofpackets that are somehow assigned to multiple classes. The trafficclassification could be based on Differentiated Service (DiffServ)or Multiple Protocol Label Switching (MPLS). Various trafficclasses are statistically multiplexed onto communications lines,which are terminated at ingress port modules of a switch. Switchingress modules examine individual packets to determines thedestined egress port of each packet and the traffic class thatthis packet belongs to. The switching fabric controls the flowsof packets through the switch to forward packets from the arrivalingress ports to their destined egress ports.Packets in computer networks

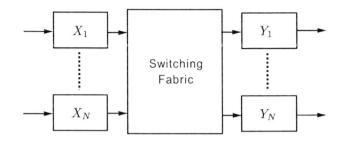

Figure 1: Packet switch general organization.

generally have variable lengths. Buthigh-speed packet switches typically use a fixed-length internalpacket as the switching unit. So ingress port modules performpacket fragmentation to generate fixed-size internal packets, andegress port modules reassemble internal packets back to theoriginal packets. The time interval for receiving one internalpacket at the ingress module is called one *time slot*. Inthis chapter, the term *packet* refers to the fixed-sizeinternal packet.Switching fabric structure and buffer management (typicallyreferred to as the queueing scheme) are two factors that have themost significant influence on switch performance. We discuss themin following sub-sections.

2.2   Switching Fabric Structures

Switching fabric structures can be classified into threecategories: *shared medium-based* structure, *sharedmemory-based* structure, and *crossbar-based* structure[35].The shared medium-based switching fabric structure uses a bus orring that is connected to all ingress and egress modules. Theshared memory-based switching fabric structure has a centralmemory that can be written to by all ingress modules and read outby all egress modules. Both the shared medium-based structure andthe shared memory-based structure have scalability problem, whichmeans that the complexity of a switching fabric grows at anunacceptable rate as the switch size increases. For an N switch, the bandwidth of the shared transmission medium or theshared memory has to be at least N times of the ingress/egressport rate, which is very difficult when the switch size N islarge or the ingress/egress port rate is high. Therefore thesetwo kinds of structures are not suitable to build large capacityswitches.The crossbar-based switching fabric structure is composed of a setof horizontal lines and a set of vertical lines. Each horizontalline is connected to one ingress module and each vertical line isconnected to one egress module. There is a cross-point betweenany horizontal line and any vertical line. When a cross-point isclosed, it connects a horizontal path to a vertical path, thuscreating a connection between a pair of ingress-egress ports. Thecrossbar allows multiple data transfers to take placesimultaneously between disjoint ingress/egress port pairs. Thisstructure is scalable because the bandwidth of crossbar does notincreases with the switch size. It is a promising switchingfabric structure to build high-speed large capacity switches.

2.3   Packet Switch Queueing Schemes

Due to the dynamic traffic load in computer networks, packetswitches need buffers to avoid losing packets. The approach formanaging buffers in a packet switch is called queueing scheme.Typical queueing schemes include output queueing (OQ), inputqueueing (IQ), virtual output queueing (VOQ), and combined inputand output queueing (CIOQ).The output queueing scheme only uses buffers at each egress moduleand no buffer at any ingress module. A packet switch using outputqueueing scheme is called an OQ switch. In an OQ switch, anyincoming packet enters an output buffer immediately during itsarrival time slot. In this sense each output port of an OQ switchis equivalent to a statistical multiplexer. The OQ switch canobtain 100% throughput performance and is able to provide QoSguarantee by applying a suitable packet scheduling policy at eachegress module. However, in order to obtain such desirableproperties, an $N \times N$ OQ switch should be able to transferup to N packets into an output buffer in each time slot, whichmeans the bandwidth of the switching fabric and the output buffersmust be at least N times of the ingress/egress port rate. Thisis not feasible for large switches with high-speed ingress/egressports.The input queueing scheme uses buffers only at each ingress moduleand no buffers at any egress module. A packet switch using aninput queueing scheme is called an IQ switch. The switching fabricof an IQ switch operates at the same rate as ingress ports, whichwill not increase with the switch size. However, the IQ switchhas the well-known *head of line (HOL) blocking* problem ifthe input buffer is a FIFO queue, which means that if the HOLpacket of an input queue is blocked, all packets in this queue arealso blocked even if some of their destined egress ports are idle.Thus, HOL blocking results in a non work-conserving switch andlimits the achievable throughput of an IQ switch.In order to solve the HOL blocking problem in IQ switches, thevirtual output queueing scheme is applied. This scheme usesseparated logical queues at each input buffer, one for each egressport. A packet switch using virtual output queueing scheme iscalled a VOQ switch. A VOQ switch is able to achieve 100%throughput by applying a suitable matching algorithm thatdetermines which ingress module transfers packet to which egressmodule in each time slot. However, without output buffers, IQswitches and VOQ switches can only transfer one packet to anegress module in each time slot. This implies that packetscheduling cannot be applied at egress modules to control thebandwidth and delay of different traffic classes, whichsignificantly limits the QoS provision capability of the switch.The combined input and output queueing scheme uses buffers at bothingress and egress modules, and a switch employs this queueingscheme is called a CIOQ switch. Due to buffers at egress modules,a CIOQ switch can transfer multiple packets to the same egressmodule in each time slot. A switch is said to have a *speedupfactor K* if up to K packets can be transferred from anyingress module to any egress module in each time slot. It has beenproved that a CIOQ switch using a switching fabric withoutinternal buffers and with a speedup factor two can achieveequivalent performance as an OQ switch.

2.4   Buffered Crossbar Switch Architecture

A block diagram of an $N \times N$ buffered crossbar switch isshown in Figure 2. The switching fabric employsthe crossbar-based structure with a buffer at each cross-point,which is referred to as a *cross-point buffer*. Thecross-point buffer between the ingress module X_i

and the egressmodule Y_j is denoted as $M_{i,j}$.The queueing scheme applied in this switch

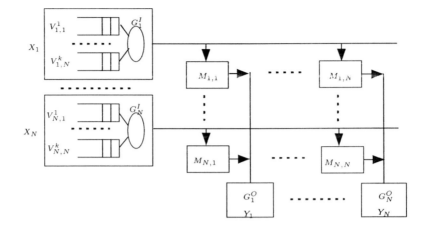

Figure 2: Buffered crossbar switcharchitecture.

architecture is acombination of VOQ and CIOQ. Input buffers at each ingress moduleare organized as one VOQ for each egress port. There may bemultiple traffic classes between a pair of ingress and egressports. We define a *flow* in the switch as the stream ofpackets of one traffic class between an ingress-egress port pair.Then the input buffers at each ingress module are organized as oneVOQ for each flow. The kth flow from X_i to Y_j is denotedby $f_{i,j}^k$ and the VOQ for this flow is denoted by$V_{i,j}^k$. All the cross-point buffers on the same crossbarvertical line can be accessed directly from the egress port thatis connected with this vertical line, thus constituting adistributed output queue for this egress port. For example,cross-point buffers $M_{i,j}$, $i = 1, 2, \cdots, N$, constitutes adistributed output queue for the egress module Y_j.To control traffic inside the switch, each ingress module $X_i$has an input scheduler G_i^I, which in each time slot selectsone packet from the input buffer to be forwarded into across-point buffer. Each egress module Y_j has an outputscheduler G_j^O, which in each time slot chooses one packet inthe distributed output queue for sending out from the egress port.The cross-point buffers are implemented as internal memory insidethe switching fabric chip and only have limited buffer space. Toavoid losing packets due to cross-point buffer overflow,credit-based flow control [17] is applied between ingressmodules and cross-point buffers. A finite pool of credits ismaintained to support each flow; that is, there is one credit poolfor each VOQ at each ingress module. Initially, all credits are inthe pool at the ingress module. Each time a packet is transferredfrom the ingress module to a cross-point buffer, one credit ismoved to the credit pool at the cross-point buffer. Each time apacket departs a cross-point buffer, one credit is returned to thearrival ingress module of that packet. The forward and backwardpropagation delay between ingress modules and cross-point buffersare denoted as d_f and d_b respectively.The buffered crossbar switch architecture has some specialfeatures. For an $N \times N$ buffered crossbar switch, because ofthe distributed output queue implemented as a set of cross-pointbuffers, any egress module can receive up to N packets in eachtime slot without speeding up the switching fabric. This impliesthat output contention will not occur in this switch architecture,therefore each input scheduler can work independently withoutcoordination with schedulers at other ingress modules. Thecross-point buffer also removes the synchronization requirementbetween ingress and egress modules. These features greatlysimplify the traffic control system and allow the switch achievehigh performance without complex implementation. It is believedthat the buffered crossbar switch architecture will be one of thedominating architectures for high-speed packet switches in thenear future [37]. Therefore, in this chapter wespecifically investigate the issue of QoS provision in bufferedcrossbar switches.

3   QoS Provision in High-Speed Packet Switches

This section briefly reviews available technologies for improving switch performance and supporting network QoS. We first discuss technologies for achieving high switch throughput and typical QoS-enforcing packet scheduling algorithms, then review the output-queueing emulation approach and its application in CIOQ and buffered crossbar switches for QoS provision. We also introduce the basic idea of the network calculus theory, which forms the basis of the modeling and analysis in following sections.

3.1   Improving Throughput in Packet Switches

For achieving high throughput in IQ/VOQ switches, the traffic control system must set up a set of connection between ingress and egress ports in each time slot, which share no common ingress or egress port. Such a set of connections is called a match. Finding a match in a packet switch is essentially a bipartite graph matching problem. There are three types of matching algorithms applied in packet switches, namely maximum size matching, maximum weight matching, and maximal matching.

The maximum size matching algorithm finds a match with the maximum number of connections. It is shown that the maximum size matching algorithm achieves 100% throughput under independent, identical, and uniform distributed arrival traffic [23]. However, a switch with the maximum size matching may become unstable under non-uniform traffic [21]. For solving this problem, each ingress/egress port pair can be assigned a weight to represent its current state. The maximum weight matching algorithm finds a match that has the maximum total weight. The longest queue first (LQF) algorithm proposed in [21] assigns the VOQ occupancy as the weight to the corresponding ingress-egress pair. It is proved that the LQF algorithm can achieve 100% throughput under both uniform and non-uniform independent and identical arrival traffic.

To simplify switch implementation, some multi-phase iterative matching algorithms are proposed. This kind of algorithms can achieve a match for which a new connection cannot be added without removing any previously found connection. Such algorithms are called *maximal matching* algorithms by convention. For example, parallel iterative matching (PIM) [1], iterative round-robin with slip (iSLIP) [22], and dual round-robin matching (DRRM) [19] are maximal matching algorithms. It is shown that a VOQ switch with a bufferless crossbar switching fabric can achieve 100% throughput under uniform independent traffic by applying any one of the above listed maximal matching algorithms.

Improving throughput of buffered crossbar switches has also attracted extensive interest recently. Nabeshima proposed the oldest packet first policy for output scheduling and the longest delayed packet first policy for input scheduling in buffered crossbar switches [26]. Javidi and his colleagues investigated the throughput performance of a buffered cross-bar switch that has one packet buffer per cross-point and uses the longest queue first input scheduling and round-robin output scheduling [16]. K. Yoshigoe and K. J. Christensen studied a parallel-polled crossbar switch with VOQs at ingress modules and a buffer at each cross-point [36]. R. Rojas-Cessa *et al.* proposed a combined input-crosspoint-output buffered switch architecture and studied the performance of this switch architecture with round-robin arbitration at both input and output [30]. L. Mhamdi and M. Hamdi [25] proposed the most critical buffer first scheduling policy for buffered crossbar switches to achieve high throughput with simpler implementation.

Although the above referenced techniques can achieve high switching throughput and low average packet delay, they are not sufficient in supporting different multimedia net-working applications. Such applications require packet switches to guarantee QoS perfor-mances, including the minimum bandwidth and the maximum packet delay for different traffic classes. Therefore, QoS-enforcing packet scheduling policies must be applied to achieve this objective.

3.2 QoS-Enforcing Packet Scheduling

Multiple packet scheduling algorithms have been proposed for QoS provision [38]. One of the most important one is Generalized Processor Sharing (GPS) [27]. A GPS server with N flows is characterized by N positive real numbers, $\phi_1, \phi_2, \cdots, \phi_N$, one for each flow, where ϕ_i can be called the *weight* of the flow f_i. Let $W_i(t_1, t_2)$ be the amount of service offered to the flow f_i in time interval $(t_1 t_2]$ and $W(t_1, t_2)$ be the total amount of service provided by the server in the same time period. Suppose the flow f_i is continuously backlogged during $(t_1, t_2]$, then the GPS server guarantees that

$$W_i(t_1, t_2) \geq \frac{\phi_i}{\phi_s} W(t_1, t_2), \tag{1}$$

where $\phi_s = \sum_{j=1}^{N} \phi_j$ and ϕ_i/ϕ_s is the reserved share for flow f_i. Suppose the flow f_i is constrained by a *leaky bucket* with parameters (P_i, ρ_i, σ_i); i.e., the amount of traffic that arrives from flow f_i during any time interval $(\tau, t]$ is given as $A_i(\tau, t) \leq \min\{P_i(t - \tau), \sigma_i + \rho_i(t - \tau)\}$, then the GPS server guarantees this flow a maximum packet delay

$$D_{max}^{GPS} = \frac{\sigma_i}{r_i}. \tag{2}$$

where r_i is the service rate allocated to this flow and $r_i \geq \rho_i$.

A GPS server is an ideal fluid model that cannot be implemented in practical packet switches. The Weighted Fair Queueing (WFQ) algorithm approximates a GPS server by serving packets in an increasing order of the packet's finish time in the GPS server. A WFQ server guarantees that the departure time of any packet from a WFQ server won't be later by more than one packet transmission time than the departure time of the same packet from the GPS server [27]. Let $d_{i,WFQ}^k$ and $d_{i,GPS}^k$ denote the departure time of the k-th packet of the flow f_i from the WFQ server and the GPS server respectively, L_{max} denote the maximal packet length, and r_i and r denote the service rate assigned to flow f_i and the total service rate of the server, respectively. Then for any k,

$$d_{i,WFQ}^k - d_{i,GPS}^k \leq \frac{L_{max}}{r}. \tag{3}$$

Thus, the WFQ algorithm guarantees a upper-bounded packet delay for the flow, which is

$$D_{max}^{WFQ} \leq \frac{\sigma_i}{r_i} + \frac{L_{max}}{r}. \tag{4}$$

Let $W_{i,GPS}(0,\tau)$ and $W_{i,WFQ}(0,\tau)$ denote respectively the amount of service offered to flow f_i by a GPS server and by a WFQ server in the time interval $(0,\tau]$. It is proved in [27] that

$$W_{i,GPS}(0,\tau) - W_{i,WFQ}(0,\tau) \leq L_{max}. \tag{5}$$

That is, the amount of service received by any flow f_i from a WFQ server won't be less than what this flow receives from a GPS server by more than one packet. This implies that a WFQ server also provides bandwidth guarantee to each flow.

A closer approximation of the GPS server–the Worst-Case Fair Weighted Fair Queueing (WF^2Q)–was proposed in [2]. It's proved that besides holding (5), a WF^2Q server also has the following property

$$W_{i,WF^2Q}(0,\tau) - W_{i,GPS}(0,\tau) \leq (1 - \frac{r_i}{r})L_{i,max}. \tag{6}$$

This implies that the service provided to a flow by a WF^2Q server cannot be ahead of the GPS server by more than a fraction of the maximal packet size, so WF^2Q provides almost identical service to each flow as the GPS server does.

However, all of the above packet scheduling algorithms assume that queueing occurs only at egress modules of a packet switch, i.e., the switch employs the output queueing scheme. Therefore, they cannot be applied directly to switches with other queueing schemes, for example CIOQ and buffered crossbar switches, where traffic contention and queueing occur at both ingress and egress modules. The additional queueing points can detract from the output scheduler's ability to provide QoS guarantees.

3.3   Output-Queueing Emulation for QoS Provision

One approach for providing QoS guarantees in CIOQ and buffered crossbar switches is *output-queueing emulation* [6] (This approach is also called *output-queueing match*). This technique was first proposed in the context of supporting QoS in CIOQ switches. The idea of emulating an OQ switch by a CIOQ switch is to achieve an identical departure time for every packet from the CIOQ switch as the departure time of the same packet from the OQ switch. Since we know that the OQ switch can guarantee minimum bandwidth and maximum packet delay for each traffic class by deploying a QoS enforcing scheduler at each egress module, then if the CIOQ switch can emulate the OQ switch, all packets have the same service order in the CIOQ switch as what they would have in the OQ switch. This implies that identical QoS performance will be guaranteed to each traffic class by the CIOQ switch as the OQ switch does.

A stable matching-based scheduling algorithm for output-queueing emulation is given in [6]. The basic idea of this scheduling algorithm is as follows. Consider the behavior of an OQ switch operating under some QoS supporting scheduling discipline. Suppose that at the end of every time slot, we know the currently scheduled departure time of every packet in the OQ switch. Then, that collection of sets of departure times from the OQ switch together with the current state of all packets in the CIOQ switch can be used to formulate a schedule of transfers across the CIOQ switch such that the departure time of the packets of the CIOQ switch exactly match those of the OQ switch. It's proved in [6] that a speedup factor of $2 - 1/N$ is necessary and sufficient for an $N \times N$ CIOQ switch to emulate an $N \times N$ OQ switch.

The development in [6] assumes that output buffers of the CIOQ switch always have sufficient memory space for any incoming packet. That is, so long as a packet is scheduled by the control algorithm to be transferred across the switching fabric in a time slot, it can enter an output buffer in that time slot. This assumption is reasonable for CIOQ switches where output buffers are implemented as memory modules outside the switching fabric. However, for buffered crossbar switches, where output buffers are implemented as on-chip memory at the crossbar cross-points and have very limited buffer space, this assumption is not valid. Therefore, the results obtained in [6] are not applicable to buffered crossbar switches.

The application of the output-queueing emulation approach in buffered crossbar switches has been studied by R. B. Magill et $al.$ [20] and S. T. Chuang et $al.$ [7]. It is proved in [20] that a buffered crossbar switch with a speedup factor two can emulate an OQ switch with FIFO output scheduling. However, FIFO scheduling even in an OQ switch is not sufficient in QoS provision. Chuang and his colleagues reported in [7] that an $N \times N$ OQ switch with QoS-enforcing scheduling policy can be emulated by a buffered cross-bar switch with a speedup factor three, or can be emulated with a $\dfrac{N}{2}$ time slot delay by a buffered crossbar switch with a speedup factor two. Based on research results obtained so far, we can see that supporting QoS in buffered crossbar switches by emulating an OQ switch has not yet been a practical approach. It either requires a speedup factor three, which significantly increases switch complexity, or can only guarantee a maximum packet delay that is associated with the switch size, which may not satisfy the QoS requirements of some networking applications.

Another option to support QoS in buffered crossbar switches is to achieve equivalent QoS performance guarantees without emulating an OQ switch. For example, although every packet does not achieve an identical departure time as an OQ switch, the flow of packets for each traffic class may achieve an identical delay upper bound in the buffered crossbar switch as in the OQ switch, thus achieving an identical worst-case QoS guarantee. The *network calculus* theory, which will be introduced in next subsection, provides an effective tool for analyzing the worst-case QoS performance. In following sections, we will apply network calculus to study the QoS provision issue in buffered crossbar switches.

3.4   Introduction to Network Calculus

In short, *network calculus* [5] can be viewed as an application of *min-plus algebra* to study network problems. We first introduce two fundamental network calculus concepts–*arrival curve* and *service curve*.

Let $R^{in}(t)$ denote the accumulated amount of traffic from a flow that arrives at a server by time t. Given a non-decreasing, non-negative function, $A(\cdot)$, the flow is said to have an *arrival curve* $A(\cdot)$ if

$$R^{in}(t) - R^{in}(s) \le A(t - s) \quad \forall\, 0 < s < t. \tag{7}$$

Intuitively the arrival curve of a flow gives the upper bound of the amount of traffic that arrives from the flow.

The traffic regulators most commonly used in practice are leaky buckets with a peak rate enforcer. A flow constrained by a leaky bucket has an arrival curve

$$A(t) = \min\{Pt, \sigma + \rho t\}, \tag{8}$$

where P, ρ, and σ are respectively the peak rate, sustained rate, and burstiness of this flow.

Let $R^{out}(t)$ be the accumulated amount of traffic of a flow that departs the server by time t. Given a non-negative, non-decreasing function, $S(\cdot)$, where $S(0) = 0$, we say that the server guarantees a *service curve* [8] $S(\cdot)$ for the flow, if for any $t \ge 0$ in the busy period of the server,

$$R^{out}(t) \ge R^{in}(t) \otimes S(t) \tag{9}$$

where $\otimes$ denotes the convolution operation in min-plus algebra, which is defined as $h(t) \otimes x(t) = \inf_{s:0 \le s \le t}\{h(t - s) + x(s)\}$. Intuitively the service curve of a flow describes the lower bound of the amount of service that the server offers to the flow.

If a server guarantees any flow i a service curve

$$\beta_{r_i, \theta_i}(t) = r_i(t - \theta_i), \tag{10}$$

the server is called a Latency-Rate (LR) server [33], and the scheduling algorithm employed by the server is called a latency-rate scheduling algorithm. The parameter θ_i and r_i are respectively the latency and service rate guaranteed to the flow i by the server. The LR server is a general server model. Many well-known schedulers, such as GPS, WFQ and WF^2Q, belong to the LR server class.

Assume that a service system consists of a series of tandem servers, $G_1, G_2, \cdots, G_n$, which respectively guarantee service curves, $S_1(t), S_2(t), \cdots, S_n(t)$, to a flow, then the service curve guaranteed by the entire system to this flow can be obtained through the convolution of the service curves guaranteed by each server; that is,

$$S(t) = S_1(t) \otimes S_2(t) \cdots \otimes S_n(t). \tag{11}$$

Convolution of LR service curves has a nice property. Suppose each scheduler, G_i, guarantees a flow a service curve, $\beta_{r_i, \theta_i}(t) = r_i(t - \theta_i)$. Then it can be proved that the convolution of these service curves is

$$\beta_{r_1, \theta_1}(t) \otimes \cdots, \otimes \beta_{r_n, \theta_n}(t) = \beta_{r, \theta_\Sigma}(t), \tag{12}$$

where

$$r = \min\{r_1, r_2, \cdots, r_n\} \quad \text{and} \quad \theta_\Sigma = \sum_{i=1}^{n} \theta_i. \tag{13}$$

Network calculus provides a mapping between the arrival curve and service curve to the bandwidth and delay performance. A service curve is a general description of the minimum service capacity offered to a flow, which essentially gives the minimum bandwidth guaranteed to the flow. The maximum packet delay of the flow can be determined from the maximal horizontal distance between the service curve and the arrival curve of the flow. That is, given $A(t)$ and $S(t)$ of a flow, the packet delay upper bound for the flow is,

$$D_{max} = \max_{t:t\geq 0}\{\min\{\Delta : \Delta \geq 0 \quad \text{and} \quad A(t) \leq S(t + \Delta)\}\}. \tag{14}$$

4   QoS Provision in Buffered Crossbar Switches

In this section, we apply network calculus to study the problem of QoS provision in buffered crossbar switches. We begin by developing a service curve-based model for traffic control in buffered crossbar switches. Then we apply this model to determine the minimum bandwidth and the maximum packet delay that can be guaranteed to a flow in the switch. We also analyze the relation between the bandwidth / delay performance for a flow and the buffer space allocated to the flow. Based on this relation we study the resource allocation issue for QoS provision in buffered crossbar switches.

4.1   Model for Traffic Control in Buffered Crossbar Switches

The traffic control system for a flow from the ingress port X_i to the egress port Y_j of a buffered crossbar switch is illustrated in Figure 3. It consists of the input scheduler G_i^I, the cross-point buffer $M_{i,j}$, and the output scheduler G_j^O. The total number of credits allocated to this flow is K. The input scheduler G_i^I can offer service to the flow only when there are credits available to this flow at the ingress module X_i. The amount of service offered to a flow by the input scheduler is determined by the combination of the input scheduling algorithm and the credit-based flow control. Therefore, it is equivalent to having a traffic controller C in front of the input scheduler G_i^I that represents the influence of credit circulation on the amount of service offered to this flow. Credits returned from the cross-point buffer credit pool for this flow are triggered by the service offered to this flow by the output scheduler G_j^O.

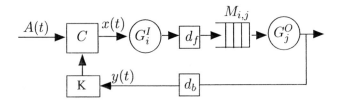

Figure 3: Traffic control system for a flow in buffered crossbar switch.

Denote the arrival curve of the flow by $A(t)$, the accumulated traffic of the flow that passes the traffic controller C by time t as $x(t)$, and the accumulated amount of credits returned to the ingress port module by time t as $y(t)$. Suppose the service curve guaranteed by the input and output schedulers to the flow by $S^I(t)$ and $S^O(t)$ respectively, and the forward and backward propagation delay between input port and cross-point buffer is d_f and d_b, respectively. Denote by G the credit circulation loop that consists of the tandem schedulers G_i^I and G_j^O, the cross-point buffer $M_{i,j}$, and the forward and backward delay elements d_f and d_b. The service curve guaranteed by the system G, $S^G(t)$, can be obtained by the convolution of the $S^I(t)$, $S^O(t)$, and the service curve caused by the round trip delay $d = d_f + d_b$; that is,

$$S^G(t) = S^I(t) \otimes S^O(t) \otimes \delta(t - d_f - d_b). \tag{15}$$

Because $x(t)$ and $y(t)$ are respectively the input and output of the system G, following the service curve definition given by (9) we have

$$y(t) \geq x(t) \otimes S^G(t). \tag{16}$$

The amount of traffic that can pass the traffic controller C is constrained by both the arrival curve, $A(t)$, and the amount of credits returned to the ingress port module, $y(t)$. Therefore,

$$x(t) \leq A(t) \quad \text{and} \quad x(t) \leq y(t) + K. \tag{17}$$

That is,

$$x(t) \leq \min\{A(t), y(t) + K\}. \tag{18}$$

The analysis of such a feedback control system can be found in [5]. Denote by $f^{(m)}$ the function obtained by $(m-1)$ fold convolutions of f, i.e., $f^{(1)} = f, f^{(2)} = f \otimes f, f^{(3)} = f \otimes f \otimes f$. Then following the techniques given in [5], we can obtain that

$$x(t) \geq A(t) \otimes \left(\inf_{m \geq 0} \left\{ (S^G(t) + K)^{(m)} \right\} \right). \tag{19}$$

Comparing (19) with the definition of service curve given by (9), we can see that the traffic controller C guarantees this flow a service curve

$$S^C(t) = \inf_{m \geq 0} \left\{ (S^G(t) + K)^{(m)} \right\}. \tag{20}$$

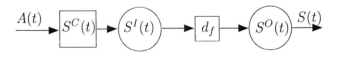

Figure 4: Service curve-based model for traffic control in buffered crossbar switches.

Therefore, the closed-loop feedback system shown in Figure 3 can be characterized by an open-loop service curve-based model shown in Figure 4. Therefore, the service curve guaranteed by the buffered crossbar switch to this flow can be calculated as

$$S(t) = S^C(t) \otimes S^I(t) \otimes S^O(t) \otimes \delta(t - d_f). \tag{21}$$

Since the packet schedulers adopted by most practical switches belong to the LR server class, we specifically study buffered crossbar switches with LR schedulers at ingress and egress modules. Assume that the input and output schedulers guarantee service curves $\beta_{r,\theta_I}(t)$ and $\beta_{r,\theta_O}(t)$ respectively to a flow. That is, both schedulers guarantees a service rate r to this flow, and the latency of this flow at input and output scheduler are θ_I and θ_O respectively. Then for this flow, we have,

$$S^G(t) = \beta_{r,\theta_I}(t) \otimes \beta_{r,\theta_O}(t) \otimes \delta(t - d_f - d_b) = \beta_{r,\theta}(t), \tag{22}$$

where $\theta = \theta_I + \theta_O + d_f + d_b$, which is the total latency of the credit circulation loop in the buffered crossbar switch. Based on (12), (13), and LR server properties given in [33] we can get

$$(S^G(t) + K)^{(m)} = (S^G(t))^{(m)} + mK = \beta_{r,m\theta}(t) + mK. \tag{23}$$

Thus, from (20), the service curve guaranteed by the controller to the flow is

$$S^C(t) = \inf_{m \geq 0} \left\{ (S^G(t) + K)^{(m)} \right\} = \inf_{m \geq 0} \left\{ \beta_{r,m\theta}(t) + mK \right\} \tag{24}$$

Let $K^* = r(\theta_I + \theta_O + d_f + d_b)$. If the total number of credits allocated to this flow is $K \geq K^*$, then for all $m \geq 0$

$$rt \leq \beta_{r,m\theta}(t) + mK, \tag{25}$$

thus

$$S^C(t) = \inf_{m \geq 0} \left\{ \beta_{r,m\theta}(t) + mK \right\} = rt. \tag{26}$$

From (21), the service curve guaranteed by the buffered crossbar switch to this flow is then

$$S(t) = r_i t \otimes \beta_{r,\theta_I}(t) \otimes \beta_{r,\theta_O}(t) \otimes \delta(t - d_f) = \beta_{r,\theta_\Sigma}(t) \tag{27}$$

where $\theta_\Sigma = \theta_I + \theta_O + d_f$.

Equation (27) implies that if the number of credits allocated to this flow is at least $r(\theta_I + \theta_O + d_f + f_b)$, which is the product of the service rate offered by input and output schedulers to the flow and the total round-trip latency of the credit circulation loop, then the credit-based flow control will not limit the amount of service offered to this flow. The buffered crossbar switch is equivalent to a latency-rate server with parameters r and θ_Σ in terms of the amount of service guaranteed to this flow. In this case, we say that sufficient number of credits are allocated to this flow.

On the other hand, if the total number of credits for the flow is $K < K^*$, then the service curve guaranteed by the traffic controller will be

$$S^C(t) = \inf_{m \geq 0} \left\{ \beta_{r,m\theta}(t) + mK \right\} = \begin{cases} rt & m\theta \leq t \leq m\theta + K/r \\ mK & m\theta + K/r < t < (m+1)\theta + K/r. \end{cases} \tag{28}$$

where $m = 0, 1, 2, 3, \cdots$. The lower bound of this service curve is $S_L^C(t) = r't$, where $r' = K/\theta < r$. Then the end-to-end service curve guaranteed to this flow is

$$S(t) = S^C(t) \otimes \beta_{r,\theta_I}(t) \otimes \beta_{r,\theta_O}(t) \otimes \delta(t - d_f), \tag{29}$$

which is lower bounded by

$$S_L(t) = S_L^C(t) \otimes \beta_{r,\theta_I}(t) \otimes \beta_{r,\theta_O}(t) \otimes \delta(t - d_f) = \beta_{r',\theta_\Sigma}(t). \tag{30}$$

Equation (28) and (30) imply that when the number of credits allocated for a flow is less than $r(\theta_I + \theta_O + d_f + f_b)$, the bandwidth actually received by this flow will be $r' = K/\theta$, which is less than r and is determined by the number of credits allocated to this flow and the total round-trip latency of the credit circulation loop. In this case, we say that the number of credits allocated for this flow is not sufficient. Without sufficient number of credits allocated to a flow, the credit circulation loop will become the bottleneck for packet forwarding in a buffered crossbar switch and will limit the bandwidth that is actually received by a flow.

4.2   Delay Performance Analysis

4.2.1   Delay Upper Bound for a Flow with Sufficient Number of Credits

Assume that the arrival traffic from a flow is constrained by a leaky bucket with parameters (P, ρ, σ), where P, ρ and σ are respectively the peak rate, sustained rate and the token bucket depth of the leaky bucket, then the arrival curve for the flow is $A(t) = \min\{Pt, \sigma + \rho t\}$. Suppose the input and output schedulers guarantee service curves $S_I(t) = \beta_{r,\theta_I}(t)$ and $S_O(t) = \beta_{r,\theta_O}(t)$ respectively to the flow, and the number of credits allocated to the flow is K.

If $K \geq r\theta = r(\theta_I + \theta_O + d_f + d_b)$, following (27), the service curve guaranteed to the flow is

$$S(t) = \beta_{r,\theta_\Sigma}(t) = \max\{0, r(t - \theta_\Sigma)\} \tag{31}$$

Denote by $R^{out}(t)$ the amount of service offered by the switch to the flow by time t, then $R^{out}(t) \geq S(t)$. For any packet that arrives from the flow at time t and suffers a delay d in the switch, $A(t) = R^{out}(t + d)$. Thus

$$\min\{Pt, \sigma + \rho t\} \geq A(t) = R^{out}(t + d) \geq S(t + d).$$

For $0 \leq t \leq \sigma/(P - \rho)$, $\min\{Pt, \sigma + \rho t\} = Pt$. Thus $Pt \geq S(t + d) = \max\{0, r(t + d - \theta_\Sigma)\}$. Because $Pt \geq 0$ for all $t \geq 0$, we only need $Pt \geq r(t + d - \theta_\Sigma)$. Thus we find that

$$d \leq \theta_\Sigma + \frac{P - r}{r} t \leq \theta_\Sigma + \left(\frac{P - r}{P - \rho}\right) \frac{\sigma}{r}. \tag{32}$$

For $t > \sigma/(P - \rho)$, $\min\{Pt, \sigma + \rho t\} = \sigma + \rho t$, thus $\sigma + \rho t \geq r(t + d - \theta_\Sigma)$, from which we find $d \leq \theta_\Sigma + \sigma/r - (r - \rho)t$. If $r < \rho$, delay d is not upper bounded. For $r \geq \rho$,

$$d \leq \theta_\Sigma + \frac{\sigma}{r} - (r - \rho)\frac{\sigma}{P - \rho} = \theta_\Sigma + \left(\frac{P - r}{P - \rho}\right) \frac{\sigma}{r}. \tag{33}$$

Therefore, from (32) and (33) we obtain that the delay upper bound for any packet of this flow is

$$D_{max} = \theta_\Sigma + \left(\frac{P - r}{P - \rho}\right) \frac{\sigma}{r} \qquad (r \geq \rho). \tag{34}$$

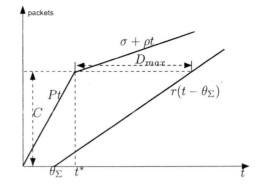

Figure 5: Delay upper bound with sufficient number of credits.

The same result can be obtained by applying (14) directly. From (14) we know that the packet delay upper bound for a flow can be determined from the maximal horizontal distance between $A(t)$ and $S(t)$ of the flow. The arrival curve $A(t)$ of the flow and the service curve $S(t)$ guaranteed to the flow with sufficient number of credits is shown in Figure 5. From this figure we can see that the delay will not be upper bounded if $r < \rho$. For $r \geq \rho$, the packet arrives at time instant t^*, which is the end of a maximal burst size, experiences the maximal delay D_{max}. Figure 5 shows that

$$t^* = \frac{\sigma}{P - \rho} \quad \text{and} \quad C = Pt^* = \frac{P\sigma}{P - \rho}.$$

Then the delay upper bound is,

$$D_{max} = \theta_\Sigma + \frac{C}{r} - t^* = \theta_\Sigma + \left(\frac{P - r}{P - \rho}\right)\frac{\sigma}{r}. \tag{35}$$

Therefore given the arrival traffic parameters, if the number of credits allocated for a flow is at least $r(\theta_I + \theta_O + d_f + f_b)$, the delay upper bound of this flow is determined by the latency and service rate parameters of input and output schedulers.

If both the input and output schedulers use the WFQ algorithm, it is known from [33] that $\theta_I = \theta_O = L(1/R + 1/r)$, then

$$D_{max} = 2L\left(\frac{1}{r} + \frac{1}{R}\right) + d_f + \left(\frac{P - r}{P - \rho}\right)\frac{\sigma}{r} \quad (r \geq \rho) \tag{36}$$

where R is the switch ingress/egress port rate and L is the internal packet length of the switch.

4.2.2   Delay Upper Bound for a Flow without Sufficient Number of Credits

Suppose a flow is not allocated sufficient credits, i.e., $K < r\theta = r(\theta_I + \theta_O + d_f + d_b)$, then from (28) and (29), the service curve guaranteed by the switch to the flow is

$$S(t) = \begin{cases} r(t - m(\theta + \theta_\Sigma)) & m\theta \leq t \leq m\theta + K/r \\ mK & m\theta + K/r < t < (m + 1)\theta + K/r. \end{cases} \tag{37}$$

where $m = 0, 1, 2, 3, \cdots$.

Figure 6 shows the arrival curve and the service curve guaranteed by the switch to this flow without sufficient number of credits. From this figure we can see that the maximum packet delay for the flow, D_{max}, occurs at a time instant t^* such that

$$Pt^* = C = \frac{P\sigma}{P - \rho} = mK, \quad m = 1, 2, 3 \cdots$$

Actually D_{max} is the maximal horizontal distance between $A(t)$ and the $S_L(t) = r't = (K/\theta)t$, which is the lower bound of the service curve guaranteed to the flow i.

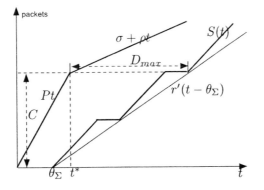

Figure 6: Delay upper bound without sufficient number of credits.

If $r' = K/\theta < \rho$, that is, $K < \rho\theta$, then the packet delay of this flow is not upper bounded.

If $r' = K/\theta \geq \rho$, that is, $K \geq \rho\theta$, then the delay upper bound for the flow is

$$D_{max} = \theta_\Sigma + \frac{C}{r'} - t^* = \theta + \left(\frac{P - r'}{P - \rho}\right) \frac{\sigma}{r'}. \tag{38}$$

4.3   Resource Allocation for QoS Provision

The delay performance analysis in the previous sub-section shows that given the arrival curve of a flow, the delay upper bound D_{max} of this flow is a function of the bandwidth r guaranteed to this flow by the switch. If $r < \rho$, i.e. the guaranteed bandwidth is less than the sustained arrival rate of the flow, the packet delay of this flow cannot be upper bounded. Equation (34) shows that the more bandwidth is allocated, the tighter is the guaranteed delay bound. The minimum possible delay bound θ_Σ, which includes scheduler latency and forward propagation delay, can be achieved when r is assigned as the peak arrival rate P. When $r = \rho$, the delay upper bound achieves the maximum possible value $D^*_{max} = T + \sigma/r$. When $P > r > \rho$, this flow is guaranteed a delay upper bound D_{max} that is between θ_Σ and D^*_{max}.

Suppose the delay budget for one flow at the switch is D_{req}, then the switch must guarantee this flow a delay upper bound no greater than D_{req}, that is,

$$D_{max} = \theta_\Sigma + \left(\frac{P - r}{P - \rho}\right) \frac{\sigma}{r} \leq D_{req}. \tag{39}$$

Given the arrival traffic profile (P, ρ, σ), the delay requirement is satisfied by guaranteeing enough bandwidth to this flow. If $D_{req} \geq D^*_{max}$, the required bandwidth is just the sustained rate of the flow, i.e., $r = \rho$. If $D_{req} < D^*_{max}$, the required amount of bandwidth is

$$r = \frac{P\sigma}{(P - \rho)(D_{req} - \theta_\Sigma) + \sigma}. \tag{40}$$

This equation implies that the require bandwidth is always less than the peak rate P and $r \to P$ as arrival traffic becomes more smooth, i.e. $\rho \to P$.

If both input and output schedulers employ the WFQ algorithm, then $\theta_I = \theta_O = L(1/R + 1/r)$ and $\theta_\Sigma = 2L(1/R + 1/r) + d_f$. Thus from (40) the required bandwidth is

$$r = \frac{P\sigma}{(P - \rho)(D_{req} - 2L(1/R + 1/r) - d_f) + \sigma} \tag{41}$$

Simple algebra manipulation shows that the required bandwidth is

$$r = \frac{P\sigma + L(P - \rho)}{(P - \rho)(D_{req} - L/R) + \sigma}. \tag{42}$$

From the relation between bandwidth guarantee and credit allocation given by (27) and (30), we know that the required number of credits for guaranteing bandwidth r to a flow is at least $C_{req} = r(\theta_I + \theta_o + d_f + d_b)$. Therefore from (40) we can get that the number of credits required to achieve a delay objective D_{req} is

$$C_{req} = \frac{P\sigma(\theta_I + \theta_o + d_f + d_b)}{(P - \rho)(D_{req} - \theta_\Sigma) + \sigma} = \frac{P\sigma\theta}{(P - \rho)(D_{req} - \theta_\Sigma) + \sigma}. \tag{43}$$

where θ which is the total round-trip latency of credit circulation loop while θ_Σ is the total packet forwarding latency in the switch. From (43) we can see that the required number of credits is upper bounded by $P\theta$, and this upper bound is approached when either $\rho \to P$ or $D_{req} \to \theta_\Sigma$.

To understand the influences of the variations of traffic parameters (P, ρ, σ) and the delay objective D_{req} on credit requirement, we calculate the derivatives of C_{req} with respective to these parameters:

$$\frac{\partial C_{req}}{\partial \sigma} = \frac{P\theta(P - \rho)(D_{req} - \theta_\Sigma)}{[(P - \rho)(D_{req} - \theta_\Sigma) + \sigma]^2}, \tag{44}$$

$$\frac{\partial C_{req}}{\partial \rho} = \frac{P\sigma\theta(D_{req} - \theta_\Sigma)}{[(P - \rho)(D_{req} - \theta_\Sigma) + \sigma]^2}, \tag{45}$$

$$\frac{\partial C_{req}}{\partial P} = \frac{\sigma\theta[\sigma - \rho(D_{req} - \theta_\Sigma)]}{[(P - \rho)(D_{req} - \theta_\Sigma) + \sigma]^2}, \tag{46}$$

$$\frac{\partial C_{req}}{\partial D_{req}} = -\frac{P\sigma\theta(P - \rho)}{[(P - \rho)(D_{req} - \theta_\Sigma) + \sigma]^2}. \tag{47}$$

Equation (44) shows that $\frac{\partial C_{req}}{\partial \sigma} > 0$ when $P > \rho$ and $D_{req} > \theta_\Sigma$, which is always true. So the required number of credits increases when the burstiness of arrival traffic increases.

The function $\frac{\partial C_{req}}{\partial \sigma}$ is a decreasing function of σ, which implies that changing of the arrival traffic burstiness around a smaller value has stronger influence on the required number of credits than the changing of burstiness around a larger value.

Equation (45) shows that $\frac{\partial C_{req}}{\partial \rho} > 0$ when $D_{req} > \theta_\Sigma$. Therefore, the required number of credits increases with the sustained arrival rate. Function $\frac{\partial C_{req}}{\partial \rho}$ is a increasing function of ρ, which implies that changing the sustained arrival rate around a larger value has stronger influence on the required number of credits than changing the sustained arrival rate around a smaller value.

Equation (46) shows that $\frac{\partial C_{req}}{\partial P} \geq 0$ when $\sigma \geq \rho(D_{req} - \theta_\Sigma)$, and $\frac{\partial C_{req}}{\partial P} < 0$ when $\sigma < \rho(D_{req} - \theta_\Sigma)$. This implies that the influence of peak rate variation on C_{req} depends on other traffic parameters σ, ρ and the delay requirement D_{req}. The function $\frac{\partial C_{req}}{\partial P}$ is a decreasing function of P, which means that changing the arrival peak rate around a smaller value has stronger influence on the required number of credits than the changing of arrival peak rate around a larger value.

Equation (47) shows that $\frac{\partial C_{req}}{\partial D_{req}} < 0$, which implies that tighter delay requirement requires more credits. The absolute value of function $\frac{\partial C_{req}}{\partial D_{req}}$ decreases when D_{req} increases, which means that changing the delay requirement around a smaller value has stronger influence on the required number of credits than the changing of delay requirement around a larger value.

In summary, to achieve a packet delay objective D_{req} for a flow in a buffered crossbar switch, both input and output schedulers of the switch must allocate sufficient bandwidth to this flow, which is given by (40). To guarantee that this bandwidth is actually received by the flow, sufficient number of credits must be allocated to the flow, which is at least the product of the allocated bandwidth and the total round-trip latency of the credit circulation loop. Since it is typical for a credit-based flow control system to set the credit number of a flow to be the buffer space allocated to the flow, the credit requirement given by (43) tells us the required cross-point buffer space for a flow.

4.4 Numerical Examples

In this subsection, we use numerical examples to illustrate the application of the developed techniques for delay analysis and resource allocation. We assume that each scheduler uses the WFQ algorithm, the internal packet length is $L = 40$ bytes, and the switch ingress/egress port rate is $R = 10$ Gb/s.

Consider two classes of traffic, video traffic and packet voice traffic, which arrive at the same ingress port of a switch. Each traffic class is an aggregation of traffic generated from a set of single traffic sources. The aggregated video traffic class is constrained by a leaky bucket with peak rate $P_v = 5.3$ Gb/s, sustained rate $\rho_v = 1.5$ Gb/s, and burstiness $\sigma_v = 140$ Mbits. The aggregated packet voice traffic class is constrained by a leaky bucket with peak rate $P_a = 3.2$ Gb/s, sustained rate $\rho_a = 1.1$ Gb/s, and burstiness $\sigma_a = 715$ Mbits.

Figure 7 shows delay objectives and the required amount of bandwidth for the video and voice traffic classes, denoted respectively by r_v and r_a. We can see that for both video and voice traffic, the required bandwidth increases when the delay objective becomes tighter,

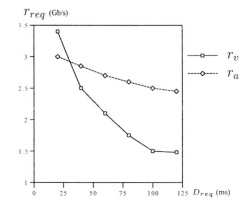

Figure 7: Delay objectives and required bandwidth for video and voice traffic classes.

and the bandwidth for video traffic r_v increases faster than the bandwidth for voice traffic r_a. When D_{req} for the voice traffic class is larger than a threshold (100 ms in this example), the required bandwidth r_v approaches the sustained arrival rate ρ_v.

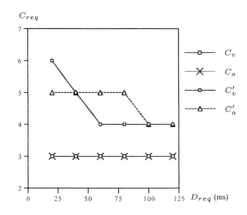

Figure 8: Delay objectives and required number of credits for video and voice traffic classes.

Figure 8 gives delay objectives D_{req}, the required number of credits for the video and voice classes when $d_f = d_b = 30$ ns, which are denoted respectively by C_v and C_a, and the required number of credits for the video and audio classes when $d_f = d_b = 150$ ns, which are denoted respectively by C'_c and C'_a. This figure shows that when the propagation delay is small (30 ns in this example), both traffic classes require the same number of credits for all delay objectives. This is because the product of bandwidth and propagation delay is small, so C_{req} does not increase much with bandwidth. When the propagation delay is not ignorable (150 ns in this example), the bandwidth delay product is larger and the required number of credits will increase with the allocated bandwidth.

5 QoS Performance Comparison between Buffered Crossbar Switches and OQ Switches

From Sections 2 and 3 we know that the OQ switch is an ideal case that achieves optimal QoS performance, but output-queueing emulation is not a practical approach for QoS provision in buffered crossbar switches. In Section 4, we presented the network calculus-based model and techniques for providing QoS in buffered crossbar switches, which can guarantee minimum bandwidth and maximum packet delay for a flow without output-queueing emulation. In this section, we compare the achievable bandwidth and delay guarantees in buffered crossbar switches with the QoS performance guaranteed by OQ switches. Toward this end, we first apply the network calculus-based techniques to model and analyze the OQ switch.

5.1 OQ Switch Modeling and Analysis

The traffic control system in an OQ switch for a flow f is shown in the Figure 9. The X_i and Y_j are respectively the arrival ingress module and departure egress module of the flow. The propagation delay from ingress to egress ports is denoted by d_f. Since the output scheduler G_j^O is the only server in the system, if d_f is ignorable, the service curve guaranteed by this system to the flow f is equal to the service curve guaranteed by the scheduler G_j^O to the flow. Suppose G_j^O is a latency-rate server with parameter (r_o, θ_o) for the flow f, then the service curve guaranteed by the OQ switch to f is

$$S^O(t) = r_o(t - \theta_o). \tag{48}$$

Since the service rate parameter of a LR service curve specifies the minimum bandwidth offered to a flow by the server [33], equation (48) implies that the minimal bandwidth guaranteed by the OQ switch to a flow is equal to the service rate, r_o, allocated to the flow at the output scheduler.

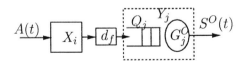

Figure 9: Traffic control system in OQ switch.

Suppose the arrival traffic from the flow f is constrained by a leaky bucket with parameters (P, ρ, σ), i.e., $A(t) = \min\{Pt, \sigma + \rho t\}$. Following (14) and similar analysis in Section 4, we obtain that the delay upper bound guaranteed to the flow f by the OQ switch is

$$D_{max}^O = \theta_o + \left(\frac{P - r_o}{P - \rho}\right)\frac{\sigma}{r_o}. \tag{49}$$

If the OQ switch employs WFQ algorithm at each output scheduler, then the latency parameter guaranteed by the output scheduler for the flow f will be $\theta_o = L(1/R + 1/r_o)$, where L and R are respectively the internal packet length and the ingress/egress port rate of the OQ switch. Therefore, the delay upper bound guaranteed to the flow is

$$D_{max}^O = L \left(\frac{1}{R} + \frac{1}{r_o} \right) + \left(\frac{P - r_o}{P - \rho} \right) \frac{\sigma}{r_o}. \tag{50}$$

5.2   QoS Performance Comparison

5.2.1   Minimum Bandwidth Comparison

Suppose the OQ switch output scheduler G_j^O allocates a service rate r_o to the flow f, then the service curve guaranteed to the flow by the OQ switch will be

$$S^O(t) = r_o(t - \theta_o). \tag{51}$$

Suppose the buffered crossbar switch offers the service rate r at both ingress and egress schedulers and allocates sufficient number of credits to the flow f, then the service curve guaranteed by the buffered crossbar switch to the flow will be

$$S^C(t) = r(t - \theta_I - \theta_E - d_f). \tag{52}$$

The latency parameter of an egress scheduler in the buffered crossbar switch is denoted by θ_E in this section to distinguish it from θ_o, the latency parameter of the output scheduler of an OQ switch.

Since the rate parameter of a LR service curve reflects the guaranteed minimal bandwidth, Comparison between (51) and (52) tells us that the buffered crossbar switch can guarantee an identical bandwidth lower bound to the flow f as the OQ switch does, if the service rate offered to the flow by ingress and egress schedulers is $r = r_o$ and sufficient cross-point buffer space to allocated the flow. Please notice that neither switching fabric speedup nor complex control algorithm is required here. The buffered crossbar switch still use the simple LR-class scheduling policy such as WFQ, which has been implemented in many practical packet switches.

5.2.2   Maximum Packet Delay Comparison

Given the arrival curve $A(t) = \min\{Pt, \sigma + \rho t\}$ for the flow f, if both the buffered crossbar switch and the OQ switch guarantee the same bandwidth to the flow, i.e. $r = r_o$, then by comparing (49) and (34) we find that the difference in the delay bounds guaranteed by the two switches is

$$\Delta D_{max} = \theta_\Sigma + \left(\frac{P - r}{P - \rho} \right) \frac{\sigma}{r} - \theta_o - \left(\frac{P - r_o}{P - \rho} \right) \frac{\sigma}{r_o} = \theta_\Sigma - \theta_o \tag{53}$$

From (53) we can see that the delay upper bound guaranteed by the buffered crossbar switch is greater than that of the OQ switch. The increment is the difference between the total packet forwarding latency in the two switches, because packets pass one more scheduler in the buffered crossbar switch than in the OQ switch.

Suppose both switches employ WFQ at each scheduler, then $\theta_I = \theta_E = \theta_o = L\left(\frac{1}{R} + \frac{1}{r}\right)$. From (53) we have

$$\Delta D_{max} = L\left(\frac{1}{R} + \frac{1}{r}\right).$$

(54)

Equations (53) and (54) imply that the difference in the delay bounds guaranteed by the two switches is associated with the allocated service rate r for the flow, the internal packet length L, and the switch I/O port rate R. Given a service rate, shorter internal packet length and higher I/O port rate lead to less increment in the guaranteed delay upper bound. Most high-speed packet switches have fast I/O port and short internal packet, for example $R > 1$ Gb/s and $L < 100$ bytes. This implies that the worst case delay performance achieved by most buffered crossbar switches can be very close to what are guaranteed by OQ switches. Given the values of L and R, equation (54) shows that ΔD_{max} is a decreasing function of r, which implies that a highly aggregated flow that requires more bandwidth in the buffered crossbar switch can be guaranteed a closer delay bound to what is achieved in the OQ switch.

5.2.3   Resource Allocation Comparison

Let D_{req} be the delay objective for a flow f. From equation (49) we derive that the required bandwidth in the OQ switch to guarantee D_{req} is

$$r^O_{req} = \frac{P\sigma}{(P - \rho)(D_{req} - \theta_o) + \sigma}.$$

(55)

Equation (43) gives the required bandwidth in the buffered crossbar switch to guarantee the same D_{req}

$$r^C_{req} = \frac{P\sigma}{(P - \rho)(D_{req} - \theta_\Sigma) + \sigma}.$$

(56)

Suppose identical LR-class scheduling policy is applied at each scheduler of both switches, we can assume that the latency parameters guaranteed by ingress/egress schedulers in the buffered crossbar switch and output schedulers in the OQ switch are equal; that is $\theta_I = \theta_E = \theta_o = \theta$. Thus, the bandwidth allocation increment is

$$\Delta r_{req} = r^C_{req} - r^O_{req} = \frac{(P - \rho)P\sigma\theta}{[(P - \rho)(D_{req} - 2\theta) + \sigma][(P - \rho)(D_{req} - \theta) + \sigma]}.$$

(57)

Equation (57) implies that more bandwidth is needed in the buffered crossbar switch than in the OQ switch to guarantee the same delay objective. The increment in bandwidth allocation is a function of the delay objective D_{req}, the traffic parameters (P, ρ, σ), and the scheduler latency parameter θ. For a given flow, the Δr_{req} is a decreasing function of D_{req}, which means that the tighter the delay objective is, the more is the bandwidth increment. Suppose both switches employ WFQ at each scheduler, then $\theta = L\left(\frac{1}{R} + \frac{1}{r}\right)$. Thus,

$$r^O_{req} = \frac{P\sigma + L(P - \rho)}{(P - \rho)(D_{req} - L/R) + \sigma} \approx \frac{P\sigma + L(P - \rho)}{(P - \rho)D_{req} + \sigma}$$

(58)

$$r_{req}^C = \frac{P\sigma + 2L(P - \rho)}{(P - \rho)(D_{req} - 2L/R) + \sigma} \approx \frac{P\sigma + 2L(P - \rho)}{(P - \rho)D_{req} + \sigma} \qquad (59)$$

We made the above approximations in (58) and (59) because the ratio L/R is ignorable for typical high-speed packet switches. Then the bandwidth allocation increment is

$$\Delta r_{req} = \frac{L(P - \rho)}{(P - \rho)D_{req} + \sigma}. \qquad (60)$$

Equation (60) shows that Δr_{req} is a decreasing function of D_{req} and an increasing function of L. This implies that buffered crossbar switches with WFQ packet scheduling should use a short internal packet length to reduce the bandwidth allocation increment for achieving identical delay guarantee performance as OQ switches.

5.3   Numerical Examples for Performance Comparison

The examples given in this subsection assume that both the buffered crossbar switch and the OQ switch apply WFQ algorithm at each scheduler and have 1 Gb/s ingress/egress rate. We consider a flow constrained by a leaky bucket with parameters $P = 3.9$ Mb/s, $\rho = 1.1$ Mb/s, and $\sigma = 143$ kbits.

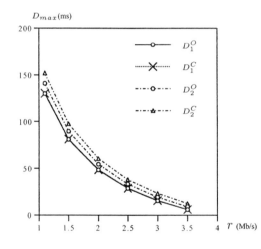

Figure 10: Delay upper bounds guaranteed by a buffered crossbar switch and an OQ switch.

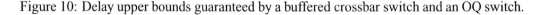

The allocated bandwidth and the guaranteed delay upper bounds for the flow in the two switches are given in Figure 10. In this figure, the D_1^O and D_1^C are respectively delay bounds guaranteed by the OQ switch and the buffered crossbar switch with an internal packet length $L = 50$ bytes; the D_2^O and D_2^C are respectively delay bounds guaranteed by the OQ switch and the buffered crossbar switch with an internal packet length $L = 1000$ bytes. From this figure we can see that D_1^O and D_1^C are indistinguishable, which means that delay upper bounds guaranteed by the two switches are very close if L is small. This figure also shows that D_2^O and D_2^C are distinct from each other, which implies that the difference in delay guarantees increases with the internal packet length L.

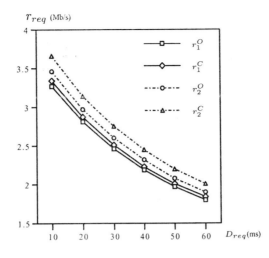

Figure 11: Bandwidth allocation in a buffered crossbar switch and an OQ switch.

The delay objectives and the required amount of bandwidth in the two switches are given in Figure 11. In this figure, the r_1^O and r_1^C are respectively the required bandwidth in the OQ switch and the buffered crossbar switch when $L = 50$ bytes; the r_2^O and r_2^C are respectively the required bandwidth in the OQ switch and the buffered crossbar switch when $L = 1000$ bytes. This figure shows that r_1^O and r_1^C are very close and r_2^O and r_2^C are more distinct. This implies that the required amounts bandwidth in the two switches for achieving the same delay objective are very close if L small, and become distinct for larger L.

6 QoS Provision in Multistage Buffered Crossbar Switches

For constructing a packet switch with a huge number of ingress/egress ports, a group of buffered crossbar switching fabrics need to be interconnected according to a certain topology. We call the switching system obtained in this way a *multistage buffered crossbar switch*, and call the switch with a single buffered crossbar switching fabric a *single-stage buffered crossbar switch*. In this section, we study QoS provision in multistage buffered crossbar switches. The model and techniques developed in Section 4 for single-stage buffered crossbar switches can be extended to the multistage case. In this section, we focus our study on the three-stage switch architecture constructed by following the Benes topology, which will be described in the following sub-section.

6.1 Multistage Buffered Crossbar Switch Architecture

Figure 12 illustrates the architecture of an $N^2 \times N^2$ multistage buffered crossbar switch constructed by interconnecting a group switching elements according to the three-stage Benês network. Each switching element is an $N \times N$ single-stage buffered crossbar switching fabric. Denote $X_i, i = 1, 2, \cdots, N^2$, as the ith ingress port and denote $Y_j, i = 1, 2, \cdots, N^2$, as the jth egress port of the multistage switch. There are N switching elements at each stage. The ith switching element at the jth stage is denoted as $E_{i,j}$ $(i = 1, 2, 3; j = 1, 2, \ldots, N)$. Each first-stage switching element has N input lines that are connected with N ingress port modules, and the collection of ingress ports connected to the same first-stage switching element is referred to as an *ingress port cluster*. Each third-stage switching element has N output lines connected with N egress port modules, and the collection of egress ports that are connected to the same third-stage switching element is referred to as an *egress port cluster*. Each output port of a first-stage switching element is connected to an input port of a distinct switching element at the middle stage. Each input port of a third-stage switching element is connected with an output port of a distinct switching element at the middle stage. Therefore, there are N parallel paths between any first-stage switching element and any third-stage switching element of the multistage switch, where each path traverses one of the N middle stage switching elements. Traffic between one ingress port cluster and one egress port cluster share the same set of parallel paths.

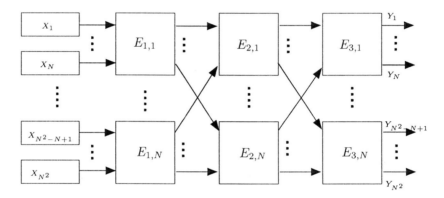

Figure 12: Multistage buffered crossbar switch architecture.

Each ingress port module has input buffers, and each switching element has a buffer at each cross-point. There is a scheduler at each ingress port module to control packets forwarded from the input buffer to cross-point buffers in the first-stage switching elements. The output port of each switching element has a scheduler to control packets forwarded from cross-point buffers of this switching element to cross-point buffers at the next stage. Credit-based flow control is applied between ingress modules and the first-stage switching elements and also applied between the first and second-stage and between the second and third-stage switching elements.

6.2   Traffic Control Model for Multistage Buffered Crossbar Switches

Various traffic control approaches can be applied in a multistage buffered crossbar switch. An end-to-end traffic control mechanism is considered in this section, which treats each class of traffic between a pair of ingress-egress ports as an end-to-end flow in the switch. Each one of such flows is assigned to one of the parallel paths between its arrival ingress port and the destined egress port according to some load balancing policy. For each end-to-end flow, there are three credit circulation loops, namely the credit circulation loop between the arrival ingress module and the first-stage switching element that this flow passes, the credit circulation loop between the first and second-stage switching elements through which this flow passes, and the credit circulation loop between the second and the third-stage switching elements through which this flow passes. There a logical queue and a credit pool for each flow at each switching element that the flow passes.

The path through which an end-to-end flow traverses a multistage buffered crossbar switch is shown in Figure 13. This path consists of the following components: the VOQ V for this flow at its arrival ingress port module, the scheduler G_0 at the ingress port module, the logical queues for this flow at the first, second, and third-stage switching elements, denoted by Q_1, Q_2, and Q_3 respectively, and the schedulers at the first, second, and third stages, denoted by G_1, G_2, and G_3 respectively. Credits allocated for this flow are circulated between each pair of adjacent stages to control the amount of service offered to this flow by the scheduler at each stage. The traffic controllers C_i ($i = 0, 1, 2$) are added in front of the corresponding schedulers to represent the influence of the credit circulation at that stage. The total number of credits allocated to this flow at the ith stage is denoted by K_i, $i = 1, 2, 3$. The forward propagation delay from the $(i-1)$-st to the ith stage is denoted by d_i^f, and the backward propagation delay from the ith to the $(i-1)$-st stage is denoted by d_i^b, $i = 1, 2, 3$.

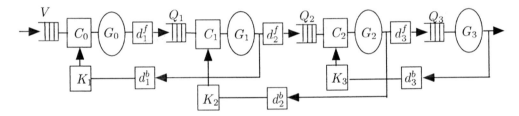

Figure 13: The path through which a flow traverses a multi-stage buffered crossbar switch.

The network calculus-based approach can also be applied to model and analyze this multistage traffic control system. Let $S_0(t)$ denote the service curve guaranteed by the ingress port scheduler, G_0, and $S_i(t)$, $i = 1, 2, 3$, be the service curves guaranteed by the first, second, and third-stage schedulers respectively. The key to obtaining the service curve guaranteed by the multistage switch to an end-to-end flow is to determine the service curve guaranteed to this flow by each traffic controller C_i, which is denoted as $S_i^c(t)$, $i = 0, 1, 2$. After obtaining $S_i^c(t)$, we can get the actual service curves guaranteed by the scheduler at each stage under the credit-based flow control, which are denoted by $S_i^*(t)$, $i = 0, 1, 2$. Toward this end, we decompose the system shown in Figure 13 into three subsystems, each contains one credit circulation loop. By applying a similar analysis we did for the single-stage case, the $S_i^c(t)$ can be calculated stage-by-stage.

We first consider the subsystem that consists of the path segment from the second-stage switching element output port to the third-stage switching element, which is shown in Figure 14. Upon comparing Figure 14 and Figure 3 we can see that this subsystem is identical to the path through which a flow traverses a single-stage buffered crossbar switch. Following the same analysis procedure as the single-stage case, this subsystem with a closed credit

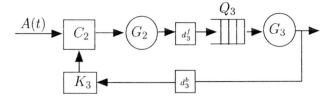

Figure 14: The path segment between the second and the third stages.

circulation loop can be modelled by an service curve-based open loop system shown in Figure 15. Suppose in this open loop system the service curve guaranteed by the schedulers G_2 and G_3 are respectively $S_2(t)$ and $S_3(t)$, then the service curve guaranteed by the traffic controller C_2 will be

$$S_2^c(t) = \inf_{m \geq 0} \left\{ (S_{F_3}(t) + K_3)^{(m)} \right\}, \tag{61}$$

where $S_{F_3}(t) = S_2(t) \otimes \delta(t - d_3^f) \otimes S_3(t) \otimes \delta(t - d_3^b)$. Therefore, the service curve guaranteed to the flow by the second-stage scheduler G_2 is

$$S_2^*(t) = S_2^c(t) \otimes S_2(t). \tag{62}$$

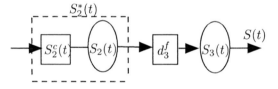

Figure 15: The model for the path segment between the second and the third stages.

Following the same procedure, the path segment between the first and the third stages can be modelled as an open loop system shown in Figure 16. Suppose the service curve guaranteed by the scheduler G_1 be $S_1(t)$, then the service curve guaranteed by the first-stage traffic controller C_1 is

$$S_1^c(t) = \inf_{m \geq 0} \left\{ (S_{F_2}(t) + K_2)^{(m)} \right\}, \tag{63}$$

where $S_{F_2}(t) = S_1(t) \otimes \delta(t - d_2^f) \otimes S_2^*(t) \otimes \delta(t - d_2^b)$, and the service curve guaranteed by the first-stage scheduler G_1 to this flow is

$$S_1^*(t) = S_1^c(t) \otimes S_1(t). \tag{64}$$

The end-to-end path for the flow, which is shown in Figure 13, can be modelled by an end-to-end open loop system shown in Figure 17. In this system, the service curve guaranteed by the traffic controller at the ingress port module C_0 is

$$S_0^c(t) = \inf_{m \geq 0} \left\{ (S_{F_1}(t) + K_1)^{(m)} \right\}, \tag{65}$$

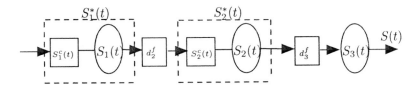

Figure 16: The model for the path segment between the first and the third stages.

where $S_{F_1}(t) = S_0(t) \otimes \delta(t - d_1^f) \otimes S_1^*(t) \otimes \delta(t - d_1^b)$, the service curve guaranteed by the ingress port scheduler G_0 to this flow is

$$S_0^*(t) = S_0^c(t) \otimes S_0(t). \tag{66}$$

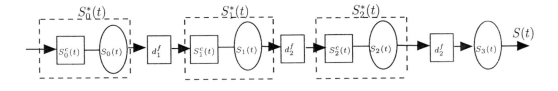

Figure 17: Model the the end-to-end path of a flow in the multistage buffered crossbar switch.

Therefore, the service curve guaranteed by the entire multistage switch to the end-to-end flow can be obtained by the convolution of the service curve actually guaranteed by the scheduler at each stage and the total forward propagation delay, i.e.,

$$S(t) = S_0^*(t) \otimes S_1^*(t) \otimes S_2^*(t) \otimes S_3(t) \otimes \delta(t - d_\Sigma^f), \tag{67}$$

where $d_\Sigma^f = d_1^f + d_2^f + d_3^f$.

6.3   Performance Analysis and Resource Allocation

In this subsection we analyze the delay performance and determine the required amount of bandwidth and buffer space for QoS provision in multistage buffered crossbar switches. Suppose that the scheduler at each stage employs a LR server, and each scheduler G_i ($i = 0, 1, 2, 3$) guarantees a service rate r and latency θ_i to an end-to-end flow, i.e.,

$$S_i(t) = \beta_{r,\theta_i}(t) = \max\{0, r(t - \theta_i)\} \quad i \in \{0, 1, 2, 3\}. \tag{68}$$

We first consider the credit circulation between the second-stage switching element output to the third-stage switch element.

$$S_{F_3}(t) = \beta_{r,\theta_2}(t) \otimes \beta_{r,\theta_3}(t) \otimes \delta(t - d_3^f - d_3^b) = \max\{0, r(t - \theta_{2,3})\},$$

where $\theta_{2,3} = \theta_2 + d_3^f + \theta_3 + d_3^b$. From (61), the service curve guaranteed by the traffic controller before the scheduler G_2 is

$$S_2^c(t) = \inf_{m \geq 0}\left\{(\beta_{r,\theta_{2,3}}(t))^{(m)} + mK_3\right\} = \inf_{m \geq 0}\left\{\beta_{r,m\theta_{2,3}}(t) + mK_3\right\}. \tag{69}$$

Comparison between equations (69) and (20) shows that they have the same form. Therefore, from a similar analysis we can get that if $K_3 \geq r(\theta_2 + d_3^f + \theta_3 + d_3^b)$, then

$$S_2^c(t) = \inf_{m \geq 0} \left\{ \beta_{r,m\theta_{2,3}}(t) + mK_3 \right\} = rt \quad \text{and} \quad S_2^*(t) = rt \otimes S_2(t) = S_2(t). \quad (70)$$

On the other hand, if $K_3 < r(\theta_2 + d_3^f + \theta_3 + d_3^b)$, then $S_2^*(t) = S_2^c(t) \otimes S_2(t) < S_2(t)$. This implies that in order to guarantee the bandwidth r to the end-to-end flow at the second-stage scheduler, the number of credits that must be allocated between the second and the third stages is at least $r(\theta_2 + d_3^f + \theta_3 + d_3^b)$.

For the credit circulation loop between the first and the second stages, we have

$$S_{F_2}(t) = \max\{0, r(t - (\theta_{1,2})\} \quad \text{and} \quad S_1^c(t) = \inf_{m \geq 0} \left\{ \beta_{r,m\theta_{1,2}}(t) + mK_2 \right\}, \quad (71)$$

where $\theta_{1,2} = \theta_1 + d_2^f + \theta_2 + d_2^b$. The service curve $S_1^c(t)$ has the same form as $S_2^c(t)$. Therefore, from similar analysis we can find that $S_1^*(t) = rt \otimes S_1(t) = S_1(t)$ if $K_2 \geq r(\theta_1 + d_2^f + \theta_2 + d_2^b)$, otherwise $S_1^*(t) = S_1^c(t) \otimes S_1(t) < S_1(t)$. That is, the number of credits that must be allocated at the first stage to guarantee bandwidth r to the end-to-end flow at that stage is at least $r(\theta_1 + d_2^f + \theta_2 + d_2^b)$.

For the credit circulation between the ingress module and the first stage, we have

$$S_{F_1}(t) = \max\{0, r(t - \theta_{0,1})\} \quad \text{and} \quad S_0^c(t) = \inf_{m \geq 0} \left\{ \beta_{r,m\theta_{0,1}}(t) + mK_1 \right\}, \quad (72)$$

where $\theta_{0,1} = \theta_0 + d_1^f + \theta_1 + d_1^b$. The $S_0^c(t)$ is also in the same form as $S_1^c(t)$ and $S_2^c(t)$. Similarly we can get that $S_0^*(t) = rt \otimes S_0(t) = S_0(t)$ if $K_1 \geq r(\theta_0 + d_1^f + \theta_1 + d_1^b)$, otherwise $S_0^*(t) = S_0^c(t) \otimes S_0(t) < S_0(t)$. This implies that to guarantee bandwidth r to the end-to-end flow at the ingress scheduler, the number of credits that must be be allocated at the ingress module to this flow is at least $r(\theta_0 + d_1^f + \theta_1 + d_1^b)$.

Put all the above analysis together we can see that if the number of credits allocated for the end-to-end flow at each stage satisfies that

$$K_1 \geq r(\theta_0 + d_1^f + \theta_1 + d_1^b), \quad K_2 \geq r(\theta_1 + d_2^f + \theta_2 + d_2^b), \quad \text{and} \quad K_3 \geq r(\theta_2 + d_3^f + \theta_3 + d_3^b),$$

then

$$S_0^*(t) = S_0(t), \quad S_1^*(t) = S_1(t), \quad \text{and} \quad S_2^*(t) = S_2(t).$$

The end-to-end service curve guaranteed to this flow by the multistage switch is then

$$\begin{aligned} S(t) &= S_0^*(t) \otimes S_1^*(t) \otimes S_2^*(t) \otimes S_3(t) \otimes \delta(t - d_\Sigma^f) \\ &= \max \left\{ 0, r[t - (\theta_0 + \theta_1 + \theta_2 + \theta_3 + d_\Sigma^f)] \right\} \\ &= \max \left\{ 0, r(t - \theta_\Sigma) \right\}, \end{aligned} \quad (73)$$

where $d_\Sigma^f = \sum_{i=1}^3 d_i^f$ and $\theta_\Sigma = \sum_{i=0}^3 \theta_i + d_\Sigma^f$.

Equation (73) implies that if the scheduler at each stage is a LR server and sufficient credits are allocated for an end-to-end flow in each credit circulation loop, then the end-to-end path through which this flow transverses the multistage switch is equivalent to a single

LR server that guarantees a service rate r and a latency θ_Σ to this flow. Here r is the service rate allocated by each stage for this flow, and θ_Σ is the summation of total scheduler latency parameters and the total forward propagation delay. This is identical to the single-stage case in the sense that the service curve guaranteed to a flow is in the form of a service curve guaranteed by a LR server if sufficient credits are allocated to this flow. Therefore, given the arrival traffic profile and a delay objective for an end-to-end flow, the required amount of bandwidth and number of credits that the multistage switch must allocate to this flow at each stage can be determined from a similar analysis as the single-stage case.

Suppose a flow f has an arrival envelope $A(t) = \min\{Pt, \sigma + \rho t\}$ and the service curve guaranteed to this flow by the multistage switch is $S(t) = \max\{0, r(t - \theta_\Sigma)\}$. From (34), the delay upper bound guaranteed to this flow by the multistage switch is

$$D_{max} = \theta_\Sigma + \left(\frac{P - r}{P - \rho}\right)\frac{\sigma}{r} \quad (r \geq \rho). \tag{74}$$

Given a delay objective D_{req}, the bandwidth that must be allocated at each stage for this flow is

$$r = \begin{cases} \rho, & \text{for } D_{req} \geq \theta_\Sigma + \sigma/r; \\ \frac{P\sigma}{(P-\rho)(D_{req}-\theta_\Sigma)+\sigma}, & \text{for } D_{req} < \theta_\Sigma + \sigma/r. \end{cases} \tag{75}$$

That is, if $D_{req} \geq \theta_\Sigma + \sigma/r$, the required bandwidth to guarantee this delay objective is just the sustained arrival rate of this flow. If $D_{req} < \theta_\Sigma + \sigma/r$, more bandwidth than the sustained rate must be allocated to achieve the delay objective.

The number of credits that must be allocated at each stage, which gives the required cross-point buffer space at that stage, for guaranteeing the allocated bandwidth r can be calculated as

$$C_{req}^1 = r(\theta_0+d_1^f+\theta_1+d_1^b), \quad C_{req}^2 = r(\theta_1+d_2^f+\theta_2+d_2^b), \quad \text{and} \quad C_{req}^3 = r(\theta_2+d_3^f+\theta_3+d_3^b). \tag{76}$$

That is, in order to actually offer the allocated bandwidth to a flow at each stage, the required cross-point buffer space for the flow at that stage is the product of the bandwidth and the total round-trip latency of the credit-circulation loop at that stage.

6.4   Numerical Examples

The examples given in this subsection assume that schedulers at each stage of the multistage switch use the WFQ algorithm, the internal packet length is $L = 40$ bytes, the I/O rate of each switching elements is $R = 10$ Gb/s, and the propagation delay between any two successive stages is 30 ns. We consider the same video and packet voice traffic classes as in the examples given in subsection 4.4 for a single-stage buffered crossbar switch; that is, the video traffic class has peak rate $P_v = 5.3$ Gb/s, sustained rate $\rho_v = 1.5$ Gb/s, and burstiness $\sigma_v = 140$ Mbits, and the packet voice traffic class has peak rate $P_a = 3.2$ Gb/s, sustained rate $\rho_a = 1.1$ Gb/s, and burstiness $\sigma_a = 715$ Mbits.

The delay objectives and the required bandwidth for each traffic class for achieving the objectives are given in Figure 18. On comparing Figure 18 with Figure 7 we can see that to guarantee the same delay objective, the amount of bandwidth required for an end-to-end flow in the multistage switch is almost equal to the required amount of bandwidth for a flow

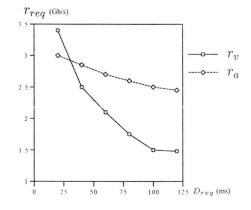

Figure 18: Delay objectives and required bandwidth for video and audio traffic classes in a multistage buffered crossbar switch.

in the single-stage switch. Therefore, the number of credits that must be allocated for an end-to-end flow at each stage of the multistage switch is also approximately equal to the number of credits required in a single-stage switch. This can be explained from equation (40) and equation (75). For the single-stage switch, $\theta_\Sigma = 2L(1/R + 1/r)$, so the required bandwidth to guarantee D_{req} is $r_s = [2L + P\sigma/(P - \rho)]/[D_{req} + \sigma/(P - \rho) - 2L/R - d_f]$. In the multistage switch, $\theta_\Sigma = 4L(1/R + 1/r)$, the required bandwidth to guarantee D_{req} is $r_m = [4L + P\sigma/(P - \rho)]/(D_{req} + \sigma/(P - \rho) - 4L/R - 3d_f)$. Therefore, when L is small (40 bytes in this example), R is large (10 Gb/s in this example), and propagation delay d_f is small (30 ns in this example), $r_m \approx r_s$. However, when the forward propagation delay cannot be neglected, we will see that more bandwidth is required in the multistage switch than in the single-stage switch to guarantee the same delay objective. Figure 19 shows the required bandwidth for a single-stage switch and a multistage switch with large forward propagation delay ($d_f = 10$ ms). In Figure 19, r_{s1} and r_{m1} are the required bandwidth for the video traffic classes in the single-stage and multistage switches respectively; r_{s2} and r_{m2} are the required bandwidth for the packet voice traffic classes in the single-stage and multistage switches respectively. We can see that more bandwidth must be allocated in the multistage switch to guarantee the same delay objective. Notice that this increase in required bandwidth is non-trivial unless the delay objective is large.

7   QoS Provision in Buffered Crossbar Switches with Traffic Aggregation

The traffic control complexity in a buffered crossbar switch increases with the number of flows that traverse the switch. Resource allocation based on individual flows may lower resource utilization due to the lack of resource sharing among flows. One approach for simplifying traffic control and improving resource utilization in buffered crossbar switches is to forward streams of packets in an aggregated manner. Typically, packet switches aggregate the set of flows arrive at an ingress port into a couple of Forwarding Equivalent

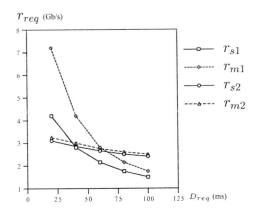

Figure 19: Comparison of required bandwidth in single-stage and multistage buffered cross-bar switches.

Classes (FEC). All flows in such an aggregated class have identical requirements on packet forwarding, thus being equivalent from the forwarding viewpoint. For example, all flows in the class have the same destined egress port and require an identical packet delay upper bound. In this section, we study the problem of aggregated resource allocation for QoS provision in buffered crossbar switches. The analysis is given in the context of a single-stage switch, but can also be extended to the multistage case.

7.1 Resource Allocation with Identical Flow Aggregation

In this subsection we study the resource allocation for an aggregated traffic class that consists of a set of flows with identical arrival curves.

Suppose a set of flows f_i, $i = 1, 2, \cdots, N$, each of which has an arrival curve $A_i(t) = \min\{Pt, \sigma + \rho t\}$, and the delay objective for each flow is D_{req}. By following (40), we can obtain that the bandwidth required by each flow to achieve D_{req} is

$$r = \frac{P\sigma}{(D_{req} - \theta)(P - \rho) + \sigma} \qquad (77)$$

where θ is the total packet forwarding latency for an individual flow. Thus, the total required bandwidth for the N flows is

$$r_\Sigma = Nr = \frac{NP\sigma}{(D_{req} - \theta)(P - \rho) + \sigma}. \qquad (78)$$

Suppose the N flows are aggregated into one class f_g, then the arrival curve for the aggregated class is

$$A_g(t) = \sum_{i=1}^{N} A_i(t) = \min\{NPt, N\sigma + N\rho t\} = \min\{P_g t, \sigma_g + \rho_g t\} \qquad (79)$$

where $P_g = NP$, $\rho_g = N\rho$, $\sigma_g = N\sigma$. The required bandwidth for the aggregated class to achieve the same delay objective D_{req} is

$$r_g = \frac{P_g\sigma}{(D_{req} - \theta_g)(P - \rho_g) + \sigma_g} = \frac{NP\sigma}{(D_{req} - \theta_g)(P - \rho) + \sigma} \tag{80}$$

where θ_g is the total packet forwarding latency for the aggregated class. By comparing (78) and (80) we can see that if $\theta_g < \theta$, then $r_g < Nr$. This implies that if the total latency parameter of the aggregated class is less than that of each individual flow, then less bandwidth is required by the aggregated class than the set of flows to guarantee the same delay objective.

The number of credits, which gives the required cross-point buffer space, for each individual flow is $C = r(\theta + d)$, and the total buffer space required for the N flows is

$$C_\Sigma = NC = Nr(\theta + d). \tag{81}$$

Similarly we get the number of credits required by the aggregated class is

$$C_g = r_g(\theta_g + d). \tag{82}$$

Since have already known from (78) and (80) that $r_g < Nr$ when $\theta_g < \theta$, then from (81) and (82) we have $C_g < NC$. This means that the aggregated class also requires less buffer space then the set of individual flows if $\theta_g < \theta$.

Equations (78) and (80) imply that the key factor for analyzing resource utilization is the latency parameters of the aggregated class and individual flows, which are determined by the scheduling algorithm employed at input and output schedulers. Suppose the WFQ algorithm is applied at each scheduler, then the switch guarantees each flow the latency $\theta = 2L\left(\frac{1}{R} + \frac{1}{r}\right)$, where R is the switch port rate and L is the internal packet length. Thus, the required bandwidth to guarantee a delay objective D_{req} for a flow is

$$r = \frac{2L(P - \rho) + P\sigma}{(D_{req} - \beta)(P - \rho) + \sigma} \tag{83}$$

where $\beta = 2L/R$. Therefore, the total amount of bandwidth required by the set of N flows is

$$r_\Sigma = Nr = \frac{2NL(P - \rho) + NP\sigma}{(D_{req} - \beta)(P - \rho) + \sigma}. \tag{84}$$

For the aggregated class, latency $\theta_g = 2L\left(\frac{1}{R} + \frac{1}{r_g}\right)$. So, the required bandwidth for achieving the same delay objective D_{req} is

$$r_g = \frac{2L(P_g - \rho_g) + P_g\sigma_g}{(D_{req} - \beta)(P_g - \rho_g) + \sigma_g} = \frac{2L(P - \rho) + NP\sigma}{(D_{req} - \beta)(P - \rho) + \sigma}. \tag{85}$$

Therefore, the difference in bandwidth requirement is

$$\Delta r = r_\Sigma - r_g = \frac{2(N - 1)L(P - \rho)}{(D_{req} - \beta)(P - \rho) + \sigma}. \tag{86}$$

Equation (86) shows that Δr is a function of the delay objective D_{req}, the arrival traffic envelope (P, ρ, σ), the number of flows in the aggregated class N, and the switch system parameter $\beta = 2L/R$. Since β is the minimum delay for forwarding any packet through the switch, $D_{req} - \beta > 0$. For any non-constant rate arrival traffic, $P - \rho > 0$. Therefore, $\Delta r > 0$, which means that for variable rate traffic, aggregation saves bandwidth to achieve an identical delay guarantee as each individual flow. Equation (86) also implies that the more flows are aggregated and the tighter the delay objective is, the more bandwidth can be save by traffic aggregation. We also notice from (86) that $\Delta r = 0$ if $P = \rho$, i.e., no bandwidth can be saved by aggregating a set of constant rate flows.

Following (82), we get the required number of credits for the aggregated class is

$$C_g = r_g(\theta_g + d) = (2L/R + d)\, r_g + 2L \qquad (87)$$

The total number of credits required by the set of flows is

$$C_\Sigma = N\,(2L/R + d) + 2NL. \qquad (88)$$

Therefore the difference in required credit numbers is

$$\Delta C = C_\Sigma - C_g = (2L/R + d)\,\Delta r + 2(N-1)L. \qquad (89)$$

Equation (89) implies that the number of credits, which corresponds to the cross-point buffer space, that can be saved by traffic aggregation is associative with Δr and N. The saved buffer space ΔC increases with Δr. It is also interesting to notice that even if $\Delta r = 0$, for example for a set of constant rate flows, $\Delta C = 2(N-1)L > 0$, which means that traffic aggregation improves buffer space utilization more than the improvement on bandwidth utilization.

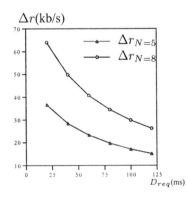

Figure 20: Difference in bandwidth requirements for aggregated class and individual flows.

Now we give a numerical example to show the impact of identical flow aggregation on resource allocation. Suppose each flow in an aggregated traffic class is constrained by a leaky bucket with peak rate $P = 3.2$ Gb/s, sustained rate $\rho = 1.2$ Gb/s, and burstiness $\sigma = 100$ Mbits. The required bandwidth for the aggregated class and the total bandwidth required by a set of flows for achieving identical delay objectives are calculated. Figure 20 shows the difference in bandwidth requirements, Δr, with the number of flows in the class $N = 5$ and $N = 8$ respectively. From this figure we can see that the improvement on bandwidth utilization increases when the delay objective becomes tighter. We can also see that the more flows are aggregated into one class, the more bandwidth can be saved by traffic aggregation.

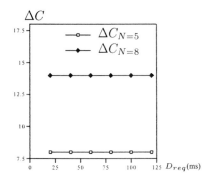

Figure 21: Difference in required numbers of credits for aggregated class and individual flows.

Figure 21 shows the difference in the numbers of credits required by the aggregated class and by the set of individual flows, ΔC, with $N = 5$ and $N = 8$. From this figure we can see that N, the number of flows aggregated into one class, is the dominating impact factor on the improvement of cross-point buffer utilization. The delay objective D_{req} has less impact on buffer space utilization than on bandwidth utilization.

7.2   Resource Allocation with General Flow Aggregation

In this subsection we analyze the resource allocation for aggregated traffic classes with general flows, i.e., the class consists of a set of flows with heterogenous arrival curves.

Assume that a set of flows, $f_1, f_2, \cdots, f_m$, are aggregated into one class f_g, each f_i has an arrival curve $A_i(t) = \min\{P_i t, \sigma_i + \rho_i t\}$. Let $x_i = \sigma_i/(P_i - \rho_i), i = 1, 2, \cdots, m$, $x_0 = 0$, and $x_1 \leq x_2 \leq \cdots \leq x_{m-1} \leq x_m$. Then the aggregated arrival curve will be

$$A_g(t) = \sum_{i=1}^{m} A_i(t) = \begin{cases} \sum_{i=1}^{m} P_i t & t < x_1 \\ \sigma_1 + \rho_1 t + \sum_{i=2}^{m} P_i t & x_1 < t < x_2 \\ \cdots \quad \cdots \quad \cdots & \cdots \\ \sum_{i=1}^{l-1}(\sigma_i + \rho_i t) + \sum_{i=l}^{m} P_i t & x_l < t < x_{l+1} \\ \cdots \quad \cdots \quad \cdots & \cdots \\ \sum_{i=1}^{m}(\sigma_i + \rho_i t) & t > x_m \end{cases} \tag{90}$$

Suppose that the service curve guaranteed to this traffic class by the switch is $S(t) = \max\{0, r(t - \theta)\}$. From (14) we know that the delay upper bound for the class can be obtained from the maximal horizontal distance between the aggregated arrival curve and

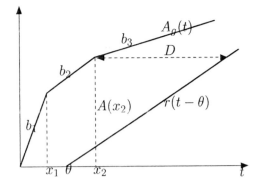

Figure 22: Delay analysis for an aggregated traffic class.

the service curve, which is illustrated in Figure 22. Define

$$b_l = \sum_{i=1}^{l-1} \rho_i + \sum_{i=l}^{m} P_i \quad \text{and} \quad b_k > r > b_{k+1}. \tag{91}$$

Then the packet arrives at the time instant x_k will experience the maximal delay. From Figure 22 we can see that the delay upper bound for this flow is

$$D_{max} = \frac{A_g(x_k)}{r} + \theta - x_k = \frac{\sum_{i=1}^{k-1}(\sigma_i + \rho_i x_k) + \sum_{i=k}^{m} P_i x_k}{r} + \theta - x_k. \tag{92}$$

Therefore, to achieve a delay objective D_{req} for the aggregated class , the required bandwidth that must be allocated to the aggregated class can be obtained from (92), which is

$$r = \frac{A_g(x_k)}{D_{req} + x_k - \theta} = \frac{\sum_{i=1}^{k-1}(\sigma_i + \rho_i x_k) + \sum_{i=k}^{m} P_i x_k}{D_{req} + x_k - \theta}. \tag{93}$$

We sort $b_1 > b_2 > \cdots > b_m$. For each b_i $(i = 1, 2, \cdots, m)$ there is one corresponding $x_i = \sigma_i/(P_i - \rho_i)$. The required bandwidth is thus,

$$r_g = \min \left\{ r : \frac{A_g(x_k)}{r} + \theta - x_k \leq D_{req} \right\}, \tag{94}$$

where x_k corresponds to the b_k such that $b_k > r > b_{k+1}$. After obtaining r_g, we can calculate the required number of credits for the aggregated class as $C_g = r_g(\theta + d)$.

As an example, we consider three flows f_1, f_2, f_3 that are aggregated into one class. All the three flows are constrained by leaky buckets with the following parameters: $P_1 = 5.4$ Gb/s, $\rho_1 = 1.5$ Gb/s, $\sigma_1 = 140$ Mbits for f_1; $P_2 = 3.2$ Gb/s, $\rho_2 = 1.2$ Gb/s, $\sigma_2 = 100$ Mbits for f_2; and $P_3 = 2.5$ Gb/s, $\rho_3 = 1.0$ Gb/s, $\sigma_3 = 75$ Mbits for f_3.

Figure 23 shows that the required bandwidth for the aggregated class, r_g, and the total amount of bandwidth required by the three flows, r_Σ, for achieving a set of delay objectives. Both r_g and r_Σ increase when D_{req} becomes tighter, but r_Σ increases faster than r_g. This implies that the aggregated traffic class requires less bandwidth than the set of individual flows, and the tighter the delay objective is, the more bandwidth can be saved by traffic

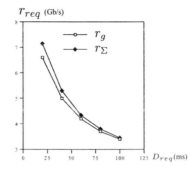

Figure 23: Delay objectives and the required bandwidth for aggregated class and individual flows

aggregation. We also notice that $r_g \rightarrow r_\Sigma$ when D_{req} is large. This is because that when the delay objective is greater than a threshold, the required bandwidth r_g will be the sustained arrival rate of the aggregated class ρ_g, the required bandwidth for each individual flow will also be the sustained arrival rate ρ_i $(i = 1, 2, 3)$, and $\rho_g = \rho_1 + \rho_2 + \rho_3$.

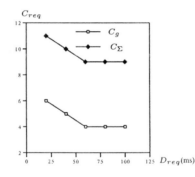

Figure 24: Delay objectives and the required number of credits for aggregated class and individual flows

Figure 24 gives the delay objectives and the required number of credits for the aggregated class, C_g, and the total required number of credits of all the three flows $C_\Sigma = C_1 + C_2 + C_3$. This figure shows that C_g is always less than C_Σ, and the difference is a constant in the range of delay objectives of this example. This implies that the improvement on cross-point buffer utilization is less sensitive to D_{req} than the improvement on bandwidth utilization.

8   Statistical QoS Provision in Buffered Crossbar Switches

The QoS guarantees discussed in previous sections are deterministic; that is, the switch guarantees that the bandwidth lower bound and the packet delay upper bound of a flow will not be violated in any case. Some networking applications can tolerate the violation of a delay upper bound with a certain probability. The applications work fine so long as the probability that the packet delay is greater than this upper bound is less than a specified value. We call such a delay upper bound a *probabilistic delay upper bound*. The arrival traffic from a flow can also be specified in a statistical way; that is, specify the amount of arrival traffic by a upper bound with a small violation probability. Such an upper bound for the arrival traffic is called an *effective arrival envelope* [4].

In this section, we analyze probabilistic delay guarantee in buffered crossbar switches and determine the required amount of bandwidth and cross-point buffer space for achieving a probabilistic delay objective for a flow. Toward this end, we first introduce the concept of effective arrival envelope and its construction.

8.1   Effective Arrival Envelope

The effective arrival envelope is defined in [4] as follows:

Let $A(t, t + \tau)$ be the amount of traffic arrives from a flow during the time interval $[t, t + \tau]$. If for all $t \geq 0, \tau \geq 0$ and a non-decreasing function $\mathcal{G}^{\varepsilon_g}(\cdot)$,

$$\Pr\left\{A(t, t + \tau) \leq \mathcal{G}^{\varepsilon_g}(\tau)\right\} \geq 1 - \varepsilon_g, \tag{95}$$

then the function $\mathcal{G}^{\varepsilon_g}(\cdot)$ is called the effective arrival envelope of this flow with violation probability ε_g.

Consider an aggregated leaky bucket constrained traffic source, where traffic generated from each single source is constrained by a leaky bucket with parameters (P, ρ, σ). Let $A_i(t_1, t_2)$ be the amount of traffic from the ith single source during the time interval $[t_1, t_2]$. Suppose $A_i(t_1, t_2)$ satisfies the following properties:

1. Additivity: for any $t_1 < t_2 < t_3$, $A_i(t_1, t_2) + A_i(t_2, t_3) = A_i(t_1, t_3)$.

2. Sub-additive bounds: each source i is regulated by a deterministic sub-additive envelope $A_i^*(t)$, such that $A_i(t, t + \tau) \leq A_i^*(\tau)$ for all $\tau \geq 0, t \geq 0$.

3. Stationarity: $\Pr\{A_i(t, t + \tau) \leq x\} = \Pr\{A_i(t', t' + \tau) \leq x\}$ for all $t \geq 0, t' \geq 0$.

4. Independence: arrival traffic from source i and j are stochastically independent for all $i \neq j$.

5. Homogeneity within a flow: all sources aggregated into one flow have identical deterministic envelops and identical delay bounds.

Approaches for constructing the effective envelope for an aggregated leaky bucket constrained traffic source with the above listed properties are given in [4]. One approach employs the Central Limit Theorem, which gives

$$\mathcal{G}^{\varepsilon}(\tau) \approx N\rho\tau + z\sqrt{N}\rho\tau\sqrt{\frac{A^*(\tau)}{\rho\tau} - 1}, \tag{96}$$

where N is the total number of single sources aggregated in one flow, z is defined by $1 - \Phi(z) = \varepsilon$ and has the approximation value $z \approx \sqrt{|\log(2\pi\varepsilon)|}$, ε is the violation probability of this effective envelope.

Another approach given in [4] for constructing effective envelopes for leaky bucket constrained traffic flows is based on Chernoff bound, which gives

$$\mathcal{G}^{\varepsilon}(\tau) = N \min\{x, A^*(\tau)\},\tag{97}$$

where $x \leq A^*(\tau)$ and is set to be the smallest value satisfying the inequality

$$\left(\frac{\rho\tau}{x}\right)^{\frac{x}{A^*(\tau)}} \left(\frac{A^*(\tau) - \rho\tau}{A^*(\tau) - x}\right)^{1 - \frac{x}{A^*(\tau)}} \leq \varepsilon^{1/N}.\tag{98}$$

To determine the effective arrival envelope for an aggregated leaky bucket constrained traffic flow by using this approach, the value of x must be first calculated from (98) numerically. Starting from $x = A^*(\tau)$, the value of x is decreased until the inequality (98) is violated. Then $G^{\varepsilon}(\tau)$ can be obtained by plugging this x value in (97).

8.2   Probabilistic Delay Bound Guaranteed by Deterministic Service Curve

Suppose the arrival traffic from a flow f is specified by an effective arrival envelope $\mathcal{G}^{\varepsilon g}(\tau)$, and the switch guarantees a deterministic service curve $S(t)$ to this flow. Let $d(t)$ be the delay for the packet that arrives at the time instant t. Let $D(t_1, t_2)$ denote the amount of traffic of the flow f that departs the switch during time interval $[t_1, t_2]$, and $B(t)$ denote the backlog of this flow at the time t. Define $t_0 = \max\{x < t, B(x) = 0\}$; that is, the flow f is continuously backlogged during the time interval $(t_0, t]$. Since the service curve $S(t)$ guaranteed to this flow gives a lower bound of the amount of service offered to this flow, then

$$D(t_0, t + d(t)) \geq S(t + d(t) - t_0).\tag{99}$$

Thus, for an arbitrary small $\Delta d > 0$,

$$\begin{aligned}
A(0, t) &\geq D(0, t + d(t) - \Delta d) \\
&\geq D(0, t_0) + D(t_0, t + d(t) - \Delta d) \\
&\geq D(0, t_0) + S(t + d(t) - \Delta d - t_0) \\
&= A(0, t_0) + S(t + d(t) - \Delta d - t_0).
\end{aligned}\tag{100}$$

Therefore,

$$A(t_0, t) \geq S(t + d(t) - \Delta d - t_0).\tag{101}$$

If

$$\mathcal{G}(t - t_0) \geq A(t_0, t),\tag{102}$$

then

$$\mathcal{G}(t - t_0) \geq S(t + d(t) - \Delta d - t_0).\tag{103}$$

Because function $S(t)$ is non-decreasing, the inequality (103) implies that

$$\begin{aligned}
d(t) &\leq \min\left\{\Delta : \Delta \geq 0 \text{ and } \mathcal{G}(t - t_0) \leq S(t + \Delta - t_0)\right\} \\
&\leq \max\left\{\min\left\{\Delta : \Delta \geq 0 \text{ and } \mathcal{G}(\tau) \leq S(\tau + \Delta)\right\}\right\} = d_{max}.
\end{aligned}\tag{104}$$

Since (102) implies (103), and (103) implies (104), the event $\{\mathcal{G}(t-t_0) \geq S(t+d(t)- \Delta d - t_0)\}$ is an subset of the event $\{d(t) \leq d_{max}\}$. Thus,

$$\begin{aligned} \Pr\{d(t) \leq d_{max}\} &\geq \Pr\{\mathcal{G}(t-t_0) \geq S(t+d(t) - \Delta d - t_0)\} \\ &\geq \Pr\{\mathcal{G}(t-t_0) \geq A(t_0,t)\} \\ &\geq 1 - \varepsilon_g. \end{aligned} \tag{105}$$

Inequalities (104) and (105) imply that when the arrival traffic of a flow is specified by an effective arrival envelope with a violation probability ε_g and the switch guarantees the flow a deterministic service curve, the probabilistic delay upper bound guaranteed for this flow can be determined from the maximal horizontal distance between the effective arrival envelope and the deterministic service curve with a violation probability ε_g.

Suppose the input and output schedulers of the buffered crossbar switch are LR servers that guarantee the flow f a service rate r and latency parameters θ_I and θ_O respectively, we know from Section 4 that if sufficient credits are allocated to this flow, i.e., $K \geq r(\theta_I+\theta_O+ d_f+d_b)$, then the service curve guaranteed by the switch to this flow will be $S(t) = r(t-\theta_\Sigma)$ where $\theta_\Sigma = \theta_I + \theta_O + d_f$.

Let $D_{max}(r)$ denote the probabilistic delay upper bound guaranteed by the allocated bandwidth r to a flow with an effective arrival envelope $G^{\varepsilon_g}(\tau)$. For each value of r, $D_{max}(r)$ can be calculated from the maximal horizontal distance between $G^{\varepsilon_g}(\tau)$ and $S(t)$. This function is a non-decreasing function of r; that is, the more bandwidth is allocated to a traffic class, the tighter is the delay bound guaranteed. Therefore, to guarantee a given delay objective D_{req}, the amount of bandwidth that must be allocated to a flow can be determined as

$$r_{req} = \min\{r : D_{max}(r) \leq D_{req}\}. \tag{106}$$

The required number of credits, which gives the cross-point buffer space requirement, will be $C_{req} = r_{req}(\theta_I + \theta_O + d_f + d_b)$.

8.3   Probabilistic Delay Bound Guaranteed by Effective Service Curve

In this subsection, the service capacity of a buffered crossbar switch is characterized in a statistical manner by using an effective service curve, which is defined in [18] and repeated below for continuity.

Given an arrival flow at a server, let $R(t)$ be the amount of arrival traffic from this flow during a time interval with length t, and $D(t)$ be amount of traffic from this flow that departs the server during a time interval with length t. Then an *effective service curve* is a non-negative real-valued function $S^\varepsilon(\cdot)$ that satisfies for all $t > 0$,

$$\Pr\{D(t) \geq R(t) \otimes S^{\varepsilon_s}(t)\} \geq 1 - \varepsilon_s. \tag{107}$$

where ε_g is the violation probability of this effective service curve.

Regarding the probabilistic delay bound for a flow whose arrival traffic is specified by an effective envelope, and is guaranteed an effective service curve, the following results are given in [18].

Assumes that there exits a number $T^{\varepsilon_b} < \infty$ such that for all $t > 0$,

$$\Pr\{\exists \tau \leq T^{\varepsilon_b} : D(t) \geq A(t - \tau) + S^{\varepsilon_s}(\tau)\} \geq 1 - (\varepsilon_s + \varepsilon_b). \tag{108}$$

Suppose that $\mathcal{G}^{\varepsilon_g}(t)$ is the effective arrival envelope of a flow and $\mathcal{S}^{\varepsilon_s}(t)$ is the effective service curve guaranteed to this flow by a server, and that T^{ε_b} satisfies (108). If $d \geq 0$ satisfies

$$\max_{\tau \leq T^{\varepsilon_b}} \left\{ \mathcal{G}^{\varepsilon_g}(\tau) - \mathcal{S}^{\varepsilon_s}(d + \tau) \right\} \leq 0, \tag{109}$$

then it is proved in [18] that for any t, the delay of a packet arrives at t, $d(t)$, satisfies the inequality

$$\Pr\left\{ d(t) \leq d \right\} \geq 1 - \varepsilon, \tag{110}$$

where $\varepsilon = \varepsilon_s + \varepsilon_b + T^{\varepsilon_b} \varepsilon_g$.

The inequality (110) implies that the probabilistic delay upper bound for a flow, whose arrival traffic is specified by an effective envelope and is guaranteed an effective service curve by the server, can also be obtained from the maximal horizontal distance between the effective arrival envelope and the effective service curve.

The above results can be applied to buffered crossbar switches to determine the amount of resources required to guarantee a probabilistic delay objective for a flow. To do this, the effective service curve guaranteed by the buffered crossbar switch to a flow must be determined first. It is known from Section 4 that if both input and output schedulers are LR servers and sufficient credits are allocated to a flow, then the service curve guaranteed to the flow is the service curve of a LR server. Therefore, the effective service curve guaranteed to a flow by a LR server can be derived as follows.

Consider a flow f_p that is guaranteed a deterministic service curve $S_p(t) = \lambda_p(t - \theta_p)$. Let $B_p(t)$ be the backlog of f_p at the time t. Define $\underline{t}_p = \max \left\{ x \leq t, B_p(x) = 0 \right\}$. For any $t > \underline{t}_p$, the flow f_p is continuously backlogged during the time interval $(\underline{t}_p, t]$, therefore,

$$D_p(t) - D_p(\underline{t}_p) \geq \lambda_p(t - \underline{t}_p - \theta_p) \quad \text{and} \quad A_p(\underline{t}_p) = D_p(\underline{t}_p). \tag{111}$$

Thus,

$$D_p(t) \geq A_p(\underline{t}_p) + \lambda_p(t - \underline{t}_p - \theta_p). \tag{112}$$

The backlog of f_p at time t satisfies that

$$B_p(t) = A_p(t) - D_p(t) \leq A_p(t) - A_p(\underline{t}_p) + \lambda_p(t - \underline{t}_p - \theta_p). \tag{113}$$

For $t \geq 0$ and $q \neq p$, define

$$\underline{t}_{qp} = \max \left\{ x \leq \underline{t}_q, B_p(x) = 0 \right\}.$$

For any $t > \underline{t}_{qp}$, the flow f_q is continuously backlogged during the time interval $(\underline{t}_{qp}, t]$, thus

$$D_p(t) - D_p(\underline{t}_q) = B_p(\underline{t}_q) + A_p(t) - A_p(\underline{t}_q) - B_p(t) \leq B_p(\underline{t}_q) + A_p(t) - A_p(\underline{t}_q). \tag{114}$$

Replacing t by $\underline{t}_q$ in (113) and using (114), we get

$$D_p(t) - D_p(\underline{t}_q) \leq A_p(\underline{t}_q) - A_p(\underline{t}_{qp}) - \lambda_p(\underline{t}_q - \underline{t}_{qp} - \theta_p) + A_p(t) - A_p(\underline{t}_q)$$
$$= A_p(t) - A_p(\underline{t}_{qp}) - \lambda_p(\underline{t}_q - \underline{t}_{qp} - \theta_p). \tag{115}$$

Assume that the service capacity left over by a flow is shared among all other active flows fairly in the sense that the extra service rate received by a flow f_p is proportional to the service rate allocated to this flow, λ_p. Let C be the total service capacity of this server. For another arbitrary flow f_q, $q \neq p$,

$$D_q(t) - D_q(\underline{t}_q) \geq \lambda_q(t - \underline{t}_q - \theta_q) + \frac{\lambda_q}{C} \sum_{p \neq q} \left\{ \lambda_p(t - \underline{t}_q - \theta_p) - [D_p(t) - D_p(\underline{t}_q)] \right\}$$

$$\geq \lambda_q(t - \underline{t}_q - \theta_q) +$$

$$+ \frac{\lambda_q}{C} \sum_{p \neq q} \left\{ \lambda_p(t - \underline{t}_q - \theta_p) - [A_p(t) - A_p(\underline{t}_{qp}) - \lambda_p(\underline{t}_q - \underline{t}_{qp} - \theta_p)] \right\}$$

$$= \lambda_q(t - \underline{t}_q - \theta_q) + \frac{\lambda_q}{C} \sum_{p \neq q} \left\{ \lambda_p(t - \underline{t}_{qp} - 2\theta_p) - [A_p(t) - A_p(\underline{t}_{qp})] \right\}.$$

$$(116)$$

If

$$t - \underline{t}_q \leq T^{\varepsilon b} \quad \text{and} \quad \forall p \neq q, \forall \tau \leq T^{\varepsilon b} : A_p(t) - A_p(t - \tau) \leq \mathcal{G}_p^\varepsilon(\tau), \tag{117}$$

then

$$D_q(t) - D_q(\underline{t}_q) \geq \lambda_q(t - \underline{t}_q - \theta_q) + \frac{\lambda_q}{C} \sum_{p \neq q} \left\{ \lambda_p(t - \underline{t}_{qp} - 2\theta_p) - \mathcal{G}_p^\varepsilon(t - \underline{t}_{qp}) \right\}. \tag{118}$$

Because $D_q(\underline{t}_q) = A_q(\underline{t}_q)$, (118) yields

$$D_q(t) \geq A_q(\underline{t}_q) + \lambda_q(t - \underline{t}_q - \theta_q) + \frac{\lambda_q}{C} \sum_{p \neq q} \left\{ \lambda_p(t - \underline{t}_{qp} - 2\theta_p) - \mathcal{G}_p^\varepsilon(t - \underline{t}_{qp}) \right\}. \tag{119}$$

Upon replacing $(t - \underline{t}_{pq})$ by the smaller value $(t - \underline{t}_q)$, it follows that

$$D_q(t) \geq A_q(\underline{t}_q) + \lambda_q(t - \underline{t}_q - \theta_q) + \frac{\lambda_q}{C} \sum_{p \neq q} \left\{ \lambda_p(t - \underline{t}_q - 2\theta_p) - \mathcal{G}_p^\varepsilon(t - \underline{t}_q) \right\}. \tag{120}$$

Comparing (120) with the definition of effective service curve given in (107), we can see that

$$S_q^\varepsilon(t - \underline{t}_q) = \lambda_q(t - \underline{t}_q - \theta_q) + \frac{\lambda_q}{C} \sum_{p \neq q} \left\{ \lambda_p(t - \underline{t}_q - 2\theta_p) - \mathcal{G}_p^\varepsilon(t - \underline{t}_q) \right\}. \tag{121}$$

That is, the effective service curve for the traffic class f_q is

$$S_q^\varepsilon(t) = \lambda_q(t - \theta_q) + \frac{\lambda_q}{C} \sum_{p \neq q} \left\{ \lambda_p(t - 2\theta_p) - \mathcal{G}_p^\varepsilon(t) \right\}. \tag{122}$$

Consider the probabilistic case, since (117) implies (118), which in turn, implies (122), we find

$$\Pr\{(122)\text{holds}\} \geq \Pr\{(117)\text{holds}\} \geq 1 - [\varepsilon_b + (Q - 1)T^{\varepsilon b}\varepsilon_g]. \tag{123}$$

That is, the violation probability of the effective service curve guaranteed to f_q is $\varepsilon = 1 - [\varepsilon_b + (Q-1)T^{\varepsilon_b}\varepsilon_g]$.

Since (110) implies that the probabilistic delay upper bound for a flow can be obtained from the maximal horizontal distance between the effective arrival envelope and the effective service curve of the flow, the probabilistic delay upper bound for the flow can be determined after getting the effective service curve guaranteed by the switch to a flow. This delay bound will be a function of r, which is denoted as $D^e_{max}(r)$, thus the required amount of bandwidth and number of credits to guarantee a delay upper bound objective D_{req} for this flow is

$$r_{req} = \min\left\{r : D^e_{max}(r) \leq D_{req}\right\}. \tag{124}$$

The required number of credits for guaranteeing this bandwidth allocation will be $C_{req} = r_{req}(\theta_I + \theta_O + d_f + d_b)$.

8.4   Numerical Examples for Statistical QoS Provision

The examples given in this subsection assume that the buffered crossbar switch uses WFQ algorithm at both input and output schedulers and each flow is allocated sufficient credits, then the service curve guaranteed to a flow with allocate bandwidth r is $r(t - \theta_\Sigma)$, where $\theta_\Sigma = 2L(1/R + 1/r) + d_f$, R is the switch I/O port rate, and L is the length of the internal switching unit used by the switch. Assume that the ingress/egress port rate is $R = 10$ Gbps and the internal packet length is $L = 40$ bytes.

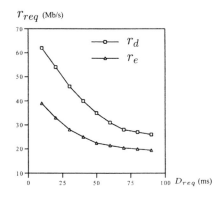

Figure 25: Required bandwidth for delay guarantees with 10^{-3} violation probability.

Consider a traffic class f_b that is aggregated by traffic from 16 single video traffic sources, each of which is regulated by a leaky bucket with parameters $(3.9\text{Mbps}, 1.1\text{Mbps}, 143\text{kbits})$. Figure 25 gives the amounts of bandwidth r_e that must be allocated to guarantee a set of probabilistic delay upper bounds with a violation probability 10^{-3}, and the required bandwidth r_d that must be allocated to guarantee the corresponding deterministic delay objectives. We can see that $r_e < r_d$, which means that if a class can accept a delay upper bound with a violation probability (10^{-3} in this example), less bandwidth is required to be allocated inside the switch. This figure also shows that for tighter delay objective, for example $D_{req} \leq 60$ ms, the difference between r_d and r_e is about $1/3$ of r_d. When the delay objective increases, the bandwidth difference decreases.

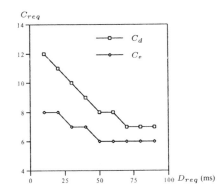

Figure 26: Required number of credits for delay guarantees with 10^{-3} violation probability.

The required number of credits C_e for guaranteeing a probabilistic delay upper bound to the flow f_b, and the required number of credits C_d for guaranteeing the corresponding deterministic delay upper bound are shown in Figure 26. We can see that $C_e < C_d$; that is, the required number of credits to guarantee a probabilistic delay objective is less than what the number of credits required to guarantee the deterministic delay objective with the same value. The tighter the delay objective is, the more credits can be saved. This is because that the required number of credits is the product of the allocated bandwidth and the total round-trip latency of the credit circulation loop, therefore less required bandwidth means fewer required number of credits.

9 Conclusions

In this chapter, we studied the problem of QoS provision in high-speed packet switches. Specifically, we focused our study on the newly developed buffered crossbar switch architecture that is expected to be widely applied in computer networks. The buffered crossbar switch employs a crossbar-based switching fabric with buffers at each cross-point, and deploys virtual output queues at each ingress module and distributed output queues for each egress port. The traffic control system of a buffered crossbar switch consists of packet schedulers at ingress and egress modules and the credit circulation between ingress modules and cross-point buffers. The buffered crossbar switch architecture has desirable features for supporting QoS provision without complex implementation.

We first developed a novel model for traffic control in buffered crossbar switches. Network calculus is applied in the model and the service capacity of each traffic control component, including packet schedulers and the credit circulation, is specified by a service curve. The arrival traffic from each flow is characterized by using an arrival curve. Based on this model we determined the service curve guaranteed to a traffic flow by the buffered crossbar switch, and analyzed the relation among this guaranteed service curve, the achievable bandwidth, and the allocated cross-point buffer space for the flow. The minimum bandwidth and the maximum packet delay of a traffic flow are the two main QoS parameters that we studied in this chapter. The service curve guaranteed to a flow describes the minimum bandwidth offered to the flow, and the maximal horizontal distance between the arrival curve and the service curve of a flow gives the maximum packet delay of that flow. We found that a certain amount of bandwidth must be allocated to a flow to guarantee a packet delay upper bound for the flow. This required amount of bandwidth must be at least the sustained arrival rate of the flow, and more bandwidth is required when the delay objective becomes tighter. We also found that sufficient cross-point buffer space must be allocated so that the allocated bandwidth can be actually received by the flow. The required buffer space is at least the product of the allocated bandwidth and the total latency of the credit circulation loop.

It is well known that the output queueing switch can achieve optimal performance for QoS provision. We applied our network calculus-based model and analysis method to compare the bandwidth and delay performances guaranteed to a flow by a buffered crossbar switch and by an output queueing switch. We found that it is possible for a buffered cross-bar switch to achieve identical worst-case bandwidth and delay guarantees as the performance guaranteed by an output queueing switch. We notices that this equivalent capability of QoS provision can be achieved with neither any switching fabric speedup nor the output-queueing emulation algorithm.

Multiple buffered crossbar switches can be interconnected to construct a multistage switch architecture. The network calculus-based model and analysis techniques developed for single-stage buffered crossbar switches can be extend to study QoS provision in multistage buffered crossbar switches. Similar results on bandwidth / delay guarantees and resource allocation were obtained for multistage switches as for single-stage buffered crossbar switches. We found that sufficient cross-point buffer space must be allocated at each stage to guarantee a required bandwidth. We also found that more bandwidth is required in a multistage switch than in a single-stage buffered crossbar switch to guarantee the delay objective. The difference in bandwidth requirement increases when the delay objective becomes tighter.

Traffic aggregation can be employed to simplify the traffic control system and improve resource utilization in buffered crossbar switches. We examined two traffic aggregation cases, namely the aggregation of flows with identical arrival profile and the aggregation of flows with heterogenous arrival profiles, to analyze their influences on resource allocation for QoS provision in buffered crossbar switches. We found that for both cases an aggregated traffic class requires less amount of bandwidth and cross-point buffer space than the set of individual flows for achieving an identical delay objective. The amount of resources saved by traffic aggregation is associated with multiple factors, including the number of flows aggregated into one class, the packet delay objective, and the arrival traffic profile of each flow.

Some networking applications require a probabilistic instead of a deterministic packet delay upperbound, i.e., the applications work fine as long as the probabilistic that the packet delay is larger than the upperbound is less than a specified number. In this chapter, we also studied the ability of buffered crossbar switches to guarantee a probabilistic delay upper bound, and determined the required amount of bandwidth and cross-point buffer space for achieving a probabilistic delay objective. The effective arrival envelope and effective service curve were applied to respectively specify the arrival traffic from a flow and the minimum service capacity offered to a flow in a statistical manner. We found that less amount of bandwidth and cross-point buffer space are required for statistical QoS provision than deterministic QoS guarantees.

Acknowledgement

The author sincerely appreciate Prof. John N. Daigle at The University of Mississippi for his invaluable advice on part of the research work discussed in this chapter.

References

[1] T. E. Anderson, "High-speed switch scheduling for local-area networks," *ACM Trans. Computer System*, vol. 11, no. 4, pp. 319–352, Nov. 1993.

[2] J. C. R. Bennett and H. Zhang, "WF^2Q: worst-case fair weighted fair queueing," *Proc. IEEE INFOCOM'96*, pp. 120–128, March 1996.

[3] J. C. R. Bennett and H. Zhang, "Hierarchical packet fair queueing algorithms," *IEEE/ACM Trans. Networking*, vol. 5, no. 5, pp. 675–689, Oct. 1997.

[4] R. Boorstyn, A. Burchard, J. Liebeherr and C. Oottamakorn "Statistical Service Assurance for traffic scheduling algorithms," *IEEE J. Select. Areas Commun.*, vol. 18, no. 12, pp. 2651–2664, Dec. 2000.

[5] J. L. Boudec and P. Thiran, *Network calculus: a theory of deterministic queueing systems for the Internet*, Springer Verlag LNCS 2050, June 2001.

[6] S. T. Chuang, A. Goel, N. McKeown, and B. Prabhakar, "Matching output queueing with a combined input/output-queued switch," *IEEE J. Select. Areas Commun.*, vol. 17, no. 6, pp. 1030–1038, June 1999.

[7] S. T. Chuang, S. Iyer, and N. McKeown, "Practical algorithms for performance guarantees in buffered crossbar switches," *Technical Report, Computer Science Department, Stanford University*, 2003.

[8] R. L. Cruz, "Quality of service guarantees in virtual circuit switched networks," *IEEE J. Select. Areas Commun.*, vol. 13, no. 6, pp. 1048–1056, August 1995.

[9] Q. Duan and J. N. Daigle, "Resource allocation for quality of service provision in buffered crossbar switches," *Proc. 2002 IEEE International Conference on Computer Communications and Networks*, pp. 509–513, Oct. 2002.

[10] Q. Duan and J. N. Daigle, "Resource allocation for statistial QoS provision in buffered crossbar switches," *Proc. 2004 IEEE International Conference on Communications*, pp. 2292–2296, June 2004

[11] Q. Duan and J. N. Daigle, "Resource allocation for QoS provision in multistage buffered crossbar switches," *Journal of Computer Networks*, vol. 46, no. 10, pp. 147–168, Oct., 2004.

[12] Q. Duan, "Performance comparison between combined input and crosspoint queueing switches and output queueing switches," *Proc. of 2004 International Conference on Computer Communication Networks*, pp. 509–513, Nov. 2004.

[13] F. H. P. Fizek and M. Reisslein, "MPEG-4 and H.263 video traces for network performance evaluation," *IEEE Network Magazine*, vol. 15, no. 6, pp. 40–54, Nov. 2001.

[14] A. Francini and F. M. Chiussi, "Providing QoS guarantee to unicast and multicast flows in multistage packet switches," *IEEE J. Select. Areas Commun.*, vol. 20, no. 8,, pp. 1589–1601, Oct. 2002.

[15] A. Francini and F. M. Chiussi, "A distributed scheduling architecture for scalable packet switches," *IEEE J. Select. Areas Commun.*, vol. 18, no. 10, pp. 2665–2683, Dec. 2002.

[16] T. Javidi, R. Magill, and T. Hrabik, "A high-throughput scheduling algorithm for a buffered crossbar switch fabric," *Proc. IEEE ICC'01*, pp. 1586–1591, June 2001.

[17] H. T. Kung and R. Morris, "Credit-based flow control for ATM networks," *IEEE Network Magazine*, vol. 9, no.2, pp. 40–48, March 1995.

[18] C. Li, A. Burchard, and J. Liebeherr, "A network calculus with effective bandwidth," *Computer Science Department Technical Report*, University of Virginia, , July 2002.

[19] Y. Li, S. Panwar, and J. Chao, "On the performance of dual round-robin switch," *Proc. IEEE INFOCOM'01*, pp. 1688–1697, April 2001.

[20] R. B. Magill, C. E. Robhrs, and R. L. Stevenson, "Output-queued switch emulation by fabrics with limited memory," *IEEE J. Select. Areas Commun.*, vol. 21, no. 4, pp. 606–615, May 2003.

[21] N. McKeown, "Achieving 100% throughput in an input-queued switch," *Proc. IEEE INFOCOM'96*, pp. 296–302, March 1996.

[22] N. McKeown and T. E. Anderson, "A quantitative comparison of scheduling algorithms for input queued switches," *Computer Networks and ISDN Systems*, vol. 30, no. 24, pp. 2309–2326, Dec. 1998.

[23] N. McKeown, "Scheduling algorithms for input-queued cell switches," Ph.D. Thesis, University of California at Berkeley, 1995.

[24] A. Mekkittiul and N. McKeown, "A practical scheduling algorithm to achieve 100% throughput in input-queued switches," *Proc. IEEE INFOCOM'98*, pp. 792–799, March 1998.

[25] L. Mhamdi and M. Hamdi, "MCBF: a high-performance scheduling algorithm for buffered crossbar switches," *IEEE Communication Letters*, vol. 7, no. 9, pp. 451–453, Sept. 2003.

[26] M. Nabeshima, "Performance evaluation of a combined input and crosspoint queued switch," *IEICE Trans. Commun.*, vol. E83-B, no.3, pp. 737–741, March 2000.

[27] A. K. Parekh and R. G. Gallager, "A generalized processor sharing approach to flow control in integrated services networks: the single-node case," *IEEE/ACM Trans. Networking*, vol. 1, no. 3, pp. 344–357, June 1993.

[28] B. Prabhakar and N. McKeown, "On the speedup required for combined input and output queued switches," *Computer System Technical Report*, CSL-TR-97-738 Nov. 1997.

[29] D. J. Reininger and D. Raychaudhuri, "Bandwidth renegotiation for VBR video over ATM networks," *IEEE J. Select. Areas Commun.*, vol. 14, no. 6, pp. 1076–1085, June 1996.

[30] R. Rojas, E. Oki, and H. J. Chao, "CIXOB-k combined input-crosspoint-output buffered packet switch," *Proc. GLOBCOM 2001*, pp. 2654–2660, Nov. 2001.

[31] D. C. Stephens, "Implementing distributed packet fair queueing in a scalable switch architecture," M.S. Thesis, Carnegie Mellon University, 1998.

[32] D. C. Stephens, H. Zhang, "Implementing distributed packet fair queueing in a scalable switch architecture," *Proc. IEEE INFOCOM'98*, pp. 282–290, March 1998.

[33] D. Stiliadis and A. Varma, "Latency-rate servers: a general model for analysis of traffic scheduling algorithms," *IEEE/ACM Trans. Networking*, vol. 6, no. 5, pp. 611–624, Oct. 1998

[34] I. Stoica and H. Zhang, "Exact emulation of an output queueing switch by a combined input output queueing switch," *Proc. IEEE IWQoS'98*, pp. 218–224, May 1998.

[35] J. Turner and N. Yamanaka, "Architectural choices in large scale ATM switches," *IEICE Transactions*, vol. E81-B, no.2, pp. 120–137, Feb. 1998.

[36] K. Yoshigoe and K. J. Christensen, "A parallel-polled virtual output queued switch with a buffered crossbar," *Proc. the 2001 Worshop on High Performance Switching and Routing*, pp. 271–275, May 2001.

[37] K. Yoshigoe and K. J. Christensen, "An evolution to crossbar switches with virtual output queueing and buffered cross points," *IEEE Network Magazine*, vol. 17, no. 5, pp. 48–56, Sept. 2003.

[38] H. Zhang, "Service disciplines for guaranteed performance service in packet-switching networks," *Proceedings of the IEEE*, pp. 1374–1398, Oct. 1995.

INDEX

A

accelerator, 119
acceptance, 13
access, viii, ix, 2, 5, 9, 13, 46, 63, 64, 67, 69, 71, 72, 74, 80, 81, 83, 88, 94, 95, 96, 102, 119, 120, 122, 130, 141, 142, 144, 146, 148, 150, 154, 161, 176, 177, 190
accommodation, 91
accounting, 13, 100, 102, 105, 107
accuracy, 120, 125, 128, 129, 145, 183, 184
achievement, 116
ACL, 54
activation, 150
ad hoc network, 161
adaptability, 144
adaptation, 16
adjustment, 120, 133
administrators, 11, 15
advertising, 3
affect, 4, 28, 120, 144
agent, 12, 59, 60, 117, 118, 121, 129, 145, 146, 147, 151, 161
aggregation, x, 99, 190, 191, 207, 223, 224, 226, 234
algorithm, 16, 20, 23, 24, 27, 28, 31, 122, 129, 131, 145, 193, 195, 196, 197, 198, 199, 200, 204, 206, 207, 209, 210, 212, 219, 222, 232, 234, 236
alternative, 2, 92, 123, 137, 153
ambassadors, 3
annotation, 61
arbitration, 13, 196
argument, 47, 148
assets, 1, 2
association, 153, 178
AT&T, 37, 38
attachment, 143
attacker, 2, 3, 4, 5, 7, 8, 9, 10, 11, 12, 14, 15, 16, 26, 34

attacks, vii, 1, 2, 3, 4, 5, 6, 7, 9, 10, 11, 12, 13, 14, 17, 19, 23, 25, 26, 31, 33, 35, 38
attention, 12, 65
authentication, 14, 15, 16, 17, 18, 22, 34
authenticity, 17, 18
authority, 12
automation, 43, 46
availability, vii, 1, 2, 3, 34, 67, 117, 142, 143, 144, 148

B

bandwidth, viii, ix, x, 3, 7, 8, 9, 13, 15, 19, 23, 26, 30, 31, 36, 64, 65, 66, 68, 69, 72, 74, 75, 76, 78, 79, 80, 81, 82, 83, 84, 85, 87, 90, 92, 93, 94, 102, 104, 105, 106, 109, 115, 116, 118, 141, 142, 143, 144, 145, 148, 153, 154, 158, 171, 178, 181, 182, 183, 186, 189, 190, 191, 192, 193, 196, 197, 200, 203, 205, 206, 207, 208, 209, 210, 211, 212, 213, 217, 218, 219, 220, 221, 222, 223, 224, 225, 226, 227, 229, 232, 233, 234, 235, 236
bandwidth allocation, 65, 211, 212, 232
bandwidth utilization, 90, 223, 224, 226
bargaining, 60
barriers, 91
behavior, 88, 90, 106, 120, 182, 183, 198
Beijing, 39
bias, 182
binding, 146, 169
black hole, 12
blocks, 5, 16, 88, 89, 90
body, 121, 125, 126
broadband, viii, 9, 63, 64, 65, 67, 69, 74, 79, 80, 81, 82, 90, 91, 92, 93, 95
browser, 6
browsing, viii, 115

C

cable television, 93
cables, 63, 64, 73, 74, 75, 76, 79, 83, 84, 93
calculus, x, 191, 195, 198, 199, 200, 209, 215, 233, 234, 235, 236
candidates, 154
case study, 4, 28
cation, 53
cell, 68, 69, 70, 93, 116, 236
channel interference, 142
channels, 64, 73, 74, 75, 76, 77, 79, 80, 83, 85, 86, 87, 89, 90, 93
circulation, 200, 201, 202, 203, 206, 207, 215, 216, 217, 218, 219, 233, 234
classes, 190, 191, 193, 194, 196, 207, 208, 219, 220, 224
classification, 45
clients, 13, 50, 51, 52, 117, 120
clustering, 23
coding, 67
coherence, 53
collaboration, 37, 42, 148
commitment, 11
commodity, 1, 34, 111
communication, 8, 18, 47, 48, 54, 55, 57, 58, 59, 79, 111, 117, 144, 146, 148, 167, 187
communication systems, 79
communications channel, 3
community, ix, 25, 64, 66, 102, 113, 186, 189, 190
compatibility, 94, 95
compensation, 133
competitive advantage, vii, 1
complexity, 28, 41, 64, 65, 67, 91, 143, 146, 158, 192, 198, 220
components, 65, 69, 74, 79, 82, 83, 95, 120, 125, 148, 152, 153, 154, 215
composition, 42
computation, 61, 120, 125, 126, 127, 137, 138
computing, vii, 117, 121, 183
concrete, 47, 48
conduct, 3, 109, 163, 183, 186
confidence, 2, 67, 106, 109, 110
confidence interval, 106, 109, 110
confidentiality, 2, 18
configuration, 73, 78, 79, 81, 82, 83, 84, 88, 144, 149, 161, 179
connectivity, vii, 1, 2, 100, 101, 142, 147, 148, 152
consensus, 66
constant rate, 223
construction, 43, 48, 51, 58, 112
consumers, 16, 43, 44, 50, 58, 59, 94, 95
consumption, 3, 8, 31, 43, 46, 47, 48, 145

context, vii, 12, 43, 45, 48, 54, 58, 67, 122, 144, 148, 149, 150, 151, 197, 221
continuity, 65, 80, 89, 96, 146, 148, 152, 229
control, x, 2, 8, 20, 33, 68, 69, 70, 86, 88, 89, 90, 91, 93, 126, 130, 133, 148, 152, 161, 189, 190, 191, 193, 194, 195, 198, 200, 201, 202, 207, 209, 210, 214, 215, 220, 233, 234, 236, 237
convergence, 125, 126, 128
conversion, 89
corporations, 42
correlation, 101, 106
corruption, 12
cost saving, 42
costs, 19, 31, 64, 65, 80, 94
coupling, 142
coverage, ix, 141, 142, 144, 145, 147, 177
covering, 49
CPU, 181, 183
credit, 66, 194, 200, 201, 202, 203, 206, 207, 215, 217, 218, 219, 223, 233, 234
customers, 42, 50, 59, 82
cycles, 122, 123, 127
cycling, 89

D

danger, viii, 115
data collection, 100
data mining, 102
data processing, 109
data set, 132, 133, 134
database, 20, 78, 148
decay, 143, 144
decision making, 48, 49, 54, 55, 57, 58, 59, 142, 143, 144, 145, 146, 154
decisions, 143, 144
decoding, 90
decomposition, 52
defects, 109
definition, 43, 45, 48, 103, 105, 201, 231
degradation, 17, 152
delivery, 8, 12, 91, 111, 153
demand, ix, 14, 45, 50, 51, 52, 71, 74, 78, 80, 81, 82, 85, 86, 93, 105, 189, 190
denial, vii, 1, 2, 3, 4, 5, 6, 7, 8, 9, 10, 11, 13, 14, 15, 16, 17, 19, 20, 21, 22, 23, 25, 26, 27, 28, 31, 34, 35, 36, 38
denial-of-service attacks, vii, 2, 3, 4, 7, 8, 11, 13, 14, 15, 16, 19, 22, 23, 25, 26, 28, 35
density, 48, 55
derivatives, 206
detection, vii, 1, 2, 3, 11, 12, 14, 15, 16, 17, 19, 20, 22, 23, 24, 25, 27, 28, 31, 33, 35, 36, 39, 93, 143, 144

detection techniques, 39
deviation, 23
differentiation, 144
dislocation, 105
distribution, 13, 42, 53, 72, 73, 74, 76, 77, 78, 80, 81, 82, 93, 100, 103, 104, 106, 109, 117, 120, 121, 122, 125, 126, 127, 130, 132, 137
division, 27, 75, 81
domain, 5, 17, 19, 20, 21, 23, 28, 45, 49, 65, 69, 77, 83, 84, 85, 118
draft, 57, 59
duplication, ix, 157, 186
duration, 90, 100, 103, 104, 105, 106

E

e-commerce, 62
emergence, 8, 9
employees, 116
encryption, 18
environment, vii, 1, 8, 12, 13, 17, 27, 28, 41, 43, 54, 116, 119, 129, 145, 162
equipment, 64, 82, 94, 95, 158
estimating, 101
evidence, 13
evolution, 95, 237
execution, 44, 118, 121, 122, 125, 126, 127, 143, 145
expectation, 106
exploitation, 8, 42
expression, 41, 109

F

fabric, x, 69, 189, 190, 191, 192, 193, 194, 195, 198, 210, 213, 233, 234, 236
failure, 112, 133
false positive, 22, 24, 25, 28, 33
feedback, 8, 12, 125, 126, 129, 138, 201
fibers, 64, 73, 74, 79, 80, 83, 91, 93
fidelity, 91, 160
financing, 111
firewalls, 2, 13, 14
flavor, 67
flexibility, 25, 35, 46, 57, 65, 79, 83, 85
flood, 10, 11, 14, 21, 25, 26, 32, 33
flooding, 3, 7, 8, 9, 10, 14, 38
fluctuations, 11, 144
fluid, 196
focusing, 12
framing, 76, 86, 88, 89
freedom, 107
frequency distribution, 76

functional architecture, 70

G

gateway node, 147
gene, 102, 111
generation, 18, 30, 55, 56, 89, 141, 154
Germany, 36
goals, 16, 48, 53, 92
GPS, 196, 197
grants, 138
graph, 195
groups, 5, 56, 67, 91, 102
growth, vii, viii, 1, 34, 115, 153
growth rate, viii, 115
guidelines, 53, 55

H

handoff, ix, 141, 142, 143, 144, 145, 146, 147, 148, 149, 150, 152, 153, 154, 155
healing, 72, 74, 81, 83
heterogeneous systems, vii, 41
highways, 69
Hong Kong, 115, 116, 138
host, 3, 7, 8, 11, 13, 14, 18, 19, 20, 22, 23, 26, 34, 149, 158, 159, 160, 164, 165, 166, 167, 168, 169, 170, 171, 172, 173, 174, 175, 176, 177, 180, 181, 183, 185
hub, 87
human resources, 100
hybrid, 72, 73, 74, 79, 81, 95, 143
hypothesis, 102, 106, 143
hypothesis test, 143

I

ideas, 42
identification, 66
identity, 14, 18, 26, 76
IDSs, 20
implementation, ix, 3, 15, 25, 54, 59, 71, 74, 79, 80, 81, 88, 94, 95, 122, 123, 128, 129, 138, 142, 152, 157, 158, 160, 161, 190, 195, 196, 233
independence, 54, 120, 143
indication, 102, 109, 142
industry, 42, 45, 57, 64, 65, 67, 72, 80, 93, 94, 95
inefficiency, 28
inequality, 228, 230
infinite, 19, 103
influence, x, 66, 190, 192, 200, 207, 215
information economy, vii, 1, 2, 3, 34

information exchange, 50
information retrieval, viii, 115, 117, 118, 119
infrastructure, vii, 1, 3, 4, 5, 11, 12, 15, 16, 17, 19, 22,
    23, 33, 35, 41, 42, 43, 49, 50, 58, 67, 74, 113, 116,
    161, 171, 176, 177
input, 18, 69, 70, 77, 88, 130, 190, 193, 194, 195, 196,
    200, 201, 202, 203, 204, 206, 207, 214, 222, 229,
    230, 232, 235, 236, 237
instability, 120
institutions, 102
integration, vii, ix, 41, 42, 46, 54, 60, 141, 142
integrity, vii, 1, 2, 11, 17, 18
intellect, 34
intelligence, 65, 72, 78
intensity, 3, 103
intentions, 14
interaction(s), 42, 50, 51, 117
interest, 25, 66, 126, 195
interface, 45, 48, 58, 77, 78, 107, 146, 153, 158, 159,
    160, 161, 163, 164, 165, 166, 168, 171, 178, 180
interference, 162
internet, 2, 3, 6, 109
interoperability, 2, 42, 94, 95
interval, viii, 30, 103, 106, 109, 115, 183, 184, 185,
    192, 196, 197, 227, 228, 229, 230
intervention, 16, 121, 163
investment, 64, 93
IP address, 8, 9, 13, 23, 26, 27, 92, 99, 111, 146, 149,
    150, 153, 161, 165, 168, 169, 170, 171, 173, 175,
    176, 177, 178, 180
IP networks, 74, 153, 161

K

knowledge, 22, 67, 102, 113, 116

L

labour, 16
language, 25, 46, 59, 61, 77
laptop, 27
latency, 148, 152, 199, 202, 203, 204, 205, 206, 207,
    209, 210, 211, 217, 219, 221, 222, 229, 233, 234
layered architecture, 70
lead, 6, 16, 76, 96, 125, 158, 211
learning, 48, 55, 62, 161
liability, 126
limitation, 168
links, 19, 27, 50, 72, 74, 78, 79, 80, 83, 100, 101, 102,
    103, 104, 106, 107, 108, 109, 111, 160, 170, 171,
    178, 182, 183, 184, 185, 186, 190
location, 19, 116, 144, 146, 151

location information, 151
logging, 131

M

management, 9, 12, 13, 15, 17, 42, 54, 55, 69, 70, 95,
    102, 108, 142, 146, 148, 152, 153, 154, 155, 177,
    192
manipulation, 206
mapping, 54, 58, 78, 130, 148, 169, 200
market, 16, 34, 43, 65, 69, 71, 72, 79, 80, 91, 93, 94,
    95, 96
marketing, 34
markets, 65
mass, 117
mathematics, 25
matrix, 69
maturation, 67
maximum price, 47
measurement, 15, 100, 102, 120, 121, 122
measures, 11, 14, 15, 27, 152, 183
media, 95
medium access control, 142
membership, 8
memory, 27, 34, 88, 89, 90, 94, 123, 133, 135, 136,
    137, 164, 186, 192, 194, 198, 236
message passing, 4, 121
methodology, viii, ix, 27, 99, 100, 157, 158, 159, 160,
    161
Microsoft, 5
military, 161
mobile phone, 116
mobility, 6, 142, 146, 148, 151, 152, 153, 154, 155,
    174
mode, 66, 88, 89, 126, 148, 151, 152, 155, 161, 171,
    174, 175, 176, 177, 186
modeling, 112, 195
models, viii, 53, 54, 60, 63, 64, 99, 105, 131, 162
modules, 162, 165, 166, 191, 192, 193, 194, 195, 196,
    197, 198, 202, 214, 233
modus operandi, 2
money, 12
monitoring, 10, 11, 12, 15, 16, 23, 34, 44, 49, 61, 62,
    74, 82, 85, 86, 100, 102, 106, 161
motivation, 42, 43
multimedia, 59, 94, 95, 196
multimedia services, 95
multiple factors, 234
multiples, 57, 66
multiplication, 145

N

NATO, 112
needs, viii, ix, 10, 18, 19, 25, 41, 42, 44, 47, 66, 67, 74, 81, 88, 91, 94, 106, 109, 116, 142, 152, 158, 163, 167, 168, 169, 171, 172, 173, 176, 178, 183, 184, 185, 186
negotiating, 46, 59, 61
negotiation, viii, 41, 43, 44, 46, 47, 48, 49, 50, 51, 52, 53, 54, 55, 56, 57, 58, 59, 60, 61, 62
network, vii, viii, ix, x, 1, 2, 3, 4, 5, 6, 7, 8, 9, 10, 11, 12, 13, 14, 15, 16, 17, 19, 20, 21, 22, 24, 26, 27, 28, 34, 35, 42, 51, 63, 64, 65, 66, 67, 68, 69, 70, 71, 72, 73, 74, 76, 77, 78, 79, 80, 81, 82, 83, 86, 87, 88, 90, 91, 92, 93, 94, 95, 96, 99, 100, 101, 102, 103, 104, 105, 106, 107, 108, 109, 111, 112, 113, 115, 116, 117, 118, 119, 141, 142, 143, 144, 145, 146, 147, 148, 149, 150, 151, 152, 153, 154, 157, 158, 159, 160, 161, 162, 163, 164, 165, 166, 167, 168, 169, 170, 171, 172, 173, 174, 175, 176, 177, 178, 179, 180, 181, 182, 183, 184, 185, 186, 187, 189, 190, 191, 195, 198, 199, 200, 209, 213, 215, 234, 236
network congestion, viii, ix, 115, 116, 118, 153
networking, vii, ix, 2, 11, 19, 34, 68, 90, 95, 158, 187, 189, 190, 191, 196, 198, 226, 234
neural networks, 143
next generation, 42, 80
node(s), 2, 9, 10, 15, 21, 28, 69, 72, 73, 74, 76, 77, 82, 83, 84, 87, 91, 93, 117, 118, 121, 143, 145, 146, 147, 152, 153, 160, 162, 163, 164, 165, 168, 169, 170, 171, 173, 174, 175, 176, 177, 178, 180, 182, 183, 185, 186, 187, 237
noise, 94, 103, 129, 162
non-repudiation, 17
North America, 66, 94

O

obligation, 50
operating system, 2, 9, 11, 27, 159, 164, 165, 186
operator, 102
optical fiber, 63, 64, 73, 74, 77, 80, 82, 83, 87, 90, 93
optimal performance, 234
optimization, 145, 190
organ, 90, 117
organization(s), 42, 45, 50, 81, 93, 107, 191, 192
orientation, 42, 57
oscillation, 126
outline, 50, 51, 57, 59
output, x, 18, 69, 77, 83, 88, 90, 159, 167, 189, 190, 191, 193, 194, 195, 196, 197, 198, 200, 201, 202, 203, 204, 206, 207, 209, 210, 211, 214, 215, 217, 222, 229, 230, 232, 233, 234, 235, 236, 237
outsourcing, vii, 41, 42, 43, 46, 49, 56, 58, 61
overload, viii, 99, 100, 102, 105, 108, 111

P

packaging, 76
packet forwarding, 91, 92, 190, 203, 206, 210, 221, 222
parameter, ix, 8, 70, 116, 118, 120, 122, 126, 137, 143, 144, 145, 199, 209, 210, 211, 222, 223
Pareto, 103
partnership, 42, 43
passive, 14, 64, 71, 100, 106
pattern recognition, 9, 143
penalties, 16
pervasive computing, 116
planning, 102
police, 116
poor, 16, 153
population, 124
ports, 9, 10, 26, 69, 80, 87, 100, 192, 193, 195, 209, 213, 214
power, 3, 10, 19, 38, 64, 120, 126, 143, 144, 145, 162
prediction, 121, 126, 128
preference, viii, 115, 120, 121, 122, 144
preparation, 43
pressure, 16
prevention, 35, 38
prices, 13, 65
principle, 6, 85
probability, viii, 115, 227, 229, 232, 233
profits, 65, 96
program, 6, 27, 28, 32, 158, 159, 161, 162, 163, 167, 169, 172, 173, 183, 186
programming, 6, 31, 113, 143
propagation, 123, 128, 129, 158, 160, 162, 201, 205, 208, 209, 215, 217, 219, 220
protocol, viii, ix, 2, 7, 8, 11, 12, 13, 14, 18, 25, 26, 33, 46, 47, 53, 54, 55, 57, 58, 59, 64, 65, 67, 68, 70, 72, 73, 74, 76, 80, 82, 84, 85, 86, 88, 90, 91, 93, 99, 100, 103, 105, 140, 144, 146, 148, 149, 152, 153, 157, 158, 159, 160, 161, 162, 169, 174, 185, 186
prototype, 3, 23, 27, 32, 33, 161

Q

QAM, 94
quality of service, ix, 13, 14, 68, 74, 105, 106, 189, 235
query, 8

R

race, 9
radio, 152
range, ix, 26, 47, 71, 80, 91, 100, 118, 120, 125, 138, 162, 175, 189, 190, 226
reading, 50, 90, 160
real numbers, 196
real time, 107, 157, 163, 171, 181, 183, 186
reasoning, 61
reception, 2
recovery, 70, 72
reduction, ix, 20, 25, 43, 108, 116
registry, 53
regression, 122
regulators, 199
relationship(s), viii, 25, 26, 43, 42, 46, 50, 51, 115, 124, 130, 148, 164, 169
reliability, 46, 117, 153
repetitions, 124
replacement, ix, 116, 119, 120, 122, 125, 129, 131
reputation, 1, 34
reservation protocol, 92
resolution, 48, 132
resource allocation, 191, 200, 221, 224, 234
resource management, 13, 159
resources, x, 3, 4, 5, 9, 10, 13, 14, 16, 22, 44, 117, 123, 145, 158, 189, 191, 230, 234
response time, 48, 100
responsibility, 11, 52, 90, 144
retrieval, viii, 115, 117, 118, 120, 129, 130, 137
revenue, 3
rights, 13, 46
risk, 19
robustness, 4, 83, 119
routing, 6, 8, 12, 15, 16, 17, 22, 23, 27, 28, 33, 35, 64, 91, 92, 93, 119, 140, 146, 149, 159, 163, 166, 168, 172, 175, 180, 181

S

sample, 20, 22, 24, 33, 124, 125, 127, 128
sample mean, 124
sampling, 15, 125
sanctions, 43
satellite, 90
scheduling, 161, 177, 191, 193, 195, 196, 197, 198, 199, 200, 210, 211, 212, 222, 235, 236, 237
search(es), 25, 32, 33, 34, 43, 46, 49, 50, 51, 52, 53, 57, 58, 130, 170
searching, vii, 41, 43, 44, 50

security, vii, 1, 2, 7, 9, 11, 13, 20, 22, 24, 34, 74, 82, 85, 86, 150
seed, 123, 161
selecting, 5
self, 72, 74, 81, 83, 117, 120, 130
semantic information, 45
semantics, 8, 45
sensing, 143, 144
sensitivity, 125, 126, 127
separation, 49, 57
series, 22, 67, 68, 82, 95, 124, 199
service provider, 43, 44, 45, 46, 49, 51, 59, 74, 78, 81, 94, 101
services, vii, 2, 3, 10, 11, 12, 13, 16, 17, 22, 26, 34, 41, 42, 43, 44, 50, 56, 58, 59, 60, 61, 63, 64, 65, 66, 67, 68, 70, 72, 74, 76, 78, 80, 82, 84, 85, 86, 87, 90, 91, 93, 95, 102, 145, 148, 153, 154, 237
set theory, 25
shape, 34, 121, 122, 131, 132
shaping, 70
shares, 85
sharing, 79, 80, 82, 84, 85, 117, 118, 220, 237
short run, 72
sign, 43
signals, 86, 88, 90, 143, 148
similarity, 48, 55, 60, 111
simulation, ix, 27, 28, 31, 113, 130, 131, 157, 158, 159, 160, 161, 162, 163, 164, 165, 168, 169, 171, 172, 173, 174, 175, 176, 178, 180, 181, 182, 183, 185
sites, 5
software, 9, 11, 12, 16, 27, 41, 42, 45, 60, 61, 62, 65, 72, 91, 92, 100, 107, 109, 111, 140, 158
spectrum, 190
speech, 66
speed, vii, x, 1, 9, 16, 33, 34, 65, 67, 69, 85, 91, 92, 93, 94, 102, 111, 127, 128, 145, 161, 173, 186, 189, 190, 191, 192, 193, 195, 211, 212, 233, 235
Sprint, 100, 101, 112
stability, 120, 129, 143, 145
stages, 53, 143, 215, 216, 217, 218, 219
standard deviation, 120, 121, 122, 123, 124, 126, 127, 128, 129, 131, 133, 137
standardization, 66, 94
standards, viii, 27, 41, 42, 79, 94, 141
starvation, 3, 6, 7
statistics, 100, 119, 158, 163, 186
stochastic model, 111
strategies, ix, 34, 58, 59, 116, 118, 119, 120, 142, 143, 144, 154
streams, 76, 77, 79, 84, 85, 87, 88, 89, 95, 120, 144, 191, 220
strength, 64, 142, 143, 144, 145, 152

stretching, 94
students, 161
subscribers, 94, 148
substitution, 124
suppliers, 116
supply, 42, 50
supply chain, 42
susceptibility, 19
switching, x, 65, 67, 68, 69, 72, 77, 78, 83, 88, 92, 189, 190, 191, 192, 193, 194, 195, 196, 198, 210, 213, 214, 215, 217, 219, 232, 233, 234
symbols, 126
synchronization, 163, 183, 184, 185, 195
systems, vii, 1, 2, 8, 9, 11, 13, 16, 22, 23, 25, 27, 34, 41, 42, 65, 66, 67, 74, 80, 81, 83, 86, 116, 117, 119, 122, 123, 131, 133, 134, 135, 136, 137, 143, 164, 235

T

tactics, 161
targets, 7, 11, 26, 59
taxonomy, 58, 62
technology, vii, ix, 1, 9, 13, 34, 64, 65, 66, 67, 74, 75, 76, 77, 80, 81, 93, 94, 95, 102, 106, 109, 141, 151, 154, 159
telecommunications, 67, 79, 93, 102
telephone, 64, 66, 67, 74, 78, 79, 80, 81, 82, 85, 86, 91, 94, 95, 102
terminals, 144
theory, viii, 99, 102, 191, 235
threats, vii, 1, 2, 13, 22, 25, 34
threshold(s), 15, 20, 22, 23, 101, 105, 143, 144, 208, 226
time, vii, viii, ix, 3, 8, 10, 12, 13, 17, 19, 20, 21, 22, 24, 26, 30, 34, 41, 42, 43, 44, 47, 48, 52, 54, 64, 65, 66, 67, 68, 69, 72, 74, 75, 76, 77, 78, 79, 83, 84, 85, 86, 90, 91, 92, 95, 100, 101, 103, 106, 109, 111, 115, 116, 117, 118, 119, 120, 121, 122, 123, 125, 126, 127, 130, 132, 133, 137, 142, 143, 144, 145, 150, 152, 153, 157, 160, 161, 163, 166, 167, 169, 171, 174, 175, 177, 183, 184, 185, 190, 192, 193, 194, 195, 196, 197, 198, 199, 201, 203, 204, 205, 225, 227, 228, 229, 230
time constraints, 54
time series, 121
timing, 127, 130
topology, 19, 21, 72, 73, 81, 83, 84, 104, 105, 171, 172, 173, 175, 178, 181, 183, 184, 185, 213
total utility, 48
tracking, 49
trade, 28, 55, 60
trade-off, 55, 60
trading, 116
traffic, viii, ix, x, 3, 4, 5, 7, 8, 9, 10, 11, 13, 14, 15, 16, 17, 19, 20, 21, 22, 23, 24, 25, 26, 28, 31, 32, 33, 34, 68, 69, 70, 76, 77, 91, 92, 99, 101, 102, 103, 104, 106, 107, 111, 116, 117, 120, 122, 125, 129, 130, 131, 132, 133, 137, 138, 140, 142, 153, 157, 158, 161, 164, 165, 177, 181, 182, 186, 189, 190, 191, 192, 193, 194, 195, 196, 197, 198, 199, 200, 201, 202, 203, 204, 206, 207, 208, 209, 211, 214, 215, 216, 217, 219, 220, 221, 223, 224, 225, 227, 228, 229, 230, 231, 232, 233, 234, 235, 237
transactions, 12, 13, 116, 132
transformation, 42
transitions, 15
translation, 148, 169
transmission, ix, 2, 8, 64, 67, 80, 85, 86, 89, 93, 141, 152, 153, 159, 160, 162, 175, 185, 190, 192, 196
transmits, 19, 84, 87, 88
transparency, 79, 119
transport, 7, 8, 66, 82, 95, 103, 105, 112, 144, 146, 152, 153, 154
transportation, 118
trend, 63, 64, 85, 91, 99
trial, 124, 125
trust, 14

U

uniform, 13, 195
user data, 66, 173

V

values, 22, 25, 45, 47, 48, 51, 91, 100, 106, 107, 109, 124, 127, 129, 130, 143, 145, 211
variable(s), 23, 25, 26, 91, 104, 180, 192, 223
variance, 103, 104, 106, 122, 137, 183, 184
variation, 13, 22, 100, 104, 207
velocity, 152
vocabulary, 56
voice, 65, 67, 79, 90, 91, 94, 95, 143, 207, 208, 219, 220

W

wavelengths, 64, 80, 83
web, viii, 41, 42, 45, 48, 56, 59, 60, 61, 62, 111, 115, 116, 118, 119, 120, 140, 159, 186
web pages, 118
web service, 41, 42, 45, 48, 56, 59, 60, 61, 62
wireless cellular network, 143
wireless LANs, 141, 142

wireless networks, ix, 2, 141, 142, 143, 145, 154
wireless sensor networks, 161
work, ix, 12, 35, 43, 46, 48, 49, 56, 58, 66, 100, 108,
    111, 116, 119, 120, 125, 131, 193, 195, 227, 234,
    235
workflow, 42
workload, 120
World Wide Web, 34, 138, 139
worms, 2
writing, 90, 160
WWW, viii, 61, 115, 116, 118, 131, 132, 140

X

X-axis, 122
XML, 48

Y

yield, 9, 10, 129, 133